The Letters of
GUSTAVE FLAUBERT
1830-1857

The Letters of
GUSTAVE FLAUBERT
1830–1857

SELECTED, EDITED, AND TRANSLATED

BY

Francis Steegmuller

THE BELKNAP PRESS OF
HARVARD UNIVERSITY PRESS
CAMBRIDGE, MASSACHUSETTS

Library of Congress Cataloging in Publication Data

Flaubert, Gustave, 1821-1880.
    The letters of Gustave Flaubert, 1830-1857.

    Bibliography: p.
    Includes index.
    1. Flaubert, Gustave, 1821-1880—Correspondence.
2. Novelists, French—19th century—Correspondence.
I. Steegmuller, Francis, 1906-
PQ2247.A23E57 1980   843'.8 [B]   79-13503
ISBN 0-674-52636-8 (cloth)
ISBN 0-674-52637-6 (paper)

To
Jean Bruneau
and
Norbert Guterman

ACKNOWLEDGMENTS

IN PREPARING the present volume I have been greatly helped by the cooperation of MM. Gallimard, who have allowed me to use the text of *Flaubert: Correspondance*, Volume I (1973) and Volume II (in preparation), edited by Jean Bruneau (Bibliothèque de la Pléiade). I am also particularly indebted to M. Jean Bruneau himself, for sharing with me some of his preparations for Volume II of that edition and for his patient clarification of many details (I have included his name or initials in a number of my notes); to Mr. Norbert Guterman, for his invaluable help in the search for literal equivalent or proper paraphrase; and to the John Simon Guggenheim Memorial Foundation for its generous grant-in-aid. My warm thanks go also to Miss Shirley Hazzard for inestimable assistance; and to the following: Mr. Jacques Barzun, Mr. Leroy C. Breunig, Mr. Steele Commager, Mr. William B. Goodman, Mr. Gordon Haight, M. Jean Hugo, Mr. Harry Levin, Mr. Ved Mehta, Mr. Walter Pistole, Mr. Gordon N. Ray, Mr. Douglas Siler, Ms. Camille Smith, Mr. Robert Sonkin, M. Jacques Suffel, Mr. Frank Tuohy, and M. and Mme Olivier Ziegel.

IT IS INTENDED that this collection of Gustave Flaubert's letters, culminating with the publication of *Madame Bovary*, will be the first of two volumes of selections from Flaubert's correspondence in English translation. The pair will replace my much shorter *Selected Letters of Gustave Flaubert* (1953). The second volume, which awaits the further editing of the French texts, will open with letters pertaining to the writing and publication of *Salammbô*, and will contain portions of the correspondence with George Sand, Guy de Maupassant, Ivan Turgenev, and other friends of Flaubert's later life, including letters written during the Franco-Prussian War.

Contents

ILLUSTRATIONS (following page 156)

Flaubert at age ten, by E. Langlois
    Photo Bibliothèque Nationale, Paris

Flaubert in adolescence, by Delaunay
    Photo Bibliothèque Nationale, Paris

Louise Colet, by Winterhalter
    Cliché des Musées Nationaux, Paris

Flaubert in his twenties, by Desandré
    Courtesy M. Jean A. Ducourneau and Dr. B. Jean

Maxime DuCamp, "the man who is excessively thin,"
    caricature by E. Giraud
    Photo Bibliothèque Nationale, Paris

Flaubert dissecting Emma Bovary, caricature by Lemot
    Photo Bibliothèque Nationale, Paris

Louise Colet (anonymous; authenticated by V. Sardou)
    Bulloz

Reflections: Gustave Flaubert's Correspondence

> What seems to me the highest and most difficult
> achievement of Art is not to make us laugh or cry,
> nor to arouse our lust or rage, but to do what
> nature does—that is, to set us dreaming.
>
> *(Letter to Louise Colet, August 26, 1853)*

I F THERE IS one article of faith that dominates the Credo of Gustave Flaubert's correspondence, it is that the function of great art is not to provide "answers." To suppose that art need respond only to such questions as we are capable of posing is, in Flaubert's view, a presumption, an egotistic fallacy. If art has a "function," it is to extend us into unimagined shocks, experiences, pleasures, reflections. Art is discovery, as much as recognition.

By no means new in Flaubert's time, the view that art should be "serviceable" in supplying a text for the management of life—a view that has played its role, too, in proposing art as an inexhaustible ground for critical theory and explication—has since then cast its shadow over much of modern thought and education. It was to be expected that such an attitude would gain credence with the onset of the industrial era; and that Flaubert would be, in 1853, aroused to its dangers. Two decades later, George Eliot was excoriating "that dead anatomy of culture which turns the universe into a mere ceaseless answer to questions." In our own era, the necessary correctives continue. There is Auden's: "A work of art is not *about* this or that kind of life; it *has* life"; and Saul Bellow's charge against intellectuals—against "the educated people of modern countries" whose "business is to reduce masterpieces to discourse."

Flaubert's letter defining "the highest and most difficult achievement of art" goes on to say:

> The most beautiful works . . . are serene in aspect, unfathomable. The means by which they act on us are various: they are motionless as cliffs, stormy as the ocean, leafy, green and murmurous as forests, forlorn as the desert, blue as the sky. Rabelais, Michelangelo, Shakespeare and Goethe seem to me *pitiless*. They are bottomless, infinite, manifold. Through small apertures we glimpse abysses whose sombre depths turn us faint. And yet over the whole there hovers an

extraordinary tenderness. It is like the brilliance of light, the smile of the sun; and it is calm, calm and strong.

When he wrote these words, Flaubert had already been at work on *Madame Bovary* for two years. He had become fully aware of the great possibilities and rich promise of his novel after his first year's labor on it: "When I think of what it can be, I am dazzled. But then, when I reflect that so much beauty has been entrusted to me—to *me*—I am terrified . . . I have been working like a mule for fifteen long years . . . Oh, if I ever produce a good book I'll have earned it!"

At that time he was thirty, and had published nothing, despite several opportunities to do so. The son of a provincial doctor, he had been raised in a household where scientific, and particularly medical, research was held to be man's noblest activity. In that ambience, the preferred pastimes of his early years—reverie, and the composition of plays to be acted by himself and his friends—were accepted with kindness but with a certain disregard. (Even so, Jean-Paul Sartre may exaggerate in ironically entitling his study of the young Flaubert *L'Idiot de la famille*.)[1] Throughout childhood, youth, and early manhood Flaubert wrote incessantly, producing work enough to fill several volumes—the earliest plays, essays and stories, then a short novel, a longer novel, half a book on Brittany, and a long, learned fantasy in dramatic form about the fourth-century St. Anthony Abbot, his age and beliefs. Almost without exception these works were of progressively greater interest and quality. But at the crucial point in writing *Madame Bovary* he looked back and saw them as mule's work. "How I congratulate myself on the prescience I had not to publish!" he wrote exultantly to his mistress, Louise Colet.

Earlier, at the age of twenty-five, when he had not yet begun *Saint Antoine*, much less *Madame Bovary*, he had rejected praise from Louise, who, herself a writer, had quickly become aware of what she called his "sure literary sense." In 1846 he wrote to her: "You disparage yourself in comparison with me, you belittle yourself—I surprise you, I astonish you—but who am I, what am I? I am nothing but a literary lizard, warming myself all day in the bright sun of Beauty. That is all."

The reader of the correspondence will appreciate such self-description: Flaubert is conspicuously a literary lizard from the beginning, warming himself in the bright suns of one great writer after another. But in the early years he had demanded, or expected, direct responses from them: each of the works he himself produced bore the stamp of one or another of these great predecessors, rather than his own. In those days he had even warned his friend Maxime DuCamp against daydreaming: "Be on your guard against la Rêverie, a vicious monster, siren of the soul, which has already devoured much of my substance." The near-simultaneity of his perceiving the possibilities of the new work he was engaged in and his realization that the highest good his fore-

---

1. Sartre possibly derived his title from "L'Idiot des Salons," a farcical skit in which Flaubert impersonated a foolish party-goer for the entertainment of his friends. (See *Journal des Goncourt*, March 29, 1862.)

fathers in art had done him had been to set him dreaming was no coincidence, but the affirmation of maturing genius. The true Flaubert was born when he recognized that his rewards from great art had come from immersion in it, as in a stream or the sea—not from requiring formulae and solutions from it as from a Sybil. "Ineptitude," he had learned, "consists in wanting to reach conclusions . . . What mind worthy of the name, beginning with Homer, ever reached a conclusion?"

IT MIGHT BE rejoined that even after the dazzling vision of his novel's potentialities, the great burden of his letters, whenever *Madame Bovary* is mentioned, is essentially a lament that he was still—especially as he approached the end of the book—working "like a mule": that, as Henry James oddly put it, in *Notes on Novelists*, "Flaubert's case was a doom because he felt of his vocation almost nothing but the difficulty." James's word "almost" is quite unsuitable here—because on those days when Flaubert did pierce through his difficulties, the glimpse of blue sky brought nothing short of ecstasy. A few years earlier, during his journey to Egypt in 1849-50, when his *cange* lay off Thebes in the sunset, with the Nile "a lake of molten steel," and the sailors singing and dancing on board, he had expressed, in his journal, a similar conscious rejoicing: "It was then, while I was observing those things, and enjoying observing them, and just as I was watching three wave-crests curling under the wind at our stern, that I felt a surge of solemn happiness that reached out toward what I was seeing, and I thanked God in my heart for having made me capable of such joy: I felt fortunate at the thought, and yet it seemed to me that I was thinking of nothing: it was a sensuous pleasure that pervaded my entire being."

Now, it was his own work, *Madame Bovary*, under way and offering its promise, that brought a comparable surge of gratitude:

> . . . it is a delicious thing to write, to be no longer yourself but to move in an entire universe of your own creating. Today, for instance, as man and woman, both lover and mistress, I rode in a forest on an autumn afternoon under the yellow leaves, and I was also the horses, the leaves, the wind, the words my people uttered, even the red sun that made them almost close their love-drowned eyes.
>
> Is this pride or piety? Is it a foolish overflow of exaggerated self-satisfaction, or is it really a vague and noble religious instinct? But when I brood over these marvelous pleasures I have enjoyed, I would be tempted to offer God a prayer of thanks if I knew he could hear me. Praised may he be for not creating me a cotton merchant, a vaudevillian, a wit, etc.! Let us sing to Apollo as in ancient days, and breathe deeply of the fresh cold air of Parnassus; let us strum our guitars and clash our cymbals, and whirl like dervishes in the eternal hubbub of Forms and Ideas.

SHORTLY AFTER the publication of *Madame Bovary*, Flaubert—the same Flaubert who is credited, or charged, with "inaugurating the modern novel"—

wrote to the critic Charles Augustin de Sainte-Beuve to deny that he was a "realist." In Sainte-Beuve's review of the novel (with its celebrated closing words: "Son and brother of eminent doctors, M. Gustave Flaubert wields the pen as others wield the scalpel. Anatomists and physiologists, I find you on every page!"), the critic, although granting him distinction in the matter of style, had nevertheless classified Flaubert among the "more or less exact observers who in our time pride themselves on conscientiously reproducing reality, and nothing but reality." "Please let me enlighten you on a purely personal point," Flaubert wrote. "I do not belong to the generation you speak of: at least, not in ways of feeling. I insist that I belong to *yours*—I mean the good generation, that of 1830. It represents everything I love. I am a rabid old Romantic—or a fossilized one, whichever you prefer."

Readers of the correspondence are made aware of Flaubert's "personal" romanticism almost from the outset. The intricacy of the pattern of *Madame Bovary*—Flaubert's revelation of the fatality of living out romantic dreams in the modern world (the dangers, the dreams, and the modern world all being depicted in "impersonal" detail)—has long been a cornerstone of literary study. And very conspicuous is the exotic "revenge" inherent in the author's subsequently turning from that novel subtitled "Patterns of Provincial Life" to the bloody, Carthaginian *Salammbô*. The coexistence of "personal" romanticism with professional "realism" is perhaps most vividly dramatized at the point in the correspondence where, after laborious days spent chronicling Emma Bovary's frustrations, Flaubert bursts out to Louise Colet in an all but untranslatable apostrophe reminiscent of Chateaubriand: "J'aurai connu vos douleurs, pauvres âmes obscures, humides de mélancolie renfermée, comme vos arrière-cours de province, dont les murs ont de la mousse."

The romantic-realistic dichotomy forms a broad supporting base for the constant self-contradiction that is one of the joys of the correspondence and a source of its great vigor. There is perhaps no better characterization of the correspondence itself than Flaubert's phrase already quoted about the "hubbub of Forms and Ideas." In the letters, almost every conceivable artistic form is examined. And Flaubert forestalled much present-day academic discourse with his simple: "Prose was born yesterday: you have to keep that in mind. Verse is the form par excellence of ancient literatures. All possible prosodic [that is, poetic] variations have been discovered; but that is far from being the case with prose." Scarcely a passage of Flaubert's correspondence is without ideas. That a novelist will deal in contradictory attitudes is not unexpected. Flaubert not only admits this trait: he flaunts it. "My basic character, whatever anyone may say, is that of the mountebank." "With my faculty of arousing myself with my pen, I took my subject seriously; *but only while I was writing.*" "You are lucky, you poets: you have an outlet in your verse. When something troubles you, you spit out a sonnet, and that relieves you"—followed exactly a month later by the corrective: "Do not imagine you can exorcise what oppresses you in life by giving vent to it in art. No. The heart's dross does not find its way on to paper: all you pour out there is ink." How many writers

might be quoted in support, contradiction, or extenuation of these outbursts—
Auden, in his poem "The Novelist"; or Yeats exclaiming over his hopeless
passion for Maud Gonne: "How much of the best I have done and still do is
but the attempt to explain myself to her?"

Flaubert had his own opinion of "Systematic thinkers": "As a rule the philosopher [he was thinking particularly of Victor Cousin] is a kind of mongrel
being, a cross between scientist and poet, envious of both. Metaphysics puts a
good deal of rancor into the blood—a very curious and most interesting phenomenon. I was considerably engrossed by it for a couple of years, but it was a
waste of time I now regret."

Flaubert might have enjoyed the Chinese sage Chuang Tzu: "Were we to tell
him we had found contradictions in what he said, he would be apt to do a most
unphilosophic thing. His students did just that, once: they confronted him to
say, 'Yesterday *that* happened, now today *this* happens: what position would
you take in such a case, Master?' And what did the Master do?—Chuang Tzu
laughed."[2]

As for critics, Flaubert says bluntly that they "write criticism because they
are unable to be artists, just as a man unfit to bear arms becomes a police spy.
I'd like to know what poets throughout the ages could have in common with
the critics who have analyzed their work." And: "Criticism occupies the lowest
place in the literary hierarchy; as regards form, almost always; and as regards
'moral value,' incontestably. It comes after rhyming games and acrostics,
which at least require a certain inventiveness."

In contrast to the massive critical and academic attention given to Flaubert's
work and to other aspects of his ideas, such reflections as these, and the cau-
tionary truths expressed in them, have been given a wide critical berth.

ATTENTIVE READERS OF *Madame Bovary* have always noticed aspects of the
novel—not only the pervasive presence of romanticism—that provide some
confirmation of Flaubert's assertion to Sainte-Beuve that he was no "realist."
There are time-sequences that do not coalesce, descriptive details that are alien
—all of them, however, achieving an effect of the liveliest realism by virtue of
what the French *flaubertiste* Jean-Jacques Mayoux has called Flaubert's "secret
rhythm"—the masterly succession of "words each exerting the proper weight
in itself and in combination with the others."[3]

In his review, Sainte-Beuve complained that "there is no goodness in the
book. Not a single character represents goodness"; and that this detracts from
the novel's "realism." Sainte-Beuve's objection has been laughed at as philis-
tine, but it does not lack validity; and there is the further question of the characters' intelligence. In *Madame Bovary* intelligence seems to be reserved solely

2. Sebastian de Grazia, "About Chuang Tzu," *Dalhousie Review*, Summer 1974. And see
The Complete Works of Chuang Tzu, translated by Burton Watson (New York: Columbia
University Press, 1968), p. 109.
3. "Flaubert et le Réel," *Mercure de France*, 15 Février-15 Mars 1934.

for the author—and, presumably, for his appreciative reader. A single questioning or self-appraising intelligence, though intermittently active as in life itself, would disrupt the book's tone. Yet even the dreariest provincial society (or even the worldliest) cannot be certain of insulating itself from an occasional flash of self-appraisal. The exclusion of both simple humanity (unless we except the aptly named Justin) and intelligent insight from the story, while a source of its power, deprives it of a measure of universality.

THE VERY EARLIEST letters in Flaubert's correspondence, those to his school friend Ernest Chevalier, are youthful and naive (Flaubert's tone to and about Chevalier was later to change, when he had outstripped him); those to the adored Alfred LePoittevin are generally rhapsodic, with interpolations of parroted cynicism; those to his literary "midwife," Louis Bouilhet, have a tone of frank camaraderie. The two series of letters to Louise Colet, separated by a three-year interval, have their similarities and their contrasts.

In 1846, within the space of six months, Flaubert lost his father, his sister, and—through marriage—his most intimate friend, who was also soon to die. When, in July of that year, he met Louise Colet for the first time, at the studio of the sculptor James Pradier, he was in a state of depression, even of shock. (He was in fact delivering his sister's death-mask to the sculptor.) For the previous two years, following an epileptoid breakdown, he had, furthermore, been celibate. Rather than participate in life, he had resolved to observe it, and, if the artistic power were granted him, to represent it. Two or three nights after meeting Louise, he was in her bed. Or, as he wrote her half-reproachfully: "Then you came along, and with the touch of a fingertip stirred everything up again."

It is to Louise Colet's retentive nature—and her daughter's need for money—that we owe the preservation and publication of approximately two hundred letters written by her celebrated lover during the first half of his life. His first letters to her, while throbbing with physical passion, nevertheless abound in half-reproaches. She had aroused his flesh *malgré lui;* he reveled in the sensuality, and resented it. Hence the peculiar tone of these love letters, for two years continually tipped with an insensitivity amounting to sadism. At this stage Flaubert has an equivocal view of Louise's destiny. He wants her to achieve her possibilities as a writer, and yet to be a "sex object" to him. He wants to confide his literary dreams to her, but scarcely to share hers. In a moving passage he repudiates her reproach that his reflections on art are what he would say to any casual acquaintance—"to someone I care nothing for." Yet he is almost never at ease in the role of a loving man. The complexity of his feelings affects his style and syntax, sometimes to the point of challenging the reader's understanding. He himself speaks of this more than once: "I feel I am writing badly—you will read this without emotion—I am saying nothing of what I want to say"; "It's strange how bad my writing is in these letters to you . . . One thing conflicts with another . . . It's as though I wanted to say three words at a time." Of all the letters, these are the most exigent for the translator—and perhaps for the reader.

After the first rupture (for which Louise eventually had the intelligence to recognize some responsibility), and the interval of Flaubert's "Voyage en Orient," the liaison was resumed on a different basis. Now it is Louise's "Memoranda," or "Mementos" (discovered by M. Jean Bruneau at Avignon in 1974) that record Flaubert's physical response: Flaubert himself refers to it less often. He tells her that he longs to make of her a "sublime hermaphrodite"; he wants her to be "a man from the waist up." And ultimately she becomes little more than a repository, a "convenient receptacle" for all he has to say about the weird novel he finds himself creating—a book so different from anything he, or any other writer, has done before, that night after night he feels compelled to chronicle its tortuous, tormenting progress. As Louise well realizes, this, from a supposed lover whom one seldom sees, again approaches a form of sadism: "In his letters, Gustave never speaks to me of anything except art—or himself." And indeed, in the almost total absence from the archive of Louise Colet's letters to Flaubert, his second series to her, especially, brings to mind the image of a man dancing with a partner from whom he remains detached. Louise's bitter complaints, and her clumsy contrivings to hold Flaubert fast, bring about the unhappy close.

THE FOREGOING PAGES may suggest why there are readers of Flaubert who from time to time turn from the novels to his correspondence. How often, in the letters, he laments that the art he produces is not the art he most admires. Flaubert's own great heroes among the artists are, in their prodigious spontaneity, his very opposites. His own power in the novels—one need only mention his celebrated and unremitting castigation of the bourgeois ("bourgeois" being defined as "anyone who thinks basely")—is achieved by the labor revealed in the letters. Whereas: "how easily the great men achieve their effects by means extraneous to Art. What is more badly put together than much of Rabelais, Cervantes, Molière and Hugo? But such quick punches! Such power in a single word! We must pile up a mass of little pebbles to build our pyramids; theirs, a hundred times greater, are hewn in monoliths." It is in his correspondence—the writing he does "after hours"—that Flaubert attains the very spontaneity he covets. In the torrential letters about "art—or himself," about the "eternal hubbub of Forms and Ideas," he enters the company of those other great men, the ones who, with such formidable effect, had set him dreaming.

I

The Billiard Table,
The Collège
1821-1840

GUSTAVE FLAUBERT was born on December 12, 1821, in the residence wing of the Hôtel-Dieu, the municipal hospital of Rouen, where his father, the eminent Dr. Achille-Cléophas Flaubert, was director and chief surgeon. For most of his first twenty-five years he lived in this contiguity with blood, suffering, and death—and with scientific research. "The dissecting room of the hospital gave on our garden. How many times my sister and I used to climb the trellis, cling to the vines, and peer curiously at the cadavers on their slabs! The sun shone on them, and the same flies that were flitting about us and about the flowers would light on them and come buzzing back to us . . . I still see my father raising his head from his dissecting, and telling us to go away." As though the continual presence of physical malfunction and destruction were not enough, an uncle saw to it that the boy observed their mental counterpart: "The first time I saw insane people was here in Rouen, in the asylum, with poor Père Parain. Sitting in cells, chained around the middle, naked to the waist, disheveled, a dozen women were screaming and tearing their faces with their nails. I was then perhaps six or seven. These are good impressions to have when young: they make a man of you." During his adolescence, he often visited the morgue.

He was a handsome boy, with the classic Norman fair hair and blue eyes; affectionate with his sister Caroline, but always in the shadow of his brother Achille. Achille, nine years his senior, was an apt and diligent student, trained almost from the cradle to follow his father into medicine, whereas Gustave's favorite childhood occupations were almost exactly those which the young Marcel Proust, another son of a doctor, would later list as his own: "reading, reverie, poetry, the theatre."

In Flaubert's case, reading was somewhat delayed. His sister Caroline, three years younger, was—with the advanced aptitude more usual in girls at that age —quick to learn her letters, putting her brother to shame. The little boy's slowness in reading and writing was a grave matter to his exigent family; and Gustave's sufferings over it are reflected in certain tales written in his adolescence. The retardation was brief, and, when overcome, evidently compensated for by a precocity of literary expression to which one of his earliest known letters—written at the age of nine (the first in the present volume)—amply testifies.

On the theme of reverie, or daydreaming, he would have much to say all his life; and his early theatre consisted of presenting and acting in his own dramas and in versions of the classics, before audiences of family and friends, using the home billiard table as a stage.

When he was eleven he became a boarder in the local lycée, the Collège Royal de Rouen, where he remained for several years. Here his friends were enthusiasts for the French Romantic writers. These students were not simply the readers, but, in many of their youthful tastes, the emulators, of literary figures—Chateaubriand, Hugo, Lamartine, Vigny, Musset—who concerned themselves with various forms of social, political, and spiritual agitation. Though typical of contemporary Romanticism throughout Europe, this ferment among French artists was credited by Musset himself, in *La Confession d'un enfant du siècle*, with a national raison d'être: reaction against the increasing flatness of French life following the years of revolution and Napoleonic drama. However, in the 1830s, while Flaubert was still a schoolboy, Balzac was beginning to publish the early volumes of his *Comédie Humaine*; and Flaubert read Balzac as well as the Romantics.

In the summer of 1836, at the seashore in Trouville, when he was almost fifteen, Flaubert conceived a passion—an "enormous" passion, he later called it—for a woman of twenty-six with a genial husband and a small child. This was Mme Maurice (Elise) Schlesinger, whose warm motherliness was in contrast to the habitually rigid demeanor of Flaubert's own mother. There is no mention of this attachment in the adolescent's letters, but in an "ideal" form Flaubert continued to cherish it, and it would eventually inspire the main thread of his third published novel, *L'Education Sentimentale*, which appeared when he was almost fifty—one of the many examples, in Flaubert's literary life, of a very early experience serving as a quarry for much later work.

As a schoolboy he wrote essays and short tales, two of which were printed in a Rouen magazine—his only work published before the appearance of *Madame Bovary*. Two other short pieces were circulated privately by a family friend. He and his schoolmates invented a grotesque character, baptized "le Garçon," a raucous amalgam of clichés and boorishness, with a particularly revolting loud laugh, whom they tirelessly impersonated among themselves. Although he already occasionally satirized the contemporary bourgeois, most of the "narrative compositions" he wrote while at the Collège Royal were gory prose melodramas, laid in the medieval settings often favored by the Romantics. Gradually these early writings became more autobiographical, infused with ennui and yearning—yearning for love and for the exotic. In later life he painted himself as having been the complete young Romantic:

> [At seventeen] I was like the cathedrals of the XVth century, lanceolated, flamboyant . . . Between the world and me there existed a kind of stained-glass window, colored yellow, with rays of fire and

golden arabesques, so that everything was reflected in my soul as on the pavement of a sanctuary, beautified, transfigured, and yet melancholy; and all who walked on it were beautiful. They were dreams— more majestic, more gorgeously costumed, than cardinals in purple robes. Such throbbings from the organ! Such hymns! And what a sweet odor of incense pouring from a thousand censers!

In 1839, his last year at the college, he participated in a student protest against the dismissal of a favorite teacher, and was expelled. The French school system allowed him to prepare for the final examination at home, and he passed it, obtaining his baccalauréat in 1840.

The present correspondence opens with the nine-year-old Flaubert already castigating (and at the same time observing) a bourgeois holiday ritual, commenting on national affairs, and discussing his own writing. In the French original the first few letters are marked by schoolboy errors of spelling and syntax; no attempt has been made to approximate these in the translation.

To ERNEST CHEVALIER[1]

[Rouen, before January 1, 1831]

Dear Friend

You are right in saying that New Year's Day[2] is stupid. My friend, they have just dismissed the greatest of them all, the white-haired Lafayette, champion of freedom in the old world and the new.[3] Friend, I'll send you some of my political and constitutional liberal speeches. You are right in saying you'll give me pleasure by coming to Rouen, you will give me a great deal. I wish you a happy 1831, my affectionate greetings to your dear family. The friend you sent me seemed a nice fellow even though I saw him only once. I'll also send you some of my comedies. If you'd like us to work together at writing, I'll write comedies and you can write your dreams, and since there's a lady who comes to see papa and always says stupid things I'll write them too. I'm not writing this letter well because I'm expecting a box of sweets from Nogent.[4] Adieu, answer me as soon as possible.

Adieu, good health; your friend for life.

Answer as quickly as possible, please.

1. Ernest Chevalier (1820-1887), a year older than Flaubert and his earliest school friend, was the son of a prosperous farmer-businessman in the nearby country town of Les Andelys. For some years he was a boarder at the lycée in Rouen. His maternal grandparents, M. and Mme Mignot, who lived in Rouen, were friends of the Flaubert family. As he grows older, Chevalier will be, along with Flaubert's older brother Achille, a "straight man" in the correspondence—the young bourgeois who advances complacently in a normal professional career.

2. Many years later, in a letter to his niece Caroline, the daughter of his long-dead sister, Flaubert would describe ritual New Year's Day visiting in the Rouen of his childhood: "In those times, on New Year's Day, Julie [the children's nurse] would take your mother and me by the hand and we'd pay our first call on Mme Lenôtre, who engulfed us in her great bonnet as she kissed us; next, père Langlois; then M. and Mme Bapeaume, Mme Lormier, Mme

3

Énault, old Mme Legros and ending with Mme LePoittevin. So many different houses and faces—I remember them all clearly. My legs still ache when I think of those long boulevards. Our four little buttocks would be icy cold, and we couldn't pry our teeth apart, stuck together with apple taffy. What a din at your grandfather's! The front door wide open from seven in the morning! A salad bowl overflowing with visiting cards; hugs and kisses all day long. And the next day, zero, absolute solitude. That's how it was." (Julie, old and blind, was still with Flaubert when this letter was written.)

3. The Liberal Lafayette had been dismissed (more precisely, his office as commander-in-chief of the National Guard had been "abolished") by the Chamber of Deputies, in compliance with the wishes of King Louis-Philippe. There was agitation throughout France following this reactionary move by the recently inaugurated "July Monarchy." During the earlier Restoration, Dr. Flaubert, suspected of "progressive ideas," had been investigated but judged not dangerous.

4. Where lived a number of aunts, uncles, and cousins on Dr. Flaubert's side of the family.

To Ernest Chevalier

[January 15, 1832]

Dear Friend

Your grandfather is a little better, the medicine papa gave him helped and we hope he'll soon be well. I'm making notes on *Don Quixote* and he says they're very good. Somebody I think Amédée has had my eulogy of Corneille printed and I am sending you a copy.[1] The billiard table is deserted, I'm not putting on any plays as you're not here. The Sunday you left seemed to me ten times as long as the others. I forgot to tell you that I'm about to begin a play to be called The miser lover, it will be about a miser who refuses to give his mistress any presents so his friend gets her away from him. All my greetings to your family, I will tell you the end of my play in another letter. Make your parents promise to come here with you for Carnival, work at your geography. I'm going to start also a History of Henry 4, Louis 13 and Louis 14. I must get to work. Answer . . . Adieu my best friend till death by God.

Good night. Your old friend.   Rouen this 15 of January
                                                in the year 1832 of Our
Answer   Lord Jesus Christ.

1. Amédée Mignot, Ernest Chevalier's uncle, finding young Flaubert's compositions precocious and amusing, had several handwritten copies made of two of them: a eulogy of Corneille and a mock treatise on constipation written partly in Latin. He circulated these as a pamphlet, entitled *Trois pages d'un Cahier d'Ecolier, ou, Oeuvres choisies de Gustave F****.

To Ernest Chevalier

February 4, 183[2]

Dear Friend

I'm answering you by return of mail. I told you I'd be writing some plays, but no, I'll write some Novels I have in mind, they are the Beautiful Andalusian, the masked ball, Cardenio, Dorothy, the moorish woman, the impertinent eavesdropper, the prudent husband. I have put aside the billiard table and

4

the scenery. In my *proverbes dramatiques*[1] there are several plays that we can do. Your grandfather is still the same. You see I was right in saying that the splendid explanation of that famous condition constipation and my eulogy of Corneille would go down to posterity. That is, down to the posterior . . .

So long. Happy New Year, kiss my ass, come to Rouen.

Your dauntless dirty-minded friend till death.

Answer.

1. A *proverbe dramatique* is a short play developed from a proverb, such as Alfred de Musset's *On ne badine pas avec l'amour*. Other well known French writers of *proverbes dramatiques* are Louis Carrogis, known as Carmontelle (1717-1806) and Michel-Theodore Leclercq (1777-1851). (J.B.)

To ERNEST CHEVALIER

Rouen, March 31, 1832

Dauntless One:

You know I told you in one of my letters that we were not having any more theatre, but the last few days we've been busy on the billiard table again. I have about 30 plays and there are many which Caroline and I act together. Be a good boy, come for Easter and stay at least a week. You'll say "What about my catechism?" but you'd set out on Sunday at six o'clock after vespers, you'd be at Rouen by eleven, and you'd leave us with great regret the next Saturday afternoon. Your grandfather is better. I have written a poem called "a mother" which is as good as the death of Louis 16. I have also done several plays, among others one called The ignorant antiquary which makes fun of stupid antiquaries and another which is called "preparations to receive the king," which is very funny.

Listen to this, there's a pupil of old Langlois's[1] named Alexis, called by everybody Jesus. The other day he almost fell into the trench. At the moment he was placing his façade on the hole the boards broke and if someone hadn't caught hold of him he'd have fallen into old Langlois's excrement. Adieu.

Answer quickly at the first opportunity.

1. Perhaps a Rouen drawing teacher. (J.B.) One of the recipients of the New Year's Day calls described on p. 3, n. 2.

To ERNEST CHEVALIER

[Rouen, before April 22, 1832]

Victory Victory Victory Victory Victory you'll be coming one of these days, my friend, the theatre, the posters, everything is ready. When you come, Amédée, Edmond, Mme Chevalier, mama, two servants and perhaps some of the medical students will come to see us act. We'll give 4 plays you don't know but you'll learn the lines quickly. The tickets for the first, second, and third performances are done, there will be regular seats, there are also roofs and decorations. The backdrop is ready, perhaps there will be 10 or twelve people.

So you must be brave and fear nothing, we'll have a doorkeeper who'll be young Lerond and his sister will be an extra. I don't know whether you have seen Poursognac,[1] we'll give it along with a play by Berquin, one by Scribe and a *proverbe dramatique* by Carmontelle, no use my telling you their titles I don't think you know them. When they told me you weren't coming I was in a frightful rage. If by any chance you didn't come I'd go to Les Andelys to get you on all fours like the dogs of King Louis Fils-Lippe (see the newspaper *La Caricature*) and I think you would do the same for me, for you and I are bound by a love that can be called fraternal. Yes, I, who have deep feelings, yes, I would walk a thousand leagues if necessary to be reunited with my best of friends, for nothing is so sweet as friendship oh sweet friendship how much has been accomplished thanks to this sentiment, without attachments how could we live. We find this feeling even in the smallest animals, without friends how would the weak live, how could widows and children subsist?

Permit me, my dear friend, these tender reflections but I swear to you I have not been trying to embellish them nor to indulge in rhetoric, but am speaking to you with the frankness of the true friend. There is almost no cholera morbus at the Hôtel-Dieu. Your grandfather is the same. Come to Rouen. Adieu.

1. Molière's *Monsieur de Pourceaugnac*. For a scene from this "comedy-ballet" see p. 193.

To Ernest Chevalier

Rouen, Friday August 14, 1835

Dear Ernest

It is with much pleasure that I can now tell you with certainty that in papa's words "We'll soon be coming to see you."

Then you will owe us a return visit, and I hope you will adopt the good habit of coming to spend a week with us. About two weeks ago I finished my *Frédégonde*, I've even recopied an act and a half. I have another drama in mind. Gourgaud is assigning me narrative compositions.[1]

Since you saw me I've read *Catherine Howard* and *La Tour de Nesle*. I've also read the works of Beaumarchais: that's the place to find new ideas. Now I am entirely absorbed in the plays of old Shakespeare, I am reading *Othello*, and then I am going to take with me for my trip the *History of Scotland* in three volumes by W. Scott,[2] then I'll read Voltaire. I am working like a demon, getting up at half past three in the morning.

I see with indignation that theatre censorship is going to be reintroduced and the freedom of the press abolished; yes, this law will be passed, for the representatives of the people are nothing but a filthy lot of sold-out wretches, they see only their own interests, their natural bent is toward baseness, their honor is a stupid pride, their soul a lump of mud; but some day, a day that will come before long, the people will unleash the third revolution; kings' heads will roll, there will be rivers of blood. At present they are depriving the man of letters of his conscience, his artist's conscience. Yes, our century is rich in bloody peripeties. Adieu, au revoir, and let us continue to devote ourselves to what is greater than peoples, crowns and kings: to the god of Art, who is ever-present, wearing his diadem, his divine frenzy merely in abeyance.

1. Henri-Honoré Gourgaud-Dugazon, professor of literature at the college. He recognized and encouraged the adolescent Flaubert's narrative gift, and became his friend and confidant. Flaubert preserved these early "narrative compositions," and they were published posthumously in his *Oeuvres de jeunesse*.
2. At this time he read both authors in French translation.

To Ernest Chevalier

[Rouen,] Saturday night [June] 24, 1837.
(St. John's Day, the longest day of the year, on which it chances that that old jokester the sun, among its other antics, dons its Sunday clothes, turns red as a carrot, draws sweat from grocers—hunting dogs—the National Guard,—and dries out the turds in the streets.)
. . .

Now that I am no longer writing, but have become an historian (so-called),[1] now that I read books, display serious tastes, and in the midst of it all preserve sufficient sangfroid and gravity to be able to look at myself in the mirror without laughing, I am all too happy when with the excuse of writing a letter I can let myself go, interrupt my work, and put off making notes, even those on M. Michelet; for the most beautiful woman is scarcely beautiful on the table of a dissecting-room, with her bowels draped over her nose, one leg minus its skin, and half a burnt-out cigar on her foot. Oh no it's a sad thing, criticism, study, plumbing the depths of knowledge to find only vanity, analyzing the human heart to find only egoism, and understanding the world only to find in it nothing but misery. Oh how much more I love pure poetry, cries from the soul, sudden transports and then deep sighs, the voices of the soul, the thoughts of the heart. There are days when I would give all the knowledge of chatterers past, present and future, all the stupid erudition of the nitpickers, hairsplitters, philosophers, novelists, chemists, grocers, academicians, for two lines of Lamartine or Victor Hugo. You see me become very antiprose, antireason, antitruth, for what is the beautiful if not the impossible, what is poetry if not barbarism—the heart of man—and where to find that heart when in most cases it is given over to the two enormous preoccupations that fill a man's life: making his fortune and living for himself, in other words compressing his heart to make it fit in somewhere between his shop and his digestion . . .

1. Adolphe Chéruel, professor of history at the college, later a well known historian himself, was multiplying Flaubert's assignments, encouraging his historical studies as Gourgaud-Dugazon was encouraging his writing of fiction. The titles of many of Flaubert's youthful tales—ancestors of the *contes* of his maturity—reveal their historical settings: *Mort du duc de Guise, Chronique normande du Xe siècle, La Peste à Florence*, etc.

To Ernest Chevalier

Rouen, Thursday, September 13, 1838

Your remarks on Victor Hugo are as true as they are unoriginal. Modern criticism now generally accepts that antithesis of body and soul so profoundly expressed in all the works of the great author of *Notre-Dame*. This man has been much attacked because he is great and arouses envy. People were at first astonished, and then they blushed, to see before them a genius as immense as any of those whom they had been admiring for centuries; for human pride doesn't enjoy paying tribute to laurels that are still green. Is not V. Hugo as great a man as Racine, Calderón, Lope de Vega and many another long admired?

I am still reading Rabelais, and have also taken up Montaigne. I even intend later to make a special philosophical and literary study of these two men. Together they mark the taking-off point, as I see it, of French literature and the French spirit.

Really I deeply value only two men, Rabelais and Byron, the only two who have written in a spirit of malice toward the human race and with the intention of laughing in its face. What a tremendous position a man occupies who places himself in that relation to the world!

· · ·

To Ernest Chevalier

[Rouen,] Sunday morning, February 24, 1839

What a fine and joyous existence is yours![1] Living from day to day, heedless of tomorrow, no worries about the future, no doubts, no fears, no hopes, no dreams—a life of merry loves and glasses of kirschwasser. A dissolute life, fantastic, artistic, jumping, hopping, bouncing, a life that goes up in its own smoke and drinks itself silly. Masked balls, restaurants, champagne, liqueurs, whores, vast clouds of tobacco—that's your life and you can't get enough of it, that's how you're wasting your days. Well, why not? You go with the wind; caprice is your only guide; when a woman passes, you follow her; you hear music, and it's on with the dance, the cancan, the chahut, squeezings and ticklings. And then the orgies! The "bacchanalian" orgies! The shrieking! The yelling! The howling! (Here a poem on "bacchanalian" orgies: I'll skip it.) You'll live this way for three years, and they will be—of course—"the happiest years of your life," the ones you'll regret when you've settled down into sobriety and sharp dealing, living splendidly, paying your taxes, a convert to the virtue of a lawfully wedded wife and to temperance societies. But what are you going to do? What do you expect to become? What will your future be? Do you ask yourself that, sometimes? No: why should you? And you are right. The future is the worst thing about the present. The question, "What are you going to do?", when it is cast in your face, is like an abyss in front of you that keeps moving ahead with each step you take. Quite apart from the metaphysical future (which I don't give a damn about because I can't believe that our body, composed as it is of mud and shit and equipped with instincts lower than those of the pig or the crab-louse, contains anything pure and immaterial, when everything around it is so polluted and ignoble)—apart from that future, there is the future of one's life. But don't think that I am undecided as to the choice of a profession: I am quite resolved to embrace none whatever. Because I despise my fellow-creatures too much to want to help them or harm them. Anyhow, I will get myself admitted to the bar, and perhaps even go on for a doctorate as a means of loafing an additional year. But very probably I shall never practise, unless perhaps to defend some famous criminal, or if a case is exceptionally horrible. As for writing . . . I am willing to bet that I will never be printed or acted. Not that I'm afraid of failure: I would simply be too disgusted with the chicaneries of publishing or the theatre. However, if I ever do take an active part in the world it will be as a thinker and de-moralizer. I will simply tell the truth: but that truth will be horrible, cruel, naked. Still, how do I know? For I am one of those people always disgusted from one day to the next, always thinking of the future, always dreaming, or rather day-dreaming, surly, pestiferous, never knowing what they want, bored with themselves and boring to everybody else. I went to the brothel for some fun and was merely bored. Magnier[2] gets on my nerves, history I find oppressive. Tobacco? My throat is raw from it. Alcohol? I am pickled in it. The only thing left is eating, and that I do for hours on end. As a result, my body is fatter but my mind emaciated. In the past I used to think, reflect, write, dash down on paper all the verve I felt in my heart. Now I no longer think, no longer reflect—even less, write. Poetry has perhaps left me, too bored to stay. Poor angel, will you never return? And yet I have a confused feeling of something stirring within me, I am in a period of transition, curious to see what the result will be, how I'll come out of it: I am moulting (in the intellectual sense). Will I be hairless, or magnificent? I wonder. We shall see. My thoughts are confused, I am unable to do any work requiring imagination, everything I produce is dry, labored, painful. I began a morality play two months ago—what I have done of it is absurd, absolutely empty of ideas. Perhaps I'll drop it. Too bad: at least I'll have had a glimpse of the sublime, but clouds came up and plunged me back into the inglorious commonplace. My life, in my dreams so beautiful, so poetic, so vast, so filled with love, will be like everyone else's—monotonous, sensible, stupid. I'll attend Law School, be admitted to the bar, and end up as a respectable assistant district attorney in a small provincial town, like Yvetot or Dieppe . . .

1. Chevalier, a year older than Flaubert, had entered the Paris Law School the previous autumn. For the prophetic aspect of this mockery of bourgeois clichés about "la vie de bohème" in the Latin Quarter, and its sequel, see Flaubert's letter to his mother from Constantinople on page 133.
2. Professor of rhetoric at the college.

To Ernest Chevalier

[Rouen,] Monday morning. [March 18, 1839]

· · ·

As to your horror of "ces dames"[1]—who are, I might say in passing, very kind-hearted, broad-minded persons—I leave to Alfred[2] the task of changing it logically into a philosophical love consistent with the rest of your moral opinions. Yes, a thousand times yes, I prefer a whore to a grisette, for of all types of human beings the grisette is what I most abominate. Such, I believe, is the name given to that wriggly, properish, coquettish, simpery, perky, stupid something that's always getting on your nerves and wanting to play passion the way she sees it played in vaudeville. No, I much prefer the ignoble that doesn't pretend to be anything else. This preference is a pose like any other, a fact I am well aware of. With all my heart I could love a beautiful, ardent woman with the soul—and the fingers—of a whore. Such is the point I have reached. Such pure and innocent tastes! . . .

You tell me you have an admiration for G. Sand; I share it keenly, and with the same reservations. I have read few things as fine as *Jacques*. Speak to Alfred about it.

At present I am reading scarcely at all. I have resumed a work I put aside a long time ago, a morality play, a ragout—I think I've told you about it already.[3]

· · ·

1. "Ces dames"—"those women"—in Flaubert's letters always means "prostitutes"; he mocks, simply by using it, a pharisaic bourgeois euphemism. Chevalier had apparently written from Paris expressing "pure" sentiments on the subject.

A grisette was a working girl, often a seamstress: more particularly, one living with a student or several students or a succession of students. Mimi, in Puccini's *La Bohème* (its libretto based on Murger's *Scènes de la vie de bohème*, 1847-49), is probably the world's best known grisette. The word originally signified a cheap gray cloth, perhaps the stuff of the girls' workaday smocks, and is now used only historically, in connection with the Latin Quarter of that period.

2. Alfred LePoittevin, of whom much more will be heard.

3. There follows a detailed synopsis of his philosophical drama, *Smarh*, in which Satan guides and misguides a mortal, commenting sardonically on human thoughts and passions. It reflects early readings in Byron, Goethe, Quinet, Spinoza, Michelet.

To Ernest Chevalier

[Rouen,] Monday afternoon,
mathematics class, July 15, 1839

· · ·

I thought I was going to have some ideas just now, and nothing has come—so what? I'm sorry, but it's not my fault if I don't have a philosophical mind, like [Victor] Cousin or Pierre Leroux or Brillat-Savarin—or like Lacenaire,[1] who philosophized also, in his own way. And a strange, deep, bitter philosophy it was. What a lesson he read Morality, what a public whipping he gave that poor desiccated prude—how he pummeled her, dragged her in the mud, in blood. I love to see men like that, like Nero, like the marquis de Sade. When you read history, when you see the same old wheels always rolling along the same old roads in the midst of ruins, turning, turning in the dusty path of the human race, those figures loom up like Egyptian priapi . . . Those monsters explain history for me, they are its complement, its apogee, its moral, its dessert. Believe me, they too are great men, immortals. Nero will live as long as Vespasian, Satan as long as J-C.

Oh, dear Ernest, apropos of the marquis de Sade, if you could find me some of the novels of that honorable writer, I'd pay you their weight in gold. I've read a biographical article about him by J. Janin, which filled me with revulsion—revulsion against Janin, needless to say: he held forth on behalf of morality, philanthropy, deflowered virgins . . .

1. Pierre-François Lacenaire, thief and assassin, guillotined in Paris in 1836. A volume of his memoirs, reflections, and poems, published after his death, was discussed with horror at the time. His name is known to present generations through his depiction by the actor Marcel Herrand in the film *Les Enfants du Paradis* (1945).

Victor Cousin was the most prominent living French philosopher and will re-enter these pages in another role. Flaubert had been reading one of his works at the college.

Pierre Leroux was a Saint-Simonian economist; Brillat-Savarin the author of *The Physiology of Taste*; Jules Janin a literary journalist.

II

The Law
1840-1843

A FTER PASSING the baccalauréat in August 1840, Flaubert was sent by his parents on his first long journey—to Corsica, via the Pyrenees and Provence, with a family friend, Dr. Jules Cloquet. Also in the party were the doctor's sister and an Italian abbé friend of the Cloquets. The company was not particularly congenial to Flaubert, but it was in Marseilles during this trip that his erotic initiation was completed[1] by the alluringly named Mme Eulalie Foucault, née Delanglade, who with her mother was co-owner, or co-manager, of the Hôtel Richelieu, rue de la Darse. Unwittingly or otherwise, Dr. Cloquet performed a service for his handsome, not virginal, but "unawakened," romantic young friend when he took him to stay in this hotel for a few days— and nights. Flaubert wrote to Mme Foucault after his return to Rouen, and kept some of her affectionate replies: Jean Bruneau thinks their style suggests that they were copied from printed models. As we shall see, Flaubert never forgot this blessedly aggressive benefactress.

In Provence, Flaubert first saw the Mediterranean and glimpsed the architecture of the ancient world. Both enchanted him and aroused his appetite. Dazzled, he returned to Rouen on November 1, 1840.

1. In their journal, the Goncourt brothers report Flaubert's telling them of having been *dépucelé* by one of his mother's maids. After that initiation came the schoolboy visits to Rouen brothels.

To Ernest Chevalier

[Rouen,] November 14, 1840.

. . .

My mind is dried up, exhausted. I'm disgusted to be back in this damned country where you see the sun in the sky about as often as a diamond in a pig's ass-hole. I don't give a shit for Normandy and la belle France. Ah! To live in Spain, in Italy, even in Provence! Some day I must buy myself a slave in Constantinople, a Georgian girl—a man who doesn't own a slave is a nonentity; is there anything more stupid than equality, especially for those who are crippled by it?—and it cripples me horribly. I hate Europe, France—my own country, my succulent motherland that I'd gladly send to hell now that I've had a glimpse of what lies beyond. I think I must have been transplanted by the winds to this land of mud; surely I was born elsewhere—I've always had what seem like memories or intuitions of perfumed shores and blue seas. I was born to be emperor of Cochin-China, to smoke 100-foot pipes, to have 6 thousand wives and 1400 catamites, scimitars to slice off heads I don't like the look of, Numidian horses, marble pools—and I have nothing but immense, insatiable desires, frightful boredom and incessant yawns. Also a broken pipe and dried-out tobacco.

Shit! Adieu; keep well. Too bad if you're shocked by the cynicism of this letter: that would be proof you're stupid, and I like to think you're not.

Dr. Flaubert had experienced no difficulty in settling his elder son, Achille, in the career he had chosen for him—medicine; Gustave he now directed to the law, overriding the boy's evident and outspoken repugnance.[1] Having obtained his baccalauréat, Flaubert would normally have proceeded to Paris and the Law School at once. Instead, his father allowed him to delay the move for two years—part of the period, apparently, to be spent in preparation. Perhaps Dr. Flaubert had already detected symptoms of poor health in Gustave, had prescribed the trip to the south for health reasons, and on his return decided to keep him under observation. This interlude at home seems to have been one of extensive daydreaming. He began a novella, *Novembre*, put it aside several times, and finished it on October 25, 1842. For a time he kept a journal. This was discovered only in 1965, and was published that year in France as *Souvenirs, notes, et pensées intimes*. An English translation of this melancholy, poetic, youthfully cynical diary, *Intimate Notebook, 1840-41*, appeared in 1967.

1. Jean-Paul Sartre's primary thesis in his study of Flaubert, *L'Idiot de la famille*, set forth in the (comparatively) early pages of that three-volume, uncompleted work, may perhaps be summarized as follows: Because of Gustave's slight delay in learning his letters, his daydreaming, his general tastes, nervousness, and impracticality (all the foregoing characteristics being in themselves products of the family environment), Dr. Flaubert considered him unworthy, unlike his older brother, to be trained in medical science. For the doctor, according to Sartre, medicine was the noblest profession, and he himself one of its noblest practitioners. Gustave was quite aware of this, and aware that his being directed to a career in the law (an inferior, less demanding profession) was a humiliation, exclusion from the dynasty of doctor-scientists; and his eventual breakdown was due primarily to that rejection rather than to mere distaste for legal studies. Sartre then proceeds to expound and analyze the use Flaubert made of the freedom to write, conferred by the breakdown.

To HENRI-HONORÉ GOURGAUD-DUGAZON

Rouen, January 22, 1842.

Mon cher Maître,

I begin by saying that I'd like an answer. I count on seeing you in April, and since your letters usually take whole trimesters and semesters to arrive, you might easily leave me without news until then. Come—surprise me, be punctual: that is a scholastic virtue you should make a point of possessing, since you have all the others. I was in Paris at the beginning of this month: I stayed two days, full of business and errands, and hadn't the time to come and embrace you. In the spring I'll come to see you some Sunday morning, and willynilly you'll have to make me a present of your entire day. Hours pass quickly when we are together; I have so many things to tell you, and you listen so well!

Now more than ever I need to talk to you, need your wisdom, your friendship. My moral position is critical: you saw that when we were last together. From you I hide nothing, and I speak to you not as to my former teacher, but as though you were only twenty and were here, facing me, beside my fireplace.

I am, as you know, studying law; that is, I have bought my lawbooks and matriculated. I'll start studying soon, and expect to pass my examination in July.[1] I continue to busy myself with Greek and Latin, and shall perhaps be busy with them always. I love the flavor of those beautiful tongues; Tacitus is for me like bronze bas-reliefs, and Homer has the beauty of the Mediterranean; the same pure blue waters, the same sun, the same horizon. But what comes back to me from moment to moment, what makes me drop my pen as I take notes, and obliterates my textbooks as I read, is my old love, the same fixed idea: writing! That is why I am not accomplishing much, even though I get up very early and go out less than ever.

I have arrived at a moment of decision: I must go forward or backward. It is a question of life and death. When I decide, nothing will stop me, even though I were booed and jeered at by everyone. You know my stubbornness and stoicism well enough to believe me. I will pass my bar examination, but I scarcely think I shall ever plead in court about a party-wall or on behalf of some poor paterfamilias cheated by a rich upstart. When people speak to me about the bar, saying "This young fellow will make a fine trial lawyer," because I'm broad in the shoulders and have a booming voice, I confess it turns my stomach. I don't feel myself made for such a completely materialistic, trivial life. On the contrary, every day I admire the poets more and more. I discover in them a thousand things that formerly I never saw. I grasp analogies and antitheses whose precision astonishes me, etc. This, then, is what I have resolved: I have in mind three novels, three tales, each of them different, each requiring a particular way of writing. This will suffice to prove to myself whether I have talent or not.

Into them I'll put everything I have in the way of style, passion and intelligence, and then we'll see.

In April I expect to have something to show you. It is that sentimental and amatory hodgepodge I spoke to you about.[2] There is no action. I wouldn't know how to give you an analysis of it, since it consists of nothing but psychological analyses and dissections. It is perhaps very fine; but I fear it may be very false, and not a little pretentious and stilted.

Adieu; I leave you, for you've perhaps had enough of this letter in which I've done nothing but speak of myself and my wretched passions. But I have nothing else to talk to you about: I don't go to dances, and don't read the newspapers.

Again adieu; all my affection.

P.S. Answer me soon. I should dearly love to correspond with you more often, for after finishing a letter to you I find myself only at the beginning of what I want to say.

1. That is, the Law School's so-called First Examination, based on study of Justinian's *Institutes* and the French *Code Civil*, which formed the program of the first year.

2. This is the hundred-page novella, *Novembre,* Flaubert's most accomplished work so far. There are only two characters, an unnamed young man and a shadowy woman, Marie, with whom he placates the "demon of the flesh." (Flaubert's nights in Marseilles were a fresh memory.) The very Romantic tone echoes that of Goethe's *Werther* and Chateaubriand's *René,* the latter probably Flaubert's favorite modern fiction at the time. There is a pervasive vagueness; character delineation and realistic detail are almost totally absent. An English translation, by Frank Jellinek, suggests the imitative beauty of Flaubert's early Romantic prose.

Jean Bruneau thinks that Flaubert's other two projects may have been an oriental tale, *Les Sept Fils du derviche,* which he never finished, and a dictionary of accepted opinions or clichés, of which more will be heard.

Gourgaud-Dugazon was now teaching at Versailles.

In the early summer of 1842 Dr. Flaubert found Gustave well enough to go to Paris for some cramming and to take the first examination for the study of law, apparently scheduled for August.

To ERNEST CHEVALIER

[Paris, July 22, 1842]

A pretty science, the Law! Ah, it's beautiful! From the literary point of view, especially. Professors Oudot and Ducoudray: they have such elegant styles! Professor Duranton: his face—the face of a true artist! and ah! what a splendid physique: pure Greek! To think that for a month I haven't read a line of poetry, listened to a note of music, daydreamed peacefully for three hours, lived a single minute! I am so harassed by it all that the other night I *dreamed* of the law! I felt ashamed at having so dishonored dreaming. I'm sweating blood and tears, but if I can't find somebody's notes on Oudot it's the end—I'll be rejected for next year. Yesterday I went to watch some other students taking their examinations; I have nothing better to do than that. Soon I too shall have to wear that filthy harness. I care nothing for the law, as long as I retain the right to smoke my pipe and watch the clouds, lying on my back with eyes half-closed. That is all I want. Do you think I have any desire to be important, a great man, a man known in an arrondissement, in a department, in three provinces, a man without flesh on his bones, a man whose digestion doesn't work? Do you think I have ambition, like bootblacks who aspire to be bootmakers, coachmen who long to be grooms, valets who yearn to be masters—the ambition to be a deputy or minister, to be decorated, to become municipal councillor? All that seems utterly dreary to me and makes my mouth water as little as a 40-sou dinner or a humanitarian speech. But it's everybody's mania. And even if only to retain some distinction (quite apart from following one's own taste)—out of mere good form and not inclination—it is well nowadays to keep to oneself and leave that sort of thing to the riffraff, who keep pushing and calling attention to themselves. As for us, we stay at home; from our balcony we watch the public go by; and if at times disgust gets the better of us, then let's just spit down on their heads, and go on talking quietly and watching the sun sink below the horizon.

Good-night to you.

To his sister Caroline

[Paris, July 25, 1842]

. . .

I dined yesterday at Monsieur Tardif's, with Monsieur and Madame Daupias.[1] Distinguished in dress and manner (like Murat), I conducted myself very well through dinner. But later the company took it into their heads to speak of Louis-Philippe, and I railed against him because of the museum at Versailles. Think of that pig, when he discovers that a picture by Gros isn't large enough to fill a wall panel, conceiving the idea of tearing off one side of the frame and adding two or three feet of canvas painted by some mediocre artist. I'd enjoy meeting that artist, just to see what he looks like. Naturally Monsieur and Madame Daupias, who are frantic *philippistes*—who attend court and therefore, like Madame de Sévigné after dancing with Louis XIV, cry "What a great king!"—were very shocked by the way I spoke of him. But as you know, the more indignant I make the bourgeois, the happier I am. So I was thoroughly satisfied with my evening. They doubtless took me for a legitimist, because I made just as much fun of the men of the opposition.

. . . Your friend Gourgaud is coming to have lunch with me today, and I write this while waiting for him. The study of law is souring my temper in the extreme; I'm constantly grumbling, growling, grousing; when I'm alone I mutter even against myself. The night before last I'd have given a hundred francs (which I didn't have) to be able to administer a good thrashing to somebody—anybody . . .

1. Tardif was Dr. Flaubert's Paris banker, who remitted Gustave his allowance.
Daupias, baron d'Alcochete, Portuguese consul-general in Paris, was one of the many types of bourgeois who drove the young Flaubert into a frenzy. In another letter to his sister Caroline he wrote: "Last night I dined at old Tardif's, who gave me 150 francs. *Le sieur* Daupias was there. You can reassure maman, I behaved well—said almost nothing; or at least I didn't rail against the infamous Louis-Philippe. What a ridiculous imbecile that baron d'Alcochete is, what a pig, what utter, wretched riffraff! He was formerly a pearl dealer, went

bankrupt, and is now a diplomat and baron with many ribbons on the lapel of his tail-coat. How I'd have loved to spit in his face, beat him up, make him die by torture befitting the lowest criminal."

But Flaubert discovered that to be permitted to take the first law examination a student had to "qualify," on the evidence of preparation done and notes made; and Professor Oudot found Flaubert's notes on the *code civil* (Oudot's specialty) inadequate. Or perhaps he discovered that they had not—as Flaubert hints in his letters—been made by Flaubert himself, but bought or borrowed. The examination was postponed until December, and Flaubert was at home again for the late summer and part of the autumn.

In the late autumn of 1842, after finishing *Novembre*, he returned to Paris, took a flat in the Latin Quarter, registered once more at the Law School, and attended lectures.

To his sister Caroline

[Paris, after December 10, 1842]

My nerves are so on edge that I have to let myself go a little in a letter to you. Next Friday I'll definitely make the appointment for my examination. I want to get it over with as soon as possible because things can't go on like this any longer. I'd end up in a state of idiocy or fury. Tonight, for example, I'm enjoying both those agreeable sensations simultaneously. I am so desperately impatient to put the examination behind me that I could weep. I think I'd even be glad if I failed, such a burden do I find this life I've been leading for six weeks. Some days are worse than others. Yesterday, for example, the weather was mild as May: all morning I had a terrible longing to take a cart and drive out into the country. I kept thinking that if I were in Déville I'd be under the shed with Neo[1] watching the rain and quietly smoking my pipe. When preparing for an examination one mustn't pay attention to all the good, delightful things that come into one's mind: I reproach myself for wasting time whenever I open my window to look at the stars (there's a beautiful moon just now) and take my mind off things a little. To think that since leaving you I haven't read a line of French, not six lines of poetry, not a single decent sentence. The *Institutes* are written in Latin and the *code civil* in something even less resembling French. The gentlemen who compiled it didn't offer much of a sacrifice to the Graces. They made it as dry, as hard, as stinking, as flatly bourgeois as the wooden benches of the Law School, where we go to harden our buttocks while hearing it explained. Those who care little about comfort—intellectual comfort, in this case—may find themselves not too badly off there; but for aristocrats like me, who are accustomed to enthroning their imaginations in seats that are more ornate, richer, and above all more softly luxurious, it's damned disagreeable and humiliating. *"There is nothing so grossly and largely offending, nor so ordinarily wronging, as the lawes."*[2]

18

1. His dog.

2. Montaigne, *Essais*, book 3, chap. 13, "De l'expérience": "Il n'est rien si lourdement et largement faultier que les loix." (The English is John Florio's; 1603.)

Flaubert finally passed his first examination on December 28, 1842, and after spending the New Year holidays at home he returned to his Paris lodgings. His letters throughout 1843 are disturbed; he loathed his law studies and dreaded the future they represented. He sought relief in various forms. He began a second novel, which he called *L'Education Sentimentale*—the title he would use again almost thirty years later for his great novel portraying an entire generation of Frenchmen. Once a week or so he left the Latin Quarter to visit friends in other parts of the city: the Schlesingers (Maurice Schlesinger, Elise's husband, was a music publisher); the Colliers, an English family he had also met in Trouville; the sculptor James Pradier and his wife; and Mme Pradier's family, the Darcets, whom the Flauberts had known in Rouen. Otherwise he was lonely: Ernest Chevalier (and Alfred LePoittevin, whom the reader will soon meet) had finished Law School and left Paris; Flaubert patronized some of the brothels whose addresses, with the names of certain girls, Alfred sent him. On one occasion he found himself in financial trouble because of bad company, and had to appeal to his father, apparently through Caroline or his mother.[1] It was a wretchedly unhappy time. In August he failed his second examination[2] and had again to reregister.

Symptoms described in a letter to Caroline on May 12, 1843, are a portent of what was to happen the following January: "How I wish I were with you! But I'm grinding away like crazy, and from now until August shall be in a perpetual fury of work. Sometimes I'm taken with fits of twitching, and fling myself about with my books as though I had the *danse de Saint-Guy*,[3] patron of tailors, or as though I were stricken with epilepsy, the falling sickness."

1. Dr. Flaubert wrote him in July:

"You are doubly silly—first to let yourself be gulled like a real provincial, a ninny letting himself be swindled by confidence men or loose women, whose usual victims must be morons or imbecile dodderers, and thank God you are neither stupid nor old; your second mistake is not to have confidence in me . . . I thought I was sufficiently your friend to merit being told anything that might happen to you, good or bad . . .

"Adieu, dear Gustave. Spare my purse a little and above all keep well and working."

2. A passage in the definitive *Education Sentimentale* (1870) perhaps evokes this occasion. Frédéric Moreau, the novel's hero, is taking a law examination:

"Standing behind the chair, he fidgeted and kept pulling on his moustache.

" 'I'm still waiting for your answer,' said the examiner. And because Frédéric's gesture apparently irritated him: 'You won't find it in your beard.' "

3. St. Vitus's dance.

To his sister Caroline

Sunday, 5 p.m. [Paris, December 3, 1843]

Bonjour, vieux rat. I gather your precious health is satisfactory, and that you are beginning to acquire a "robust constitution." Continue to take care of yourself, so that soon, in a month, when I come to Rouen,[1] I'll find you more vigorous and flourishing than ever. If you continue well, what a time we'll have at Trouville next summer! You know my vacation begins in June. May God make it as good as I hope to make it long.

. . .

You are expecting details about Victor Hugo. What can I tell you? He is a man who looks like many another, with a rather ugly face and a rather common appearance. He has magnificent teeth, a superb forehead, no eyelashes or eyebrows. He talks little, gives the impression of being on his guard and not wanting to give himself away; he is very polite and a little stiff. I greatly like the sound of his voice. I enjoyed watching him from close by; I looked at him with astonishment, as I would at a casket of gold and royal diamonds, thinking of everything that has come out of him—that man who was sitting on a little chair beside me; I kept looking at his right hand, which has written so many splendid things. There was the man who ever since I was born has done more than any other to make my heart throb; the man whom I have loved best, perhaps, of all those whom I do not know! Some of the conversation was about executions, revenge, thieves, etc. The great man and I did most of the talking, and I no longer remember whether what I said was good or stupid, but I said rather a lot. As you see, I go quite often to the Pradiers'. It's a house I very much like; one doesn't feel at all constrained there; it's my kind of place . . .

1. For the New Year holidays.

III

Breakdown, Travel, Mourning
1844-1846

LATE IN DECEMBER 1843, Flaubert left Paris to spend the New Year holidays—"twelve days at the most," he wrote his sister—in Rouen. The exact date of the dramatic and decisive event which now soon occurred is not certain. In January he apparently returned to Paris and his studies as planned, and then for some reason went back again to Normandy. It seems to have been during that second stay that the prospect of resuming the frustrations of the Law School finally became more than his nerves could bear. One late January night, returning in a carriage with his brother Achille from a visit to Deauville to inspect the site being considered for the construction of a summer cottage, he fell to the floorboards, stricken with epilepsy. At home, cared for by his father, he suffered more attacks.

A few months earlier, he had confided to Alfred LePoittevin (who had been writing him cynical letters about the law, not designed to improve his morale) his intention of telling his father that although he would finish Law School he was determined never to practise; and Alfred had replied: "If I were capable of pitying anyone, I would pity you, buried as you are under law books. I long to know how things will end, and how Father will take your resolution to make your diploma the end of your active life." The onset of epilepsy spared Flaubert the need to announce his resolution. That aspect of his future had solved itself.

To Ernest Chevalier

[Rouen, February 1, 1844]

Dear Ernest

Without suspecting it, you came close to going into mourning for the worthy who is writing you these lines. Yes, old man; yes, young man; I barely escaped paying my respects to Pluto, Rhadamanthus and Minos. I am still in bed, with a seton in my neck—a collar even stiffer than the kind worn by an officer of the National Guard—taking countless pills and infusions, and above all plagued by that specter, a thousand times worse than all the illnesses in the world, called a diet. Know then, dear friend, that I had a cerebral congestion, a kind of attack of apoplexy in miniature, accompanied by nervous symptoms which I continue to display because it's good form to do so. I very nearly popped off in the midst of my family (with whom I had come to spend two or three days to recover from the horrible scenes I had witnessed at Hamard's [in Paris]).[1] They bled me in three places at once and I finally opened my eyes. My father wants to keep me here a long time and observe me carefully; my morale is good, however, because I don't know what worry is. I'm in a rotten state; at the slightest excitement, all my nerves quiver like violin strings, my knees, my shoulders, and my belly tremble like leaves. Well, c'est la vie, *sic est vita*, such is life. I shall probably not be returning to Paris, except for two or three days toward April, to give up my flat and attend to a few small matters. I'll be sent to the seashore early this year and will be made to take a lot of exercise and above all keep very quiet. No doubt I'm boring you frightfully with this tale of my woes, but what can I do? If I'm already suffering from old men's illnesses, I must be allowed to drivel on the way they do . . .

1. Emile Hamard, a school friend, of whom Flaubert had a poor opinion; the future husband of Caroline Flaubert. The "horrible scenes" were apparently scenes of frantic grief: Hamard's mother had just died, leaving him an orphan and alone; his only brother had died the year before. But Hamard's grief seems scarcely sufficient reason for Flaubert's return to Rouen. The true reason is not known. Perhaps there had been further health-warnings.

To Ernest Chevalier

[Rouen,] June 7 [1844]

. . .

As to your faithful servant, he is better, without being precisely well. Not a day goes by that I don't see, every once in a while, what looks like a tangle of filaments, or a burst of fireworks, passing before my eyes.[1] That lasts varying lengths of time. Still, my last big attack was lighter than the others. I still have my seton, a pleasure I don't wish on you, and I am still deprived of my pipe— a horrible torture, one not inflicted on the early Christians. And they say the emperors were cruel!!! You see how history is written, dear sir! *Sic scribitur historia!* I am still not allowed to go about by myself . . .

My father has bought a house outside Rouen, at Croisset. We are going there to live next week. Everything is upside down because of the move; we'll be rather uncomfortable there this summer, surrounded by workmen, but next summer I think it will be superb. I go boating with Achille . . .

1. Later, in a letter to Louise Colet, Flaubert wrote more fully about the sensations he experienced during a seizure:
"Each attack was like a hemorrhage of the nervous system. Seminal losses from the pictorial faculty of the brain, a hundred thousand images cavorting at once in a kind of fireworks. It was a snatching of the soul from the body, excruciating. (I am convinced I died several times.) But what constitutes the personality, the rational essence, was present throughout; had it not been, the suffering would have been nothing, for I would have been purely passive, whereas I was always conscious even when I could no longer speak. Thus my soul was turned back entirely on itself, like a hedgehog wounding itself with its own quills."

To EMMANUEL VASSE DE SAINT-OUEN[1]

[Rouen, January 1845]

. . . I rarely leave my room. I see nobody except Alfred Le Poittevin. I live alone, like a bear. All summer I spent boating and reading Shakespeare, and since we returned from the country I have been reading and working a certain amount, studying Greek and reviewing my history. My illness has brought one benefit, in that I am allowed to spend my time as I like, a great thing in life. For me I can imagine nothing in the world preferable to a nice, well heated room, with the books one loves and the leisure one wants.[2] As for my health, it is in general better, but in these devilish nervous illnesses recovery is so slow as to be almost imperceptible. I'll be on a diet for a long time to come. But I am patient, and meanwhile time passes. I have suffered a good deal, pauvre vieux, since that last night we spent together reading Petronius. I had a seton in my neck which hurt horribly. I almost lost my right hand because of a burn, which has left a great red scar,[3] and to cap it all have had three teeth pulled . . .

1. A school friend, now studying Cretan history.

2. In August he would write to Ernest Chevalier: "I have never spent better years than the two just ended, because they have been the freest, the least constrained, of my life. I have sacrificed much for this freedom! And I would sacrifice more."

3. In the course of a treatment, Dr. Flaubert had spilled boiling water on the hand, which remained permanently scarred and half-stiffened—"like the hand of a mummy," Flaubert said.

Raised to revere the medical profession, Flaubert was learning—literally at first-hand—the fallibility of doctors, to which he would allude more than once in his correspondence and to which he would give formidable illustration in *Madame Bovary*. Sartre points out that the figure of the great Larivière at the conclusion of that novel, commonly accepted as a reverential portrait of Flaubert's father, appears on examination to be quiet mockery. There is no doubt that the man Flaubert revered his father always; Flaubert the artist, however, registered the irreverent truth.

A year after his first attack, Flaubert finished *L'Education Sentimentale*.[1]
On March 3, 1845, his sister Caroline married Emile Hamard, and a month later the couple set out (from Nogent-sur-Seine, where they were visiting cousins) on the conventional wedding trip to Italy. They were accompanied by Dr. and Mme Flaubert and by Gustave, now considered well enough to travel. Caroline herself was frail and had never been farther from Rouen than Paris; her father wanted to satisfy himself that she could stand the rigors of the road. His plan was that they would all stay together as far as Genoa—whence, if all went well, the young couple would continue alone to Florence, Rome, and Naples and the others return to France via Switzerland. But by the time they reached Genoa Caroline was exhausted and ill. Dr. Flaubert briefly thought that the Hamards could perhaps still continue to Naples if he and the others went with them; but Caroline did not improve, Mme Flaubert wept, Dr. Flaubert himself developed an eye infection, and in the end they all turned back together. During the trip Flaubert suffered two attacks.

His chief correspondent during the journey was Alfred LePoittevin. With the exception of one schoolboy note written when he was sixteen and already joking about a brothel, these are the earliest of his letters to LePoittevin to have been preserved, and from them can be gauged the importance of this apparently charming and pitiable young man in Flaubert's early life.

Alfred LePoittevin was the voluptuary, Romantic-minded son of a rich Rouen cotton manufacturer. His parents were close friends of Dr. and Mme Flaubert (each father was the godfather of the other's son); he was devoted to literature and philosophy; and he had a four-year seniority which qualified him to be cast by Flaubert in the role of substitute for the close older brother that Achille might have been but was not. Alfred's father, like Dr. Flaubert, ordered his son to study law, and like Flaubert Alfred obeyed; but he was without ambition or Flaubert's creative gift, and when his disgust for his enforced profession took the upper hand he did not go on to better things, but wasted himself in whoring, alcohol, a cynical marriage, and, eventually, languor and resignation to early death from tuberculosis.

Before Alfred's departure for Paris and Law School, he and the adolescent Flaubert had been inseparable; Alfred had shared Flaubert's passion for his literary heroes, had perhaps introduced him to some of them; two of Flaubert's works of that time, *Agonies* and *Mémoires d'un fou*, are dedicated to Alfred. Flaubert went to Paris just as Alfred returned to Rouen to practise; only after Flaubert's breakdown were they reunited, and during his convalescence the intimacy was resumed, Alfred already alcoholic, practising law *à contrecoeur*, writing occasional poetry and prose. Now, in 1845, separated from Alfred yet again while traveling, Flaubert let his heart overflow, writing often in the particular tone and vocabulary, a compound of cynicism and rhapsody, which Alfred inspired and which had infused much of Flaubert's early, Romantic fiction.

1. This early novel, three times the length of the graceful *Novembre*, and with a good-sized cast of characters, is Flaubert's most ambitious fiction in a contemporary setting before *Madame Bovary*. It is an awkward attempt at objective narration, which repeatedly, and in the end definitively, relapses into Romantic effusion. There are reflections on art, and longings for exotic scenes, which resemble passages in the correspondence. In its story of two young school friends, Henry and Jules, who follow different paths, this primitive *Education Sentimentale* contains one of the themes of Flaubert's novel of 1870 to which he would give the same title. Like *Novembre* and the rest, it remained among his unpublished juvenilia until after his death. There is an English translation by Douglas Garman.

To ALFRED LEPOITTEVIN

Nogent-sur-Seine, April 2, [18]45.

It is truly wrong for you and me to part, to disrupt our work and our intimacy. Each time we have done so we have found ourselves the worse for it. Once again, at this last separation, I felt a pang; it was less of a shock to me than other times, but still very depressing. For three months we were happy together, alone, each of us alone in himself and with the other. There is nothing in the world to equal those strange conversations we have beside that sooty fireplace where you come and sit—isn't it so, dear poet? Plumb the depths of your life and you will admit, as I do, that we have no better memories; that is, no memories of things more personal, more profound, and all the more tender for being exalted.

I enjoyed seeing Paris again; I looked at the boulevards, the rue de Rivoli, the sidewalks, as though I were back among them after being away a hundred years; and I don't know why, but I felt happy in the midst of all that noise and all that human flood. (But I have no one with me, alas! The moment you and I part, we set foot in some strange land where people do not speak our language nor we theirs.) No sooner was I off the train than I put on my city shoes, boarded a bus, and began my visits. The stairs of the Mint left me breathless, because there are a hundred of them and also because I remembered the evenings, gone never to return, when I used to climb them on my way to dinner. I greeted Mme and Mlle Darcet,[1] who were in mourning; I sat down, talked for half an hour, and then decamped.

Everywhere I went I walked in my own past, pushing through it as though striding knee-deep against the current of a flowing, murmuring river. I went to the Champs-Elysées, to see the two women[2] with whom I used to spend entire afternoons (which I probably wouldn't do now, I've become such a lout). The invalid was still half-lying in an armchair. She greeted me with the same smile and the same voice. The furniture was still the same, and the rug no more worn. In exquisite affinity, one of those rare harmonies that can be perceived only by the artist, a street-organ began to play under the windows, just as it used to when I would be reading them *Hernani* or *René*. Then I made my way to the home of a great man.[3] Alas! He was away. "Monsieur Maurice left just this afternoon for London." You may imagine that I was put out, that I'd have liked to see someone for whom I feel such unconquerable affection. Maurice's clerk found me taller; what do you say to that?

Having got Mme Pradier's address from Panofka, I hurried to the rue Laffitte and asked the concierge of No. 42 for the apartment of that lost lady. Ah! What an interesting study it was! How well I handled myself—at once bourgeois and vulgar gallant! I approved her conduct, declared myself the champion of adultery, perhaps even surprised her by my indulgence. She was certainly extremely flattered by my visit, and invited me to lunch on my return. The whole scene begs to be written, detailed, painted, carved. I would do it for a man like you if it weren't that I hurt my finger the other day, and it forces me to write slowly and hampers me at every word.

I pitied the baseness of all the people who have attacked that poor woman because she spread her legs to admit a prick other than the one officially designated for the purpose. They have taken away her children, taken away everything. She lives on six thousand francs a year in a furnished flat, no maid—wretchedness. When I saw her the time before last she was in her glory—two salons, purple silk chairs, gilded ceilings. When I came in she had been weeping, having learned that morning that the police had been following her for two weeks. The father of the young man with whom she had her affair is afraid that she'll "get him in her clutches" and is doing everything he can to break up this illicit union. Do you see the beauty of it? The father, terrified of the gold-digger? And the son, nervous and uneasy? And the girl, pitilessly prosecuted?

We leave tomorrow from Nogent, and go down immediately to Arles and Marseilles. We'll visit the Midi at leisure on our way back from Genoa, after leaving Caroline. So write me in five or six days at the latest, and address your letter to Marseilles. I'll get to see Mme Foucaud, née Eulalie de Langlade; that will be singularly bitter and funny, especially if I find her grown ugly, as I expect. A bourgeois would say "If you go, you'll be greatly disillusioned." But I have rarely experienced disillusion, having had few illusions. What a stupid platitude, always to glorify the lie and say that poetry lives on illusions! As if disillusion weren't a hundred times more poetic in itself! Both words are immensely inept, really.

Today my boredom was terrible. How beautiful are the provinces and the chic of the comfortably-off who inhabit them! Their talk is of *The Wandering Jew*[4] and the polka, of taxes and road improvements. The *neighbor* is a wonderful institution. To be given his full social importance he should always be written in capitals: NEIGHBOR.

Since leaving you, my physical and moral health have been quite good. Only the sore on my tongue is growing larger. What a joke, haha.[5]

Good-bye, dear, very dear, friend. Are you working on your novel? Write it carefully: shit us some good shit. Write me soon, and make it a long one.

Adieu, je t'embrasse.

I saw nothing on the boulevard, and did nothing obscene.

1. Jean-Pierre-Joseph Darcet, chemist and official of the Paris Mint, whom the Flauberts had known in Rouen, had recently died. The Darcets lived on an upper floor of the Mint itself (the Hôtel de la Monnaie on the Quai des Grands Augustins). Their other daughter, Louise (sometimes called Ludovica), whom Flaubert speaks of in later paragraphs, had recently been repudiated by her husband, the sculptor James Pradier, because of adultery.

2. Gertrude and Henriette Collier, daughters of a British naval officer then living in Paris. Flaubert had met them during the summer of 1842 at Trouville and had seen something of them in Paris during his years at the Law School.

3. Maurice Schlesinger.

4. The novel by Eugène Sue, the best-seller of the moment.

5. Apparently a venereal infection or a symptom resulting from a "cure."

To Alfred LePoittevin

Marseilles, Tuesday night,
[April] 15 [1845] Ten o'clock.

Ah! Ah! Ah! Picture to yourself a man catching his breath after a steep climb, a horse resting after a long gallop—picture anything you like, as long as it conveys the idea of liberty, emancipation, relief—and you will picture me writing to you. The longer I go, the more I feel myself incapable of living the life of everybody, of sharing family pleasures, warming to others' enthusiasms, blushing at what shocks them. I try the best I can to keep the sanctum of my heart concealed: useless effort! Alas! The beams pierce through and disclose the God within. Deep down I am serene, but on the surface everything agitates me. It is easier to command one's heart than one's face. By everything you hold sacred, if you hold anything sacred—by everything true and grand—oh my dear sweet Alfred, I conjure you in the name of heaven, in my own name, never travel with anyone! Anyone! I wanted to see Aigues-Mortes and I did not see Aigues-Mortes, nor the Sainte-Baume with the cave where Magdalen wept, nor the battlefield of Marius, etc. I saw nothing of any of those, because I was not alone, I wasn't free. This is the second time I've seen the Mediterranean like a grocer on holiday. Will the third time be better? It goes without saying that I'm "delighted with my trip," and always in jovial mood—factors favorable to my eventual "establishment" in life, should I ever wish to be established.

. . . Just now, walking along the shore, I recited to myself passages from your novel: I thought of you again at the Arena in Nimes and under the arches of the Pont du Gard: that is, in those places I felt a peculiar craving for your presence—because when we are far from one another there is in each of us something one might say lost, indefinite, incomplete.

. . . [At Nimes] I saw the Arena again, which I first saw five years ago. What have I done since then (words that could be equally well followed by an exclamation point or a question mark). I saw my[1] wild fig tree, growing between the courses of the Velarium, but it was dry, leafless, not rustling; I climbed to the highest tiers, thinking of all who shouted and applauded there—and then it was time to leave. Just as I begin to identify with nature or with history I'm suddenly snatched away—it's enough to give me bloody guts. On the way to the Pont du Gard I saw two or three wagons of gypsies. At Arles I went with Hamard to the Café de la Rotonde and treated a policeman to a glass of kirsch. Do you sense the sublimity of the scene? I stared at all the young girls—some of them were exquisite, two especially. On Sunday I went to Mass to have a more leisurely look. I saw one, especially, pale and thin, with a warm moistness about her. I walked in the theatre, in the Arena, I spoke with a whore from the brothel opposite the theatre—the old theatre where they played the *Rudens* and the *Bacchides*, where Ballio and Labrax[2] ejaculated their insults and belched their obscenities. I didn't "go upstairs." I didn't want to spoil the poetry of it. (In Avignon, too, I talked with whores in the street.) I'll tell you about it all later.

At Marseilles I couldn't find that admirable big-breasted female[3] who gave me such blissful interludes there. She and her mother no longer have the Hôtel Richelieu. I passed it, saw the steps and the door. The shutters were closed: the hotel is abandoned—I could barely recognize it. Isn't that symbolic? The shutters of my heart, too, have been closed a long time, now,[4] its steps deserted; it was a tumultuous hostelry once, but now it is empty and echoing like a great tomb without a corpse! With a little more effort and a little more will I could

27

perhaps have found out where she lives. But the information I was given was so sketchy that I let it go. I lacked eagerness: I always lack eagerness except where art is concerned. Not to mention that I have a strong aversion to revisiting my past; and yet my pitiless curiosity drives me to probe everything, to dig down to the last layers of mud . . . [Five years ago] I returned to the hotel after dinner (it was my last night) and fired four rounds with her. Today I'm writing to you—a superior occupation.

I read nothing, write nothing, and think just about as much. My health remains the same. My stomach is in good shape and I have developed a surprising appetite.

Write to me in Genoa . . .

Take good care with your novel. I don't approve of the idea of a second part. While you're at it, exhaust the subject. Condense it into a single part. Unless there's a better opinion, that's the one I think good.

Adieu, dear and great man, *dimidium animae meae*[5] . . .

1. "My" because the same fig tree appears in Flaubert's notes on his earlier trip, which Alfred had apparently read or listened to.
2. Comedies by Plautus, and two of his characters.
3. Eulalie Foucault.
4. Since his first attack, Flaubert had been living chastely (see p. 33).
5. "Half of my soul."

To Alfred LePoittevin

Genoa, May 1 [1845], St. Philip's Day.

(I should have gone to the French consulate today and left my card.[1] That would have been a way to put myself into the government's good graces and perhaps be given the Cross of the Legion of Honor. Let's get ourselves noticed, why don't we: let's push, climb, kiss the right asses, give thought to "establishing" ourselves, take wives, "arrive," etc.)

It is nine o'clock: they have just fired the evening gun. My window is open, the stars are shining, the air is warm; and you, old friend? Where are you? Are you thinking of me? Since my last letter reached you I've been going through agonies, suffering as I haven't suffered for years. You'll need all the intellectual intensity you're capable of to understand it. My father was thinking of continuing as far as Naples, so I thought I'd be going too. But thank God we're not going. We're returning, through Switzerland. In three weeks, a month at the latest, we'll be back in Rouen—(good old Rouen, which could be invaded by foreign troops, pillaged and sacked, without my shedding a tear. I've groaned with boredom on every one of its paving stones, yawned with depression on its every street-corner.) Do you understand what my fear was? You grasp what I mean? This trip, though very comfortable, has been too crass from the poetic point of view for me to want to prolong it. In Naples I would have experienced such exquisite sensations that the thought of having them spoiled in a million ways was terrible. When I go, I want to get to know that old antiquity to its very marrow. I want to be free, on my own, alone or with you, not with others. I want to be able to sleep under the stars, set out without knowing when I'll return. Then I'll let my thoughts flow without hindrance or reticence before they cool off, giving them all the time they need to boil away at their ease; I'll take on the color of whatever I see, identify myself with it utterly and passionately. Travel should be a serious occupation. Taken otherwise, unless one stays drunk all day, it is one of the most galling things in life and also one of the silliest. If you knew how continually I am frustrated (never intentionally, of course), everything I'm snatched away from, all the possibilities I'm forced to miss, you would be almost indignant—even you, who never let yourself become indignant about anything, like La Rochefoucauld's *honnête homme.*[2] Of course I conjure you to say nothing of all this to anyone. Despite my best efforts, it may have become all too apparent. Say the opposite: that I'm happy and have been having a charming trip.

I have seen a truly beautiful road, the Corniche, and am now in a beautiful city, a truly beautiful city, Genoa. You walk on marble; everything is marble —stairs, balconies, palaces. The palaces touch one another; walking in the street you look up and see the great patrician ceilings, all painted and gilded. I go into many of the churches, listen to the singing and the organ, watch the monks, look at the chasubles, the altars, the statues. There was a time when I would have indulged in many more reflections than I do now, though I don't know what they would have been: perhaps I would have reflected more and looked less. Now I open my eyes to everything, naively and simply, which is perhaps better.

. . . On the way from Fréjus to Antibes we went over the Esterel, and on the right I saw the immortal Auberge des Adrets. I gazed at it religiously, remembering that it was from there that the great Robert Macaire[3] took his flight toward the future, that out of that house came the greatest symbol of the epoch —the motto, one might say, of our age. Types like that aren't created every day: since Don Juan, I don't know of one who looms so large. A propos of Don Juan, this is the place to come and think about him: one enjoys imagining him as one strolls in these Italian churches, among the statues, in the rosy light coming through the red curtains, glimpsing the shadowy necks of the kneeling women. They all wear great white veils and long gold or silver earrings. It must be good to fuck there, in the evening, hidden behind the confessionals, at the hour when they're lighting the lamps. But all that isn't for us. We are made to feel it, to talk about it, but not to do it. How is your novel? Coming along? Are you happy about it? I am eager to see it as a whole. Think only of Art, of that and that alone, because that's all there is. Work! God ordains it. To me that seems clear.

. . . I expected a letter from you here—I need one . . . You promised to write me often . . .

Adieu, dear Alfred. You know I love you and think of you.

1. May 1 was officially celebrated as the name day of Louis-Philippe.

2. La Rochefoucauld: "Le vrai honnête homme est celui qui ne se pique de rien."

3. The bandit-hero of the popular melodrama, *L'Auberge des Adrets*, by Benjamin, Saint-Amant, and Paulyanthe. It was first produced in Paris in 1823, thus antedating by seven years Victor Hugo's *Hernani*, generally considered—on a different literary level—the "first" Romantic play. In Jean Bruneau's words, Robert Macaire is "le type romantique du révolté contre la société, sur le mode héroï-comique." As such he was immensely appealing to the young Flaubert, who perhaps saw the play in Rouen. He imitated it in some of his earliest writings. The three authors of *L'Auberge des Adrets*, and the play itself, are burlesqued in the film *Les Enfants du Paradis*.

To Alfred LePoittevin

Milan, May 13 [1845]

Once again I have left my dear old Mediterranean!! I bade it farewell with a strange sinking of the heart. The morning we were to leave Genoa I went out of the hotel at six o'clock as though to take a stroll. I hired a boat and had myself rowed as far as the entrance of the harbor, to look one last time at the blue waters I so love. The sea was running high. I let myself be rocked with the boat, thinking of you and missing you. And then, when I began to feel I might be seasick, I returned to shore and we set out. I was so depressed for the next three days that more than once I thought I would die. I mean that literally. No matter how great an effort I made, I could not utter a word. I begin to disbelieve that people die of grief, because I am alive.

I saw the battlefields of Marengo, Novi, and Vercelli, but I was in such a pitiable state of mind that it all left me unmoved. I kept thinking of those ceilings in the Genoa palaces, and the proud fucking one would do under them. I carry the love of antiquity in my entrails. I am moved to the deepest depths of my being when I think of the Roman keels that once cut the changeless, eternally undulant waves of this ever-young sea. The ocean is perhaps more beautiful. But here the absence of tides which divide time into regular periods seems to make you forget that the past is far distant and that centuries separate you from Cleopatra. Ah! When will you and I stretch out on our bellies on the sands of Alexandria, or sleep in the shade of the plane trees of the Hellespont?

You are wasting away with boredom, you say? Bursting with anger, dying of depression, stifling? Have patience, oh lion of the desert! I myself suffered a long period of suffocation: the walls of my room in the rue de l'Est still echo with the frightful curses, the foot-stampings, the cries of distress I gave vent to when I was alone there. How I roared in that room! And how I yawned! Train your lungs to use only a little air: they will expand all the more joyfully when you're on the high peaks and have to breathe hurricanes. Think, work, write, roll up your sleeves and cut your marble, like the good workman who refuses to be diverted from his task and keeps at it with sweat and good humor. It is in the second part of an artist's life that travel is beneficial: in his earlier years the would-be traveler should cleanse his mind of everything subjective, original,

30

individual. So think what a long wandering in the Orient will mean to you a few years from now! Give your muse free rein, ignore human concerns, and each day you'll feel your mind expanding in a way that will astonish you. The only way not to be unhappy is to shut yourself up in Art and count all the rest as nothing. One's pride, if it is well founded, makes up for everything else. As for me, I've really been fairly well since resigning myself to perpetual illness. You're aware, aren't you, that there are many things lacking in my existence? That I had it in me to be as lavish as the richest men in the world, every bit as tender as the greatest lovers, every bit as sensual as the most unbridled libertines? However, I do not regret the absence of riches, or love, or the flesh, and everyone is astonished to see me behaving so sensibly. I have said an irrevocable farewell to the practical life. My nervous illness was the transition between two states. From now until a day that is far distant I ask for no more than five or six quiet hours in my room, a good fire in winter, and a pair of candles to light me at night.

You distress me, my dear sweet friend (there should be another word, because for me you are not what is commonly meant by "friend," even in the best sense); you distress me when you speak of your death. Think of what would become of me. A wandering soul, like a bird flying over the flooded earth, I would have not the tiniest stone, not a square inch of ground, where I could rest my weariness. Why are you going to spend a month in Paris? You'll be even more bored than in Rouen. You'll return even more exhausted. Besides, are you sure that steam baths are really so good for your head, oh Moechus?[1]

I long to see what you have written since I left. In four or five weeks we'll read it over together, alone, by ourselves and sufficient unto ourselves, far from the world and from the bourgeois, holed up like bears, growling under our layers of fur. I still think about my oriental tale, which I shall write next winter. For the past few days I have had an idea for a rather good play about an episode of the Corsican war which I read in a history of Genoa. I have seen a picture by Breughel, *The Temptation of Saint Anthony*, which made me think of arranging the subject for the theatre. But that would need someone very different from me. I would certainly give the entire collection of the *Moniteur*, if I had it, and a hundred thousand francs besides, for that picture, which most people undoubtedly think bad.

. . . As you recommend, and as I promised, I will go and lunch with Mme Pradier, but it is doubtful that I'll do more than that, unless she invites me *very* openly. Sex games have nothing more to teach me. My desire is too universal, too permanent, too intense, for me to have desires. I don't use women as means to an end: I do what the poet in your novel does—I use them only as objects of contemplation.

1. Adulterer, fornicator.

To Alfred LePoittevin

Geneva, May 26 [1845], Monday, 9 P.M.

Two days ago I saw Byron's name written on one of the pillars of the dungeon where the prisoner of Chillon was confined. The sight afforded me exquisite joy. I thought more about Byron than about the prisoner, and no ideas came to me about tyranny and slavery. All the time I thought of the pale man who came there one day, walked up and down, wrote his name on the stone, and left.

One would have to be very daring or very stupid to write one's name in such a place after that. The stone is scratched and stained in a hundred places. In the midst of all the obscure names there I saw those of Victor Hugo and George Sand. It gave me bad feelings towards them: I thought they had more taste. Also, written in pencil, I read: "Mme Viardot, née Pauline Garcia,"[1] and that made me laugh. Mme Viardot née Pauline Garcia dreaming of the misfortunes poetized by the master and wanting the public to know about it I found truly grotesque. It "excited my hilarity," as we say in parliamentary style.

Byron's name is scratched on one side, and it is already black, as though ink had been rubbed into it to make it show. It does in fact stand out on the gray column, and one sees it the minute one enters. Below the name, the stone is a little eaten away, as though the tremendous hand which rested there had worn it with its weight. I was sunk in contemplation before those five letters.

This evening, just now, I lit my cigar and walked to a little island attached to the shore of the lake opposite our hotel, called the Ile Jean-Jacques because of Pradier's statue which stands there. This island is a favorite promenade, where they have music in the evening. When I arrived at the foot of the statue, the brasses were playing softly. One could scarcely see; people were sitting on benches, facing the lake, at the foot of tall trees whose tops were almost still, just slightly swaying. Old Rousseau, motionless on his pedestal, listened to it all. I shivered; the sound of the trombones and flutes went to my very entrails. After the andante came something merry, full of fanfares. I thought of the theatre, the orchestra, boxes full of powdered women, all the thrills of fame, and of this paragraph of the *Confessions:*[2] . . . The music continued a long time. From symphony to symphony I put off returning to the hotel; finally I left. At the two ends of Lake Geneva there are two geniuses who cast shadows loftier than those of the mountains: Byron and Rousseau, two "sly ones who would have made very good lawyers."[3]

You tell me that you are falling more and more in love with nature. My own passion for it is becoming uncontrollable. At times I look on animals and even trees with a tenderness that amounts to a feeling of affinity: I derive almost voluptuous sensations from the mere act of seeing—when I see clearly. A few days ago I met three poor idiot women who asked me for alms. They were horrible, disgusting in their ugliness and cretinism; they could not speak, they could scarcely walk. When they saw me they began to make signs to tell me that they loved me; they smiled at me, lifted their hands to their faces and sent me kisses. At Pont-l'Evêque my father owns a pasture where the caretaker has an imbecile daughter; the first times she saw me she too displayed a strange attachment to me. I attract mad people and animals. Is it because they sense that I understand them, because they feel that I enter into their world?

.   .   .

We crossed the Simplon last Thursday. It is the most beautiful thing I have seen in nature so far. You know that beautiful things cannot stand description. I missed you badly; I'd have liked you to be with me, or else I'd have liked to be in the soul of those tall pines that hung, all snowy, over the rim of the precipices. I kept measuring myself against that immensity.

.   .   .

It's a singular thing, the way I have drawn away from women. I am satiated with them, as those must be who have been loved too much. Or perhaps it is I who have loved too much. Masturbation is the cause of that: moral masturbation, I mean. Everything has gone out of me; everything has returned and entered into me. I have become impotent as a result of those magnificent effluvia that have seethed in me too furiously ever to flow. It is now two years since I last had coitus; and, in a few days, a year since I performed any lascivious act. I no longer experience in the presence of any skirt even the desire that springs from curiosity, that impels you to strip the veil from the unknown and look for something new. I must have fallen very low, since the sight of a brothel inspires me with no urge to enter it. I approve your project about the trip with a whore. That would indeed be tremendously ironic, and worthy of a great man like you.[4]

.   .   .

1. The singer, sister of Malibran. It is not clear whether at this time Flaubert knew who she was. He became acquainted with her later, through Turgenev.

2. Here Flaubert (mis)quotes from memory the opening words of a paragraph in which Rousseau looks back on a moment of youthful fiasco from the height of his triumph with his opera, *Le Devin du village*.

3. Alfred LePoittevin's father had said of Flaubert: "He's a sly one; he'd make a good lawyer."

4. Alfred's plan which Flaubert "approved" was this (written in reply to Flaubert's May 1 letter from Genoa):

"Le Havre and Honfleur, for many reasons, still play strangely on my emotions. I dreamed of love there when I was very young, of that love which I would refuse today, wherever it might come from, in whatever form. Today I enjoy it as buffoonery, the most exquisite kind of all, but I like to think back on the past, when I *believed!* . . . Of those women, some are married, others still available. It's a strange thing: my sensuality is of the wild, impetuous kind, yet I cannot give a kiss that is not ironic. I don't know what you will think of a project I intend to carry out when I can: it is to spend three days in Le Havre or Honfleur with a whore I'll choose *ad hoc*. We'll eat, drink, take walks, and sleep together. I'll greatly enjoy taking her to places where, being still young, I *believed* . . . I'll pay her off when we get back. I am like that Greek who could never laugh again after going down into Trophonius's cave."

33

To Alfred LePoittevin

Croisset, Tuesday night, half-past 10.
[June 17, 1845]

Back in my cave!

Back in my solitude! By dint of being in a bad way, I'm in a good way. I shan't be wanting any change in my circumstances for a long time. What do I need, after all? Liberty and leisure, isn't it so? I have deliberately weaned my-self from so many things that I feel rich in the midst of the most absolute des-titution. I still have some way to go. My sentimental education[1] isn't finished, but I may graduate soon. Have you sometimes thought, dear sweet friend, how many tears the horrible word "happiness" is responsible for? If that word didn't exist we would sleep more serenely and live in greater peace. I am still prey, sometimes, to strange yearnings for love, although I am disgusted by it down to my very entrails. They would perhaps pass unnoticed if I could pay less attention to them; but I'm forever on the watch, spying on the workings of my heart.

I have had no return of the depression of five years ago. Do you remember the state I was in one whole winter, when I used to come to you Thursday afternoons after leaving Chéruel's class, in my big blue overcoat? My feet would be soaked from the snow, and I'd warm them at your fire.

My youth has really been a bitter one, and I would not care to relive it. But now my life seems to be arranged in a regular way. Its horizons are less wide, alas!—less varied, especially; but perhaps it is the more intense for being re-stricted. My books are here on the table before me, everything is calm, the rain is dropping softly on the leaves, and the moon is passing behind the great tulip tree, a black silhouette against the deep blue sky.

I have thought about Pradier's advice. It is good: but how to follow it? And where would I stop? If I were to take it seriously, and really throw myself into physical pleasure, I'd be humiliated. But that is what I would have to do, and what I will not do. Normal, regular, rich, hearty copulation would take me too much out of myself, disturb my peace. I would be re-entering active life in the physical sense, and that is what has been detrimental to me each time I've tried it. Besides, if it were destined to be, it would be.

. . . Adieu, carissimo—answer me soon, as you promised . . .

1. Flaubert's words are "mon éducation sentimentale." "Sentimental Education," the literal English translation of the term as the title of Flaubert's novel, is misleading: the book treats of the illusion of romantic love.

To Alfred LePoittevin

[Croisset, July 1845]

. . .

I am still dissecting Voltaire's plays. It is tedious, but may be useful to me later. One does come on some astonishingly stupid lines. I keep doing a little

Greek. I have finished Herodotus's *Egypt.* Three months from now I hope to be reading him easily; and in a year, with patience, Sophocles. Also, I'm reading Quintus Curtius. What a lad, that Alexander! The sculptural beauty of his life! He gives the impression of a magnificent actor, continually improvising the play he is starring in. The life of that man was pure art. I saw in one of Voltaire's notes that he preferred the Marcus Aureliuses and the Trajans to Alexander. What do you say to that: good, isn't it? I'll show you several passages from Quintus Curtius that I think you'll find worthy of your esteem, including the entry into Persepolis and the enumeration of Darius's troops. Today I finished Shakespeare's *Timon of Athens.* The more I think about Shakespeare the more overwhelmed I am. Remind me to tell you about the scene where Timon uses the dishes from his table to show his contempt for his parasites.

We'll be neighbors this winter,[1] old man. We'll be able to see each other every day—we'll plan some projects. We'll talk beside my fire while the rain falls or the snow blankets the roofs. No, I don't look on myself as one to be pitied when I think that I have you, that we still have time to ourselves, whole free hours. Bare though a rock may be, it isn't bleak when seaweed comes and clings to it, refreshing the granite with the drops of water sparkling in its tufts. If you were to disappear, what would be left to me? What would I have in my inner life—my real life?

Answer me quickly. You should write me more often and more fully. When do you return? Soon? Last night in bed I read the first volume of Stendhal's *Le Rouge et le Noir.* A distinguished mind, it seems to me—a mind of great delicacy. The style is French. But is it *style,* true style, as it used to be, unknown today?[2]

. . . Adieu, dear Alfred. Try, if you possibly can, and for love of me, to watch the drinking . . .

1. When the Flauberts would move back to the Hôtel-Dieu from the riverside house at Croisset (then well outside the city), which had so far been used only for summer residence. These winter plans were to be sadly disrupted.
2. One recalls Stendhal's words to Balzac: "While composing the *Chartreuse,* to acquire the tone, I used to read two or three pages of the *code civil* every morning," and Flaubert's remarks concerning the *code* (see p. 18).

To ALFRED LePOITTEVIN

[Croisset,] Tuesday night, September 16 [1845]

.   .   .

I am very eager to read your story . . . Work, work, write—write all you can while the muse bears you along. She is the best battle-steed, the best coach to carry you through life in noble style. The burden of existence does not weigh on our shoulders when we are composing. It is true that the fatigue and the feeling of desertion that follow are all the more terrible. Let it be so, however.

Two glasses of vinegar and one of wine are better than one of reddish water. As for me, I no longer feel the glowing enthusiasm of youth, nor those dreadful old waves of bitterness. The two have merged, and the result is a single, universal tone, made up of everything, ground together and compounded. I notice that I seldom laugh any more, and no longer suffer from depressions. I am ripe. You speak of my serenity, dear friend,[1] and are envious of it. It is true that it might seem surprising. Ill, agitated, prey a thousand times a day to moments of terrible anxiety, without women, without wine, without any of the tinsel the world offers, I continue my slow work like a good workman who rolls up his sleeves and sweats away at his anvil, indifferent to rain or wind, hail or thunder. Formerly I was not like that. The change came about naturally. My will, too, played a certain role. It will take me further, I hope. My only fear is lest it give way, for there are days when my torpor is frightening. I think I have finally come to understand one thing, one great thing. That is, that for people like you and me happiness is in the *idea*, nowhere else. Seek out what is truly your nature, and be in harmony with it. *"Sibi constet,"* says Horace. That is everything. I swear to you that I think neither about fame nor—very much—about art. I try to pass the time in the least boring way possible, and I have found it. Do as I do. *Break with the outside world*, live like a bear—a polar bear—let everything else go to hell—everything, yourself included, except your intelligence. There is now such a great gap between me and the rest of the world that I am sometimes surprised to hear people say the most natural and simple things. It's strange how the most banal utterance sometimes makes me marvel. There are gestures, sounds of people's voices, that I cannot get over, silly remarks that almost give me vertigo. Have you sometimes listened closely to people speaking a foreign language you didn't understand? That is my case. Precisely because I want to understand everything, anything at all sets me wondering. Still, it seems to me that this astonishment is not stupidity. The bourgeois, for example, is for me something unfathomable.

· · ·

Everyone is quite well here. Adieu; answer quickly.

1. Alfred had recently written him: "I say nothing about my morale: it continues as low as ever, just as listless and exhausted. It seems one doesn't shake off boredom and one's disgust with things. If the supreme good is action, then I'm a bloody long way from it. I admire your serenity. Does it come from your being less distracted than I, less harried by external things? Or is it simply that you are stronger? You are lucky to be able to save yourself by a means that I too might have had at my command, but which so far I haven't felt any urgent need to clutch hold of."

"Everyone is quite well here" . . .
Within a few months the Flaubert family was shattered by two deaths. On January 15, 1846, Dr. Flaubert died, at sixty-one, following an operation by his son Achille for "a deep abscess in the thigh." Caroline, who had come to Rouen for the delivery of her first child, gave birth to a daughter on January

21; after a few days she developed an infection; she lingered, and died on March 22.

After Caroline's death, Flaubert and his mother moved out of the Hôtel-Dieu and took the baby girl—to be baptized Caroline—with them to Croisset; Hamard came to live in a small house adjoining.

"The good, intelligent man we have lost; the tender, noble soul that is gone," Flaubert wrote to Ernest Chevalier. Flaubert unquestionably loved and admired his exigent father; and yet following the doctor's disappearance the epileptic attacks immediately began to decrease in frequency.

Maxime DuCamp, who now enters the correspondence and will continue to occupy a prominent place in it, was introduced to Flaubert in Paris during the years of law study: Flaubert considered DuCamp's friendship the only good that came to him during that time. A year younger than Flaubert, and like him the son of a prominent doctor, DuCamp had lost both parents and lived in Paris with his grandmother. He had some independent means, and was trying his hand at various kinds of writing. In contrast to Flaubert, he was worldly and efficient, with a wide-ranging curiosity and a force of ambition that would eventually take him into the French Academy. At this moment of new crisis in Flaubert's life DuCamp was planning a trip to the "Orient"—what is now called the Middle East.

To Maxime DuCamp

[Rouen, March 15, 1846]

Hamard has just left my room, where he was standing sobbing beside the fire. My mother is a weeping statue.

Caroline speaks to us, caresses us, says gentle and affectionate things to all of us. Her memory is going, her ideas are confused; she didn't know whether it was I or Achille who had gone to Paris.[1] What grace there is about the sick, what strange movements they make! The baby sucks and cries. Achille says nothing, not knowing what to say. What a house! What a hell!

My own eyes are dry as marble. It is strange how sorrows in fiction flood me with facile emotion, while actual sorrows remain hard and bitter in my heart, crystallizing there as they come.

It seems that calamity is upon us, and that it will not leave until it has glutted itself on us.

Once again I'm to see the house draped in black; once again I'm to hear the hobnailed boots of the undertaker's men—ignoble sound!—descending the stairs.

I prefer to have no hope, but rather to direct my thoughts to the grief that is coming. Dr. Marjolin arrives tonight. What can he do?

I had a premonition last night that when I next saw you I would not be gay.

1. Flaubert had just seen DuCamp in Paris, where he had gone to enlist the aid of highly placed medical friends of the family concerning his brother Achille's succession to his father's post in the Rouen hospital. Certain doctors on the staff had tried to block the appointment, charging underqualification and favoritism. Flaubert would always be proud of the successful role he played in this episode of "practical life."

To Maxime DuCamp

[Croisset,] Wednesday morning [March 25, 1846]

Mon cher vieux, I didn't want you to come here. I was afraid of your affection. It was enough for me to see Hamard, without seeing you. Perhaps you would have been even less calm than we were. In a little while I'll send you a call: I count on you. It was yesterday at eleven o'clock that we buried her, poor girl. They dressed her in her wedding-gown, with bouquets of roses, immortelles and violets. I watched beside her all night. She lay on her bed, in that room where you heard her play her piano. She seemed much taller and much more beautiful than when she was alive, with the long white veil coming down to her feet.[1] In the morning, when everything was done, I gave her a long last farewell kiss in her coffin. I bent over her, and as I lowered my head into the coffin I felt the lead buckle under my hands. It was I who attended to the casts. I saw the great paws of those louts touching her and covering her with plaster. I shall have her hand and her face. I shall ask Pradier to make me her bust and will put it in my room. I have her big colored shawl, a lock of her hair, her table and writing-desk. That is all—all that remains of those we love!

Hamard insisted on coming with us. There, in the cemetery (I used to walk just outside the walls with my class, and it was there that Hamard saw me for the first time), he knelt at the edge of the grave, threw kisses to her, and wept. The grave was too narrow, the coffin wouldn't fit. They shook it, pulled it, turned it this way and that; they took a spade and crowbars, and finally a gravedigger trod on it—just above Caroline's head—to force it down. I was standing at the side, holding my hat in my hand; I threw it down with a cry.

I'll tell you the rest when we're together, for I'd write it all too badly. I was as tearless as a tombstone, but seething with anger. I wanted to tell you all this, thinking it would give you pleasure. You are sufficiently intelligent, and love me enough, to understand that word "pleasure," which would make the bourgeois laugh.

We have been back in Croisset since Sunday. (What a journey, alone with my mother, and the baby crying!) The last time I left Croisset was with you: you remember. Of the four who lived here then, two remain. The trees are still leafless, the wind is blowing, the river is high; the rooms are cold and bare.

My mother is better than one would think she could be. She busies herself with her daughter's child, sleeps in her room, rocks her, does everything she can. She is trying to turn herself into a mother again. Will she succeed? The reaction has not yet set in, and I dread its coming.

We face some bad trouble because of the child.[2] It is no longer possible to settle things privately; we must go to court. Even if there is no hitch, it will take three months. Also—and this is the most pressing—we must find a place to live in Rouen.[3]

I am crushed, numb. I greatly need to resume a quiet existence: the grief and the worry have been suffocating. When can I return to my austere life of tranquil art and long meditation? I laugh with pity at the vanity of the human will, when I think that for the past six years I have wanted to learn Greek, and that circumstances have been such that I haven't yet got as far as the verbs.

Adieu, dear Maxime. Je t'embrasse tendrement.

It goes without saying that this letter is for you alone, and nothing in it should go any further.

1. Recalling this scene in a later letter to Louise Colet, Flaubert adds the following: "I was reading Montaigne; my eyes kept turning from my book to the corpse; her husband and the priest were snoring; and I kept telling myself, as I saw all this, that forms disappear, that the idea alone remains; and I kept feeling thrills at turns of phrase in the Montaigne, and reflected that he too would be forgotten. It was freezing, the window was open because of the odor, and from time to time I got up to look at the stars, calm, radiant, eternal."
2. Hamard was showing signs of mental derangement.
3. For the following winter.

To Maxime DuCamp

[Croisset,] Tuesday, 2 p.m.
[April 7, 1846]

I have taken a large sheet of paper with the intention of writing you a long letter; perhaps I shall send you only three lines; we'll see how it goes. The sky is gray, the Seine yellow, the grass green; the trees are just beginning to bud; it is spring, the season of joy and love. "But there is no more spring in my heart than there is on the highroad, where the wind wearies the eyes and the dust rises in whirling clouds." Do you remember where that comes from? From my old *Novembre*. I was nineteen when I wrote it, almost six years ago. It is strange, how I was born with little faith in happiness. While still very young I had a complete presentiment of life. It was like a nauseating smell of cooking escaping through a ventilator: you don't have to eat it to know it would make you vomit. This is not a complaint, however; my recent bereavements have saddened me but not surprised me. Without feeling them any the less acutely, I have analyzed them as an artist. This task has revived my grief in a melancholy way. Had my expectations been greater, I'd have cursed life. That is just what I have not done. You would perhaps consider me heartless were I to tell you that I do not consider my present state the most pitiable of all. When I had nothing to complain of, I felt much sorrier for myself. This, after all, may be only a question of practice. The soul expands with suffering, thus enormously increasing its capacity; what formerly filled it to the point of bursting now barely covers the bottom. At least I have one great consolation, one firm basis of support: I don't see what further trouble can befall me . . .

To Alfred LePoittevin

[Croisset,] Sunday night, 10:30.
[May 31, 1846]

Not having asked me for advice, it would be proper for me to give none.[1] So we won't speak about that. There are many things which I foresee. Unfortunately, I am farsighted; I think you are deluded, enormously so—as indeed one is when one takes any Step. Are you sure, oh great man, that you'll not end up becoming a bourgeois? In all my artistic hopes, I was at one with you. It is that aspect that distresses me.

Too late! Let be what will be. I will always be here for you. Remains to be seen whether you will be there for me. Don't protest or explain! Time and things are stronger than ourselves. An entire volume would be needed to develop even the least significant word on this page. No one wishes for your happiness more than I, and no one is more doubtful of it. Because in your very seeking it you are doing something abnormal. If you love her, so much the better; if you don't love her, try to love her.

Will we still share those arcana of ideas and feelings, inaccessible to the rest of the world? Who can say? No one.

Come and see me, or I'll come to see you whenever you wish. Only write me at least a day in advance, because at present I come occasionally to Rouen to help with the move.

I have said nothing to Hamard, as he is away and won't be back until Tuesday morning. If you can, try to come on Tuesday: that would be quite convenient for me.

Adieu, Carissimo.

1. Flaubert had just learned of Alfred's engagement. His syntax itself betrays his agitation.
Alfred's fiancée was Louise de Maupassant, daughter of a family long acquainted with the LePoittevins and the Flauberts. Both the LePoittevins and the Maupassants were of the prosperous Norman bourgeoisie, with pretensions to noble quarterings. Alfred's marriage would take place on July 6. The following November 9, Alfred's sister, Laure LePoittevin, would marry Louise de Maupassant's brother Gustave; they would become the parents of Guy de Maupassant.

To Ernest Chevalier

[Croisset,] June 4, [1846]
Thursday night.

. . .

I'll give you some news of what is happening here. Achille has succeeded my father as resident director of the Rouen hospital: so there he is, settled in the finest medical position in Normandy. The rest of us are living at Croisset, which I never leave and where I work as much as I can, which is not very much, but a step toward something more. This winter we shall spend four months in Rouen: we have taken an apartment at the corner of the rue de

Buffon. Here at Croisset we are almost settled, thank God—it has been another sad task. I have quite a nice room, with a little balcony where I can smoke my morning pipe.

Do you want me to tell you something that will make you utter an "Oh" followed by several exclamation points? It is the marriage—of whom? Of a young man of your acquaintance—not me, rest assured; but of a certain Le-Poittevin, to Mademoiselle de Maupassant[1] . . . At this point you will give yourself over to astonishment and reverie . . . The "holy nuptials" will be celebrated in a fortnight, I believe. The contract was to have been signed last Tuesday. After the wedding they will make a trip to Italy and next winter they will live in Paris. So there is one more lost to me, and doubly so—first because he is marrying, and second because he will live elsewhere. How everything vanishes! How everything vanishes! The leaves are unfurling again on the trees, but where is the month of May that will give us back the lovely flowers we have lost, and the fragrance of our early manhood? I don't know whether you feel the same, but I have the sensation of being inordinately aged, older than an obelisk. I have lived enormously, and when I'm sixty shall probably feel very young: that's what is so bitterly absurd about it all.

My poor mother remains inconsolable. You have no conception of such grief. If there is a God, you must admit he isn't always in the kindest of moods. Mme Mignot wrote me this morning to tell me she'll soon be coming to spend a few days here; I am immensely grateful to her. My courage isn't always equal to the task of carrying, alone, the burden of this great despair that nothing can lighten. Adieu, old friend; I embrace you with all my heart.

1. Deletions in the autograph here. Ernest Chevalier, going over Flaubert's letters in the eminence of his later life (he became a Senator), destroyed some and censored others.

IV

Louise Colet I
1846-1848

FLAUBERT'S VISITS to the salon of the sculptor James Pradier during his dreary terms at the Law School had received the all-important blessing of Alfred LePoittevin. "I strongly urge you to cultivate that house," Alfred wrote him on November 26, 1843. "There is much to be gained there—useful friends at the very least, a mistress perhaps." We have seen that in 1845 Flaubert found the Pradiers separated, and wrote to Alfred of Pradier's advice that he take a mistress. Then came the double bereavement in Rouen, and Alfred's marriage.

One afternoon in late July 1846, Flaubert paid Pradier a professional visit. The sculptor had already undertaken to carve a bust of Dr. Flaubert; now Flaubert brought with him the death mask of his sister Caroline and a cast of her hand, for the same purpose.

That day in Pradier's studio a beautiful woman was posing for the sculptor. Flaubert was introduced to her: Madame Louise Colet.

Flaubert had certainly heard or read about the poet Louise Colet, although at that time he may not have known her entire story.

She was eleven years his senior, born Louise Révoil in 1810 at Aix-en-Provence, where when quite young she reigned as a local muse. At twenty-four she arrived in Paris as the bride of Hippolyte Colet, an assistant professor at the Conservatory of Music. After winning a French Academy poetry prize and being awarded a government pension, she met the celebrated Victor Cousin—whose works Flaubert had studied at the Collège Royal. Philosopher and professor of philosophy, Cousin was now Minister of Education. Within a short time after Cousin's encounter with Louise, Hippolyte Colet had received promotion, Louise had been awarded a second Academy prize, and her pension had been increased. She also became pregnant (after five years of childless marriage); and when the gossip columnist Alphonse Karr suggested in print that for this, too, her "protector" might be responsible, she called on the slanderer and attempted to stab him with a kitchen knife. Karr gleefully publicized the assault, and thereafter there was always an aroma of ridicule about Louise, although—thanks in part to her beauty[1] and to her continued liaison with Cousin—her work continued to be published and she moved in literary society.

Louise Colet was uncritical toward her own work and remained a very minor poet; but she was sometimes perceptive regarding the work of others, and could write journalism that suited the taste of the time. She was a feminist, and in the face of difficulties, caused both by her own tiresome personality and by the pressures of contemporary society on women, could display considerable courage; but one of her greatest aptitudes was for intrigue, and in pursuit of her ends she exploited whomever and whatever she could. Victor Cousin believed that he was indeed the father of Louise's daughter, Henriette—a belief in which Louise, and apparently Hippolyte as well, encouraged him. The truth of the matter seems not to be known, but Cousin's belief resulted in material advantages to the household. At the time she met Flaubert in Pradier's studio, Louise's fortunes were at a lower ebb than usual: Hippolyte was sick; despite Cousin's help the Colets were in debt, and they were anything but harmonious; with Cousin, too, Louise had been quarreling.

As Flaubert himself was later to say, the meeting at Pradier's was "predestined." It seems likely that on seeing the handsome young man, Louise, never bashful, quickly showed herself available. Long ill, long celibate, Flaubert had recently lost father, sister, and, through marriage, his most intimate friend. It is evident from the letters that he was stimulated by the dual presence of the sculptor, known to be lascivious, and his beautiful model; in that atmosphere he felt himself, as he was to put it later, "sliding down the slope." The day he knew Louise would next be posing, he deliberately stayed away, but returned the day after, foreseeing the immediate outcome. They spent the next few nights and days together. Then he returned to Croisset.

IN THE PAGES immediately following, Flaubert's first several letters to Louise are translated almost in their entirety. All were written from Croisset within a month of their meeting in Pradier's studio; all derive from their first few days together and from a second, brief tryst in Paris about three weeks later. Primarily they are love letters, passionately—and repeatedly—conveying the erotic sensations Louise inspires. They are the only such effusions Flaubert is known to have written, and they contrast strongly with the flowing, openhearted letters to male friends that precede and follow them. Flaubert himself was impressed by the difficulty he experienced in expressing his feelings to Louise: "It's strange how bad my writing is in these letters to you . . . One thing conflicts with another . . . It's as though I wanted to say three words at a time." Almost immediately he proceeded to intersperse the erotic messages with reminiscences, artistic and literary ideas, and reflections on men and women that he regarded as expressions of candor—all of which provide a foretaste of the rich intellectual content of later letters, but which naturally displeased Louise, who would have preferred pages more exclusively amatory.

There is a reason for this. Reading these first letters to Louise, one recalls Flaubert's words to Alfred LePoittevin about plunging into physical pleasure: "That is what I will not do." With Louise he had, in fact, taken that plunge, and the equivocal tone in the letters from the outset betrays his resentment at having been seduced from a principle. The cruelty displayed, for example, in speculating to Louise about her own death, in explaining his gift of flowers, in asking her to forward his letter to a former mistress, is doubtless largely unconscious—Flaubert himself seldom admits to more than "tactlessness"; but it would be obtuse to accuse Flaubert of mere insensitivity: the reader will be put in mind of his earlier expression of admiration for the works of the marquis de Sade. Concerning her behavior with her young and quite peculiar lover, Louise, on her side, was later to write (in her "Memoranda"; all but a few of her letters to Flaubert have been lost): "I was exasperated, went to extremes, and was not very intelligent about charming him."

1. See Appendix I, "A Self-Portrait of Louise Colet."

To Louise Colet

[Croisset,] Tuesday midnight. [August 4-5, 1846]

Twelve hours ago we were still together, and at this very moment yesterday I was holding you in my arms! Do you remember? How long ago it seems! Now the night is soft and warm; I can hear the great tulip tree under my window rustling in the wind, and when I lift my head I see the moon reflected in the river. Your little slippers are in front of me as I write; I keep looking at them. Here, locked away by myself, I have just put away everything you gave me. Your two letters are in the little embroidered bag, and I am going to reread them as soon as I have sealed mine. I am not writing to you on my ordinary writing-paper—that is edged with black and I want nothing sad to pass from me to you. I want to cause you nothing but joy, and to surround you with a calm, endless bliss—to repay you a little for the overflowing generosity of the love you have given me. I am afraid of being cold, arid, selfish—and yet, God can see what is going on within me at this moment. What memories! And what desire! Ah! Our two marvelous carriage rides; how beautiful they were, particularly the second, with the lightning flashes above us. I keep remembering the color of the trees lit by the streetlights, and the swaying motion of the springs. We were alone, happy: I kept staring at you, and even in the darkness your whole face seemed illumined by your eyes. I feel I am writing badly—you will read this without emotion—I am saying nothing of what I want to say. My sentences run together like sighs, to understand them you will have to supply what should go between. You will do that, won't you? Every letter, every turn of my handwriting will set you dreaming? The way the sight of your little brown slippers makes me dream of the movements of your feet when they were in them, when the slippers were warm from them. The handkerchief, too, is there; I see your blood. I wish it were completely red with it.

My mother was waiting for me at the station. She wept at seeing me return. You wept to see me leave. In other words, such is our sad fate that we cannot move a league without causing tears on two sides at once! Grotesque and sombre thought! Here the grass is still green, the trees are as full, the river as

45

placid, as when I left; my books are open at the same pages; nothing is changed. External nature shames us, her serenity is a rebuke to our pride. No matter—let us think of nothing, neither of the future nor of ourselves, for to think is to suffer. Let the tempest in our hearts blow us where it will at full sail, and as for reefs—we'll simply have to take our chance with them.

. . . On the train I read almost an entire volume.[1] More than one passage moved me, but of that I will talk with you more fully later. As you can well see, I am unable to concentrate. Tonight I am far from being a critic. I wanted only to send you another kiss before sleeping, to tell you I love you. No sooner had I left you—and increasingly as I was borne farther and farther away—than my thoughts flew back toward you, more swiftly even than the smoke I saw billowing back from the train. (My metaphor implies the idea of fire: forgive the allusion.) Here: a kiss, quickly—you know the kind—the kind Ariosto[2] speaks of—and another, and another! Still another, and finally one more just under your chin on the spot I love, where your skin is so soft, and another on your breast, where I lay my heart. Adieu, adieu. All my love.

1. A volume by Louise Colet?
2. Jean Bruneau suggests that Flaubert may mean Aretino, author of erotic sonnets.

To Louise Colet

[Croisset, August 6 or 7, 1846]

I am shattered, numb, as though after a long orgy; I miss you terribly. There is an immense void in my heart. Formerly I was calm, proud of my serenity. I worked keenly and steadily from morning to night. Now I cannot read, or think, or write. Your love has made me sad. I can see you are suffering; I foresee I will make you suffer. Both for your sake and for my own I wish we had never met, and yet the thought of you is never absent from my mind. In it I find an exquisite sweetness. Ah! How much better it would have been to stop short after our first ride together! I had forebodings that things would turn out as they have! The next day, when I didn't come to Phidias', it was because I already felt myself sliding down the slope. I wanted to stop: what pushed me? So much the worse! So much the better! God did not give me a merry constitution; no one senses more keenly than I the wretchedness of life. I believe in nothing—not even in myself, which is rare. I devote myself to Art because it gives me pleasure to do so, but I have no faith whatever in beauty, any more than in anything else. So the part of your letter in which you speak of patriotism, poor darling, would have made me laugh if I had been in a gayer mood. You will think that I am hard, I wish I were. All those who cross my path would benefit from my being so, and so would I, with my heart that's been cropped close—like meadow grass in autumn by all the passing sheep. You would not believe me when I told you I was old. Alas, yes, for every sensation that enters my soul turns sour, like wine poured into jars too often used. If you knew all the inner forces that have consumed me, all the mad desires that have passed through my head, everything I have tried and experienced in the way of sensations and passions, you would see that I am not so young! It is you who are a child, you who are fresh and new, you whose candor makes me blush. The grandeur of your love fills me with humility; you deserved someone better than I. May lightning strike me, may all possible curses fall upon me if ever I forget that! You ask me whether I despise you because you gave yourself to me too quickly. Have you really been able to suspect that? *Never, never:* whatever you do, whatever may happen, I am devoted to you for life, to you, to your daughter, to anything and anyone you wish. That is a vow. Remember it. Use it. I make it because I can keep it.

Yes, I desire you and I think of you. I love you more than I loved you in Paris. I can no longer do anything; I keep seeing you in the studio, standing near your bust, your long curls stirring on your white shoulders, your blue dress, your arm, your face—everything. Ah! Now *strength* is beginning to circulate in my blood. You seem to be here; I am on fire, my nerves tremble . . . you know how . . . you know the heat of my kisses.

Ever since we said we loved each other, you have wondered why I have never added the words "for ever." Why? Because I always sense the future, the antithesis of everything is always before my eyes. I have never seen a child without thinking that it would grow old, nor a cradle without thinking of a grave. The sight of a naked woman makes me imagine her skeleton. As a result, joyful spectacles sadden me and sad ones affect me but little. I do too much inward weeping to shed outward tears—something read in a book moves me more than a real misfortune. When I had a family, I often wished I had none, so that I might be freer, free to live in China or among savages. Now that my family is gone, I long for it, and cling to the walls that still retain the imprint of its shadow. Others would be proud of the love you lavish on me, their vanity would drink its fill of it, and their male egotism would be flattered to its inmost depths. But after the moments of frenzy have passed, my heart swoons with sadness, for I say to myself: "She loves me and I love her too, but I do not love her enough. If she had never known me, she would have been spared all the tears she is shedding." Forgive me, forgive me in the name of all the rapture you have given me. But I have a presentiment of immense unhappiness for you. I fear lest my letters be discovered, that everything become known. *I am sick and my sickness is you.*

You think that you will love me for ever, child. For ever! What presumption on human lips! You have loved before, have you not? So have I. Remember that you have said "for ever" before. But I am bullying you, hurting you. You know that my caresses are fierce. No matter: I should rather inject some disquiet into your happiness now than deliberately exaggerate its extent, as men always do, to make you suffer the more when it ends—who knows? You will thank me later, perhaps, for having had the courage not to be more tender. Ah! If I lived in Paris, if every day of my life could be passed at your side— yes, then I'd let myself be swept away by this current, without crying for help! I should find in you, for my heart, my body and my mind, a daily gratification that would never weary me. But apart, destined to see each other only rarely, how frightful! What a prospect! What can we do? Still—I cannot imagine how I was able to leave you. But that is how I am; there you see my wretched character. If you were not to love me, I should die; but you do love me, and I am writing you to stop. I am disgusted by my own stupidity. But in whatever direction I look I see only unhappiness! I wish I might have come into your life like a cool brook to refresh its thirst, not as a devastating torrent. At the thought of me your flesh would have thrilled, your heart smiled. Never curse me! Ah, I shall love you well before loving you no longer. I shall always bless you—your image will stay with me, all imbued with poetry and tenderness, as last night was bathed in the milky vapor of its silvery mist.

Sometime this month I'll come to see you and will stay an entire day. In two weeks or less I shall be with you. When Phidias writes[1] I will come at once, I promise . . .

You want me to send you something I have written. No, you would find everything too good. Have you not given me enough, without literary praise? Do you want to make me completely fatuous? Nothing I have here is legible; you couldn't decipher it, with all its crossings-out and inserts—I have never had anything properly recopied. Aren't you afraid of spoiling your style by associating with me? You'd like me to publish something immediately; you'd like to stimulate me; you'd end by getting me to take myself seriously (may the Lord preserve me from that!). Formerly the pen ran quickly over my paper; now as it runs it tears. I cannot write a sentence, I keep changing my pen, because I can express nothing of what I want to say. Come to Rouen with Phidias, pretend you met him here by chance, and visit me here. That will satisfy you more than any possible description. Then you'll think of my rug and of the great white bearskin I stretch out on during the day, as I think of your alabaster lamp and how I watched its dying light flickering on the ceiling. Did you understand, that night, that I was waiting for it to go out? I didn't dare; I am timid, despite my cynicism—or perhaps because of it. I told myself I'll wait till the candle dies. Oh! Such forgetfulness of everything! Such exclusion of the rest of the world! The smooth skin of your naked body! And the hypocritical pleasure I took in my resentment as your other guests stayed, and stayed! I shall always remember your look when you were at my knees on the floor, and your ecstatic smile when you opened the door and we parted. I went down through the shadows on tiptoe like a thief. Wasn't I one? And are they all as happy, when they flee with their loot?

I owe you a frank explanation of myself, in response to a page of your letter which makes me see that you harbor illusions about me. It would be cowardly of me (and cowardice is a vice that disgusts me, in whatever aspect it shows itself) to allow these to persist.

My basic character, whatever anyone may say, is that of the mountebank. In my childhood and my youth I was wildly in love with the stage. I should perhaps have been a great actor if I had happened to be born poorer. Even now, what I love above all else, is *form*, provided it be beautiful, and nothing beyond it. Women whose hearts are too ardent and whose minds too exclusive do not understand this religion of beauty, beauty considered apart from emotion. They always demand a cause, an end. I admire tinsel as much as gold: indeed, the poetry of tinsel is even greater, because it is sadder. The only things that exist for me in the world are splendid poetry, harmonious, well-turned, singing sentences, beautiful sunsets, moonlight, pictures, ancient sculpture, and strongly marked faces. Beyond that, nothing. I would rather have been Talma than Mirabeau, because he lived in a sphere of purer beauty. I am as sorry for caged birds as for enslaved human beings. In all of politics, there is only one thing that I understand: the riot. I am as fatalistic as a Turk, and believe that whether we do everything we can for the progress of humanity, or nothing at all, makes no whit of difference. As for that "progress," I have but an obtuse comprehension of muddy ideas. I am completely out of patience with everything pertaining to that kind of language. I despise modern tyranny because it seems to me stupid, weak, and without the courage of its convictions. But I have a deep cult of ancient tyranny, which I regard as mankind's finest manifestation. I am above all a man of fantasy, caprice, lack of method. I thought long and *very seriously* (don't laugh, it is a memory of my best hours) of becoming a Mohammedan in Smyrna. The day will come when I will go and settle somewhere far from here, and nothing more will be heard of me. As for what ordinarily touches men most closely, and for me is secondary— I mean physical love—I have always kept it separate from this other. I heard you jeer at J.J.[2] on this account the other day: his case is mine exactly. You are the only woman whom I have both loved and possessed. Until now I used women to satisfy desires aroused in me by other women. You made me untrue to my system, to my heart, perhaps to my nature, which, incomplete in itself, always seeks the incomplete.

I loved one woman from the time I was fourteen until I was twenty, without telling her, without touching her;[3] and after that I went three years without feeling sexual desire. At one time I thought I should continue so until I died, and I thanked God. I wish I had neither body nor heart, or rather, I wish I might be dead, for the figure I cut on this earth is infinitely ridiculous. That is what makes me mistrustful and fearful of myself.

You are the only woman to whom I have dared to try to give pleasure, the only one, perhaps, to whom I have given it. Thank you, thank you for that! But will you understand me to the end? Will you be able to bear the burden of my spleen, my manias, my whims, my prostrations and my wild reversals? You tell me, for example, to write you every day, and if I don't you will reproach me. But the very idea that you want a letter every morning will prevent me from writing it. Let me love you in my own way, in the way my nature demands, with what you call my originality. Force me to do nothing, and I will do everything. Understand me, do not reproach me. If I thought you frivolous and stupid like other women, I would placate you with words, promises, vows. That would cost me nothing. But I prefer to express less, not more, than the true feelings of my heart.

The Numidians, Herodotus says, have a strange custom. They burn the scalps of their infant children with coals, to make them less sensitive to the action of the sun, which is so fierce in their country. And of all people on earth they are the healthiest. Imagine that I was brought up in the Numidian way. Wouldn't it be too easy to say to me: "You don't feel anything! The sun itself doesn't warm you!" Have no fear: my heart is none the worse for being calloused. Don't misunderstand me, however: when I probe myself I don't think myself better than my neighbor. Only, I have some perspicacity, and a certain delicacy in my manners.

Evening is falling. I have spent my afternoon writing to you. When I was eighteen, back from a trip to the Midi, I wrote similar letters for six months to a woman I didn't love.[4] I did it to force myself to love her, to play a role with conviction. Now it is the exact opposite; the antithesis is complete.

One last word: in Paris, there is a man[5] who is at my service, devoted to me unto death; active, bold, intelligent, a great and heroic nature compliant to my every wish. In case of need, count on him as you would on me. Tomorrow I expect your poems, and in a few days your two volumes. Farewell, think of me; yes, kiss your arm for me. Every evening now I read some of your poems. I keep looking for traces of yourself in them; sometimes I find them.

Adieu, adieu; I lay my head on your breasts and look up at you, as to a madonna.

11 P.M.

Adieu, I seal my letter. This is the hour when, alone amidst everything that sleeps, I open the drawer that holds my treasures. I look at your slippers, your handkerchief, your hair, your portrait, I reread your letters and breathe their musky perfume. If you could know what I am feeling at this moment! My heart expands in the night, suffused with a dew of love!

A thousand kisses, a thousand, everywhere—*everywhere.*

1. About the bust of Dr. Flaubert. Because of his mother, Flaubert needed a pretext to go to Paris. "Phidias," of course, was Pradier.
2. The critic Jules Janin.
3. Elise Schlesinger.
4. Eulalie Foucault.
5. Maxime DuCamp.

To Louise Colet

[Croisset,] Saturday-Sunday, midnight.
[August 8-9, 1846]

The sky is clear, the moon is shining. I hear sailors singing as they raise anchor, preparing to leave with the oncoming tide. No clouds, no wind. The river is white under the moon, black in the shadows. Moths are playing around my candles, and the scent of the night comes to me through my open windows. And you, are you asleep? Or at your window? Are you thinking of the one who thinks of you? Are you dreaming? What is the color of your dream? A week ago we were taking our beautiful drive in the Bois de Boulogne. What an abyss since that day! For others, those charming hours doubtless went by like those that preceded them and those that followed; but for us it was a radiant moment whose glow will always brighten our hearts. It was beautiful in its joy and tenderness, was it not, poor soul? If I were rich I would buy that carriage and put it in my stable and never use it again. Yes, I will come back, and soon, for I think of you always; I keep dreaming of your face, of your shoulders, your white neck, your smile, of your voice that is like a love-cry, at once impassioned, violent, and sweet. I told you, I think, that it was above all your voice that I loved.

This morning I waited a whole hour on the quay for the postman: he was late today. How many heartbeats that red-collared fool must be the cause of, all unknowing! Thank you for your good letter. But do not love me so much, do not love me so much. You hurt me! Let me love you. Don't you know that to love excessively brings bad luck to both? It's like over-fondled children: they die young. Life is not made for that. Happiness is a monstrosity; they who seek it are punished.

Yesterday and the day before, my mother was in a frightful state; she had funereal hallucinations. I stayed by her side. You don't know what it is, the burden of such despair that has to be borne alone. Remember those last words, if ever you think yourself the unhappiest of women. There is one who is more unhappy than it is possible to be: one step further lies death or madness.

Before I knew you, I was calm; I had become so. I was entering a vigorous period of moral health. My youth is over. My nervous illness, which lasted two years, was its conclusion, its close, its logical result. To have had what I had, something very serious must have happened earlier inside my brain pan. Then everything became itself again. I had experienced a clear vision of things —and of myself, which is rarer. I was living soundly, according to my particular system, devised for my particular case. I had arrived at an understanding of everything within myself, I had sorted it all, classified it all, with the result that I was more at peace than at any previous period of my existence, whereas everyone imagined the opposite—that now I was to be pitied. Then you came along, and with the touch of a fingertip stirred everything up again. The old dregs were set boiling once more; the lake of my heart began to churn. But the tempest is for the ocean; ponds, when they are disturbed, produce nothing but unhealthy smells. I must love you to tell you this. Forget me if you can, tear your soul from your body with your two hands and trample on it, to obliterate the traces I left there.

Come, don't be angry. No, I embrace you, I kiss you. I feel crazy. Were you here, I'd bite you; I long to—I, whom women jeer at for my coldness—I, charitably supposed to be incapable of sex, so little have I indulged in it. Yes, I feel within me now the cravings of wild beasts, the instincts of a love that is carnivorous, capable of tearing flesh to pieces. Is this love? Perhaps it is the opposite. Perhaps in my case it's the heart that is impotent.

My deplorable mania for analysis exhausts me. I doubt everything, even my doubt. You thought me young, and I am old. I have often spoken with old people about the pleasures of this earth, and I have always been astonished by the brightness that comes into their lackluster eyes; just as they could never get over their amazement at my way of life, and kept saying "At your age! At your age! You! You!" Take away my nervous exaltation, my fantasy of mind, the emotion of the moment, and I have little left. That's what I am underneath. *I was not made to enjoy life.* You must not take these words in a down-to-earth sense, but rather grasp their metaphysical intensity. I keep telling myself that I'll bring you misfortune, that were it not for me your life would have continued undisturbed, that the day will come when we shall part (and I protest in advance). Then the nausea of life rises to my lips, and I feel immeasurable self-disgust and a wholly Christian tenderness for you.

At other times—yesterday, for example, when I had sealed my letter—the thought of you sings, smiles, shines, and dances like a joyous fire that gives out a thousand colors and penetrating warmth. I keep remembering the graceful, charming, provocative movement of your mouth when you speak—that rosy, moist mouth that calls forth kisses and sucks them irresistibly in. What a good idea I had, to take your slippers. If you knew how I keep looking at them! The bloodstains are fading: is that their fault? We shall do the same: one year, two years, six, what does it matter? Everything measurable passes, everything that can be counted has an end. Only three things are infinite: the sky in its stars, the sea in its drops of water, and the heart in its tears. Only in that capacity is the heart large; everything else about it is small. Am I lying? Think, try to be calm. One or two shreds of happiness fill it to overflowing, whereas it has room for all the miseries of mankind.

You speak of work. Yes, you must work; love art. Of all lies, art is the least untrue. Try to love it with a love that is exclusive, ardent, devoted. It will not fail you. Only the Idea is eternal and necessary. There are no more artists as they once existed, artists whose loves and minds were the blind instruments of the appetite for the beautiful, God's organs by means of which he demonstrated to himself his own existence. For them the world did not exist; no one has ever known anything of their sufferings; each night they lay down in sadness, and they looked at human life with wonder, as we contemplate ant-hills.

You judge me from a woman's point of view: am I supposed to complain of your judgment? You love me so much that you delude yourself about me; you find in me talent, intelligence, style. In me! In me! You'll make me vain, and I was proud of not being so! See: you have already lost something as a result of meeting me. Your critical sense is forsaking you, and you imagine this person who loves you is a great man. Would that I were, to make you proud of me! (It is I who am proud of *you.* I keep telling myself: "But she loves me! Is it possible? *She!"*) Yes, I wish that I could write beautiful things, great things, and that you would weep with admiration of them. I think of you at a performance of a play by me, in a box, listening, hearing the applause. But I fear the contrary— that you will weary of constantly raising me to your level. When I was a child I dreamed of fame like everyone else, no more nor less; in me good sense sprouted late, but it is firmly planted. So it is very doubtful that the public will ever have occasion to read a single line written by me; if this happens, it will not be before ten years, at least.

I don't know what led me to read you something; forgive that weakness. I could not resist the temptation to make you think highly of me. But I was sure of success, wasn't I? What puerility on my part! It was a sweet idea you had, that we should write a book together; it moved me; but I do not want to publish anything. This is a stand I have taken, a vow I made to myself at a solemn period in my life. I work with absolute disinterestedness and without ulterior motive or concern. I am not a nightingale, but a shrill warbler, hiding deep in the woods lest I be heard by anyone except myself. If I make an appearance, one day, it will be in full armor; but I shall never have the assurance. Already my imagination is fading, my zest is not what it was. I am bored by my own sentences; and if I keep those that I have written it is because I like to surround myself with memories, just as I never sell my old clothes. I go and look at them sometimes in the attic where I keep them, and dream of the time when they were new and of everything I did when I was wearing them.

By the way—so we'll christen the blue dress together. I'll try to arrive some evening about six. We'll have all night and the next day. We'll set the night ablaze! I'll be your desire, you'll be mine, and we'll gorge ourselves on each other to see whether we can be satiated. Never! No, never! Your heart is an inexhaustible spring, you let me drink deep, it floods me, penetrates me, I drown. Oh! The beauty of your face, all pale and quivering under my kisses! But how cold I was! I did nothing but look at you; I was surprised, charmed. If I had you here now . . . Come, I'll take another look at your slippers. They are something I'll never give up; I think I love them as much as I do you. Whoever made them, little suspected how my hands would tremble when I touch them. I breathe their perfume; they smell of verbena—and of you in a way that makes my heart swell.

Adieu, my life, adieu my love, a thousand kisses everywhere. Phidias has only to write, and I will come. Next winter there will no longer be any way for us to see each other, but [if Phidias writes between now and the beginning of the winter][1] I'll come to Paris for at least three weeks. Adieu, I kiss you in the place where I *will* kiss you, where I wanted to; I put my mouth there, je me roule sur toi, mille baisers. Oh! donne-m'en, donne-m'en!

1. Clarification suggested by J.B.

To Louise Colet

[Croisset,] Sunday morning. 10 o'clock.
[August 9, 1846]

My child, your infatuation is carrying you away. Calm, calm. You are putting yourself into a state—into a rage against yourself, against life. I told you I was more reasonable than you. Do you think that I too am not to be pitied? Be more sparing with your cries; they are torturing me. What do you want me to do? Can I leave everything here and live in Paris? Impossible. If I were entirely free I would, for with you in Paris I wouldn't have the strength to go into exile—a project of my youth, which I shall carry out some day. For I want to live in a place where no one loves me or knows me, where the sound of my name causes only indifference, where my death or my absence costs no one a tear. I have been too much loved, you see; you love me too much. I am satiated with affection, and I keep wanting it, alas! You tell me that what I needed was a banal kind of love. I needed either no love at all, or yours, for I cannot imagine one more complete, more full, more beautiful. It is now ten o'clock; I have just received your letter and sent you mine, the one I wrote last night. Scarcely awake, I am writing you again without knowing what I am going to say. You must see that I am thinking of you. Don't be angry with me when you receive no letter from me. It is not my fault. Those are the very days when I am perhaps thinking of you most of all. You are afraid I am ill, dear Louise. People like me can be ill with impunity; they do not die. I have had every kind of illness and accident, horses have been killed under me, carriages have overturned, and I have never been scratched. I am fated to live a long life and to see everything perish around me and in me. In my soul I have already attended a thousand funerals; my friends leave me one after the other, they marry, move away, change; when we meet we barely recognize each other, find scarcely anything to say. What irresistible impulse drove me toward you? For an instant I saw the abyss, realized its depth, and then vertigo swept me over. But how *not* love you, you who are so sweet, so good, so noble, so loving, so beautiful? I keep remembering your voice, when you spoke to me the night of the fireworks. They blazed for us, that night, a dazzling inauguration of our love.

Your apartment resembles one I had in Paris for almost two years at 19 rue de l'Est.[1] When you pass that way, look up at the second floor. From there too there was a view over Paris. On summer nights I used to look up at the stars, and in winter at the luminous mist of the great city floating above the houses. Just as from your windows, I saw gardens, roofs, the surrounding hills. When I walked into your house it seemed to me I was reliving my past, that I had returned to one of those beautiful, sad twilights of 1843, when I would sit at my window for a little air, utterly bored, deathly depressed. If only I had known you then! Why could that not have been? I was free, alone, without family or mistress, for I have never had a mistress. You will think that I am lying. I have never been more scrupulously truthful, and this is the reason why: the grotesque aspects of love have always kept me from indulging in it. At times I have wanted to give pleasure to women, but the idea of the strange spectacle I must be presenting at that moment made me laugh so much that all my desire melted under the fire of irony, which sang a hymn of bitter derision within me. It is only with you that I have not yet laughed at myself. But when I see you so intense, absolute in your passion, I am tempted to cry out to you: "No! No! You are making a mistake! Take care! Not this man!"

Heaven made you beautiful, devoted, intelligent; I should like to be other than I am, to be worthy of you. I wish my heart were newer and fresher. Ah! Do not revive me too much: I'd blaze up like straw. You will think I am selfish, that I fear you. I admit it: I am terrified of your love, because I feel it is devouring us both, especially you. You are like Ugolino in his prison; you devour your own flesh to appease your hunger.

Some day, if I write my memoirs—the only thing I shall write well, if ever I settle down to it—you will have a place in them, and what a place! For you are making a wide breach in my existence. I had surrounded myself with a wall of stoicism; one look from you blew it to pieces, like a cannon ball. Yes, I often think I hear your dress rustling behind me on my rug; I tremble, and turn around—and it's my curtain rustling in the wind, as though you were entering the room. I keep seeing your lovely white forehead; you know, don't you, that your forehead is sublime? Too beautiful even to be kissed; pure, noble, eloquent of what is within. Do you go to Phidias', to that studio where I saw you the first time, among the marbles and the casts?

He should be coming soon. I await a letter from him which will give me a pretext to go to Paris for a day. Then early in September I will find another, to go to Mantes or Vernon. After that, we shall see. But what is the good of getting accustomed to seeing each other, loving each other? Why treat ourselves to the luxury of affection, if afterwards we must be miserable? What is the good? But what else can we do?

Adieu, my darling; I have just gone down into the garden and gathered this little rose I send you. I kiss it; put it quickly to your mouth, and then—you know where . . . Adieu! A thousand kisses. I am yours from night to day, from day to night.

1. Not the present rue de l'Est, but an old street, since demolished, near the Law School and the Luxembourg Gardens.

To Louise Colet

[Croisset,] Tuesday afternoon. [August 11, 1846]

You would breathe love into a dead man. How can I not love you? You have powers of attraction to make stones rise up at your voice. Your letters stir me to my entrails. So have no fear that I'll forget you! You must know that one doesn't turn away from natures like yours—natures that are deep and emotional, and stir the emotions of others. I hate myself, I could beat myself, for having hurt you. Forget everything I said in my letter of Sunday. I was addressing myself to your virile intellect; I had thought you could disregard the prompting of your heart and understand me in intellectual terms. You saw too many things where there were not that many to see; you exaggerated everything I said. You perhaps thought that I was acting the part of a third-rate Antony.[1] You call me a Voltairean and a materialist. God knows whether I am or not! You speak also of my "exclusive tastes in literature, which should have made you guess what I am like when it comes to love." I try in vain to find the meaning of that. I remain completely baffled. On the contrary: whatever I admire, I do so sincerely and if I am worth anything it is thanks to this pantheistic faculty, and to my very "intransigence" that offended you. Come, let's talk no more about it. I was wrong, I was foolish. I did with you what in the past I have done with those I loved best: I bared my soul, and the acrid dust that rose from its most secret recesses stuck in their throats. How many times, without wanting to, I brought tears to the eyes of my father, who was so intelligent, so perceptive! But he understood nothing of my idiom—like you, like the others. I have the infirmity of being born with a special language, to which I alone have the key. I am not in the least unhappy, not at all blasé: everybody finds me gay by nature, and I absolutely never complain. I don't really think I'm an object of pity, for I envy nothing and want nothing. Come, I'll torment you no longer; I'll touch you gently, as one does a child one fears to injure: I'll turn all my stings inward, on myself. If he's not too angry, the porcupine doesn't always pierce you. You say I analyze myself too much: I find that I don't know myself well enough—every day I discover something new. I travel within myself as in a country unknown, even though I have traversed it many times. You are not grateful for my frankness. (Women want you to deceive them: they force you to, and if you resist they blame you.) You tell me that I didn't show myself in that light at first. But think back. Remember all the things I said at our first dinner. You even exclaimed: "So you excuse everything! For you there is no good or evil!" No, I never lied to you; I loved you instinctively, and I did not set out deliberately to please you. Everything happened because it was fated to happen. Mock my fatalism if you will, and tell me I'm behind the times in being a Turk. Fatalism is the Providence of evil: it is the Providence whose evidence one sees, and I believe in it.

The tearstains I find on your letters—all from tears caused by me: I'd like to redeem them with so many cups of my blood. I am angry with myself: it increases my self-disgust. If I didn't think you liked me, I would abhor myself. But that's always the way: you bring suffering to those you love, or they to you. How can you reproach me for saying "I wish I had never known you?" I can imagine nothing more affectionate. Do you want me to tell you something comparable? It is something I said the day before my sister died—it came out spontaneously and revolted everyone. We were talking about my mother, and I said: "If only she could die!" And as everyone protested, I said: "Yes: if she wanted to throw herself out the window I'd open it for her." It seems that isn't the sort of thing one says in polite society; it sounded strange or cruel. But what the devil does one say when one's heart is full to bursting? Ask yourself whether there are many men who would have written you that letter that hurt you so. Few, I think, would have had the courage and the disinterested self-abnegation. You must tear up that letter, my love, and never think of it again;

56

or, reread it from time to time, when you feel strong.

About letters: when you write me on a Sunday, post it early: you know the offices close at two. Yesterday I didn't get one. I was afraid of I don't know what. But today both came, and the little flower with them. Thank you for the idea of the mitten: if only you could send yourself with it! If I could hide you in the drawer of the cabinet beside me—how carefully I'd lock you in!

Come, laugh! Today I'm gay, I don't know why: the sweetness of your letters of this morning has entered my blood. But don't give me any more commonplaces like these: that it is money that has kept me from being happy, that if I had worked I'd be better off. As though one had only to be an apothecary's boy, a baker or a wine merchant not to be discontented here below! All that has been said to me too often by countless Philistines for me to want to hear it from your lips. That sort of thing doesn't become them: they aren't made for it. But I am grateful that you approve my literary silence. If I am fated to say something new, it will emerge by itself, when the time comes. Oh! How I should love to write great things, to please you! How I should love to thrill you with my style. Though I do not long for fame (and in this respect I am more naive than the fox in the fable) I should love to have some for you, to toss it to you like a bouquet: it would be yet another caress, a soft bed where your mind would bask in the sun of my glory. You find me handsome: I wish I were handsome in the way of Greek youths—I wish my hair were curly, black, falling on ivory shoulders; I wish I were strong, pure. But when I look at myself in the glass and think that you love me, I find myself revoltingly common. My hands are hard; I am knock-kneed, narrow-chested. If only I had a voice, and could sing—oh! how I would modulate those long inhalations that must now evaporate as sighs. If you had known me ten years ago, I was fresh, fragrant;[2] I breathed life and love; but now I see even my maturity beginning to fade. Why weren't you the first woman I knew? Why wasn't it in your arms that I first felt the intoxication of the body and the blissful spasms that hold us in ecstasy?

I regret all my past: I feel I should have held it in reserve, waiting, even without knowing why: then I could have given it to you when the time came. But I never suspected anyone could love me. (Even now that seems unnatural. Love for me! How strange!) And like a prodigal seeking to ruin himself in a single day, I gave away all my riches, great and small. I loved unspeakable things—and furiously. I idolized vile women, I sacrificed at all the altars and drank from every cask. Ah! My moral treasures! I tossed gold pieces out the window to passersby, or sent them skimming over the water. The following comparison, which is actually only a simple analogy, will give you my picture. When I was in Paris I squandered six or seven thousand a year, yet went without dinner three times a week. It is the same with my feelings: on what would gorge a regiment, I starve to death. Indigence is in my nature, but don't think of me as being in desperate straits. I used to be, but no longer. There was a time when I was unhappy. The reproaches you send me today might have been justified then.

I will write to Phidias; I don't quite know how to say that he should make it sound urgent that I come immediately. Is he perhaps in the country? Where? When does he get back? I'll arrive one evening, and spend the night and the next day until seven: that's a promise. From Thursday on, address your letters to me like this: M. DuCamp, c/o M. G. Fl., because the letters I receive from you are supposedly from him, and when he is here it would seem odd if I were to get them just the same. I might be questioned, etc. However, if you feel the slightest distaste for this, don't do it: I don't give a damn. I am discreet for your sake. I'm sure that if I so much as uttered your name, I'd blush and all would become obvious.

. . . You wanted me to send you something concerning us. Here is a page written about this time 2 years ago (it is a fragment of a letter to a friend):[3]

> . . . From her eyes flowed a lustrous fluid that seemed to enlarge them; they were motionless, fixed. Her naked shoulders (for she wore no fichu, and her dress seemed loose about her), her naked shoulders were pale silvery-gilt, smooth and firm like yellowed marble. Blue veins coursed through her burning flesh. Her pulsing breast rose and fell, and my own chest was filled with the breath she was retaining. That lasted a century. The entire earth had vanished. I saw only the pupils of her eyes, which dilated more and more: I heard only her breathing—the only sound in the silence into which we were plunged.
>
> And I took a step forward; I kissed her on her eyes, which tasted moist and sweet. She looked at me in astonishment. "Will you love me?" she said. "Will you really love me?" I let her speak without replying. I held her in my arms, and felt her heart beating against me.
>
> She broke away. "Tonight I'll come back. Now let me go, let me go. Until tonight!" She ran out.
>
> At dinner she kept her feet on mine, and now and again touched my elbow, turning her face the other way.

Does that ring true?

. . . I haven't the heart for work. I do nothing; I walk up and down in my study, lie on my green leather sofa and think of you. Afternoons, especially, I find fatiguingly long. I am tired of thinking; I'd like to be completely simple, and love you like a child, or else be a Goethe or a Byron.

As soon as I have a letter from Phidias, I'll leave my friend (even though he's coming here particularly to see me), and come running. You can see that I no longer have heart, will, anything. I am a limp, fond thing, entirely at your command. In daydream I live in the folds of your dress, in the fine curls of your hair. I have some of those here: how good they smell! If you knew how I think of your sweet voice—of your shoulders and their fragrance that I love.

. . . I wanted to work today, and not write you until tonight. I couldn't: I had to surrender.

So: adieu, adieu: a great long kiss on your mouth.

Midnight. I have just reread your letters, looked at everything again. I send you a last kiss for the night. I have just written to Phidias. I think I have made him understand that I want to come to Paris right away. I'll mail it in Rouen tomorrow, along with this. I hope to get there in time so you'll have this tomorrow evening.

Adieu. A thousand kisses without end. Till soon, my lovely—till soon.

1. The hero of the melodrama of the same name by the elder Dumas.

2. Flaubert wrote Louise about his earlier appearance in another letter: "It was ten years ago that you should have known me. My face had a distinction it has lost, my nose was less bulbous and my forehead unlined. There are still moments when, if I look at myself, I seem all right, but much of the time I think of myself as being the very picture of a bourgeois. Do you know that when I was a child, princesses stopped their carriages to take me in their arms and kiss me? One day when the duchesse de Berry was in Rouen, driving along the quays, she noticed me in the crowd: my father was holding me up so that I could see the procession. Her calèche was moving very slowly. She stopped it and obviously enjoyed seeing me and kissing me. My poor father came home very happy about that triumph—it was certainly the only one I'll ever have." And Mrs. Tennant (Gertrude Collier: see p. 26, n. 2) wrote of the young Flaubert as she knew him as a lycéen at Trouville: "At that time Gustave Flaubert looked like a young Greek. He was in mid-adolescence, tall and slender, lithe and graceful as an athlete."

3. Actually a passage from L'Education Sentimentale (first version). It naturally aroused Louise's jealousy (see p. 65).

To Louise Colet

[Croisset,] Wednesday night. [August 12, 1846]

Today you will have gone all day without a letter from me. Once again you must have doubted me, poor love. Forgive me. The fault lies not in my will but in my memory; I thought I had until one o'clock for the last mail from Rouen, whereas actually it was only until eleven. But if you're still holding a little grudge against me I hope to make it disappear on Monday—I have great hopes for Monday! Phidias will please write to me. I count on having his note not later than Sunday.

How I love the plan you propose for the celebration! It brought tears of affection to my eyes. Yes, you do love me; to doubt it would be a crime. And as for me, if I do not love you, what can my feeling for you be called? Each letter you send me penetrates more deeply into my heart. Particularly the one of this morning; it was of an exquisite charm. It was gay, kind, beautiful, like yourself. Yes, let us love each other, let us love each other since no one has ever loved us.

I shall arrive in Paris at four or quarter-past. Thus, before half-past four I shall be at your house. Already I see myself climbing your stairs: I hear the sound of the bell. . . . "Is Madame at home?" "Come in." Ah! I'm relishing them in advance, those twenty-four hours. But why must every joy bring me pain? I already think of our separation, of your sadness. You will be sensible, won't you? For I feel I'll be more depressed than the first time.

I am not one of those in whom possession kills love; rather, it kindles it. With regard to everything good that has happened to me I am like those Arabs who, one day each year, still turn in the direction of Granada and lament the beautiful place no longer theirs.

A little earlier today I happened to be walking in the rue du Collège; I saw people on the steps of the chapel; it was Prize Day; I heard the cries of the pupils, the sound of applause and a band. I went in. There it all was again, just as in my time. The same hangings in the same places. It made me remember the smell of the wet oak leaves they used to put on our heads;[1] I thought of the delirium of joy that always gripped me that day, for two months of complete freedom lay open before me. My father was there, and my sister, and friends now dead, gone, or changed. I felt a great pang as I left. The ceremony was less colorful; there were few people as compared to the crowd that filled the church ten years ago. There was less noise, there was no singing of the *Marseillaise*, which I used to bellow madly as I banged the benches. The fashionable crowd no longer attends. I remember that formerly it was full of women got up in great style; actresses would come, kept women with titles.[2] They sat upstairs, in the galleries. How proud we were when they looked at us! Some day I will write about all this, the modern young man, his soul unfurling at sixteen with an immense love that makes him lust for wealth, fame, all the splendors of life—all the overflowing, sad poetry of the heart of an adolescent —this is a new vein which no one has yet explored. Oh Louise! What I am going to say is hard, yet it is born of the deepest, most intense sympathy and pity. If ever you are loved by some poor boy who finds you beautiful, a boy such as I was, timid, gentle, trembling, who fears you and yet seeks you out, who avoids you and yet pursues you, be kind to him, do not reject him; let him only kiss your hand and he will die of ecstasy. Drop your handkerchief, he will take it and sleep with it, press it to him and weep. The spectacle I just saw has reopened the tomb in which my mummified youth has lain sleeping; I've had a whiff of its faded breath. My soul has been haunted by something like those forgotten melodies that come back to us at twilight, during those slow hours in which memory, like a ghost among ruins, stalks our thoughts. But women will never experience any of this, and certainly they will never express it. They love, they love perhaps more than we, more strongly, but not so boldly. And then, is it enough to be possessed by a feeling, to express it? Has a drinking song ever been written by a drunken man? It is wrong to think that feeling is everything. In the arts, it is nothing without form. All this is to say that women who have loved a great deal do not know love, because they have been too immersed in it; they do not have a *disinterested* appetite for the Beautiful. For them, love must always be linked with something, with a goal, a practical concern. They write to ease their hearts—not because they are attracted by Art, which is a self-sufficient principle, no more needful of support than a star. I know very well that this is not what you think, but it is what I think. Some day I will explain these ideas to you clearly, and shall hope to convince you— you, a born poet. Yesterday I read your story *Le Marquis d'Entrecasteaux*. It is written in a good, sober, vivid style; one feels it; it shows true talent. I especially like the opening, the walk, and the scene with Madame d'Entrecasteaux alone in her room, before her husband comes in. As for myself, I keep studying a little Greek. I am reading Chardin's travels to keep up my oriental studies, and to help me with an oriental story I've been planning for a year and a half. But for some time past my imagination has been losing strength. How could it soar, poor little bee? It caught its feet in a pot of jam, and is sinking there up to its neck. Adieu, my beloved; resume your usual life, go out, invite your friends, do not refuse to see the people who were there with me on Sunday. I would like to see them again myself. I don't know why. When I love, my feeling is like a flood that spreads over everything around me.

. . . No: let's not go back to the rue de l'Est together. The very thought of the Latin Quarter nauseates me. Adieu, a thousand kisses. And—yes—a thousand of Ariosto's[3] kind—and the way we know how to give them.

1. Wreaths for the prize-winners, as in Andrew Marvell's "How vainly men themselves amaze/To win the palm, the oak, or bays."
2. Fashionable courtesans sometimes adopted *titres de noblesse,* calling themselves "comtesse," "marquise," etc. But Flaubert probably exaggerates the frequency with which such glamorous creatures attended graduation ceremonies at his provincial lycée.
3. See p. 46, n. 2.

To Louise Colet

[Croisset,] Thursday night, 11 o'clock.
[August 13, 1846]

Your letter of this morning is sad, full of sorrow and resignation. You offer to forget me if that is what I want. You are sublime! I knew you were good, wonderfully good, but I did not know you were so noble. I repeat: I feel *humble* at the contrast I see between us. Do you know that you write me cruel things? And the worst is that it was I who provoked them. You are returning blow for blow—a reprisal. What I want of you, I do not know. But what I want of myself is to love you, to love you a thousand times more. Oh! If you could read my heart you would see the place I have given you there! I can see that you are suffering more than you admit. Your letter sounds strained—you had been weeping before writing it, hadn't you? It sounds crushed, in it I sense the lassitude that grief brings, I hear the faint echo of a voice that has been sobbing. Admit it, tell me right away that you were having a bad day, that it was because my letter had not come. Be frank, not proud; do not do as I have done all too often. Do not restrain your tears, they then fall back into the heart, you know, and leave deep wounds.

Something occurs to me which I must say. I am sure you think me selfish. The thought grieves you, and you are convinced it is true. Is it because I seem so? About selfishness, you know, everyone deludes himself. I am selfish like everyone else—less so than many, perhaps, and perhaps more than others. Who knows? Besides, "selfish" is a word that everyone applies to his neighbor without really knowing what he means by it. Who is not selfish, to a greater or lesser degree? From the idiot who wouldn't give a sou to redeem the human race, to the man who dives beneath the Ice to rescue a stranger, do we not all seek, according to our various instincts, to satisfy our natures? Saint Vincent de Paul obeyed an appetite for charity, Caligula an appetite for cruelty. Everyone takes his enjoyment in his own way and for himself alone. Some direct all activity toward themselves, making themselves the cause, the center, the end of everything; others invite the whole world to the banquet of their souls. That is the difference between prodigals and misers: the first take their pleasure in giving, the second in keeping. As for ordinary selfishness (what we usually mean by the word), although it is extremely repugnant to my spirit, I confess that if I could buy it I should give everything to have it. To be stupid, selfish, and have good health are three requirements for happiness, though if stupidity is lacking, all is lost. But there is also another kind of happiness, yes, there *is* another, for I have seen it, you have made me feel it; you have shown me, in the air, its shining light; before my eyes I have seen the glistening hem of its garment. I hold out my hands to grasp it . . . and then you yourself begin to shake your head and suspect it's but a phantom. (What a stupid mania I have for speaking in metaphors that say nothing!) What I mean is, I am beginning to feel that you too have sadness in your heart, that deep sadness which comes of nothing, and which, rooted in the very substance of being, increases as that substance itself is aroused. I warned you: my misery is contagious. I am infected! Woe to the one who touches me!

Oh, what you wrote me this morning is lamentable and painful: I pictured your poor face, sad at the thought of me, sad because of me. Yesterday I was so happy, confident, serene, joyful as the summer sun between two showers. Your mitten is here. It smells sweet, making me feel that I am still breathing the perfume of your shoulder and the sweet warmth of your bare arm. Come! Here are thoughts of voluptuousness, thoughts of caresses, overwhelming me again; my heart leaps up at the thought of you. I covet all your being, I invoke my memory of you to quench this need that is crying in my very depths. Why are you not here! But—Monday, yes? I await the letter from Phidias. If he writes me, everything will be as we agreed.

Do you know what I am thinking of? Of your little boudoir, where you work, where . . . (no word here; the three dots say more than all the eloquence in the world). I keep seeing your pale, intense face as you lay on the floor, your head in my lap . . . and the lamp! Oh! Never break it; keep it, light it every night, or rather at certain solemn moments of your inner life, when you are beginning or finishing some great work. An idea! I have some water from the Mississippi. It was brought to my father by a sea captain, who gave it to him as a great treat. I want you, when you have written something you think fine, to wash your hands in it; or else I will pour it on your breast, baptising you in the name of my love. I am wandering, I think; I don't know what I was speaking of before I thought of that bottle. The lamp, wasn't it? Yes, I love it, I love your house, your furniture; everything, except that frightful caricature in oil hanging in your bedroom. I think also of that worthy Catherine who served us dinner, of Phidias' jokes, of everything, a thousand foolish details that amuse me. But do you know the two pictures of you that predominate? In the studio, standing, posing, the light falling on you from the side, when I was looking at you and you at me. And then the night at the hotel—I see you lying on my bed, your hair streaming over my pillow, your eyes raised, your face pale, your hands joined, flooding me with wild words. When you are dressed, you are fresh as a bouquet. In my arms you're a warm sweetness that melts and intoxicates. And I? Tell me how I seem to you, what sort of picture of me comes to your mind? . . . What a wretched lover I am! Will you believe me when I tell you that what happened to me with you never happened before? (I had been exhausted for three days, taut as a cello string.) If I were a man of great self-esteem I'd have been bitterly chagrined. I was, for you. I feared you might suppose things that you would consider odious; other women would perhaps have found me insulting; they would have thought me cold, or re-pelled, or depleted. I was grateful to you for your spontaneous intelligence, which kept you from being surprised, whereas I myself was surprised by it as by something inconceivable and monstrous. I must indeed have loved you, and deeply, since my initial reaction with you was the opposite of what it had always been with other women.

You would like to transform me into a pagan, O my muse! You who have Roman blood in your veins. But try as I might, any effort in that direction would be useless, for deep in my soul is the Northern fog that I breathed at my birth. I carry within me the melancholy of the barbarians, with their instinct for migration and their innate disgust for life—which made them leave their own country as though by so doing they could take leave of themselves. They loved the sun, all those barbarians who went to Italy to die; they had a fren-zied longing for light, for blue sky, for a warm, vibrant existence. They dreamed of joyful days, full of love, love that would be to the heart what the juice of ripe grapes is to the hand that squeezes them. I've always had a tender sympathy for them, as one has for ancestors. In their tumultuous history, didn't I find the whole mute, obscure story of myself? Alaric's cries of joy on entering Rome found their parallel, fourteen centuries later, in the secret rav-ings of a poor child's heart. Alas! No, I am no man of antiquity: men of an-tiquity didn't have sick nerves like mine! Nor you: you are neither Greek nor Latin; you are beyond that—you have passed through Romanticism. Though today we may be reluctant to admit it, Christianity contributed to the growth of these aspirations, at the same time poisoning them by associating them with painful inner conflict. The human heart can be enlarged only by being lacer-ated.

You tell me ironically, in connection with the article in the *Constitutionnel*, that I have little regard for patriotism, generosity, and courage. Oh no! I love the conquered, but also I love conquerors. That is perhaps difficult to under-stand, but it's true. As to the idea of a fatherland—that is, a certain portion of the earth's surface drawn on a map and separated from others by a red or blue line—no! My fatherland is for me the country I love, that is, the one I dream of, the one in which I feel at home. I am as Chinese as I am French, and rejoice not at all in our victories over the Arabs,[1] because I'm saddened by their defeats. I love that fierce, enduring, hardy people, the last example of primitive society. I like to think of them as they pause for rest at noon, lying in the shade under the bellies of their camels, smoking their chibouks and jeering at our fine civilization; and I enjoy thinking how their jeering enrages us. Where am I? Whither do I roam?—as a tragic poet of the school of Delille[2] would put it. In the Orient, God help me! Farewell, my sultana! To think that I haven't even a silver-gilt perfume-burner to light when you come to sleep in my couch! What a shame! But I'll offer you all the perfumes of my heart. Farewell; one long, very long, kiss, and others besides.

1. In Algeria, where Abd-el-Kader had "rebelled" after the French "conquest."
2. Jacques Delille (1738-1813), a poet of "sensibility."

To Louise Colet

[Croisset,] Friday night, 1 o'clock.
[August 14-15, 1846]

How beautiful they are, the poems you send me! Their rhythm is as gentle as the caresses of your voice when you murmur my name among your other endearments. Forgive me if I think them the best you've done. It wasn't pride I felt when I saw they had been written for me; no: it was love, tenderness. Yours are the seductions of a siren, fatal even to the most callous. Yes, my beautiful one, you've enwrapped me in your charm, infused me with your very self. Oh! if I have perhaps seemed cold to you, if my sarcasms are harsh and hurt you, I want to cover you with love when I next see you, with caresses, with ecstasy. I want to gorge you with all the joys of the flesh, until you faint and die. I want you to be astonished by me, to confess to yourself that you had never even dreamed of such transports. I am the one who has been happy, now I want you to be the same. When you are old, I want you to recall those few hours. I want your dry bones to quiver with joy when you think of them. Not yet having received Phidias' letter (I await it with impatience and annoyance) I cannot be with you Sunday evening. And even if I could, we wouldn't have the night together. Besides, you'll be entertaining friends. I'd have to dress, and consequently should need luggage. I want to come without anything, without bundles or bags, to be freer, unencumbered.

I understand perfectly your wish to see me again in the same place, with the same people; I too should like that. Don't we always cling to our past, recent though it may be? In our appetite for life we feast again on past feelings and dream of those yet to come. Confined strictly to the present, the soul is stifled; the world is too small for it. I often think of your alabaster lamp and the chain it hangs from. Look at it when you read this, and thank it for lending me its light.

DuCamp (he is the friend I mentioned in one of my earlier letters) arrived today—he is to spend a month. (Continue to address your letters to him, as you did your last.)[1] He brought me your portrait. The frame is of carved black wood and sets off the engraving very well. It is facing me as I write, leaning gently against a cushion on my chintz sofa, in the corner between two windows—just where you would be sitting if you came here. This sofa is the one I slept on so many nights in the rue de l'Est. During the day I would lie on it when I was tired, and refresh my heart with some great poetic dream, or the memory of an old love. I shall leave the picture there like that; no one will touch it. (The other one is in my drawer, with your bag, on top of your slippers.) My mother has seen it; she likes your face, thinks you pretty. You have an "animated, open, pleasant expression," she says. I pretended to her that proofs of the engraving happened to be delivered one afternoon when I visited you, and that you presented some of them to the people who happened to be there.

You ask me whether the few lines I sent you were written for you; you would like to know for whom; you are jealous. For no one—like everything I have written. I have always forbidden myself ever to put anything of myself into my works, and yet I have put in a great deal. I have always tried not to make Art subservient to the gratification of any particular person. I have written very tender pages without love, and burning pages with no fire in my blood. I imagined, I recollected, and I combined. What you read is a memory of nothing at all. You predict that some day I'll write beautiful things. Who knows? (*That is my favorite motto.*) I doubt it; my imagination is withering. I am becoming too fastidious. All I ask is to be able to continue to admire the masters with that innermost rapture for which I would gladly sacrifice everything, everything. But as for becoming a master myself, never: I am sure of it. I have immense deficiencies: I have no inborn gift, to begin with, and I lack perseverance in my work. Style is achieved only by dint of atrocious labor, fanatical and unremitting stubbornness. Buffon's saying is a great blasphemy;[2] genius is not "a long patience." But there is some truth in it, more than is generally believed, especially nowadays.

This morning I read poems in your volume with a friend who came to see me.[3] He's a poor fellow who gives lessons here for a living and who is a poet, a true poet, who writes superb and charming things and will remain unknown because he lacks two requirements: bread and time. Yes, we read you, we admired you.

Do you think I don't find it sweet to be able to say to myself: "Nevertheless she's mine, mine!" On Sunday two weeks will have passed since you knelt on the floor and gazed at me with sweetly eager eyes; I was looking at your forehead, thinking of all that lay behind it, staring at your face, with infinite wonder at the lightness and thickness of your hair.

I wouldn't like you to see me now: I am frighteningly ugly. I have an enormous boil on my right cheek, which has half closed one of my eyes and swollen the entire upper part of my face. I must look ridiculous. If you saw me thus, love might draw back, for it is alarmed at the grotesque. But don't worry, I'll be all right when we meet; just as I was, the way you love me.

Tell me whether you use the verbena. Do you put it on your handkerchiefs? Put some on your shift. But no—don't use perfume; the best perfume is yourself, your own natural fragrance. Perhaps I shall have a letter tomorrow.

Adieu, I bite your lip: is the little red spot still there?

Adieu, a thousand kisses. Perhaps on Monday I'll taste the sweetness of yours again.

Yours, body and soul.

1. Louise had been sending her letters to DuCamp in Paris, who forwarded them to Croisset in envelopes addressed in his own hand. But see p. 58.

2. "Le génie n'est qu'une plus grande aptitude à la patience." Attributed to the naturalist Georges Louis Leclerc de Buffon (1707-1788) by Hérault de Séchelles, in the latter's *Voyage à Montbard.*

3. This is the first mention in the present correspondence of Louis Bouilhet (1822-1869), whose "liaison" (as he himself called it) with Flaubert—intimacy in life and work—began about now. The two men, who grew to look strikingly alike, had been rivals in accomplishment at the Rouen lycée—which Bouilhet, whose family was poor, had attended with scholarship aid; and Bouilhet had later been among Dr. Flaubert's medical students. He had subsequently been dismissed from the Hôtel-Dieu—as Flaubert had been from the lycée—because of participation in a student protest, and was now devoting himself to poetry, earning his living in a Rouen tutoring school. Increasing esteem and affection for Bouilhet gave Flaubert some consolation for the "defection" of Alfred LePoittevin.

To Louise Colet

[Croisset, August 17, 1846]

An evil spell is on us! It is always so. Isn't it enough to want something in order not to obtain it? That is the law of life. Impossible for me to be in Paris tonight. My head is all wrapped in wet poultices, because of the frightful boils I have all over my body. I'm lying down, unable to move, and write you from that position. But I am applying remedies more desperate than you can imagine. We'll laugh about them together. I dare not believe I'll arrive in Paris tomorrow, Tuesday: I might, but don't count on it. So it will be for Wednesday, at the same time.

It was impossible for me yesterday, Sunday, to send you a line. I was counting on my brother's servant—my brother comes here for dinner once a week—but yesterday he didn't turn up. I share the disappointment and anxiety you'll be feeling at half past four today when I don't arrive. But forgive me. I am suffering more than you. Come, my lovely, a little patience: in a few hours you'll see me.

. . . Adieu. I am furious, but kiss you on the mouth—adieu—all yours, yours.

To Louise Colet

[Croisset,] Tuesday morning. [August 18, 1846]

Here I am on my feet, thanks to my stubbornness. By following my own instinct I rid myself in 2 days of what would have lasted a week. And that against everybody's opinion. Only scars are left.

I'll arrive at your house tomorrow between half-past four and five. I'm counting on it. *It is sure*—unless the devil himself takes a hand in it this time. He's taken a hand in so many of my affairs that he might well meddle in this one. So: until tomorrow. Shall we go and take Phidias out for dinner? What's your feeling? Think it over carefully beforehand. Ah—in thirty hours I'll be setting out! Pass swiftly, Today! Pass swiftly, Long Night!

It is raining now: the sky is gray. But I have the sun in my soul.

Adieu—I'd love to fill these 4 little pages, but the postman will soon be arriving, so I'll quickly close this and seal it.

A thousand loves.

The real ones tomorrow. Tomorrow I'll be touching you. Sometimes I think it's a dream I have read about somewhere, and that you don't really exist.

To Louise Colet

[Croisset,] Thursday, 1 o'clock in the morning.
[August 20-21, 1846]

Alone, now! All alone! It's a dream. Oh, how far away they are, those hours that are barely the past! There are whole centuries between a little while ago and now. A little while ago I was with you, we were together. Our poor ride in the Bois! How dreary the weather was last night when I left you. It was raining. There were tears in the air. The weather itself was sad.

I keep thinking of our last "reunion" at the hotel, with your silk dress open, and the lace coiling over your breast. Your entire face was smiling, wonderstruck with love and ecstasy. How your sweet eyes shone! Twenty-four hours ago: remember! Oh, the impossibility of recapturing any part of a thing that is gone! Adieu, I am going to bed now, and before sleeping I'll read there the letter you wrote me while waiting for me. Adieu, adieu, a thousand lovekisses. Were you here, I'd give you more of the kind I gave you. I am still longing for you, my thirst unquenched! Adieu, adieu.

To Louise Colet

[Croisset,] Friday night, midnight.
[August 21-22, 1846]

Last night I wrote you a note, and send it with this letter.

. . . Forty-eight hours ago . . . you filled my heart with such gladness that some of it remains, even though you're no longer with me. The memory of you is radiant, sweet, poignant. I keep seeing the joyful expression on your lovely face when I was looking into it from very close. Do you know, I'll end by not being able to live without you—a thought that sometimes makes my head spin. When I see you in my mind's eye you draw me irresistibly and it makes me dizzy. What will happen? No matter: let us love each other. It's so sweet, so good. I haven't a single word to say to you, I am so full of you. Except the eternal words: I love you.

. . . Our wonderful dinner together the night before last (the night before last: already so far away)! Afterwards, when I gave you my arm, I was so at peace, oblivious of everything! And then alone in my room, when I felt your body against mine . . . Ah, don't accuse me again of having eyes only for the wretchedness of life . . . weren't we happy? And when we were riding in the carriage, talking, hand in hand, I dreamed of what our existence might have been if conditions were different—if I lived permanently in Paris, if you were alone, if I were free. We were like a young couple on their honeymoon—rich, handsome . . . Imagine what a life like that would be—sweet, full, working together, loving each other . . .

Today I have done nothing. Neither written nor read a line. I unpacked my *Temptation of Saint Anthony*[1] and hung it on my wall; that is all. I am very fond of this picture. I had wanted it for a long time. For me the tragic grotesque holds immense charm, it corresponds to the intimate needs of my nature, which is buffoonishly bitter. It doesn't make me laugh, but sets me dreaming. I recognize it wherever it exists.

. . . Adieu. I kiss you everywhere. Think of me: I think of you. Or rather no; think less about me; work, be sensible, be happy in your thoughts. Return to your muse, who consoled you on your worst days. I am for days of happiness.

Adieu. I kiss you on the lips.

1. An engraving by Jacques Callot of the subject Flaubert had seen painted by Breughel in Genoa. The engraving now hangs in the Flaubert pavilion at Croisset.

To Louise Colet
[Croisset, Sunday, August 23, 1846]

.   .   .

Do you know you are cruel? You reproach me with not loving you, and point, as evidence, to my always leaving. That is wrong of you. How can I stay? What would you do in my place? You always speak to me of your sorrows: I know they are genuine, I have seen proof; and feel it in myself, which makes it the more convincing. But I see evidence of another sorrow, a sorrow constantly at my side; this one never complains, it even smiles, and, alongside it, yours, however exaggerated it may be, will never be more than what a flea-bite is to a burn, a spasm to a death-agony. I am caught in a vise. The two women I love most are driving me with double rein: the bit is in my heart, and they are pulling on it with their love and grief. Forgive me if this angers you yet again. I no longer know what to say to you: I hesitate, now. When I speak to you I'm afraid of making you cry, and when I touch you, of wounding you. You remember my violent caresses, how strong my hands were: you were almost trembling. I made you cry out two or three times. But be more reasonable, poor child I love: stop grieving over chimeras.

You reproach me for my habit of analyzing. But you attribute to my words a wicked subtlety they do not have. You dislike the cast of my mind: the rockets it sends up displease you: you'd like me to be more consistent, more uniform, in my affections and my language. That it should be you, you! who are now doing as others do, as everybody does—blaming me for the only good thing about me, my leaps and starts, my naive outbursts. Yes, you too want to prune the tree. Its branches may be unruly, but they are thick and leafy, and they reach out in all directions to breathe the air and the sun. You want to tame that tree, to make it into a charming espalier that would be trained against a wall: true, it would then bear lovely fruit, which a child could pick without a ladder. What do you want me to do? I love in my way: whether more than you, or less, God knows. But I love you, and when you say that I have perhaps done for vulgar women what I have done for you . . . I have done it for *no one*—no one: I swear it. You are absolutely the first and only woman whom I have ever been willing to travel to see—whom I have loved enough to do that for—because you are the first to love me as you love me. No: no one before you has ever wept the same tears, or looked at me in that sad and tender way. Yes: the memory of Wednesday night is my most beautiful memory of love. Were I to become old tomorrow, it is that memory that would make me regret what I had lost.

. . . Adieu. This is your name-day.[1] As a bouquet I send you my best kisses.

1. St. Louis's Day is August 25.

To Louise Colet

[Croisset,] Monday night. [August 24, 1846]

I shan't be able to write you tomorrow, dearly beloved, nor perhaps the day after; but Friday at the latest (I'll try to make it Thursday) you'll have a long letter from me. We[1] set out tomorrow morning (I'll see that it's not until after the postman comes), for a little trip to a region nine leagues from here. We won't be back until Wednesday night. We are going to visit some old Gothic abbeys—Jumièges, where Agnès Sorel is buried, Saint-Wandrille, etc. I shall be thinking of you throughout this trip, and missing you. If you knew how long my days are now, and how cold my nights, bereft as they are of all the joys of love!

.   .   .

In the sublime cynicism of your love you are taking pleasure in the hypothesis of a child who may be born. You desire a child—admit it. You are wishing for one, as yet another bond that would unite us, as a contract, sealed by fate, that would weld together our two destinies. Oh! It is only because you are you, dear and too tender friend, that I am not angry with you for a wish that poses such an appalling threat to my happiness. I, who have sworn to myself that I will never again link any being to my own: I, to give birth to another! If it happens I'll not complain. Since the heart is so idiotically illogical, who knows whether as a man I may not experience a spasm of divine joy? Yes, I'm sure I would love that child of ours. If you died I'd bring it up, and all my affection would probably be transferred to it. But the very idea sends a shiver up my spine. And if to prevent its coming into the world I had to leave the world, the Seine is right here, and I'd jump in this very moment with a 36-pound cannonball attached to my feet.

Don't be afraid that I would be reproachful or harsh with you. After all, you have your share of suffering. And so mine will keep silent and out of sight. I confess that in two weeks I shall perhaps be relieved of an enormous weight. My lack of precaution will hang over my soul like the sword of Damocles. In all our future ecstasies I will always keep this possible danger in mind. No matter! That is not the best part of our love. It's only the sauce, as Rabelais would say: the meat is your soul. You wept, the first time on Wednesday; you thought I wasn't happy, isn't it so? I was, though, more so than I have ever been, as happy as I could be. I shall be happier still, for I love you more and more; I want to keep telling you so and proving it to you.

1. Flaubert and Maxime DuCamp. DuCamp had not yet met Louise. Soon, however, after Louise's husband returned to Paris following a summer's absence, DuCamp would be doubly used as the lovers' post office; and later, when relations soured, he would become the repository of their mutual complaints. DuCamp soon became exasperated with Louise, a fact she quickly sensed despite what seems to have been prolonged courtesy on his part. For Flaubert to tell her, at this early date, that he could not write her because he was off on a walk with DuCamp was the first step toward making DuCamp a target of Louise's eventual invective in her letters to Flaubert. DuCamp was "a bad influence," he "came between" them, he "turned Flaubert against" her.

To Louise Colet

[Croisset,] Wednesday, 10 P.M. [August 26, 1846]

.   .   .

What would I learn from those wonderful newspapers you so want me to take each morning, with my bread and butter and cup of coffee? Why should I care what they say? I have very little curiosity about the news, politics bores me to death, and the literary articles stink. To me it's all stupid-making and irritating . . . Yes, newspapers disgust me profoundly—I mean the ephemeral, things of the moment, what is important today and won't be tomorrow. This is not insensitivity. It is simply that I sympathize as much, perhaps even more, with the past misfortunes of those who are dead and no longer thought of— all the cries they uttered, now unheard. I feel no more pity for the lot of the modern working classes than for that of the ancient slaves who turned the millstones. I am no more modern than I am ancient, no more French than Chinese; and the idea of *la patrie*, the fatherland—that is, the obligation to live on a bit of earth colored red or blue on a map, and to detest the other bits colored green or black—has always seemed to me narrow, restricted, and ferociously stupid. I am the brother in God of everything that lives, from the giraffe and the crocodile to man, and the fellow-citizen of everyone inhabiting the great furnished mansion called the universe . . . Poetry is a free plant. It grows where no one has ever seeded it. The poet is simply the patient botanist who scales mountains to gather it.

And now that I have unburdened my heart—for we have returned to this subject several times without your wishing to understand it—let's talk about ourselves, and kiss each other, sweetly and lingeringly, on the lips.

Yesterday and today we had a splendid walk. I saw ruins, ruins which I loved in my youth, which I already knew, and had often visited with those who are no more. I thought of them, and of those other dead whom I never knew, and whose empty graves I was walking on. I have a particular love for the vegetation that grows in ruins. That invasion of man's work by nature as soon as his hand is no longer there to defend it rejoices me immensely and profoundly. Life comes to superimpose itself on Death: it makes plants grow in petrified skulls; and on the stone where one of us has carved his dream the Life Principle reasserts itself with every new blossoming of the yellow wallflowers. I find it a sweet thought that one day I'll help tulips grow. Who knows? The tree at whose feet I'll be laid may bear splendid fruit. I'll perhaps make superb manure, a superior kind of guano.

. . . It gave you pleasure, poor angel, the name-day bouquet I sent you! It wasn't my idea to put those eloquent flowers in my letter: I was unaware of their symbolic meaning. It was DuCamp who taught it to me and advised me to make use of it. I thought that bit of childishness would amuse your heart. It greatly amused mine!

. . . I often think of our dear Bois de Boulogne. You remember our first ride, on July 30th? How Henriette[1] was sleeping on the cushions? And the gentle motion of the springs; and our hands—and our glances, even more closely entwined. My heart was warm and soft. I saw your eyes shining in the dark. Your pupils stared into mine, and I drank their long emanations with a kind of ecstasy. When will all that happen again? Who knows? Who knows? Oh, never accuse me of forgetting—never! That would be unspeakably cruel. Keep loving me, for my love is constant. Adieu, a thousand kisses on your lovely throat, on those breasts you offer to my lips, smiling so sweetly as you say, "So you like me? You love me?" Do I like you! Do I love you! A deaf man who saw me writing you would know the answer: he would only have to *look* at my body. Once more adieu, a thousand loves. Don't be afraid, my dear: I have your letter telling me that your blood should come on the 10th.[2]

1. Louise Colet's six-year-old daughter.
2. See p. 75, n.2.

Such are Flaubert's first "love" letters to Louise Colet. Barely a month had passed since their first meeting at Pradier's, and already Flaubert had offended by waiting almost three weeks before making the short trip to Paris to see her again. Forced to realize that for him "affair" seemed to mean chiefly "correspondence," she responded by sharpening her tone.

During the eighteen months of this, the first of their two liaisons, Flaubert would write Louise about one hundred letters, but he managed to see her only six times. Baffled and irritated by the contrast between Flaubert's eloquent and undoubted passion and his prolonged absences, Louise had to struggle also with his many other inconsistencies; and she continued to object to the amount of extraneous matter—so she found it—with which he filled the pages he sent her.

The letters which follow reflect, perhaps explain—and to some extent excuse —Louise's growing acerbity. In them, Flaubert will continue—to our advantage, if not to hers—to reveal his attitudes on art and literature, on sex and politics; and, above all, to reveal himself.

To Louise Colet

[Croisset,] Sunday, 2 p.m. [August 30, 1846]

Anger! Good God! Vituperation, invective! Lurid language! What does it mean? That you like disputes, recriminations, all the bitter daily wrangling that ends by making life a real hell? I don't understand. You complain of my hard words, but it seems to me that I never sent you any to equal these. Perhaps you'll say I have written you even more harshly: everyone has his illusions. But in your letter of this morning I see something more, a deliberate intent to be nasty, or to seem so. Who knows? Perhaps it's a trial, a ploy. Your never-ending reproach is that I'm always posing, theatrical, vain, that I parade my sorrows like a swashbuckler displaying his scars. According to you I keep hurting you to my heart's content, pretending to weep in order to draw tears from you. What an atrocious idea! How can you love me if you see me as such a wretch? If so, you must despise me—perhaps you really do despise me? You are no doubt already having regrets, you see that you made a mistake, and I'm the one who's to blame for your lost illusion. But remember that my very first words were a cry of warning to you; and when our enthusiasm swept us both away I never stopped telling you to save yourself while there was still time. Was that vanity? Was that arrogance? I might have done the opposite—lied, told you how wonderful I was, acted the sublime. You would have believed me. Then you would have thought me good, precisely because I was being a hypocrite.

What shall I tell you? What shall I do? I'm at a loss. It takes courage to write to you, knowing that whatever I say wounds you. The caresses that cats give their females draw blood, and an exchange of jabs is part of their pleasure. Why do they keep doing it? Nature impels them: I must be the same as they.

72

Every word of mine is a wound I give you: every loving impulse is taken as an insult. Ah, my poor dear Louise, nothing prepared me for anything like this, not even my most far-reaching anticipations of possible misfortunes.

How could you think I would love you the less if you had a child by me? On the contrary, I would love you more. A thousand times more. Wouldn't you be much more closely bound to me, by our common suffering, by my gratitude, even pity? That last word still shocks you, perhaps. But don't take it in its banal, narrow sense: think of its most personal, emotional, disinterested implications. You think that because of this continual fear of a new life that might result from a moment of inattention, you and I will no longer know rapture and divine forgetfulness? To tell the truth, I see this very rapture as a disturbing concomitant of love, because it is always followed by remorse. Why confuse your anxiety over an impending disaster with the happiness you give me? Usually I may not be blessed with common sense, as you keep telling me, but in this case it doesn't seem to me that I'm the one who lacks it. If I cared only for my own enjoyment, if all I asked of love were merely physical pleasure, then my behavior would be different: surely that is obvious to anyone. Come, darling, I am not yet as coarse as you say. There is something I love even more than your lovely body, and that is your self. Do you know what you lack, or rather what you sin against? Discernment. You find hidden meanings where they don't exist, in places where no one dreamed of concealing them. You exaggerate everything, you magnify, you carry things much too far. Where the devil did you ever get the idea that I wrote you anything like this: "I never loved the women I possessed, and those I loved never granted me anything"?[1] I simply told you that for six years I loved a woman who never in her life knew it. That would have seemed stupid to her. It seems so to me, now. After that, until I met you, I never loved, because I didn't want to love, that's all. Don't think I belong to that vulgar race of men who feel disgust after pleasure, love existing for them only as lust. No: in me, what rises doesn't subside so quickly. If moss grows on the castles of my heart as soon as they are built, at any rate it takes time for them to fall into ruin, if they ever do so completely.

Jeer at me as much as you like—at my life, at that boundless vanity you have just discovered (you are the Christopher Columbus of that discovery), at my pantheist beliefs. In all that, there is not the slightest wish to impress you or to seem original. I don't make a show of extravagance. If I'm extravagant, so much the worse—or the better.

. . . One has to be obsessed with eccentricity to find it in me, who lead the most bourgeois, the most obscure life in the world. I shall die in my corner without anyone being able, I hope, to blame me for a wicked deed or a bad line, the reason being that I do not make others my concern and will do nothing to make myself theirs. It is difficult for me to detect "extravagance" in so commonplace a life.

But beneath that existence lies another, a secret *other*, all radiant and illuminated for me alone. One that I display to no one, because it would arouse laughter. Is that so unreasonable?

Have no fear that I show your letters to anyone at all No: you can be sure of that. DuCamp knows only that I write to a woman in Paris who will perhaps need his help next winter with our letters. He sees me writing to you every day. But he doesn't yet know your name. He behaves similarly in matters of his own, and neither of us asks questions of the other. He merely lent me, the other day, the seal that has his motto.

I'm sorry Phidias isn't coming. He is a splendid man and a great artist, yes, a great artist, a real Greek, the most ancient of all the moderns. A man who doesn't let himself worry about anything—not politics, nor socialism, nor Fourier, nor the Jesuits, nor the University. Instead, he rolls up his sleeves like a good workman and is there to do his job from morning till night, desiring to do it well and loving his art. That is everything, love of art. But I'll stop: this must be irritating you again; you don't like to hear me say that I worry more about a line of verse than about any man, and that I'm more grateful to the poets than to saints and heroes. In old Rome, no one would have been shocked had a man approached Horace and said: "Oh, my good Flaccus, how is your ode to Melpomene coming along? Tell me about your passion for the little Persian boy whom Pollion has let you have: will you be writing about him in Asclepiadics or iambics? Everything you say is much more interesting to me than the Parthian war or the Pontifical College or the Valerian Law they want to bring up again." In other words, there was something of greater conse- quence than the men who were dying for their country or praying for it or working to make it more prosperous: namely, the men who were celebrating it in verse. Because only they survive. New worlds have been discovered where they can be read. Printing was invented to spread their fame. Ah! Yes, the love of Glycera or Lycoris will outlive future civilizations. Like a star, Art watches undisturbed as the world spins round. Shining in its blue immensity, the Beau- tiful keeps its place in the firmament. But all this is annoying you. So what shall I tell you? That I kiss you . . .

1. But see p. 49.

To Louise Colet

[Croisset,] Sunday night. [September 13, 1846]

I am very worried about your health, poor darling, about your vomiting and that cursed blood that doesn't come. I beg you to make sure of your con- dition as quickly as possible. Ask your doctor. If he has any intelligence he will understand immediately. Or consult another one, some competent doctor who doesn't know you. Tell him it happens with you sometimes, and ask him what one can do to make certain. Before making that journey,[1] you should know how things stand, no? And if you don't try what I advise (a remedy to bring on the Redcoats),[2] how will you know why they are staying away? Quite often something in the mind is enough to keep them back, almost any kind of emo- tion. You would be mad to travel down there to prevent a danger that may not exist. I think this advice very sensible. I beg you, beseech you, to follow it. And burn this letter, it is more prudent. We must think of everything. Don't do anything rash, don't tempt misfortune: you know how that monster lies in wait for his victims. If you like, I'll procure and send you an opinion, one that I guarantee in advance will be good. Think about all this and answer me promptly.

I am depressed, troubled, a mass of nerves. I feel the way I did two years ago, horribly on edge. Everything wounds me, tears me to pieces. Your last two letters made my heart beat almost to bursting. They move me so, when I unfold them and your perfume rises from the paper and the fragrance of your caressing words penetrates me to the heart. Spare me; you make me giddy with your love! We must convince ourselves, however, that we cannot live together. We must resign ourselves to a flatter, more pallid existence. I wish that you would accustom yourself to this; I want the thought of me to comfort you, not consume you; to console you, not drive you to despair. What can we do, darling? It must be so. We cannot continue with these convulsions of the soul. The despondency that follows is a kind of death. Work, think of other things. You have so much intelligence: use a little of it to become more serene. I am at the end of my strength. I had plenty of courage for myself: but for two! My role is to sustain everyone, and I am exhausted. Don't distress me with your outbursts, which make me curse myself without seeing any remedy.

. . . I must scold you about something that shocks and scandalizes me, namely how little you care about Art now.[3] You care about fame—so be it: I approve; but Art, the only true and good thing in life! Can you compare any earthly love to it? Can you prefer the adoration of some relative beauty to the cult of the True? Let me say this: there is only one good thing about me, only one thing in myself that I think estimable—I can *admire*. You adulterate the Beautiful with a mass of extraneous things—the useful, the agreeable, and who knows what else. Tell the Philosopher[4] to explain to you the idea of Pure Beauty as he expounded it in his course in 1819, and as I conceive it. We'll speak about it next time.

I am now reading an Indian play, *Sakountala*,[5] and studying some Greek. It isn't going very well, my poor Greek: your face keeps coming between the book and my eyes.

Adieu, chérie; be good, love me *well* and I will love you *much:* for that's what you want, my voracious darling. A thousand kisses and a thousand tender thoughts.

---

1. Louise was apparently planning, rather precipitately, to visit a *faiseur d'anges*—an abortionist—in some distant town.

2. "Les Anglais sont débarqués"—"The Redcoats have landed"—is an expression of relief well known to French lovers. Louise's Redcoats landed a day or two later. Flaubert had confided his anxiety to Maxime DuCamp, who wrote him on September 20: "My sincere congratulations to you, and to her too, whatever she may say." Several subsequent delays of the same kind are chronicled in the course of the correspondence.

3. For a remark made by Louise a few days earlier, when the lovers had met in Mantes (be-

tween Paris and Rouen)—the remark that triggered the present upbraiding—see p. 92.

4. Victor Cousin.

5. A "mytho-pastoral drama" in seven acts by the Sanskrit poet Kalidasa—"abounding," says the *Encyclopaedia Britannica*, "in stanzas of exquisite tenderness and fine descriptive passages."

To Louise Colet

[Croisset,] Monday, 10 p.m. [September 14, 1846]

. . .

If I were in Paris . . . how I would love you! I would sicken, die, stupefy myself, from loving you; I would become nothing but a kind of sensitive plant which only your kisses would bring to life. No middle course! Life! And life is precisely that: love, love, sexual ecstasy. Or, something which resembles that but is its negation: namely, the Idea, the contemplation of the Immutable—in a word, Religion, in the broadest sense. I feel that you are too lacking in that, my love. I mean, it seems to me that you do not greatly adore Genius, that you do not tremble to your very entrails at the contemplation of the beautiful. It is not enough to have wings: they must bear you aloft. One of these days I will write you a long literary letter. Today I finished *Sakountala*. India dazzles me. It is superb. My studies of Brahminism this winter have nearly driven me crazy. There have been moments when I thought I'd lost my wits . . .

To Louise Colet

[Croisset,] Friday, 10 p.m. [September 18, 1846]

. . .

You tell me, my angel, that I have not initiated you into my inner life, into my most secret thoughts. Do you know what is most intimate, most hidden, in my heart, and what is most authentically myself? Two or three modest ideas about art, lovingly brooded over; that is all. The greatest events of my life have been a few thoughts, a few books, certain sunsets on the beach at Trouville, and talks five or six hours long with a friend now married and lost to me.[1] I have always seen life differently from others, and the result has been that I've always isolated myself (but not sufficiently, alas!) in a state of harsh unsociability, with no exit. I suffered so many humiliations, I so shocked people and made them indignant, that I long ago came to realize that in order to live in peace one must live alone and seal one's windows lest the air of the world seep in. In spite of myself I still retain something of this habit. That is why I deliberately avoided the company of women for several years. I wanted no hindrance to my innate moral precept. I wanted no yoke, no influence. In the end I no longer desired women's company at all. Stirrings of the flesh, throbbings of the heart, were absent from my life, and I was not even conscious of my sex. As I told you, I had an overwhelming passion when I was little more than a child. When it ended I decided to divide my life in two parts: to put on one side my soul, which I reserved for Art, and on the other my body, which was to live as best it could. Then you came along and upset all that. So here I am, returning to a human existence!

You have awakened all that was slumbering, or perhaps decaying, within me! I had been loved before, and intensely, though I'm one of those who are quickly forgotten and more apt to kindle emotion than to keep it alive. The love I arouse is always that felt for something a little strange. Love, after all, is only a superior kind of curiosity, an appetite for the unknown that makes you bare your breast and plunge headlong into the storm.

As I said, I have been loved before, but *never the way you love me;* nor has there ever been between a woman and myself the bond that exists between us two. I have never felt for any woman so deep a devotion, so irresistible an attraction; never has there been such complete communion. Why do you keep saying that I love the tinselly, the showy, the flashy? "Poet of form!" That is the favorite term of abuse hurled by utilitarians at true artists. For my part, until someone comes along and separates for me the form and the substance of a given sentence, I shall continue to maintain that that distinction is meaningless. Every beautiful thought has a beautiful form, and vice versa.[2] In the world of Art, beauty is a by-product of form, just as in our world temptation is a by-product of love. Just as you cannot remove from a physical body the qualities that constitute it—color, extension, solidity—without reducing it to a hollow abstraction, without destroying it, so you cannot remove the form from the Idea, because the Idea exists only by virtue of its form. Imagine an idea that has no form—such a thing is as impossible as a form that expresses no idea. Such are the stupidities on which criticism feeds. Good stylists are reproached for neglecting the Idea, the moral goal; as though the goal of the doctor were not to heal, the goal of the painter to paint, the goal of the nightingale to sing, as though the goal of Art were not, first and foremost, Beauty!

Sculptors who create real women, with breasts that can contain milk and thighs that suggest fecundity, are accused of sensualism. Whereas, were they to carve wads of drapery and figures flat as signboards, they would be called idealists, spiritualists. "Yes, he does neglect form, it's true," people would say, "but he is a thinker!" Whereupon the bourgeois, with cries of joy, would outdo themselves to admire what bores them. It's easy, with the help of conventional jargon, and two or three ideas acceptable as common coin, to pass as a socialist humanitarian writer, a renovator, a harbinger of the evangelical future dreamed of by the poor and the mad. Such is the modern mania: one blushes to be a writer. If you merely write verse or a novel, merely carve marble, shame! That was acceptable previously, before the poet had a "social mission." Now every piece of writing must have its moral significance, must teach its lesson, elementary or advanced; a sonnet must be endowed with philosophical implications, a play must rap the knuckles of royalty, and a watercolor contribute to moral progress. Everywhere there is pettifoggery, the craze for spouting and orating: the muse becomes a mere pedestal for a thousand unholy desires. Poor Olympus! They'd be capable of planting a potato patch on its summit! If it were only the mediocrities who were involved, one would let them do as they liked. But no—vanity has banished pride, and caused a thousand little cupidities to spring up where formerly a single, noble ambition prevailed. Even men of parts, great men, ask themselves: "Why not seize the moment? Why not impress these people now, hour after hour, instead of being admired by them later?" Whereupon they mount the tribune. They join the staff of a newspaper, and there we see them lending the weight of their immortal names to ephemeral theories.

They intrigue to overthrow some minister who would topple without them —when with a single line of satirical verse they could make his name a synonym for infamy. They concern themselves with taxes, customs-duties, laws, peace and war! How petty all this is! How transient! How false and secondary! All these wretched things excite them—they attack all the crooks, gush over every decent action no matter how commonplace, cry their eyes out over every poor fellow who is murdered, every dog that's run over—as though this were the sole purpose of their lives. To me it seems finer to stand at a distance of several centuries and thrill whole generations, fill them with pure pleasures. Who can measure the ecstasy that Homer has inspired, or count the tears that the excellent Horace has changed into smiles? To speak only of myself, I am grateful to Plutarch because of evenings he gave me at the lycée, evenings filled with warlike ardor, as though the clash of armies were in my very soul.

1. Alfred LePoittevin.
2. Flaubert had read Hegel's *Aesthetics*. (J.B.)

To Louise Colet

[Croisset,] Tuesday, 10 a.m. [September 22, 1846]

. . .

Thank you for your letter of this morning. I was waiting for the postman on the quay, looking unconcerned and smoking my pipe. I love that postman! I've left orders in the kitchen that he's to have a glass of wine to refresh him. He likes this house and is very punctual. Yesterday he brought me nothing, so he got nothing.

You send me everything you can find to gratify my love for you; you pass on to me all the tributes you receive. I read Plato's[1] letter with the keenest possible concentration; I found many things in it, very many. Essentially, he's a man whose heart, despite all he may do to make it appear serene, is cold and empty; his life is dreary, without radiance, I am sure. But he greatly loved you and still does, with a love that is deep and lonely; he will feed on it a long time. I found his letter painful; I looked into the very depths of this colorless existence, filled with tasks undertaken without enthusiasm and carried out with a dogged obstinacy which is the only thing that keeps him going. Your love brought him a little joy. He clung to it with an old man's hunger for life. You were his last passion, and the only thing that reconciled him to himself. He is, I think, jealous of Béranger—the life and fame of this latter can scarcely afford him much pleasure.[2] As a rule the philosopher is a kind of mongrel being, a cross between scientist and poet, envious of both. Metaphysics puts a lot of rancor into the blood—a very curious and very interesting phenomenon. I was considerably engrossed by it for a couple of years, but it was a waste of time I now regret.

You wrote something very true: "Love is a great comedy, and so is life, when you're not playing one of the roles." Only I won't concede that it makes you laugh. About a year and a half ago I experienced a living illustration of this, something that happened spontaneously, I mean. I preferred not to witness the very end. At that time I often visited a family in which there was a charming young girl,[3] marvelously beautiful—of a very Christian, almost Gothic, beauty, if I can put it that way. She was a pure spirit, easily susceptible to emotion; one moment she'd be crying, the next laughing, like sunshine after a shower. The feelings of this lovely, innocent creature were entirely at the mercy of my words. I can still see her lying against her pink cushion and looking at me, as I read, with her great blue eyes. One day we were alone, sitting on a sofa; she took my hand, twined her fingers in mine; this I let her do without thinking (most of the time I'm a great innocent), and she gave me a look which still makes me shiver. Just then her mother entered, took in everything, and smiled at what she thought was the acquisition of a son-in-law. I'll not forget that smile—the most sublime thing ever seen. It was a compound of indulgent benevolence and genteel vulgarity. I am sure that the poor girl had been carried away by an irresistible affectionate impulse, one of those moments of mawkish sentimentality when everything within you seems to be melting and dissolving—a voluptuous anguish that would fill you with delight if only it didn't bring you to the verge of sobs and tears. You cannot conceive the terror I felt. I returned home shattered, reproaching myself for being alive. I don't know whether I exaggerated the situation, but even though I did not love her I'd gladly have given my life to redeem that sad, loving look to which I had not responded.

. . . What a horrible invention the bourgeois is, don't you agree? Why is he in the world? And what is he doing there, poor wretch? For my part, I cannot imagine how people unconcerned with art can spend their time: how they live is a mystery to me.

You are perhaps right in what you say about excessive reading killing the imagination, the individual element, the one thing, after all, that has some value. But I'm engaged in a number of tasks I must finish; and besides, these days I am continually afraid to write—afraid of botching my outlines, so I put off doing anything with them.

. . . Adieu; it's time for me to leave you. I am yours, dear love, I who love you and kiss your breasts. Look at them, and say: he is dreaming of your roundness, and his desire rests its head on you.

1. Victor Cousin, now 54.

2. Pierre-Jean Béranger (1780-1857), the writer of sentimental verse, enjoyed such immense popularity that, in 1828, when for the second time he was fined and imprisoned for satires against the regime, the fine was paid by popular subscription.

3. Henriette Collier.

To Louise Colet

[Croisset,] Sunday morning, 11 a.m. [September 27, 1846]

. . .

You're surprised that I judged the Philosopher so accurately, without knowing him? That's because, in spite of appearances, I've had considerable experience. You didn't want to believe that, when I told you at the very beginning. I am ripe. Early ripe, it's true, because I have lived in a hothouse. I never pose as a man of experience—that would be too stupid. But I observe a great deal, and never make conclusions—an infallible way not to be mistaken. In a personal affair[1] I once got the better of some supposedly astute people of importance, which gave me a very poor opinion of their abilities. Practical life is loathsome to me: the mere necessity of sitting down in a dining room at fixed hours fills my soul with a feeling of wretchedness. But when I participate in it (in practical life), when I sit down (at table), I know how to behave like anyone else.

You'd like me to meet Béranger. I should like it, too. He is a grand old man; I find him appealing. But—and now I speak of his works—he is immensely unfortunate in the kind of people who admire him. There are tremendous geniuses who have but one defect, one vice—that of being especially appreciated by the vulgar, by people susceptible to cheap poetry. For thirty years Béranger has been the inspiration for the love life of students and the erotic dreams of traveling salesmen. I know perfectly well he doesn't write for them, but it's those people in particular who appreciate him. Say what you will, popularity, which seems to give genius greater scope, actually vulgarizes it; authentic Beauty is not for the masses, especially in France. *Hamlet* will always give less pleasure than *Mademoiselle de Belle-Isle*.[2] Béranger expresses no passions that *I* feel, no dreams that *I* dream; his poetry is not mine. I read him historically; he is a man of another age. He was right for his time, but is no longer right for ours. The happy, carefree love that he so joyously celebrates in his garret window is very foreign to us who are young today; we can admire it as we might admire the hymn of some extinct religion, but it cannot move us. I've heard so many fools, so many narrow-minded bourgeois, sing his songs about beggars and the "God of the good folks" that he must really be a great poet to have kept my esteem despite all the hullabaloo. For my own consumption I prefer geniuses a little less agreeable to the touch, more disdainful of the people, more reserved, more haughty in their manner and their tastes; or else the only man who can take the place of all others, my adored Shakespeare, whom I am now going to start reading from one end to the other, and whom I shall not abandon this time until the volumes fall apart in my hands. When I read Shakespeare I become greater, wiser, purer. When I have reached the crest of one of his works I feel that I am high on a mountain: everything disappears, everything appears. I am no longer a man, I am an *eye*. New horizons loom, perspectives extend to infinity. I forget I have been living like other men in the barely discernible hovels below, that I've been drinking from all those distant rivers that appear smaller than brooks, that I have participated in all the confusion of the anthill. Long ago, in a burst of happy pride (I should dearly love to recapture it), I wrote a sentence that you will understand. Speaking of the joy experienced in reading the great poets, I said: "I often felt that the rapture they kindled in me made me their equal and raised me to a level with themselves" . . .[3]

1. The matter of securing Achille Flaubert's succession to his father's post at the Hôtel-Dieu.
2. A play by Alexandre Dumas.
3. From *Novembre*.

To Louise Colet

[Croisset,] Monday morning. [September 28, 1846]

No! Once again, no! I protest, I swear: others may feel nothing but contempt after possession, but I am not like them, and I glory in not being so. On the contrary, for me possession breeds affection. If I weren't afraid of shocking you yet again, I'd say—indeed I *will* say: "Je suis comme les cigares, on ne m'allume qu'en tirant."[1]

. . . As for Mme Foucaud,[2] she is certainly the one I knew. Is your cousin sufficiently reliable to be entrusted with a letter? Can I be sure he'll deliver it? For I feel like writing to Mme Foucaud. She's an old acquaintance; don't be jealous of her. You shall read the letter if you like, on condition you don't tear it up. Your word will be enough. If I thought of you as a commonplace woman I should not tell you all this. But what you dislike, perhaps, is precisely the fact that I treat you like a man and not like a woman. Try to put some of your intelligence into your relations with me. Later your heart will thank your mind for this. I thought at first that I would find in you less feminine personality, a more universal conception of life. But no! The heart, the heart! That poor heart, that kind heart, that charming heart with its eternal graces, is always there, even in the noblest and greatest women. As a rule men do everything they can to vex the heart, to make it bleed. They steep themselves with subtle sensuality in all those tears that they themselves don't shed, in all those little agonies they see as proofs of their strength. If I had a taste for that sort of pleasure it would be easy for me to enjoy it with you.

But no, I should like to make of you something entirely apart—neither friend nor mistress. Each of those categories is too restricted, too exclusive— one doesn't sufficiently love a friend, and one is too idiotic with a mistress. It is the intermediate term that I seek, the essence of those two sentiments combined. What I want, in short, is that, like a new kind of hermaphrodite, you give me with your body all the joys of the flesh and with your mind all those of the soul. Will you understand that? I fear it isn't clear. It's strange how bad my writing is, in these letters to you; I put no literary vanity into it. One thing conflicts with another. It's as though I wanted to say three words at a time.

. . . In writing this to you, I'm inaugurating my new armchair, in which I am destined to spend long years—if I live. What will I write in it? God knows. Will it be good or bad, tender or erotic, sad or gay? A little of each, probably— adding up to nothing. No matter: may this inauguration bless all my future work! Winter has come, the rain is falling, my fire is burning: now comes the season of long hours shut indoors. Soon now the silent, lamp-lit evenings, watching the wood burn and listening to the wind. Adieu, bright moonlight on the green grass, blue nights all spangled with stars. Adieu, my darling: I kiss you with all my soul . . .

1. A pun. To light (allumer) a cigar, one "draws" (tire); but tirer here refers to the expression tirer un coup—perform the sexual act. The more he makes love to a woman the more he is attracted. (J.B.)

2. Flaubert had written to Louise a week before: "By the way, while I think of it, ask your cousin, since he lived in Cayenne, to give you news of two people, M. Brache and Mme Foucaud de Langlade. The latter must have left there some time ago." Flaubert's spelling of the lady's name varies.

To Louise Colet

[Croisset,] Wednesday, 9 p.m. [September 30, 1846]

. . .

So what the devil do you want me to talk to you about if not Shakespeare, if not what lies closest to my heart? That I have more imagination than heart, as you remark, I should like very much to believe; but I doubt it, for I feel I have very little. When I consider my plans on the one hand and Art on the other, I echo the cry of Breton sailors: "Oh God, how vast the sea, and how small my boat!" Is it possible that you reproach me for the innocent affection I feel for an armchair? If I spoke to you about my shoes I think you'd be jealous of them. Come! I love you dearly all the same, and I kiss you on the lips, my darling. One more kiss between the breasts, and one on each finger. Take care of your hands, and let your nails grow longer. You know you promised. Adieu, adieu, a thousand warm caresses.

To Louise Colet

[Croisset,] Saturday, 8 a.m. [October 3, 1846]

. . .

Come now, smile, kiss me. Stop being hurt because I speak to you about Shakespeare rather than myself. It's simply that he strikes me as more interesting. And what should one speak of (I ask you once more) if not what fills one's mind? As for me, I fail to understand how those people exist who are not from morning to night in an aesthetic state. I have enjoyed more than many the pleasures of family, as much as any man of my age the pleasures of the senses, more than many the pleasures of love. But I know of no delight to compare with that given me by some of the illustrious dead whose works I have read or seen. The three finest things God ever made are the sea, *Hamlet*, and Mozart's *Don Giovanni.* Are you going to be offended again by all this? You mustn't be, for such a reproach doesn't represent your true feelings. It may surge up at a moment of nervous irritation, but cannot persist forever in the depths of your heart . . .

To Louise Colet

[Croisset,] Wednesday morning. [October 7, 1846]

. . .

How rapturous your letter is, how ardent, how heartfelt! Because I tell you I'll soon be coming, you approve everything in me, you shower me with caresses and praise. You no longer reproach me for my whims, my love of rhetoric, the refinements of my selfishness, etc. But should anything arise to prevent my coming, the whole thing would begin over again, would it not? Oh, my child, my child, how young you still are! Love is a springtime plant that perfumes everything with its hope, even the ruins to which it clings. I don't mean by this that you're a ruin, my darling. I mean that though you claim to be older than I in years, you are younger. You think of me a little as Madame de Sévigné thought of Louis XIV: "Oh, what a great king!" because he danced with her. Because you love me you think me handsome, intelligent, sublime; you predict great things for me. No, no, you're mistaken. Once I had all those ideas about myself. Every moron has dreamed of being a great man, and every donkey who ever peered at himself in the water of the stream he was crossing has enjoyed the sight and been sure he was a handsome horse. I lack many qualities, many of the very best, that are needed if one is to do something good. I have written a few pages here and there that are excellent, but no complete work. I have a book in mind[1] now that would show me whether I am any good. But this book may never be written. Too bad: it would have meant a lot to those who read it.

Among navigators there are some who discover worlds, who add new continents to the earth and new constellations to the heavens: they are the masters, eternally splendid. Others belch terror from their vessels' guns and wax rich and fat from their plunder. Still others leave home to seek gold and silk under foreign skies. And still others merely let down their nets to catch salmon for gourmets and cod for the poor. I am the obscure and patient pearl-fisher, who dives deep and comes up empty-handed and blue in the face. A fatal attraction draws me down into the abysses of thought, down to those innermost recesses that never lose their fascination for the strong. I shall spend my life watching the ocean of art where others are sailing or fighting; and from time to time I'll entertain myself by plunging to the bottom in search of green or yellow shells. No one will want them, so I'll keep them for myself alone, and use them to cover the walls of my hut.

1. Jean Bruneau thinks that this may still be the oriental tale, Les Sept Fils du derviche, mentioned on p. 16, n.2.

To Louise Colet

[Croisset,] Thursday, 10 p.m. [October 8, 1846]

. . .

I should love to have you here tonight—kiss your lips, to pass my hands through your lovely curls, lay my head on your breast—even though this last is forbidden since you saw that in my letter to Mme Foucaud I spoke of hers. So you found that letter a little too tender? I shouldn't have thought so. On the contrary, it seemed to me there were moments of insolence in it, and that the general tone was slightly condescending. You say that I seriously loved that woman. It is not so. Only when I was writing to her, with my faculty of arousing myself with my pen, I took my subject seriously; but *only while I was writing.* Many things that leave me cold when I see them or when others talk about them enrapture me, irritate me, or hurt me if I speak of them, and especially if I write. That is one of the effects of my mountebank nature. My father finally forbade me to imitate certain people (he was persuaded that I suffered greatly in doing it—which was true, though I denied it), among others an epileptic beggar I met one day at the seashore. He told me his story: he had begun as a journalist, etc. It was superb. No question that when I acted out that chap I was inside his skin. Impossible to imagine anything more hideous than the spectacle I made at that moment. Do you understand the satisfaction it gave me? I am sure you don't.

To return to that worthy creature, I have given you the entire truth about her. I had other adventures, more or less droll. But even at the time, those bits of foolishness didn't touch my heart very closely, and I had only one true passion. I already told you of it. I was barely 15, and it lasted until I was 18. And when I saw that woman again after several years I had difficulty in recognizing her. I still see her sometimes, but rarely, and I look at her with the same astonishment the émigrés must have felt on coming back to their dilapidated châteaux: "Is it possible I lived here?" And one tells oneself that these ruins haven't always been ruins, and that this derelict hearth, now exposed to rain and snow, was once a place where people warmed themselves.[1] There would be a magnificent story to write, but I am not the man who will do it, nor will anyone else—it would be too marvelous. The story of a modern man from age 7 to 20. Whoever accomplishes this task will remain as eternal as the human heart itself. When you like, I'll tell you something of this unknown drama that I have observed both in myself and in others. Something similar must take place in women, though I can scarcely believe it. I've never yet met one willing to show me frankly the ashes of her heart: they want to make you believe it's all glowing fire; and they actually believe that themselves . . .

1. Editors have thought that Flaubert wrote thus about Elise Schlesinger to forestall Louise Colet's jealousy of an old love. Elsewhere he speaks of her only with affection and regard, culminating in his portrayal of her as Mme Arnoux in the definitive *Education Sentimentale*.

To Louise Colet

[Croisset,] Wednesday, 11 p.m. [October 14, 1846]

.   .   .

Since my father and sister died, I have had no ambition left. They carried off my vanity in their shrouds, and they keep it. I don't know whether a single line by me will ever be printed. I am not like the fox who said the grapes he couldn't reach were too sour; instead, I am no longer hungry. Success doesn't tempt me. What does tempt me I can provide—my own approval. And even that I shall perhaps dispense with eventually, as I ought to have done with that of others. So I transfer all that to you. Work, meditate, meditate above all; condense your ideas—you know that lovely fragments are no use. Unity, unity, that is everything. The *whole*: that's what's lacking in all writers today, great and small. A thousand fine bits, no complete work. Compress your style: weave a fabric soft as silk and strong as a coat of mail. Forgive this advice, but I'd like to give you everything I desire for myself.

. . . I am working quite hard at the moment. I have several things I want to finish, things that bore me but with which I continue in the hope of extracting something from them later on. But next spring I'll really start to write again. I keep putting it off. A subject to write about is for me like a woman one is in love with: when she is going to yield, one trembles and is afraid. It's a voluptuous terror. One dares not attain one's desire.

. . . You mention Albert Aubert and M. Gaschon de Molesnes. Despise all those scamps. Why worry about the chatter of such magpies? It's a waste of time to read criticism. I pride myself on my ability to uphold the thesis that there hasn't been a single piece of good criticism since criticism was invented; that it serves no purpose except to annoy authors and blunt the sensibility of the public; and finally that critics write criticism because they are unable to be artists, just as a man unfit to bear arms becomes a police spy. I'd like to know what poets throughout the ages could have in common with the critics who have analyzed their work. Plautus would have laughed at Aristotle had he known his rules; Corneille fought against those strictures. Voltaire, despite himself, felt the pinch of Boileau. We should all have been spared much that's bad in modern drama had it not been for W. Schlegel; and when the translation of Hegel is completed God knows where we'll go. And when to these you add the journalists, who aren't even equipped to hide their leprous jealousy under a show of learning!

There. I've let my hatred for criticism and critics carry me away. Those wretches have left me no room to kiss you; but that's what I do anyway, despite them. So, with their permission, a thousand great kisses on your lovely forehead, and on your eyes, so sweet, and on . . .

To Louise Colet

[Croisset,] Friday, midnight. [October 23, 1846]

No, I do not scorn fame: one doesn't scorn what one cannot attain. More than many another's, my heart has been set pounding by that word. I used to spend long hours dreaming resounding triumphs for myself; the clamor would thrill me as though I really heard it. But, I don't know why, one fine day I awoke relieved of this desire, more completely than if it had been fulfilled. Then I saw myself in smaller dimension, and devoted all my faculties to observation of my nature—to sounding its depth, and especially to discovering its limitations. The poets I admired loomed all the grander, being now at a greater distance, and I truly enjoyed that humility, which might have maddened another man to death. For a gifted person to seek success is wanton self-mutilation, and to seek fame is perhaps self-destruction. For there are two classes of poet. The greatest, the rare true masters, are microcosms of mankind: not concerned with themselves or their own passions, discarding their own personality, they are, instead, absorbed in that of others; they reproduce the Universe, which is reflected in their works, scintillating, varied, manifold, like an entire sky mirrored in the sea with all its stars and all its azure. Then there are others, whose slightest cry is melodic, whose every tear wrings the heart, and who have only to speak of themselves to remain eternal. They might well have been unable to go further had they undertaken any different sort of work; they may lack breadth, but they have ardor and verve; had they been born with different temperaments, they might not have had genius. Byron belongs to this class, Shakespeare to the other. Indeed, who can tell me what Shakespeare loved, hated, or felt? He is a terrifying colossus: one can scarcely believe he was a man. Now, as for fame, one wants it pure, real, permanent, like that of those demigods: one stretches and strains, attempting to reach their level; one prunes the capricious naivetés and instinctive fantasies of one's talent, making them fit into a conventional type, into a ready-made mold. Or else one has the presumption to believe that it is enough to say, like Byron and Montaigne, what one thinks and feels, in order to create fine things. This latter course is perhaps the wisest for original people, because we would often have many more qualities if we didn't strive after them, and anyone capable of writing correctly would produce a superb book by setting down his memoirs, if he did so with complete sincerity. Thus—to revert to myself—I saw that I was neither of sufficient stature to produce genuine works of art, nor eccentric enough to be able to fill volumes with my *self* alone. And not having the ability needed to attain success, nor the genius to conquer fame, I am condemned to write solely for myself, for my own private diversion, as one smokes or rides on horseback. It is almost certain I shall never have a line printed; and my nephews (I say nephews in the proper sense, not wanting family posterity any more than I count on having any of the other variety) will probably make three-cornered hats for their grandchildren with my fantastic novels, and shades for their kitchen candles from my oriental tales, dramas, mystery plays, and the other twaddle I write out seriously, line by line, on good white paper. There, my dear Louise, once and for all, you have the essence of what I think concerning this subject and myself.

.   .   .

Today I've done nothing but think of you. This morning when I went to bed I thought of the thrill I experienced in bed at Mantes when I felt your thigh on my belly and your waist within my arms; and the impression of that thought stayed with me all day. But you don't want me to talk about all that. (What *am* I to talk to you about?) So let's talk of other things. You are right. It would have been better for you not to love me. Happiness is a usurer: for the loan of fifteen minutes of love it makes you pay with a whole cargo of misery . . .

To Louise Colet

[Rouen,] Friday, 4 p.m. [December 11, 1846]

.   .   .

To deny the existence of lukewarm affections because they *are* lukewarm is to deny that the sun sometimes shines when it isn't high noon. There is as much truth in halftones as in violent colors. In my youth I had a true friend who was devoted to me, who would have given his life and his fortune for me, but wouldn't have got up half an hour earlier than usual to please me, or accelerated any of his actions. When you observe life with a little attention, you see cedars as being a little less tall and bushes somewhat higher. All the same, I don't like the habit some people have of disparaging great enthusiasms or minimizing sublime impulses that surpass nature. Thus Vigny's book, *Servitude et grandeur militaires*, shocked me a little at first glance because I saw in it a systematic depreciation of blind devotion (the cult of the Emperor, for example), of man's fanaticism for man, in favor of the abstract, dry idea of duty, a concept I've never been able to grasp and which does not seem to me inherent in human entrails. What is noble in the Empire is adoration of the Emperor, a love that is exclusive, absurd, sublime, truly human. That is why I have little understanding of what *la Patrie*, the fatherland, is for us today. I can readily grasp what it was for the Greek, who had only his city, for the Roman who had only Rome, for the savage tracked down in his forest, for the Arab pursued to his very tent. But for us . . . Don't we, at bottom, feel just as Chinese or English as French? Aren't all our dreams of foreign places? As children we long to live in a land of parrots and candied dates, we're nurtured on Byron and Virgil, on rainy days we yearn for the Orient, or we want to go and make our fortunes in India, or grow sugarcane in America. *La Patrie* is the earth, the universe, the stars, the air. It is thought itself: that is, the Infinite within our breasts. But quarrels between one nation and another, between canton and arrondissement, between man and man, interest me little, and engage me only when represented in great pictures with crimson backgrounds.

. . .

To Louise Colet

[Rouen, end of December, 1846 (?)]

It is impossible for me to continue any longer a correspondence that is becoming epileptic. Change it, I beg. What have I done to you that you should unfold before me, with all the pride of grief, the spectacle of a despair for which I know no remedy? If I had betrayed you, publicly displayed you as my mistress, sold your letters, etc., you could scarcely write me things more atrocious or more distressing.

What have I done, good God? What have I done? You know quite well I cannot come to Paris. You seem to want to force me to answer you brutally; I am too well bred to do so, but it seems to me I have restated this often enough for you to bear it in mind.

I had formed quite a different idea of love. I thought it was something independent of everything, even of the person who inspired it. Absence, insult, infamy—all that does not affect it. When two persons love, they can go ten years without seeing each other and without suffering from it.[1]

You claim that I treat you like "a woman of the lowest class." I don't know what "a woman of the lowest class" is, nor of the highest class, nor of the next-highest. Women are relatively inferior or superior by reason of their beauty and the attraction they exert on us, that's all. You accuse me of being an aristocrat, but I have very democratic ideas on this subject. It's possible, as you say, that it is in the nature of moderate affections to be enduring. But in saying that, you condemn your own, for it is anything but moderate. As for myself, I am weary of grand passions, exalted feelings, frenzied loves, and howling despairs. I love good sense above all, perhaps because I have none.

I fail to understand why you are repeatedly offended, and sulk. You are at fault in this, for you are kind, most charming and lovable, and one cannot help holding it against you that you wantonly spoil it all.

Calm yourself, work, and when we meet again welcome me with a good laugh and tell me you've been silly.

1. "What a sentence!" Louise wrote in the margin here.

To Louise Colet

[Rouen,] Monday, 3 o'clock. [January 11, 1847]

.   .   .

There are certain bourgeois satisfactions that are disgusting, and some ordinary joys whose vulgarity I find repugnant. That is why I have always taken against Béranger, with his lovers in their garrets and his idealization of the mediocre. I have never understood why, as he puts it, "at twenty you're happy in a garret." Would one be unhappy in a palace? Isn't it the poet's function to transport us elsewhere? I don't like to come upon grisette-love, a porter's lodge, and my threadbare overcoat in the realm where I go to forget all that. Let people who are happy among such things remain among them, but to represent them as being beautiful, no, no. I still prefer to dream of swansdown divans and hummingbird-feather hammocks, even if I suffer in doing so.

What an extraordinary idea of yours, that someone should continue *Candide!* Is it possible? Who will do it, who *could* do it? There are some works so overpoweringly great (and *Candide* is one of them), that their weight would crush anyone who tried to take them on. Giant's armor: the dwarf who put it on his back would be flattened before taking a single step. You do not admire enough, you do not respect enough. You have a genuine love of art, but not the religion of art. If you experienced a deep and pure delight in the contemplation of masterpieces, you would not sometimes make these peculiar strictures about them. Still, as you are, one cannot help loving you and feeling drawn to you despite oneself.

Adieu. Thine.

To Louise Colet

[Paris, *ultima*, April 30, 1847]

I have never before been so conscious of how little talent I possess for expressing ideas in words. You ask me for a frank, clear explanation. But haven't I given you just that a hundred times, and, if I dare say so, in every letter for many months? What can I say now that I haven't said before?

You want to know whether I love you, so that everything can be cleared up once and for all. Isn't that what you wrote me yesterday? It is too big a question to be answered by a "Yes" or a "No." Still, I will try to do that, so you'll no longer accuse me of always being evasive. I hope that today you'll at least be fair: you don't spoil me in that respect.

For me, love is not and should not be in the foreground of life; it should remain in the back room. Other things in the soul take precedence over it— things which seem to me nearer the light, closer to the sun. So, if you look upon love as the main dish of existence, the answer is No. As a seasoning, Yes.

If you mean by "loving" to be exclusively preoccupied with the loved one, to live only through him, to see, of everything there is to see in the world, only him, to be full of the idea of him, to have your heart overflow with him, the way a little girl's apron is so full of flowers that they continually overflow even though she holds the corners in her mouth and squeezes it tightly with both hands—to feel, in a word, that your life is tied to his life and that this has become an integral organ of your soul—then, No.

If you mean by "loving" the desire to take, from this double contact, the foam that floats on the surface, without stirring the dregs that may be at the bottom; a union combining affection and pleasure; meetings filled with delight and partings free of despair (if the truth be known, even when one kisses, in their coffins, those one has loved the best, one doesn't "despair"); the ability to live without one another—since it is quite possible to live severed from everything one covets, orphaned of all one's loves, bereft of all one's dreams—yet when together experiencing moments of rapture that make you smile as though you were being tickled in some strange way; in short, the feeling that this happened because it was fated, and will end because everything must end (it being solemnly agreed, in advance, that neither will blame the other), and the determination, in the midst of this joy, to go on living as before, or perhaps a little better than before, with this additional resting-place for your heart when it is tired (not that it makes you feel any happier at facing the world each morning);—if you grant that it is possible to be in love and yet realize how immensely pitiful are the rewards of love as compared with the rewards of art, and feel an amused and bitter scorn for everything that drags you down to earth;—if you admit that it is possible to be in love and yet feel that a line of Theocritus is more intoxicating than your most precious memories, and feel too that you could easily make great sacrifices (I mean of the things generally considered most precious: life, money) whereas small compromises are difficult—then: Yes.

Ah, when I saw you, poor pretty darling, setting sail on this ocean (remember my first letters), didn't I warn you: "No! Stay where you are! Stay on shore, meager though your existence there may be!"

Now, put out of your mind your suppositions concerning the outside influences you think are acting on me—my mother, Phidias, Maxime. None of it is true—the part about Maxime no more than the rest. I don't know that anyone up until now has ever made me do anything either good or bad, or even been responsible for a single one of my opinions. Not that I'm inflexible: in these cases I simply act naturally, without being aware of what I do.

As for your differences with Maxime, you must remember that in this whole affair he came to you to serve your interests, not his own. He may have been hurt (since he bruises easily—something in which he and I differ, you see, despite the "pact" that binds us, as you put it) by a number of vehement things you wrote him, or he may be tired of being put to use so often on my account. The role of confidant may be honorable, but it isn't always amusing. Besides, you slander him: he was completely devoted to you. If the need arose, he would be so again.

One thing. You keep coming back to the intellectual differences between us, to Nero, etc. (Nero!) Let's talk no more about this: it would be more sensible.

Quite apart from the fact that I find it difficult to produce explanations of this kind, they upset me horribly. Yes—incredibly. Because they touch too closely on what lies at the very deepest part of my self.

. . . If this letter wounds you, if it's the "blow" you have been expecting, it still seems to me not so harsh as all that. You kept begging me so persistently to strike you! Blame only yourself. You asked me, on your knees, to insult you—but no, I send you my affection . . .

The heading on that letter of April 30, 1847, including the word *ultima,* is in Louise Colet's hand. *Ultima* because she believed, or pretended to believe, that it was the last letter Flaubert would write her. He was to leave the next day with Maxime DuCamp for a three-months' walking tour in Brittany, and the affair seemed to be over. In March, Louise had made scenes at Flaubert's Paris hotel, at Maxime DuCamp's house, and at the railway station—all of which, Flaubert wrote her, made him look ridiculous. Since then they had exchanged several "ultimas," of which this one was, in fact, Flaubert's last only in the sense of being written on the eve of his departure. From Brittany he wrote Louise a number of times, sending her a flower from Chateaubriand's grave, begging her for letters, and assuring her for the thousandth time that he "had never meant to hurt her."

Flaubert and DuCamp were in Brittany until late July. In Brest and several other towns they met, by prearrangement, Mme Flaubert, who had come down from Normandy with her granddaughter Caroline and the baby's nurse; and over certain carriageable stretches of the route the hikers traveled with her, then diverging and rejoining her from time to time. "The poor woman now has only me," Flaubert wrote Ernest Chevalier from Saint-Malo on July 13, "and it would have been cruel to leave her behind . . . [Maxime and I] have had some good moments in the shadow of old châteaux, and smoked our long pipes in many a crumbling moat overgrown with weeds and perfumed with the scent of broom. And the sea! The sea! The fresh air, the fields, the freedom— I mean real freedom, the kind that consists in saying what you like, thinking aloud together, and walking at random, as oblivious of the passing of time as of the drifting smoke of your pipe."[1]

The two travelers had agreed to write a joint account of their trip, DuCamp to do the even-numbered chapters and Flaubert the uneven; and this they accomplished on their return. They called their narrative *Par les champs et par les grèves—Over Field and Shore—*and had two fair handwritten copies made of the manuscript. Flaubert much later allowed a magazine to print a few of his pages, on Celtic archaeology; posthumously, all his chapters were printed. DuCamp's chapters were published only recently, in the "Club de l'honnête homme" edition of Flaubert's works. Although Flaubert once said, of his part of *Par les champs,* that it was the first thing he had ever written carefully, the general tone is casual and "occasional." A few of his passages stand out, particularly one describing the friends reading *René* aloud as they sat by the lake near Chateaubriand's Château de Combourg.

After Flaubert returned to Croisset he resumed his correspondence with Louise; but the affair was foundering. About this time, or perhaps even before leaving for Brittany, he began to enjoy the company of another, less exigent Louise on his trips to Paris—Louise Pradier, the sculptor's discarded wife, who also permitted DuCamp and a number of others certain liberties. (Pradier was kept in ignorance of this particular instance of Flaubert's obedience to his own earlier advice to take a mistress.) Louise Colet quickly suspected the new affair, and added it to her list of complaints.

1. Flaubert could not resist adding, to tease the now very respectable Chevalier, formerly one of the tumultuous band at the lycée: "If you are still in Corsica next summer [he had been appointed assistant public attorney in Ajaccio], you will probably have the honor of a visit from the young Maxime DuCamp, who plans to go to Sardinia as well. I'd love to come with him and drop into your courtroom some morning, to make a shambles of the place—belch behind the door, upset the inkwells, and shit in front of His Majesty's bust: in short, burst in on you like the Garçon."

To Louise Colet

[Croisset, November 7, 1847]

. . .

You reproach me for speaking of art with you, "as though I were speaking with someone I care nothing for." So you speak about art with people for whom you care nothing? You regard this subject as quite secondary, a kind of entertainment, something between politics and the day's news? Not I! Not I! The other day I saw a friend who lives outside France.[1] We were brought up together; he reminisced about our childhood, my father, my sister, the college, etc. Do you think that I spoke to him about the things closest to me, or even those that I have the highest regard for—my loves and my enthusiasms? I was very careful not to, I assure you, for he would have trampled them underfoot. The spirit observes the proprieties too, you know. He bored me to death, and at the end of two hours I was longing for him to go—which doesn't mean that I'm not devoted to him, and don't love him, if you call it loving. What is there worth discussing except Art? But who is there to talk of Art with? The first person who happens along? You are luckier than I, then, for I never find anyone. You want me to be frank? Well then, I will be. One day, our day together in Mantes, under the trees, you told me that you "wouldn't exchange your happiness for the fame of Corneille." Do you remember that? Is my memory correct? If you knew how those words shocked me, how they chilled the very marrow of my bones! Fame! Fame! What is fame? It is nothing. A mere noise, the external accompaniment of the joy Art gives us. "The fame of Corneille" indeed! But—to *be* Corneille! To feel *one's self* Corneille! But then I have always seen you lump art together with other things—patriotism, love, what you will—a lot of things which to my mind are alien to it and, far from augmenting its stature, in my opinion diminish it. This is one of the chasms that exist between you and me. It was you who exposed it, and revealed it to me.

. . .

1. Ernest Chevalier.

To Louise Colet

[Croisset, March 1848]

I thank you[1] for the concern you felt for me during the recent events,[2] and on this occasion as on preceding ones I beg your pardon for the worry and distress I caused you. Your letter reached me only after a delay of seven days. That was the fault of the mails, which as you may imagine functioned very badly all last week.

You ask my opinion concerning what has just taken place. Well, it is all very funny. The expressions on the faces of the discomfited[3] are a joy to see. I take the greatest delight in observing all the crushed ambitions. I don't know whether the new form of government and the resulting social order will be favorable to Art. That is a question. It cannot be more bourgeois or more worthless than the old. As for being more stupid, is it possible? I am glad that it improves the prospects for your play. A good play is well worth a king.[4] I'll come to applaud at the first performance, as I already told you. I'll be there, you'll see me, I'll do my best, and gladly.

What is the good of coming back endlessly to DuCamp and the grievances real or not that you hold against him?[5] You must realize that this has long been painful to me. Your persistence, in bad taste from the start, has become cruel.

Also, why all your preambles to telling me the "news"?[6] You could have given it to me outright from the beginning, without circumlocutions. I spare you the reflections it inspires in me and the feelings it arouses. There would be too much to say. I pity you, I pity you greatly. I suffered for you, and—more to the point—"I have seen it all." You understand, don't you? It is to the artist that I speak.

Whatever may happen, count on me always. Even though we may no longer see each other or write, there will always be a bond between us that will not be effaced, a past whose consequences will endure. My "monstrous personality," as you so amiably call it, does not obliterate in me every last decent feeling— *human* feeling, if you prefer. One day you will perhaps realize this, and regret having expended so much vexation and bitterness on my account.

Adieu, je vous embrasse.

1. Flaubert uses the formal *vous* instead of the familiar *tu* of previous letters.
2. The Revolution of 1848: more particularly, the abdication of Louis-Philippe on February 24 and the proclamation of the Second French Republic by Lamartine. Flaubert had gone to Paris to witness some of the events, and briefly joined Maxime DuCamp in a company of the National Guard (which supported the "reform" of the government).
3. The monarchists.
4. Louise Colet's five-act play in verse, *Madeleine*. There had been earlier references to it

in the correspondence: Louise had hoped that it might be performed at the Comédie Française, with Rachel in the leading rôle. Its "better prospects" under the new Republic were perhaps due to its subject, "une famille en 1793." It was never produced.

5. DuCamp had lost all esteem—if he had ever had any—for Louise Colet. In December 1847 he had written to Flaubert: "The Muse has written me a very calm letter. She says she is resigned [to the end of the liaison with Flaubert] and is going to get to work. Bad news for literature."

6. Louise, who was frequenting liberal exiles from various countries, was pregnant by a Polish refugee named Franc. Their son died in infancy.

In the spring of 1848 there occurred what might be called the second act—the first having been Alfred LePoittevin's marriage—of what Flaubert was always to consider the greatest loss of his life. Alfred, now the father of a son and living with his wife in the country, had been slowly wasting away from tuberculosis.

To MAXIME DuCAMP

[Croisset,] Friday night. [April 7, 1848]

Alfred died on Monday at midnight. I buried him yesterday, and am now back. I watched beside him two nights (the second time, all night), I wrapped him in his shroud, I gave him the farewell kiss, and saw him sealed in his coffin. I was there two days—very full days. While I sat beside him I read Creuzer's *Religions of Antiquity*. The window was open, the night splendid. I could hear a cock crowing, and a night-moth circled around the tapers. I shall never forget all that, or the look on Alfred's face, or, the first night at midnight, the far-off sound of a hunting-horn that came to me through the forest.

On Wednesday I walked all afternoon, with a dog that followed me without being summoned. (It was a bitch that had become attached to Alfred and always accompanied him when he walked alone. The night before his death she howled frightfully and couldn't be quieted.) From time to time I sat on the moss; I smoked, I stared up at the sky. I lay down behind a heap of cut broom and slept.

The last night I read *Les Feuilles d'automne*.[1] I kept coming upon poems that were his favorites or which had special meaning for me in the circumstances. Now and then I got up, lifted the veil covering his face, and looked at him. I was wrapped in a cloak that belonged to my father and which he had worn only once, the day of Caroline's wedding.

At daybreak, about four o'clock, the attendant and I began our task. I lifted him, turned him, covered him. The feeling of the coldness and rigidity of his limbs stayed in my fingertips all the next day. He was horribly decomposed; the sheets were stained through. We wrapped him in two shrouds. When it was done he looked like an Egyptian mummy in its bandages, and I was filled with an indescribable sense of joy and relief on his account. There was a whitish mist, the trees were beginning to be visible through it. The two tapers shone in the dawning whiteness; two or three birds sang, and I recited to myself this sequence from his *Bélial*:[2] "Il ira, joyeux oiseau, saluer dans les pins le soleil levant"—or rather I heard his voice saying it to me, and for the rest of the day was deliciously obsessed by it.

He was laid in the coffin in the entry, where the doors had been removed and where the morning air poured in, freshened by the rain that had started to fall. He was carried to the cemetery on men's shoulders. It was almost an hour's walk. From behind, I saw the coffin swaying like a rolling boat. The service was atrociously long. In the cemetery the earth was muddy. I stood by the grave and watched each shovelful as it fell: there seemed to be a hundred thousand of them. When the hole was filled I walked away, smoking, which Boivin didn't think proper.

I returned to Rouen on the box of a carriage with Bouilhet. The rain beat down, the horses went at a gallop, I shouted to urge them on, we were back in 43 minutes—5 leagues. The air did me much good. I slept all night and most of today, and had a strange dream, which I wrote down lest I lose it.[3]

That, dear Max, has been my life since Tuesday evening. I have had marvelous intimations and intuitions, and flashes of untranslatable ideas. A host of things have been coming back to me, with choirs of music and clouds of perfume.

As long as he was capable of doing anything, he read Spinoza in bed each night until one in the morning.

On one of his last days, when the windows were open and the sun was coming into the room, he said: "Close it! It is too beautiful—too beautiful!"

There were times, dear Max, when I thought intensely of you, recalling and comparing sad memories.[4]

. . . Adieu, dear Max. All my affection. I embrace you, and long to see you, for I need to speak with you of incomprehensible things.

1. By Victor Hugo; a Bible of the young Romantics.
2. See p. 96.
3. The dream is lost.
4. Flaubert knew that the lively, efficient DuCamp had detested the languid, decadent, subtle Alfred and had been jealous of Flaubert's love for him. In 1844, during Flaubert's first year of convalescence, DuCamp had sent him, from Rome, a long letter of encouragement, warning him, however, that association with Alfred was doing him no good. "You, who have a most brilliant intelligence, have been aping someone corrupt, that 'Greek of the Late Empire,' as he calls himself. And now, I give you my word, Gustave, he is laughing at you, and doesn't believe a word of anything he has told you. Show him this letter and see if he dares deny what I say."

Flaubert later wrote to a correspondent:[1] "Ten years ago I lost the man I loved most in the world, Alfred LePoittevin. During his last illness, he spent his nights reading Spinoza. I have never known anyone (and I know many people) of so transcendental a mind as this friend I speak of. We sometimes spent six hours on end talking about metaphysics. We flew *high* sometimes, I assure you. Since his death I no longer *talk* with anyone at all. I chatter, or remain silent. What a necropolis is the human heart!"

Doubtless fearing that scabrous passages might become known, the LePoittevin family demanded that Flaubert return to them Alfred's manuscripts, apparently including his letters, that were in his possession. "The first great aesthetico-sentimental fury of my life," he wrote Louise Colet in 1853, "was six years ago, over an expurgated edition of Molière, compiled by a priest . . . The second was when [Alfred LePoittevin's family] refused to give me, or rather demanded that I return, certain of his manuscripts." Some of Alfred's poems and letters (the latter much censored), and his "philosophical tale," *Une Promenade de Bélial*, resembling in subject Flaubert's earlier *Smarh*, were first printed only in 1909 and 1910, by the Flaubert scholar René Descharmes, to whom they were confided by Alfred's son, Louis LePoittevin. Several passages have been restored by Jean Bruneau in Pléiade, I, and by Sartre in *L'Idiot de la famille*.

1. To Mlle Leroyer de Chantepie, November 4, 1857.

To Ernest Chevalier

Croisset, Monday, July 4 [1848]

I seem fated, poor Ernest, each time I write you to give sad news.[1] You have read in the newspapers of the atrocities that have been taking place in Paris.[2] DuCamp was struck by a bullet in the calf of his right leg and will be laid up for at least a month: I am told his wound is slight but am not entirely reassured.

While that was taking place the rest of us were coping with a different kind of shock.

Hamard returned from Paris a month ago announcing his intention of becoming an actor and making his debut at the Comédie Française in two weeks. (In the last four months he has squandered thirty thousand francs, not to mention his silver and diamonds, which he gave to the Republic, etc. etc.) In short, completely mad. He came here to claim his daughter. But my mother was advised to keep her away from him because of his condition, and we left hurriedly for Forges, the first place that occurred to us. There, since my mother trembled at the sound of every carriage that arrived in town, she begged shelter from M. and Mme Beaufils, who welcomed her in a way I'll never forget— perfectly. Meanwhile his family wanted to have him committed and his uncle petitioned that he be declared incompetent. But unfortunately the outbreak in Paris kept the police from doing anything. When he learned that action was being taken against him he temporarily regained his sanity. He petitioned that my mother be obliged to return his child; but the judge decided that she should keep her until the hearing on the issue of incompetence. We reached an amicable settlement, and now he has consented that my mother should keep the child until January, and they are going to stay proceedings about his incompetence. Six months from now he will, I hope, be completely insane and will almost certainly be declared incompetent. I spare you countless details, horrible for my mother . . .

And you, what has become of you? Have you a little peace? As for me, as you may imagine, I am living in hell; all conceivable blows are falling on my head. At each new misfortune I think the limit has been reached, but they keep coming and coming! And I haven't told you everything . . .

1. Flaubert had recently written Chevalier about Alfred LePoittevin's death.

2. The workers' revolution of June 24-26 (the "June days") against the recently installed republic. It was bloodily suppressed by the National Guard, now progovernment. The "atrocities" referred to by Flaubert were probably those committed by both sides (J.B.), including the murder of General Bréa and the Archbishop of Paris by the insurgents. Flaubert considered himself nonpolitical, and he was of course vehemently antibourgeois from the aesthetic point of view; but at moments of danger from the Left he feared for his bourgeois foundations. The events of 1848 form part of the story of *L'Education Sentimentale* (1870).

To LOUISE COLET

[Croisset, August 25, 1848]

Thank you for the gift.[1]
Thank you for your very beautiful poem.
Thank you for the remembrance.

Yours, G.

Friday night.

1. A lock of Chateaubriand's hair. Chateaubriand had died on July 4. Louise had probably been given the memento by her neighbor and friend, Mme Récamier, Chateaubriand's companion.

V

Voyage en Orient
1849-1851

NOW, with Alfred LePoittevin dead, the connection with Louise Colet at an end, and the weeks in Brittany as evidence that Maxime DuCamp was a congenial traveling companion, Flaubert's thoughts turned to the "Orient"— to Egypt and the Middle East—where he had always longed to go, and where DuCamp had recently been and was eager to go again. For some years the two friends had spoken of making such a journey together. "You asked me the other day how I spend my time with DuCamp," Flaubert wrote in September 1846 to Louise, who was jealous that Maxime should be spending a month at Croisset. "For three days we've been tracing on the map a great tour of Asia which would take six years and cost us—the way we have conceived it— 3 million 600 thousand and some francs." Money was one of the hindrances to even a more modest tour: financially, Flaubert was largely dependent on his mother—and for company, as we have seen, she was dependent on him. It took time and careful plotting to get Mme Flaubert to contemplate the venture itself and the separation. She consented only after Flaubert and DuCamp persuaded Dr. Achille Flaubert and Dr. Jules Cloquet to advise her that travel in warm countries would benefit Gustave's health. The route was to be Egypt, Palestine, perhaps Persia, then Greece, Italy, and home.

In his memoirs Maxime DuCamp describes the preparations for the trip. "I wanted us to enjoy every possible advantage while traveling, and had asked the government to assign us missions that would recommend us to French diplomatic and commercial agents in the Orient. Need I say that these missions were to be, and were, entirely unpaid? My request was granted. Flaubert—one can scarcely refrain from smiling—was charged by the Ministry of Agriculture and Commerce with the task of collecting, in the various ports and caravan centers, any information that he thought might interest Chambers of Commerce." DuCamp's mission (of his own choosing) was to photograph monuments and inscriptions. He secured letters of introduction to officials of the Egyptian government; and he had a special map of Egypt prepared, a copy of which was to be left with Mme Flaubert so she could follow their progress. A servant, a Corsican named Sassetti, was hired for the journey.

Meanwhile, shortly before Alfred's death, Flaubert had begun a work which he thought, for the first time, might be worthy of publication—the appearance "in full armor" that was the only kind of literary debut he was willing to envisage. Inspired by the painting of the Temptation of St. Anthony about which he had written to Alfred LePoittevin from Genoa in 1845, and Callot's engraving of the same subject that he had bought and hung on his wall, it would "bring to life," as Jean Bruneau has put it, "the religious world of the Fourth Century A.D., with all its beliefs, heresies and legends."[1] He resolved to complete it before setting out.

He would show the Anchorite tempted not merely by sins of the world and the flesh, but by forbidden intellectual and spiritual concepts: by the pagan schools of philosophy, by the dogmas of all the heretical Christian sects, and the doctrines of non-Christian religions. To familiarize himself with these he made use of his old classical and Indian studies, and embarked on wide new reading. Jean Seznec[2] has shown that for a single episode in *La Tentation de Saint Antoine*—the procession of the fallen gods, about one-seventh part of the whole—Flaubert read, reread or consulted at least sixty ancient texts, histories, and scholarly commentaries. The work would be in dramatic form, each seductive belief and way of thought hurled at the saint by its spokesman. The cast of characters became enormous, the work so long that when he finally finished it, in September 1849, and read it aloud to Maxime DuCamp and Louis Bouilhet, they listened to him—so DuCamp says in his memoirs—for thirty-two hours.

> The hours that Bouilhet and I spent listening to Flaubert chant his lines—we sitting there silent, occasionally exchanging a glance—remain very painful in my memory. We kept straining our ears, always hoping that the action would begin, and always disappointed, for the situation remains the same from beginning to end. St. Anthony, bewildered, a little simple, really quite a blockhead if I dare say so, sees the various forms of temptation pass before him and responds with nothing but exclamations: "Ah! Ah! Oh! Oh! Mon dieu! Mon dieu!" . . . Flaubert grew heated as he read, and we tried to grow warm with him, but remained frozen . . . After the last reading—it was almost midnight—Flaubert pounded the table: "Now: tell me frankly what you think."
>
> Bouilhet was a shy man, but no one was firmer than he once he decided to express his opinion; and he said: "We think you should throw it into the fire and never speak of it again."
>
> Flaubert leapt up and uttered a cry of horror . . . He repeated certain lines to us, saying "But that is beautiful!"
>
> "Yes, it is beautiful . . . There are excellent passages, some exquisite evocations of antiquity, but it is all lost in the bombast of the language. You wanted to make music and you have made only noise."
>
> Mme Flaubert long held our frankness against us. She thought we were jealous of her son, and she let us know it.

DuCamp's account, written after the deaths of both Bouilhet and Flaubert, is perhaps overcolored; but he and Bouilhet unquestionably did advise Flaubert to put *Saint Antoine* away. Flaubert, crushed, bowed to their opinion. He was sick at heart as he made himself ready to travel. After an emotional parting from his mother, he set off with DuCamp in late October, via Marseilles and Alexandria, for Cairo.[3] There they would hire a sailing boat, a *cange*, and its crew, and explore both banks of the Nile.

1. In *Dizionario critico della letteratura francese* (Unione tipografico-editrice torinese, 1973), article "Flaubert."

2. In *Les Sources de l'épisode des dieux dans La Tentation de Saint Antoine (Première version, 1849).* (Paris, 1940.)

This first version of the *Tentation,* earliest of three composed at different periods of Flaubert's life (see pp. 224, n.2 and 228, n.2), is much the longest. There is no English translation.

3. Two "Mementos" of Louise Colet (see note to Appendix I):

"Memento of October 28, 1849. 9:30 o'clock. Alone. Today Ferrat told me that Gustave will be passing through Paris on his way to embark on that long trip to the Orient. He is leaving without writing me, without seeing me, without telling me what he has done with my letters and my keepsakes. Oh! How somber, these amours broken off forever, leaving no trace! No trace in the *man's* heart: in mine, the wounds never close, and bleed eternally. Is it possible that two beings should have loved one another, loved sincerely, merged each in the other—and that one of the two should break away like this, forget all—*all*, mon Dieu!—about those marvelous hours! He lacks even the poetic, natural curiosity which after a few years makes us yearn for another view of sites and monuments that have impressed us."

"Memento of Tuesday, December 4, 1849. Saturday morning (the 1st of the month), I saw in a newspaper that Maxime and Gustave had set sail for Egypt. Heartache, the wound reopens! Not a word of farewell! And now the sea lies between us . . . In the evening, a visit from Ferrat . . . How I am suffering, mon Dieu! I couldn't keep from crying in front of Ferrat. I spoke of Gustave in the midst of my tears. I am too wretched. I wish I were dead . . ."

To his mother

[Alexandria, November 17, 1849]

. . .

When we were two hours out from the coast of Egypt I went into the bow with the chief quartermaster and saw the seraglio of Abbas Pasha like a black dome on the blue of the Mediterranean. The sun was beating down on it. I had my first sight of the Orient through, or rather in, a glowing light that was like melted silver on the sea. Soon the shore became distinguishable, and the first thing we saw on land was a pair of camels led by their driver; then, on the dock, some Arabs peacefully fishing. Landing took place amid the most deafening uproar imaginable: negroes, negresses, camels, turbans, cudgelings to right and left, and ear-splitting guttural cries. I gulped down a whole bellyful of colors, like a donkey filling himself with hay. Cudgelings play a great role here; everyone who wears clean clothes beats everyone who wears dirty ones, or rather none at all, and when I say clothes I mean a pair of short breeches. You see many gentlemen sauntering along the streets with nothing but a shirt and a long pipe. Except in the very lowest classes, all the women are veiled, and on their noses they wear ornaments that hang down and sway from side to side . . . On the other hand, if you don't see their faces, you see their entire bosoms. As you change countries, you find that modesty changes its place, like a bored traveler who keeps shifting from the outside to the inside of the stage-coach. One curious thing here is the respect, or rather the terror, that everyone displays in the presence of "Franks," as they call Europeans. We have had bands of ten or twelve Arabs, advancing across the whole width of a street, break apart to let us pass. In fact, Alexandria is almost a European city, there are so many Europeans here. At table in our hotel alone there are thirty, and the place is full of Englishmen, Italians, etc. Yesterday we saw a magnificent procession celebrating the circumcision of the son of a rich merchant. This morning we saw Cleopatra's Needles (two great obelisks on the shorefront), Pompey's column, the catacombs, and Cleopatra's baths. Tomorrow we leave for Rosetta, whence we shall return in three or four days. We go slowly and don't get overtired, living sensibly and clad in flannel from head to foot, even though the temperature indoors is sometimes thirty degrees.[1] The heat is not at all unbearable, thanks to the sea breeze.

Soliman Pasha,[2] the most powerful man in Egypt, the victor at Nezib, the terror of Constantinople, happens just now to be in Alexandria instead of Cairo. We paid him a visit yesterday, and presented Lauvergne's letter. He received us very courteously. He is to give us orders for all the provincial governors of Egypt and offered us his carriage for the journey to Cairo. It was he who arranged about our horses for tomorrow. He is charming, cordial, etc. He apparently likes the way we look. In addition, we have M. Galis, chief of the army engineers, Princeteau Bey, etc. Just to give you an idea of how we are to travel, we have been given soldiers to hold back the crowd when we want to photograph: I trust you are impressed. As you see, poor old darling, conditions couldn't be better. As for ophthalmia: of the people one sees, only the very lowest orders (as the expression goes) suffer from it. M. Willemin, a young doctor who has been in Egypt five years, told us this morning that he has not seen a single case among the well-to-do or Europeans. That should reassure you. Don't worry, I'll come back in good shape. I have put on so much weight since I left that two pairs of my trousers are with M. Chavannes, a French tailor, being let out to accommodate my paunch.

So—goodbye, old lady. I was interrupted during the writing of this letter by the arrival of M. Pastré, the banker who is to send us our money as we need it and will ship home any packages, in case we buy a mummy or two. Now we are going to our friend Soliman Pasha to pick up a letter from him about tomorrow's expedition: it is addressed to the Governor of Rosetta, seeing to it that he puts us up in his house—i.e., in the fort, apparently the only place to stay. We had intended to push on as far as Damietta. But as we have been told that would be too tiring on horseback because of the sand, we've given up the idea. We'll go to Cairo by boat. As you see, we're not stubborn; it's our principle to follow the advice of experts and behave like a pair of little saints. Goodbye, a thousand kisses, kiss the baby for me, send me long letters . . .

1. Réaumur. 86° Fahrenheit.
2. François Sève, a former colonel in the French army, taken into the Egyptian service in 1815 (after Waterloo) by Mohammed Ali. The latter, viceroy of Egypt, revolted against his sovereign, the Turkish sultan; and his forces, under Soliman Pasha, defeated the Turks in the battle of Nezib (or Nisib) in 1839. A number of other officials mentioned by Flaubert were also Frenchmen, given the title "bey" or "pasha" in the Egyptian service.

To his mother
Alexandria, Thursday, [November] 22 [1849]

My darling—I am writing you in white tie and tails, pumps, etc., like a man who has been paying a call on a prime minister: in fact we have just left Artin Bey, Minister of Foreign Affairs, to whom we were introduced by the [French] consul and who received us splendidly. He is going to give us a *firman* with his seal on it for our entire journey. It is unbelievable how well we are treated here —it's as though we were princes, and I'm not joking. Sassetti keeps saying: "Whatever happens, I'll be able to say that once in my life I had ten slaves to serve me and one to chase away the flies," and that is quite true.

. . .

Friday morning. [November 23]

We set out at daybreak last Sunday, saddled and booted, harnessed and armed, with four men running behind us, our dragoman on his mule carrying our coats and supplies, and our three horses, which were ridden with simple halters. They looked like nags but were on the contrary excellent beasts; with two pricks of the spur they were off at a gallop, and a whistle brought them up short. To make them go right or left you had only to touch their neck. The desert begins at the very gates of Alexandria: first sandy hillocks covered here and there with palms, and then dunes that stretch on endlessly. From time to time you see on the horizon what looks like great stretches of water with trees reflected in them, and at their farthest limit, where they seem to touch the sky, a gray vapor that appears to be moving in a rush, like a train: that is the mirage, known to all, Arabs and Europeans—people familiar with the desert as well as those seeing it for the first time. Now and then you come upon the carcass of some animal on the sand—a dead camel three-quarters eaten by jackals, its guts exposed and blackened by the sun; a mummified buffalo, a horse's head, etc. Arabs trot by on their donkeys, their wives bundled in immense black or white veils: you exchange greetings—"Taieb"—and continue on your way. About eleven o'clock we lunched near Abukir, in a fort manned by soldiers who gave us excellent coffee and refused *baksheesh* (a wonder!). The beach at Abukir is still littered, here and there, with the wreckage of ships.[1] We saw a number of sharks that had been washed up, and along the water's edge our horses trod on seashells. We shot cormorants and water-magpies, and our Arabs ran like hares to pick up those we wounded: I brought down a few birds myself—yes, *me!*—something new, what? The weather was magnificent, sea and sky bluest blue, an immensity of space.

At a place called Edku (you will find it on your map) we took a ferry and there our runners bought dates from a camel-driver whose two beasts were laden with them. A mile or two farther on, we were riding tranquilly along side by side, a hundred feet in front of our runners, when suddenly we heard loud cries from behind. We turned, and saw our men in a tumult, jostling and shoving one another and making signs for us to turn back. Sassetti dashed off at a gallop, velvet jacket flying; and digging our spurs into our horses we followed after to the scene of the conflict. It was occasioned, we discovered, by the owner of the dates, who had been following his camels at a distance and who, coming upon our men and seeing that they were eating dates, had thought they had stolen them and had fallen on them with his cudgel.

But when he saw us three ruffians descending upon him with rifles slung over our saddles, roles were reversed, and from the beater he became the beaten. Courage returned to our men, and they fell upon him with their sticks in such a way that his backside was soon resounding with blow after blow. To escape, he ran into the sea, lifting up his robe to keep it dry, but his assailants followed. The higher he lifted his robe, the greater the area he exposed to their cudgels, which rattled on him like drumsticks. You can't imagine anything funnier than that man's black behind amid the white foam churned up by the combat. The rest of us stood on the shore, laughing like fools; my sides still ache when I think of it . . . Two days later, coming back from Rosetta, we met the same camels as they were returning from Alexandria. Perceiving us from afar, the owner hastily left his beasts and made a long detour in the desert to avoid us—a precaution which diverted us considerably. You would scarcely believe the important role played by the cudgel in this part of the world; buffets are distributed with a sublime prodigality, always accompanied by loud cries; it's the most genuine kind of local color you can think of.

At six in the evening, after a sunset that made the sky look like melted vermilion and the sand of the desert like ink, we arrived at Rosetta and found all the gates closed. At the name of Soliman Pasha they opened, creaking faintly like doors of a barn. The streets were dark, and so narrow that there was barely room for a single horseman. We rode through the bazaars, where each shop was lit by a glass of oil hanging from a cord, and arrived at the barracks. The [local] pasha received us on his sofa, surrounded by negroes who brought us pipes and coffee. After many courtesies and compliments, we were given supper and shown to our beds, which were equipped with excellent mosquito-netting . . . The next morning while we were washing, the pasha came into our room, followed by the regimental doctor, an Italian who spoke French perfectly and did us the honors of the city. Thanks to him we spent a very agreeable day. When he learned my name and that I was the son of a doctor, he said he had heard of Father and had often seen his name cited. It was no small satisfaction to me, dear Mother, to think that Father's memory was still beneficial to me, serving as a kind of protection at this distance. That reminds me that in the depths of Brittany, too, at Guérande, the local doctor told me he had quoted Father in his thesis. Yes, poor darling, I think constantly of those who are gone; as my body continues on its journey, my thoughts keep turning back to bury themselves in days past.

. . . All morning was taken up with things to do in Rosetta. By the way, when you write to Rouen will you please make inquiries about M. Julienne, who invented those fuel-saving devices for steam pumps? What is his address? Would he like to enter into correspondence with M. Foucault, manager of rice production at Rosetta, to whom I spoke of this invention and who would be glad to hear more? . . . I promised to do this, and would like to keep my word[2] . . .

1. From the naval battle of August 1, 1798, when Vice-Admiral Horatio Nelson destroyed the French fleet?
2. This is one of Flaubert's very rare references to anything that might be thought of as relating to his "mission." Nevertheless, in this same letter he urges his mother, when addressing her envelopes to him, to write "my name, title, and 'Cairo, Egypt,' " the "title" being: "Chargé d'une mission en Orient"—doubtless because the official designation was proving so useful.

To Louis Bouilhet
Cairo, Saturday night, 10 o'clock.
December 1, 1849.

Let me begin by kissing both your dear cheeks and blowing onto this paper all my "inspiration," so as to bring your "spirit" close to me. I imagine that you must be thinking quite a bit about us. For we think quite a bit about you, and miss you a hundred times a day. Yesterday, for example, my dear sir, we were in a whorehouse. But let's not jump ahead. At the present moment the moon is shining on the minarets—all is silence but for the occasional barking of dogs. My curtains are pulled back, and outside my window is the mass of the trees in the garden, black against the pale glimmer of the night. I am writing on a table with a green cloth, lit by two candles, and taking my ink from an ointment jar: near me, about ten millimeters away, are my ministerial instructions, which seem to be waiting impatiently for the day I'll use them as lavatory paper. Behind the partition I hear the young Maxime, preparing solutions for his negatives. Upstairs sleep the mutes, namely Sassetti and the dragoman—the latter, if truth be known, one of the most arrant pimps, ruffians and old bardashes[1] that could ever be imagined. As for my gracious self, I am wearing a large white cotton Nubian shirt, trimmed with little pompoms and of a cut whose description would take up too much space here. My head is completely shaved except for one lock at the occiput (by which Mohammed lifts you up on Judgment Day) and adorned with a tarboosh which is of a screaming red and made me half die of heat the first days I wore it. We look quite the pair of orientals—Max is especially marvelous when he smokes his *narghile* and fingers his beads. Considerations of safety limit our sartorial splurges: in Egypt the European is accorded greater respect than the native, so we won't dress up completely until we reach Syria.

And you, what are you up to in our wretched birthplace, which I occasionally surprise myself daydreaming about with affection? I keep thinking of our Sundays at Croisset, when I would hear the sound of the iron gate and look up and see first your walking-stick, then your notebook, and finally you. When shall we be back chatting endlessly before the fire in my green armchairs? What of *Melaenis?*[2] And the plays? Send me volumes. Until further notice write me to Cairo, and don't forget to put on the address: "Chargé de mission en Orient."

. . . I am sure that as an intelligent man you don't expect me to send you an account of my trip . . . In a word, this is how I sum up my feelings so far: very little impressed by nature here—i.e. landscape, sky, desert (except the mirages); enormously excited by the cities and the people. Hugo would say: "I was closer to God than to mankind." It probably comes of my having given more imagination and thought, before coming here, to things like horizon, greenery, sand, trees, sun, etc., than to houses, streets, costumes and faces. The result is that nature has been a rediscovery and the rest a discovery. There is one new element which I hadn't expected to see and which is tremendous here, and that is the grotesque. All the old comic business of the cudgeled slave, of the coarse trafficker in women, of the thieving merchant—it's all very fresh here, very genuine and charming. In the streets, in the houses, on any and all occasions, there is a merry proliferation of beatings right and left. There are guttural intonations that sound like the cries of wild beasts, and laughter, and flowing white robes, and ivory teeth flashing between thick lips, and flat negro noses, and dusty feet, and necklaces, and bracelets! Poor you! The pasha at Rosetta gave us a dinner at which there were ten negroes to serve us—they wore silk jackets and some had silver bracelets; and a little negro boy waved away the flies with a kind of feather-duster made of rushes. We ate with our fingers, the food was brought one dish at a time on a silver tray—about thirty different dishes made their appearance in this way. We were on divans in a wooden pavilion, windows open on the water. One of the finest things is the camel—I never tire of watching this strange beast that lurches like a turkey and sways its neck like a swan. Their cry is something that I wear myself out trying to imitate—I hope to bring it back with me—but it's hard to reproduce —a rattle with a kind of tremulous gargling as an accompaniment.

. . . The morning we arrived in Egypt . . . we had scarcely set foot on shore when Max, the old lecher, got excited over a negress who was drawing water at a fountain. He is just as excited by little negro boys. By whom is he *not* excited? Or, rather, by *what?* . . . Tomorrow we're to have a party on the river, with several whores dancing to the sound of *darabukehs* and castanets, their hair spangled with gold piastres. I'll try to make my next letter less disjointed—I've been interrupted twenty times in this one—and send you something worthwhile. The day before yesterday we were in the house of a woman who had arranged to have two others there for us. The place was dilapidated and open to all the winds and lit by a nightlight—we could see a palm tree through the unglazed window, and the two Turkish women wore silk robes embroidered with gold. This is a great place for contrasts: splendid things gleam in the dust. I performed on a mat that a family of cats had to be shooed from—a strange coitus, looking at each other without being able to exchange a word, and the exchange of looks is all the deeper for the curiosity and the surprise. My brain was too stimulated for me to enjoy it much otherwise. These shaved cunts make a strange effect—the flesh is hard as bronze, and my girl had a splendid arse.

Goodbye . . . Write to me, write to my mother now and then . . .

December 4, Post scriptum. For you alone.

To amuse the crowd, Mohammed Ali's jester took a woman in a Cairo bazaar one day, set her on the counter of a shop, and coupled with her publicly while the shopkeeper calmly smoked his pipe.

On the road from Cairo to Shubra some time ago a young fellow had himself publicly buggered by a large monkey—as in the story above, to create a good opinion of himself and make people laugh.

A marabout died a while ago—an idiot—who had long passed as a saint marked by God; all the Moslem women came to see him and masturbated him —in the end he died of exhaustion—from morning to night it was a perpetual jacking-off. Oh Bouilhet, why weren't you that marabout?

Quid dicis of the following fact: some time ago a *santon* (ascetic priest) used to walk through the streets of Cairo completely naked except for a cap on his head and another on his prick. To piss he would doff the prick-cap, and sterile women who wanted children would run up, put themselves under the parabola of his urine and rub themselves with it.

Goodbye—this morning I had a letter from my mother—she is very sad, poor thing. Go and talk to her about me . . .

1. Bardash: a catamite. (O.E.D.) The dragoman was named Joseph.
2. Before Flaubert's departure, Bouilhet had begun his *Melaenis*, a very long narrative poem about a dancer in ancient Rome. Flaubert's question about its progress was to bring, in Bouilhet's letters, long passages of the poem, on which Flaubert would comment at length in his replies. Most of these comments have been omitted from the present volume.

To his mother

Cairo, January 5, 1850.

Your fine long letter of the 16th reached me as a New Year's present last Wednesday, dear old darling. I was paying an official call on our consul, when he was handed a large packet. He opened it immediately, and I seized the envelope that I recognized among a hundred others. (I was itching to open it, but manners, alas! forbade.) Fortunately, he showed us into his wife's salon, and as there was a letter for her too, from her mother, we gave each other mutual permission to read almost before saying how do you do . . .

.   .   .

I'm bursting to tell you my name. Do you know what the Arabs call me? Since they have great difficulty in pronouncing French names, they invent their own for us Franks. Can you guess? Abu-Chanab, which means "Father of the Moustache." That word, *abu*, father, is applied to anyone connected with the chief detail under discussion—thus for merchants selling various commodities they say Father of the Shoes, Father of the Glue, Father of the Mustard, etc. Max's name is a very long one which I don't remember, and which means "the man who is excessively thin." Imagine my joy when I learned the honor being paid to that particular part of myself.

. . . Often when we have been out since early morning and feel hungry and don't want to take time to return to the hotel for lunch, we sit down in a Turkish restaurant. Here all the carving is done with one's hands, and everyone belches to his heart's content. Dining room and kitchen are all one, and behind you at the great fireplace little pots bubble and steam under the eye of the chef in his white turban and rolled-up sleeves. I am careful to write down the names of all the dishes and their ingredients. Also, I have made a list of all the perfumes made in Cairo—it may be very useful to me somewhere. We have hired two dragomans. In the evening an Arab storyteller comes and reads us stories, and there is an effendi whom we pay to make translations for us.

.   .   .

A few days ago I spent a fine afternoon. Max stayed at home to do I forget what, and I took Hasan (the second dragoman we have temporarily hired) and paid a visit to the bishop of the Copts for the sake of a conversation with him. I entered a square courtyard surrounded by columns, with a little garden in the middle—that is, a few big trees and a bed of dark greenery, around which ran a trellised wooden divan. My dragoman, with his capacious trousers and wide-sleeved jacket, walked ahead; I behind. On one of the corners of the divan was sitting a scowling old personage with a long white beard, wearing an ample pelisse; books in a baroque kind of handwriting were strewn all about him. At a certain distance were standing three black-robed theologians, younger and also with long beards. The dragoman said: "This is a French gentleman (*cawadja fransaoui*) who is traveling all over the world in search of knowledge, and who has come to you to speak of your religion." Such is the kind of language they go in for here. Can you imagine how I talk to them? A while ago, when I was looking at seeds in a shop, a woman to whom I had given something said: "Blessings on you, my sweet lord: God grant that you return safe and sound to your native land." There is much use of such blessings and ritual formulas. When Max asked a groom if he wasn't tired, the answer was: "It's enough for me to see the pleasure in your eyes."

But to return to the bishop. He received me with many courtesies. Coffee was brought, and I soon began to ask questions concerning the Trinity, the Virgin, the Gospels, the Eucharist—all my old erudition of *Saint Antoine* came back in a flood. It was superb, the sky blue above us, the trees, the books spread out, the old fellow ruminating in his beard before answering me, myself sitting cross-legged beside him, gesticulating with my pencil and taking notes, while Hasan stood motionless, translating aloud, and the three other theologians, sitting on stools, nodded their heads and interjected an occasional few words. I enjoyed it deeply. That was indeed the old Orient, land of religions and flowing robes. When the bishop gave out, one of the theologians replaced him; and when I finally saw that they were all somewhat flushed, I left. I am going back, for there is much to learn in that place. The Coptic religion is the most ancient of existing Christian sects, and little or nothing is known about it in Europe (so far as I know). I'm going to talk with the Armenians, too, and the Greeks, and the Sunnites, and especially with Moslem scholars.

We're still waiting for the return of the caravan from Mecca. It is too good an event to miss, and we shall not leave for Upper Egypt until the pilgrims have arrived. There are some bizarre things to see, we have been told: priests' horses walking over prostrate bodies of the faithful, all kinds of dervishes, singers, etc.

. . .

Max's days are entirely absorbed and consumed by photography. He is doing well, but grows desperate whenever he spoils a picture or finds that a plate has been badly washed. Really, if he doesn't take things easier he'll crack up. But he has been getting some superb results, and in consequence his spirits have been better the last few days. The day before yesterday a kicking mule almost smashed the entire equipment.

. . .

When I think of my future (that happens rarely, for I generally think of nothing at all despite the elevated thoughts one should have in the presence of ruins!), when I ask myself: "What shall I do when I return? What path shall I follow?" and the like, I am full of doubts and indecisions. At every stage in my life I have put off facing my situation in just this same way; and I shall die at eighty before having formed any opinion concerning myself or, perhaps, without writing anything that would have shown me what I could do. Is *Saint Antoine* good or bad? That is what I often ask myself, for example: who was mistaken—I or the others? However, I worry very little about any of this. I live like a plant, suffusing myself with sun and light, with colors and fresh air. I keep eating, so to speak; afterwards the digesting will have to be done, then the shitting; and the shit had better be good! That's the important thing.

. . . You ask me whether the Orient is up to what I imagined. Yes, it is; and more than that, it extends far beyond the narrow idea I had of it. I have found, clearly delineated, everything that was hazy in my mind. Facts have taken the place of suppositions—with such perfection that it is often as though I were suddenly coming upon old forgotten dreams.

To Louis Bouilhet

At noon today came your fine long letter that I was so hoping for. It moved me to the very guts and made a crybaby of me. How constantly I think of you, you precious bastard! How many times a day I evoke you and miss you! . . . When we next see each other many days will have passed—I mean many things will have happened. Shall we still be the same, with nothing changed in the communion of our beings? I have too much pride in both of us not to think so. Carry on with your disgusting and sublime way of life, and then we'll see about beating those drums that we've long been keeping so taut. I'm looking everywhere for something special to bring you. So far I have found nothing, except that in Memphis I cut two or three branches of palm for you to make into canes for yourself. I'm greatly giving myself over to the study of perfumes and to the composition of ointments. Yesterday I ate half a pastille so heating that for three hours I thought my tongue was on fire. I haunt the Turkish baths. I devoured the lines from *Melaenis.* Come, let's be calm: no one incapable of restraint was ever a writer—at this moment I'm bursting—I'd like to let off steam and use you as a punching bag—everything's mixed up and jostling everything else in my sick brain—let's try for some order[1] . . .

De Saltatoribus

We have not yet seen any dancing girls; they are all in exile in Upper Egypt. Good brothels no longer exist in Cairo, either. The party we were to have had on the Nile the last time I wrote you fell through—no loss there. But we have seen male dancers. Oh! Oh! Oh!

That was us, calling you. I was indignant and very sad that you weren't here. Three or four musicians playing curious instruments (we'll bring some home) took up their positions at the end of the hotel dining room while one gentleman was still eating his lunch and the rest of us were sitting on the divan smoking our pipes. As dancers, imagine two rascals, quite ugly, but charming in their corruption, in their obscene leerings and the effeminacy of their movements, dressed as women, their eyes painted with antimony. For costume, they have wide trousers and an embroidered jacket. The latter comes down to the epigastrium, whereas the trousers, held up by an enormous cashmere girdle folded double several times, begin only about at the pubis, so that the entire stomach, the loins, and the beginning of the buttocks are naked, seen through a black gauze held tight against the skin by the upper and lower garments. This ripples on the hips like a dark, transparent wave with every movement they make. The music is always the same, and goes on for two hours without stopping. The flute is shrill, the drumbeats throb in your breast, the singer dominates all. The dancers advance and retreat, shaking the pelvis with a short convulsive movement. A quivering of the muscles is the only way to describe it; when the pelvis moves, the rest of the body is motionless; when the breast shakes, nothing else moves. In this manner they advance toward you, their arms extended, rattling brass castanets, and their faces, under the rouge and the sweat, remain more expressionless than a statue's. By that I mean they never smile. The effect is produced by the gravity of the face in contrast to the lascivious movements of the body. Sometimes they lie down flat on their backs, like a woman ready to be fucked, then rise up with a movement of the loins similar to that of a tree swinging back into place after the wind has stopped. In their bowings and salutations their great red trousers suddenly inflate like oval balloons, then seem to melt away, expelling the air that swells them. From time to time, during the dance, the impresario, or pimp, who brought them plays around them, kissing them on the belly, the arse, and the small of the back, and making obscene remarks in an effort to put additional spice into a thing that is already quite self-evident. It is too beautiful to be exciting. I doubt whether we shall find the women as good as the men; the ugliness of the latter adds greatly to the thing as art. I had a headache for the rest of the day, and I had to go and piss two or three times during the performance—a nervous reaction I attribute particularly to the music—I'll have this marvelous Hasan el-Belbeissi come again. He'll dance the Bee dance for me, in particular. Done by such a bardash as he, it can scarcely be a thing for babes.

Speaking of bardashes, this is what I know about them. Here it is quite accepted. One admits one's sodomy, and it is spoken of at table in the hotel. Sometimes you do a bit of denying, and then everybody teases you and you end up confessing. Traveling as we are for educational purposes, and charged with a mission by the government, we have considered it our duty to indulge in this form of ejaculation. So far the occasion has not presented itself. We continue to seek it, however. It's at the baths that such things take place. You reserve the bath for yourself (five francs including masseurs, pipe, coffee, sheet and towel) and you skewer your lad in one of the rooms. Be informed, furthermore, that all the bath-boys are bardashes. The final masseurs, the ones who come to rub you when all the rest is done, are usually quite nice young boys. We had our eye on one in an establishment very near our hotel. I reserved the bath exclusively for myself. I went, and the rascal was away that day! I was alone in the hot room, watching the daylight fade through the great circles of glass in the dome. Hot water was flowing everywhere; stretched out indolently I thought of a quantity of things as my pores tranquilly dilated. It is very voluptuous and sweetly melancholy to take a bath like that quite alone, lost in those dim rooms where the slightest noise reverberates like cannon shot, while the naked *kellaks* call out to one another as they massage you, turning you over like embalmers preparing you for the tomb. That day (the day before yesterday, Monday) my *kellak* was rubbing me gently, and when he came to the noble parts he lifted up my *boules d'amour* to clean them, then continuing to rub my chest with his left hand he began to pull with his right on my prick, and as he drew it up and down he leaned over my shoulder and said "baksheesh, baksheesh." He was a man in his fifties, ignoble, disgusting—imagine the effect, and the word "baksheesh, baksheesh." I pushed him away a little, saying "làh, làh" ("no, no")—he thought I was angry and took on a craven look—then I gave him a few pats on the shoulder, saying "làh, làh" again but more gently—he smiled a smile that meant, "You're not fooling me—you like it as much as anybody, but today you've decided against it for some reason." As for me, I laughed aloud like a dirty old man, and the shadowy vault of the bath echoed with the sound.

. . . A week ago I saw a monkey in the street jump on a donkey and try to jack him off—the donkey brayed and kicked, the monkey's owner shouted, the monkey itself squealed; apart from two or three children who laughed—and me, who found it very funny—no one paid any attention. When I described this to M. Belin, the secretary of the consulate, he told me of having seen an ostrich trying to violate a donkey. Max had himself jacked off the other day in a deserted section among some ruins and says he never enjoyed himself more.

Enough lubricities.

By means of *baksheesh* as always (*baksheesh* and the big stick are the essence of the Arab: you hear nothing else spoken of and see nothing else) we have been initiated into the fraternity of the *psylli*, or snake-charmers. We've had snakes put around our necks, around our hands, incantations have been recited over our heads, and our initiators have breathed into our mouths, all but inserting their tongues. It was great fun—the men who engage in such sinful enterprises practise their vile arts, as M. de Voltaire puts it, with singular competency.

. . . We speak with priests of all religions. The people here sometimes assume really beautiful poses and attitudes. We have translations of songs, stories and traditions made for us—everything that is most folkloric and oriental. We employ scholars—literally. We look quite dashing and are quite insolent and permit ourselves great freedom of language—our hotelkeeper thinks we sometimes go a little far.

One of these days we're going to consult the sorcerers—all part of our quest for the old ways of life here.

Dear fellow, how I'd love to hug you—I'll be glad to see your face again . . . Go and see my mother often—help her—write to her when she's away—the poor woman needs it. You'll be performing an act of the highest evangelism, and—psychologically—you'll witness the shy, gradual expansion of a fine and upright nature. Ah, you old bardash—if it weren't for her and for you, I'd scarcely give a thought to home . . .

1. Here follows an account, similar in most details to those written by many travelers, of visits to the Pyramids and the Sphinx. "The Second Pyramid," Flaubert writes, "has its apex all covered with the droppings of the eagles and vultures that are constantly flying around the top of these monuments. It reminded me of words from *Saint Antoine*: 'The gods, with heads of ibises, have their shoulders whitened with the droppings of birds.' Maxime kept repeating: 'I saw the Sphinx fleeing toward Libya; it was galloping like a jackal.' "

DuCamp, on the other hand, writes in his memoirs: "When we reached the Sphinx . . . Flaubert reined in his horse and cried, 'I have seen the Sphinx fleeing toward Libya; it was galloping like a jackal,' and he added: 'That's from Saint Antoine.' "

In any case, both were highly excited by the great monuments at Giza, and Flaubert wrote to Bouilhet: "We don't have emotions as *po-hé-tiques* as that every day, thank God; it would kill us."

To his mother

Between Minia and Assiut. February 23, 1850.

. . .

Now I come to something that you seem to enjoy reverting to and that I utterly fail to understand. You are never at a loss for things to torment yourself about. What is the sense of this: that I must have a job—"a small job," you say. First of all, *what* job? I defy you to find me one, to specify in what field, or what it would be like. Frankly, and without deluding yourself, is there a single one that I am capable of filling? You add: "One that wouldn't take up much of your time and wouldn't prevent you from doing other things." There's the delusion! That's what Bouilhet told himself when he took up medicine, what I told myself when I began law, which nearly brought about my death from suppressed rage. When one does something, one must do it wholly and well. Those bastard existences where you sell suet all day and write poetry at night are made for mediocre minds—like those horses equally good for saddle and carriage—the worst kind, that can neither jump a ditch nor pull a plow.

In short, it seems to me that one takes a job for money, for honors, or as an escape from idleness. Now you'll grant me, darling, (1) that I keep busy enough not to have to go out looking for something to do; and (2) if it's a question of honors, my vanity is such that I'm incapable of feeling myself honored by anything: a position, however high it might be (and that isn't the kind you speak of) will never give me the satisfaction that I derive from my self-respect when I have accomplished something well in my own way; and finally, if it's for money, any jobs or job that I could have would bring in too little to make much difference to my income. Weigh all those considerations: *don't knock your head against a hollow idea.* Is there any position in which I'd be closer to you, more yours?[1] And isn't not to be bored one of the principal goals of life?

1. Flaubert's reminder to his mother that his having no job would keep him close to her was possibly effective: there seem to have been no further suggestions that he seek "une petite place."

To Louis Bouilhet

March 13, 1850. On board our *cange*, 12 leagues beyond Assuan.[1]

In six or seven hours we are going to pass the Tropic of that well known personage Cancer. It is 30 degrees in the shade at this moment, we are barefoot and wearing nothing but shirts, and I am writing to you on my divan, to the sound of the *darabukehs* of our sailors, who are singing and clapping their hands. The sun is beating down mercilessly on the awning over our deck. The Nile is flat as a river of steel. On its banks there are clusters of tall palms. The sky is blue as blue. O pauvre vieux! pauvre vieux de mon coeur!

What are you up to, there in Rouen? It's a long time since I had any of your letters, or rather I have so far had only one, dated the end of December, which I answered immediately. Perhaps another has arrived in Cairo and is being sent on to me. My mother writes that she sees you very seldom. Why is that? Even if it bores you too much, go once in a while anyway, for my sake, and try to tell me everything you can about what is going on in my house in every conceivable respect. Have you been in Paris again and seen Gautier and Pradier? What has happened to the trip to England for your Chinese story? *Melaenis* must be finished? Send me the end, you bloody bastard. I often growl out some of your lines, if you want to know. I must without further delay withdraw as vociferously as possible the objection I made to your word *vagabond* as applied to the Nile:

"Que le Nil vagabond roule sur ses rivages."

There is no designation more just, more precise and at the same time more all-embracing. It is a crazy, magnificent river, more like an ocean than anything else. Sandy beaches extend as far as the eye can see on both its banks, furrowed by the wind like sea shores; it is so enormous that one doesn't know where the current is, and sometimes you feel enclosed in a great lake. Ah! But if you expect a proper letter you are mistaken. I warn you seriously that my intelligence has greatly diminished. This worries me: *I am not joking*—I feel very empty, very flat, very sterile. What am I to do once back in the old lodgings? Publish or not publish? The *Saint Antoine* business dealt me a heavy blow, I don't mind telling you. I've tried in vain to do something with my oriental tale, and for a day or two I played with the story of Mykerinos in Herodotus (the king who slept with his daughter). But it all came to nothing. By way of work, every day I read the *Odyssey* in Greek. Since we've been on the Nile I have done four books; we are coming home by way of Greece, so it may be of service to me. The first days on board I began to write a little; but I was not long, thank God, in realizing the ineptitude of such behavior; just now it's best for me to be all eyes. We live, therefore, in the grossest idleness, stretched out all day on our divans watching everything that goes by: camels, herds of oxen from Sennar, boats floating down to Cairo laden with negresses and with elephants' tusks. We are now, my dear sir, in a land where women go naked— one might say with the poet "naked as the hand,"[2] for by way of costume they wear only rings. I have lain with Nubian girls whose necklaces of gold piastres hung down to their thighs and whose black stomachs were encircled by colored beads—they feel cold when you rub your own stomach against them. And their dancing! Sacré nom de Dieu!!! But let us proceed in proper order.

From Cairo to Benisuef, nothing very interesting.

. . . At a place called Begel el-Teir we had an amusing sight. On the top of a hill overlooking the Nile there is a Coptic monastery, whose monks have the custom, as soon as they see a boatload of tourists, of running down, throwing themselves in the water, and swimming out to ask for alms. Everyone who passes is assailed by them. You see these fellows, totally naked, rushing down their perpendicular cliffs and swimming toward you as fast as they can, shouting: "Baksheesh, baksheesh, cawadja christiani!" And since there are many caves in the cliff at this particular spot, echo repeats "Cawadja, cawadja!" loud as a cannon. Vultures and eagles were flying overhead, the boat was flashing through the water, its two great sails very full. At that moment one of our sailors, the clown of the crew, began to dance a naked, lascivious dance that consisted of an attempt to bugger himself. To drive off the Christians he showed them his prick and his arse pretending to piss and shit on their heads (they were clinging to the sides of the *cange*). The other sailors shouted insults at them, repeating the names of Allah and Mohammed. Some hit them with sticks, others with ropes; Joseph rapped their knuckles with his kitchen tongs. It was a *tutti* of cudgelings, pricks, bare arses, yells and laughter. As soon as they were given money they put it in their mouths and returned home the way they had come. If they weren't greeted with a good beating, the boats would be assailed by such hordes of them that there would be danger of capsizing.

In another place it's not men who call on you, but birds. At Sheik Sa'id there is a tomb-chapel built in honor of a Moslem saint where birds go of their own accord and drop food that is given to them—this food is then offered to poor travelers—You and I, "who have read Voltaire," don't believe this. But everyone is so backward here! You so seldom hear anyone singing Béranger's songs! ("What, sir, the benefits of civilization are not being introduced into this country? Where are your railway networks? What is the state of elementary education? Etc.")[3]—so that as you sail past this chapel all the birds flock around the boat and land on the rigging—you throw them bits of bread, they wheel about, pick it up from the water, and fly off.

At Kena I did something suitable, which I trust will win your approval: we had landed to buy supplies and were walking peacefully and dreamily in the bazaars, inhaling the odor of sandalwood that floated about us, when suddenly, at a turn in the street, we found ourselves in the whores' quarter. Picture to yourself, my friend, five or six curving streets lined with hovels about four feet high, built of dried gray mud. In the doorways, women standing or sitting on straw mats. The negresses had dresses of sky blue; others were in yellow, in white, in red—loose garments fluttering in the hot wind. Odors of spices. On their bare breasts long necklaces of gold piastres, so that when they move they rattle like carts. They call after you in drawling voices: "Cawadja, cawadja," their white teeth gleaming between their red or black lips, their metallic eyes rolling like wheels. I walked through those streets and walked through them again, giving *baksheesh* to all the women, letting them call me and catch hold of me; they took me around the waist and tried to pull me into their houses—think of all that, with the sun blazing down on it. Well, I abstained. (Young DuCamp did not follow my example.) I abstained deliber-

115

ately, in order to preserve the sweet sadness of the scene and engrave it deeply in my memory. In this way I went away dazzled, and have remained so. There is nothing more beautiful than these women calling you. If I had gone with any of them, a second picture would have been superimposed on the first and dimmed its splendor.

I haven't always made such sacrifices on the altar of art. At Esna in one day I fired five times and sucked three. I say it straight out and without circumlocution, and let me add that I enjoyed it. Kuchuk Hanem is a famous courtesan. When we reached her house she was waiting for us; her confidante had come to the *cange* that morning escorted by a sheep all spotted with yellow henna and with a black velvet muzzle on its nose, following her like a dog—it was quite a sight. Kuchuk had just left her bath. She was wearing a large tarboosh topped with a gold plaque containing a green stone, and with a loose tassel falling to her shoulders; her front hair was platted in thin braids that were drawn back and tied together; the lower part of her body was hidden in immense pink trousers; her torso was entirely naked under purple gauze. She was standing at the top of her staircase, with the sun behind her, sharply silhouetted against the blue background of the sky surrounding her. She is a regal-looking creature, large-breasted, fleshy, with slit nostrils, enormous eyes, and magnificent knees; when she danced there were formidable folds of flesh on her stomach. She began by perfuming our hands with rosewater. Her bosom gave off a smell of sweetened turpentine, and on it she wore a three-strand golden necklace. Musicians were sent for and she danced. Her dancing isn't at all up to that of the famous Hasan I mentioned earlier. Still, it was very agreeable and of quite a bold style. In general, beautiful women dance badly. (I except a Nubian we saw at Assuan—but that was no longer Arab dancing; more ferocious, more frenetic, tigerish, negroid.)

That night we visited her again. There were four women dancers and singers, *almehs*. (The word *almeh* means "learned woman," "bluestocking," but has come to signify "whore"—which goes to show, Monsieur, that in all countries literary ladies . . . !!!) The party lasted from six to half-past ten, with intermissions for fucking. Two rebec players sitting on the floor made continual shrill music. When Kuchuk undressed to dance, a fold of their turbans was lowered over their eyes, to prevent their seeing anything. This modesty gave a shocking effect. I spare you any description of the dance, I'd write it too poorly. To be understood it has to be illustrated with gestures—and even that would be inadequate.

When it came time to leave, I didn't. Kuchuk wasn't too eager to have us spend the night with her, out of fear of thieves who might well have come, knowing there were foreigners in the house. Maxime stayed alone on the divan and I went downstairs with Kuchuk to her room. We lay down on her bed, made of palm branches. A wick was burning in an antique-style lamp hanging on the wall. In an adjoining room guards were talking in low voices with the serving woman, an Abyssinian Negress whose arms were scarred by plague-sores. Kuchuk's little dog slept on my silk jacket.

116

I sucked her furiously, her body was covered with sweat, she was tired after dancing, she was cold. I covered her with my fur pelisse, and she fell asleep, her fingers in mine. As for me, I scarcely shut my eyes. My night was one long, infinitely intense reverie. That was why I stayed. Watching that beautiful creature asleep (she snored, her head against my arm; I had slipped my forefinger under her necklace), I thought of my nights in Paris brothels—a whole series of old memories came back—and I thought of her, of her dance, of her voice as she sang songs that were for me without meaning and even without distinguishable words. That continued all night.[4] At three o'clock I got up to piss in the street—the stars were shining. The sky was clear and immensely distant. She awoke, went to get a pot of charcoal and for an hour crouched beside it warming herself, then she came back to bed and fell asleep again. As for the *coups,* they were good—the third especially was ferocious, and the last tender—we told each other many sweet things—toward the end there was something sad and loving in the way we embraced.

At 7 in the morning we left. I went shooting with one of the sailors in a cotton field, under palm trees and *gazis.*[5] The countryside was lovely. Arabs, donkeys and buffalo were making their way to the fields. The wind was blowing through the fine branches of the *gazis,* whistling as it does through rushes. The mountains were pink, the sun was rising. My sailor walked ahead of me, bending to pass under bushes, and with a silent gesture pointing out to me the turtledoves he saw on the branches. I killed one, the only one I sighted. I walked pushing my feet ahead of me, and thinking of similar mornings—of one among others, at the marquis de Pomereu's at Le Héron, after a ball. I hadn't gone to bed, and in the morning went out in a boat on the pond, all alone, in my lycée uniform. The swans watched me pass, and leaves from the bushes were falling on the water. It was just before the beginning of term. I was fifteen.

In my absorption of all those things, *mon pauvre vieux,* you never ceased to be present. The thought of you was like a constant vesicant, inflaming my mind and making its juices flow by adding to the stimulation. I was sorry (the word is weak) that you were not there—I enjoyed it all for myself and for you —I was excited for both of us, and you came in for a good share, you may be sure.

. . . Just now we have stopped for lack of wind; the flies are stinging my face. Young DuCamp has gone off to take a picture. He is doing quite well—I think we'll have a nice album. As regards vice, he is calming down; it seems to us that I am inheriting his qualities, for I am growing lewd. Such is my profound conviction. When the brain sinks the prick rises. That isn't to say that I haven't collected a few metaphors. I have had a few stirrings. But how to make use of them, and where? . . .

1. Flaubert writes in a postscript: "Max insists that for the sake of elegance I add: 23°39' North Latitude. We are now exactly under the Tropic, but I don't see it."

2. Alfred de Musset, *Namouna, Conte Oriental:* "Hassan était donc nu,—mais nu comme la main." (J.B.)

3. For the significance of these "quotations," see p. 245, n.5.

4. In his travel notes Flaubert added a detail that was later to raise objections in a certain quarter: "I was facing the wall, and without changing my position I amused myself killing the bedbugs that were crawling on it." (See p. 181.)

5. A kind of low-growing palm.

To Louis Bouilhet

Between Girga and Assiut, June 2, 1850.

. . .

I have given much thought to many things since we parted, pauvre vieux. Sitting on the divan of my *cange*, watching the water flow by, I ruminate about my past life, sometimes quite intensely. Many forgotten things come back to me, like snatches of songs sung by one's nurse in childhood. Am I about to enter a new period? Or is it the beginning of complete decadence? And from the past I go dreaming into the future, where I see nothing, nothing. I have no plans, no idea, no project, and, what is worse, no ambition. Something—the eternal "what's the use?"—sets its bronze barrier across every avenue that I open up in the realm of hypothesis. Traveling doesn't make one gay. I don't know whether the sight of ruins inspires great thoughts, but I should like to know the source of the profound disgust that fills me these days when I think of making myself known and talked about. I don't feel within me the *physical strength* to publish, to run to the printer, to choose paper, to correct proofs, etc. And what is that, beside the rest? Better to work for yourself alone. Do as you like and follow your own ideas, admire yourself and please yourself: isn't that the main thing? And then the public is so stupid. Besides, who reads? And what do they read? And what do they admire?

Ah, blessed peaceful times, blessed times of powdered wigs! You lived with complete assurance, poised on your high heels, twirling your cane! But beneath *us* the earth is trembling. Where can we place our fulcrum, even assuming that we possess the lever? The thing we all lack is not style, nor the dexterity of finger and bow known as talent. We have a large orchestra, a rich palette, a variety of resources. We know many more tricks and dodges, probably, than were ever known before. No, what we lack is the intrinsic principle, the soul of the thing, the very idea of the subject. We take notes, we make journeys: emptiness! emptiness! We become scholars, archaeologists, historians, doctors, cobblers, people of taste. What is the good of all that? Where is the heart, the verve, the sap? Where to start out from? Where to go? We're good at sucking, we play a lot of tongue games, we pet for hours: but—the real thing! To ejaculate, beget the child!

. . . Yes, when I return I shall resume—and for a good long time, I hope—my old quiet life at my round table, between my fireplace and my garden. I shall continue to live like a bear, not giving a damn about my country, about critics, or anyone at all. Those ideas revolt young DuCamp, whose head is full of quite different ones; that is, he has very active plans for his return and intends to throw himself into demoniacal activity. At the end of next winter, in eight or nine months from now, we'll talk about all this.

I am going to make you a very frank confession: I pay no more attention to my mission than to the King of Prussia. To "discharge my duties" properly I should have had to give up my journey—it would have been absurd. I do stupid things now and then, but not of that enormity, I trust. Can you see me in every town, informing myself about crops, about production, about consumption? "How much oil do you shit here? How many potatoes do you stuff into yourselves?" And in every port: "How many ships? What tonnage? How many arrivals? How many departures?" And ditto, ditto. *Merde!* Ah, no! Frankly—was it possible? And after committing a sufficient number of such turpitudes (my title itself is quite enough of one), if I had taken certain steps and if my friends had spoken for me and if the Ministry had been well disposed, I should have won the Legion of Honor! *Tableau!* Great satisfaction for my uncle Parain!!! No, no, a thousand times. I want none of it: I honor myself so much that nothing can honor me. (Pompous words!)

. . .

I have seen Thebes:[1] it is very beautiful. We arrived one night at nine, in brilliant moonlight that flooded the columns. Dogs were barking, the great white ruins looked like ghosts, and the moon on the horizon, completely round and seeming to touch the earth, appeared to be motionless, resting there deliberately. Karnak gave us the impression of a life of giants. I spent a night at the feet of the colossus of Memnon, devoured by mosquitoes. The old scoundrel has a good face and is covered with graffiti. Graffiti and bird-droppings are the only two things in the ruins of Egypt that give any indication of life. The most worn stone doesn't grow a blade of grass; it falls into powder, like a mummy, and that is all . . . Often you see a tall, straight obelisk, with a long white stain down its entire length, like a drapery—wider at the top and tapering toward the base. That is from the vultures, who have been coming there to shit for centuries. It is a very handsome effect and has a curious symbolism. It is as though Nature said to the monuments of Egypt: "You will have none of me? You will not nourish the seed of the lichen? *Eh bien, merde,* I'll shit on you."

In the rock tombs at Thebes (among the most curious and fascinating things you can imagine) we discovered some pharaonic bawdy which proves, Monsieur, that in all ages of the world man has gone to perdition, has "aimé la fillette," as our immortal songwriter[2] puts it. It is a picture showing men and women at table, eating and drinking, couples with an arm around each other's waist and playing tongue games. There are some charming, lewd profiles, marvelous facial expressions of bourgeois on a spree. Nearby are two young girls in transparent dresses, the most whorish shapes imaginable, playing the guitar with a lascivious air. It's a bordello scene from a dirty Palais Royal picture of 1816. It gave us a good laugh and something to think about. Such thoughts make one dizzy, Monsieur! It's all so modern that one is tempted to believe that condoms were known at the time of Sesostris.

119

At Esna I saw Kuchuk Hanem again, it was sad, I found her changed. She had been sick. I fired only one shot. The day was heavy and overcast, her Abyssinian servant was sprinkling water on the floor to cool the room. I stared at her for a long while, so as to be able to keep a picture of her in my mind. When I left, we told her we would return the next day, but we did not. I intensely relished the bitterness of all that; that's the main thing, and I felt it in my very bowels. At Kena I had a beautiful whore who liked me very much and told me in sign language that I had lovely eyes. Her name is Hosna et-Taouilah, which means "the beautiful tall one"; and there was another, fat and lubricious, on top of whom I enjoyed myself immensely and who smelled of rancid butter.

I saw the Red Sea at Koseir. It was a journey that took four days going and five for the return, on camelback and in a heat that in the middle of the day rose to over 45 degrees Réaumur. That was a bit scorching: occasionally I longed for some beer, especially since our water smelled of sulphur and soap in addition to the taste of goat given it by the skins. We rose at three in the morning and went to bed at nine at night, living on hard-boiled eggs, dry preserves, and watermelons. It was real desert life. All along the route we came upon the carcasses of camels that had died of exhaustion. There are places where you find great sheets of sand which seem to have been turned into a kind of pavement, areas smooth and glazed like the threshing-floor of a barn: those are the places where camels stop to piss. With time the urine varnishes the sand and levels it like a floor. We had taken some cold meat with us, but in the middle of the second day had to abandon it. The odor of a leg of mutton we left on a stone immediately attracted a vulture, which began to fly round and round it.

We met great caravans of pilgrims going to Mecca (Koseir is the port where they take ship for Jidda, whence it is only three days to Mecca). Old Turks with their wives carried in baskets; a whole veiled harem called out to us like magpies as we passed; a dervish wearing a leopard-skin.

The camels in a caravan go sometimes one behind the other, sometimes all advancing on one broad front. When you see, foreshortened on the horizon, all those swaying heads coming toward you, it is like a horde of ostriches advancing slowly and gradually drawing together. At Koseir we saw pilgrims from the depths of Africa, poor negroes who have been on the march for a year, even two years. There are some curious sights. We also saw people from Bukhara, Tartars in pointed caps, who were preparing a meal in the shade of a shipwrecked boat made of red Indian wood. As for pearl-fishers, we saw only their canoes. Two men go in each canoe, one to row and one to dive, and they go out onto the open sea. When the diver returns to the surface he is bleeding from ears, nostrils, and eyes.

The day after my arrival I bathed in the Red Sea. It was one of the most voluptuous pleasures of my life. I lolled in its waters as though I were lying on a thousand liquid breasts that caressed my entire body.

That night Maxime, out of courtesy, and to honor his host, gave himself an attack of indigestion. We were lodged in a separate pavilion where we slept on divans and had a view of the sea. We were served by a young negro eunuch who had a very stylish way of carrying the tray of coffee cups on his left arm. The morning we were to leave . . . I sat by myself, looking at the sea. Never will I forget that morning. I was stirred by it as though by an adventure; because of all the shells, shellfish, madrepores, corals, etc. the bottom of the sea is more brilliant than a spring meadow covered with primroses. As for the color of the surface of the water, all possible tints passed through it, iridescent and melting together, from chocolate to amethyst, from pink to lapis lazuli and the palest green, and were I a painter I'd have been very embarrassed, thinking to what degree the reproduction of those real colors (admitting that were possible) would seem false.

We left Koseir that afternoon at four, very sadly. My eyes were wet when I embraced our host and climbed back on to my camel. It is always sad to leave a place to which one knows one will never return. Such are the *mélancolies du voyage:* perhaps they are one of the most enriching things about traveling.

As to any change we may have undergone during our separation, I do not think, *cher vieux,* that if there is one it will be to my advantage. You will have gained by solitude and concentration; I shall have lost by diffusion and daydreaming. I am becoming very empty and very barren. I feel it. It is overtaking me like a rising tide. Perhaps this is due to being physically active. I cannot do two things at once. Perhaps I have left my intelligence behind, with my drawstring trousers, my leather divan, and your company, dear sir. Where will all this lead us? What shall we have accomplished in ten years? As for myself, it seems to me that if I fail in the next thing I undertake, I might as well drown myself. Once so dauntless, now I am becoming excessively timid—and in the arts timidity is the worst possible thing and the greatest sign of weakness.

. . .

Well, I hope you will agree that this letter is a veritable document and that I'm a good fellow. Send me an answer to Beirut, where we'll be toward the end of July, then at Jerusalem. Work hard, try not to be too bored, don't do too much fornicating; conserve your strength: an ounce of sperm lost is worse than ten pounds of blood. By the way, you ask me if I consummated that business at the baths. Yes—and on a pockmarked young rascal wearing a white turban. It made me laugh, that's all. But I'll be at it again. To be done well, an experiment must be repeated.

Farewell, old man of the pen!

. . . [P.S.] 5 June. Tomorrow is the sixth, birthday of the great Corneille! What a session at the Rouen Academy! What speeches! . . . The Academicians in full dress: white tie! Pomp! Sound traditions! A brief report on agriculture!

---

1. The travelers explored Thebes on the return downstream to Cairo. Earlier, when the *cange* stopped briefly at Thebes on the way upstream, Flaubert had recorded in his travel notes a moment of particular élan:

"Monday, 4 March . . . We have passed Luxor. I was cleaning my glass when we sighted

Luxor on the left: I climbed on to the roof of the cabin. The seven columns, the obelisk, the French House, Arabs sitting beside the water near an English *cange*. The caretaker of the French House calls out that he has a letter for us . . . We stop. Among the people at the landing, a negro, swathed like a mummy—all cartilage, desiccated, with a small, dirty *takieh* [cap] on the top of his head; women are bathing their feet in the river, a donkey has come down to drink.

"Sunset over Medinet Habu. The mountains are dark indigo (on the Medinet Habu side); blue over dark gray, with contrasting horizontal stripes of purplish red in the clefts of the valleys. The palms are black as ink, the sky is red, the Nile has the look of a lake of molten steel.

"When we arrived off Thebes our sailors were drumming on their *darabukehs*, the mate was playing his flute. Khalil was dancing with his castanets: they broke off to land.

"It was then, while I was observing those things, and enjoying observing them, and just as I was watching three wave-crests curling under the wind at our stern, that I felt a surge of solemn happiness that reached out toward what I was seeing, and I thanked God in my heart for having made me capable of such joy: I felt fortunate at the thought, and yet it seemed to me that I was thinking of nothing: it was a sensuous pleasure that pervaded my entire being."

2. Béranger.

To Louis Bouilhet

Cairo, June 27 [1850]

Here we are back in Cairo. That is all the news I have to tell you, dear good friend, for after my last letter nothing of interest happened on our trip. In a few days we leave for Alexandria, and at the end of next month, if all goes well, we'll be not far from Jerusalem.

Leaving our little boat put me into a frightful melancholy.[1] Back in the hotel here in Cairo my head was buzzing, as though after a long journey by stagecoach. The city seemed empty and silent, though actually it was busy and full of people. The first night of my arrival here (last Tuesday), I kept hearing the soft sound of oars in the water—that cadenced accompaniment to our long dreamy days for the past three months. The city palm trees looked to me like brooms used for sweeping public lavatories. I relived the entire trip, and in my heart I felt a bitter sweetness that was like the taste of a belch after good wine— when you say to yourself: "Well, that was it."

. . . A bizarre psychological phenomenon! Back in Cairo (and since reading your good letter), I have been feeling myself bursting with intellectual intensity. The pot suddenly began to boil! I felt a burning need to write! I was wound up tight.

. . .

Your idea for a Chinese tale seems to me excellent in general. Can you send me the outline? Once you have decided on your main ideas for local color, do no more reading and begin to write. *Let's not get lost in archaeology*—a widespread and fatal tendency, I think, of the coming generation . . . Poor wretches that we are, we have, I think, considerable taste because we are profoundly historical: we admit everything, and adopt the point of view of whatever we are judging. But have we as much inner strength as we have understanding of others? Is fierce originality compatible with so much breadth of mind? Such are my doubts concerning the artistic spirit of the times, that is, concerning the few artists there are. At least, if we do nothing good we shall perhaps have paved the way for a generation that will have our fathers' boldness (I'm looking for another word) along with our own eclecticism. That would surprise me —the world is going to become bloody stupid and from now on will be a very boring place. We're lucky to be living now.

You won't believe that Max and I talk constantly about the future of society. For me it is almost certain that at some more or less distant time it will be regulated like a college. Schoolmasters will make the laws. Everyone will be in uniform. Mankind will no longer commit barbarisms as it writes its insipid theme, but—what wretched style! What lack of form, of rhythm, of spirit! . . .

No matter. God will always be there, after all. Let us hope that He will always hold the upper hand and that the old sun will not perish. Last night I reread Paulus's apostrophe to Venus [in *Melaenis*], and this morning I upheld (as I did at eighteen) the doctrine of Art for Art's Sake against a Utilitarian— a good man, however. I resist the torrent. Will it carry us along with it? No— rather than that, let us beat ourselves to death with a leg of our own writing table! "Let us be strong! Let us be beautiful! Let us wipe off on the grass the dust that soils our gold buskins!"[2] Or not wipe them—I haven't the slightest idea what makes me quote this. So long as there is gold underneath, who cares about the dust on top? . . . Literature! That old whore! We must try to dose her with mercury and pills and clean her out from top to bottom, she has been so ultra-screwed by filthy pricks!

· · ·

1. A fuller account of the Egyptian portion of the journey is contained in *Flaubert in Egypt*. (See bibliography.)
2. A slightly inaccurate quotation from his own *Saint Antoine*.

To Louis Bouilhet

Jerusalem, August 20, 1850.

I can certainly say, like Sassetti: "You won't believe me, Monsieur, but when I caught sight of Jerusalem I must confess it gave me a funny feeling." I checked my horse, which I had spurred on ahead of the others, and stared at the holy city, quite astonished at the sight. It looked very near; the walls were in much better state than I expected. Then I thought of Christ, and saw him climbing the Mount of Olives. He was wearing a blue robe, his temples were beaded with sweat. And I thought of his entry into Jerusalem, the shouting, the green palm branches, etc.—Flandrin's fresco that we saw together in Saint-Germain-des-Prés, the day before I left.

· · ·

The Holy Sepulchre is the agglomeration of all possible execrations. Within this tiny space, four churches: Armenian, Greek, Latin, and Coptic. All heartily insulting and cursing one another, each quarrelling with its neighbors over candlesticks, rugs, pictures—and what pictures! It's the Turkish Pasha who keeps the keys to the Holy Sepulchre. When you want to visit it, you must get them from him. I find that quite striking. On the other hand, it's the most humane solution. If the Holy Sepulchre were given over to the Christians, they would unfailingly massacre each other. Such cases have been known.

"Tanta religio! etc.," as gentle Lucretius said.[1]

. . . After my first visit to the Holy Sepulchre I returned to the hotel bone-tired and disgusted. I took up a Saint Matthew and read the Sermon on the Mount, my heart expanding as though nothing had ever touched it before. That relieved the cold, sour feeling I had experienced. Everything possible has been done to make the holy places ridiculous. It's all whorish to the last degree: hypocrisy, cupidity, falsification, impudence, yes: but as for holiness, go fuck yourself. I resent not having been moved: I wanted nothing better than to be so —you know me. Still, I do have one relic that I'll keep. Here is the story. The second time I was in the Holy Sepulchre I was in the Sepulchre itself, a small chapel all lit by lamps and full of flowers stuck in china vases of the kind you see decorating dressmakers' mantelpieces. There are so many lamps crammed one next to the other that it's like the ceiling of a lamp shop. The walls are marble. Facing you is a grimacing Christ in bas-relief, life-size and horrible, his ribs painted red. I was staring at the holy stone; the priest opened a cupboard, took out a rose, laid it on the stone of the Sepulchre, and proceeded to say a prayer, blessing the flower. I was flooded with a wry kind of sentimentality. I thought of the pious souls who would have been enchanted by such a present in such a place, and how wasted it was on me. My lack of proper response caused me no tears, I had no regrets, but there came over me that strange feeling which two men like you and me experience when we are alone beside our fire, straining with all the might of our souls to explore the ancient abyss represented by the word "love," and imagining what it might be—if it were possible. No, at that moment I was neither Voltairean nor Mephistophelian nor Sadist. On the contrary, I was being quite simple. I was examining the question in all sincerity, and remained quite calm even in my imaginings.

. . .

At Beirut we made the acquaintance of a splendid fellow, Camille Rogier, the Postmaster of the place. He is a painter from Paris, one of Gautier's cronies, who lives here in native style. Very intelligent: we enjoyed meeting him. He has a pretty house, a pretty cook (male), and an enormous prick, compared with which yours is a mere tack. When he was at Constantinople, its reputation was such that Turks came to his house mornings especially to see it. (Gospel.) He treated us to a morning of nymphets. I fucked three women, four shots in all, three before lunch and one after dessert. At the end, I even proposed doing it with their bawd, but, because I had refused when she offered herself earlier, she made it her turn to say no. Still, I'd have enjoyed pulling that one off, to crown the day's work and give me a good opinion of myself. Young DuCamp only fired once—his prick was sore from the remains of a chancre he picked up from a Walachian girl in Alexandria. I revolted the Turkish women by my cynicism in washing my prick in full view of the company. Which didn't prevent them from quite affably accepting the postilion position. (In a country where all travel is on horseback, there's nothing surprising about that.) Which in turn goes to show, dear Sir, that women are women everywhere: say what you will, upbringing and religion make no difference: they only cover up a little: they conceal, conceal, that's all. The damsels weren't bashful about downing alcohol. I remember one of them, with a spray of jasmine in her frizzy black hair; she seemed to me to smell very sweet as I ejaculated inside her. She was slightly snub-nosed, and there was a bit of matter beside the inner pupil of her right eye. This was in the morning: she probably hadn't had time to wash. These were Society ladies, as we would call them at home; through the kind agency of the procuress they do these tricks for fun and a little money . . .

Nota bene, under the seal of the greatest secrecy: Μαξίμ ουάντεδ τοῦ σόδομάϊζ ε βάρδασ ιν ϑη γρόττο οφ Ιερεμία.——Θάτς ε λαϊ!²
P.S. No! No! It's true. What think you of our young friend? Adieu, je t'embrasse. À toi.

1. Lucretius, *De natura rerum*, Book I, 1.101: "Tantum religio potuit suadere malorum!" ("Such are the crimes to which religion leads.")
2. In the original, the "Greek" is an accusation by Flaubert, consisting of the following French words written in Greek characters: "Maxime a voulu sodomiser un bardache dans la grotte de Jérémie," followed by Maxime's denial, also in "Greek": "C'est faux!" In the present "translation," English words in Greek characters have been substituted. Flaubert's P.S. is written in normal French.

To Louis Bouilhet

Damascus, September 4, 1850.

"You too, Brutus!"—which doesn't mean that I'm a Caesar!

You too, poor fellow, whom I so admired for your unshakeable faith! . . . In the midst of my lassitudes, my discouragements and my nausea you were always the seltzer water that helped me digest life. I used to soak myself in you as in a tonic bath. When I was alone and full of self-pity I used to say to myself: "Look at him!" and then I would return to my work with new strength. You were my great moral example, my continual edification. Is the saint now to fall from his niche? Don't stray from your pedestal!

Are we idiots, perhaps? Maybe so, but it is not up to us to say it, still less to believe it. However, we should by now have finished with our migraines and our failures of nerve. One thing is our ruin, one stupid thing shackles us: "taste"—good taste. We have too much of it—or rather, we worry about it more than we should. Fear of bad taste engulfs us like a fog (a dirty December fog that suddenly appears, freezes your guts, stinks, and stings your eyes), to such a point that we stand still, not daring to advance. Don't you realize how captious we are becoming, that we have our own poetics, our own ready-made ideas, our own rules? . . . What we lack is daring. Oh for the time of my youth, when I dashed off a five-act play in three days! With our scruples we resemble those poor believers who daren't live for fear of hell and who wake their confessor early in the morning to unburden their consciences of having had a miscarriage in a dream. Let's worry less about results. The thing is to keep fucking, keep fucking: who cares what child the muse will give birth to? Isn't the purest pleasure in her embraces?

To do badly, to do well—what's the difference? As for myself, I have renounced thinking of posterity—a wise move. My stand is taken. Unless some excessively literary wind begins to blow in a few years, I am resolved not to "make the presses groan" with any elucubration of my brain. You and my mother and others (for it is a wonderful thing, how no one will let people live as they like) used to scold me for my manner of life. Just wait a bit till I come back, and see whether I don't resume it. I'll burrow into my hole, and though the world crumble I'll not budge out of it. I have just sent back without even looking at them several silk scarves that were brought me to choose from. I had only to raise my eyes and decide, but the thought of the effort so overpowered me in advance that I sent the merchants away without buying anything. Had I been the sultan, I'd have thrown them out the window: I was full of rancor toward anyone trying to force me into any activity whatever. But let's get back to our bottles, as old Michel[1] says.

If you think that your worry is going to worry me a long time, you're mistaken. I have shared the burden of greater worries; I fear nothing in that line. If the bedroom in the Hôtel-Dieu now sheltering the young Juliette Flaubert[2] could recount all the disgust that two young men gave vent to there throughout twelve years, I think the establishment would collapse on the heads of its present bourgeois occupants. Poor Alfred! Astonishing how much I think of him, and all the unshed tears for him my heart still holds! How we talked! We looked each other in the eye. We *soared*.

Be careful: one comes to enjoy worrying about things—it's a kind of addiction. What's the matter with you? How I should like to be there, to kiss you on the forehead and kick you in the tail! What you are feeling now is the result of the long labor you put into *Melaenis*. Do you think a poet's brain is like a cotton-spinning machine, which perpetually turns out stuff without fatigue or intermittence? Come now, little man! Head up! Give yourself a good talking-to in the mirror. Is it the state of society at the moment that's upsetting you? It's natural for the bourgeois to worry about it behind his counter; and I too have moments of adolescent fears. *Novembre* keeps recurring to me. Am I approaching a Renaissance, or would this be decrepitude in the guise of a second bloom? Still, I have recovered (though not without pain) from the terrible blow dealt me by *Saint Antoine*. I can't boast that I'm not still staggering a little from it, but I'm no longer sick about it, as I was for the first four months of this trip. I was seeing everything through the veil of despondency cast over me by that disappointment, and I kept repeating the same inept words you now send me: "What's the use?"

However, I am making progress (?) (Perhaps you'd rather I wrote about travel—fresh air, wide horizons, blue skies?) Every day I feel myself becoming more sensitive, more easily moved. The slightest thing brings a tear. My heart plays the very whore, gushingly receptive to anything and everything. Insignificant details stir my guts. I keep falling into endless reveries and distractions. I continuously feel as though I'm a little drunk, and along with that I'm more and more inept and incapable of understanding anything that's explained to me. My memory fails me more and more often. Then, great literary frenzies. I promise myself some sprees when I get back. There you have it.

You do well to think about the *Dictionary of Accepted Opinions.*[3] Such a book, covering the field *completely,* and opening with a good preface in which we would indicate just how the work was intended to reconcile the public to tradition, to order and conventional morality, and written in such a way that the reader couldn't tell whether or not we were pulling his leg—that would perhaps be a strange book, and it might well have some success, for it would be very topical.

If the presidential election of 1852[4] doesn't result in a great debacle, if the bourgeois emerge triumphant, we may remain bogged down in our stupid state for another century. In that case the public, weary of politics, may seek diversion in literature, may want to escape from action into fantasy. Might our day then come? If on the contrary we are precipitated into the future, who can tell what kind of Poetry will spring up? There will certainly be poetry, so let's not lament or curse; let's just accept everything, learn to be tolerant . . .

In Jerusalem I read a socialist book (*Essai de philosophie positive*, by Auguste Comte).[5] It was lent me by a raging Catholic, who insisted that I read it to see how dangerous Positivism is. I skimmed a few pages: it is deadly stupid. As I expected, in fact. It contains vast mines of the comic, whole Californias of the grotesque. And perhaps something else, as well. That is possible. One of the first subjects I intend to study on my return is "those deplorable utopias which are agitating our society and threatening to reduce it to ruins." Why not accommodate ourselves to the goal proposed to us? It's as good as any other: looking at things impartially, there have been few more fertile. *Ineptitude consists in wanting to reach conclusions.* We tell ourselves: "But our point of departure is uncertain—which of the two will win out?" I see a past in ruins and a future in bud; the one is too old, the other too young: all is confusion. But that amounts to misunderstanding the nature of all transitions—wanting twilight to be either noon or midnight. What do we care what tomorrow will look like? We see only the face labeled Today. It grimaces horribly—and is thereby all the more expressive of Romanticism.

When has the Bourgeois ever loomed larger than now? What is Molière's Bourgeois in comparison? M. Jourdain doesn't come ankle-high to the first merchant you'll meet in the street. And the envious mug of the proletariat? And the young man on the make? And the Judge? And everything that's fermenting in the brains of the brainless, everything simmering in the hearts of rogues?

Yes, stupidity consists in wanting to reach conclusions. We are a thread, and we want to know the whole cloth. It recalls the eternal discussions about the decadence of art. Now we spend our time telling ourselves: "We're completely finished, we're at the last gasp," etc. What mind worthy of the name, beginning with Homer, ever reached a conclusion? Let's accept the picture. That's how things are. So be it . . .

Now I must go to bed. It is eleven o'clock. I can hear the water plashing into the basin in the courtyard. It reminds me of the sound of the fountain at Marseilles, in the Hôtel Richelieu, while I was fucking that worthy Mme Foucaud, née de Langlade. Ten years ago . . . !

1. Montaigne.
2. The daughter of Flaubert's brother, Dr. Achille Flaubert.
3. Flaubert long cherished this project. Over the years he compiled such a dictionary, and he had planned to make it the second part of his last, unfinished novel, *Bouvard et Pécuchet*. It is commonly printed in editions of that work. In English it exists also as a separate volume, *The Dictionary of Accepted Ideas*, translated by Jacques Barzun. (See bibliography and p. 175 et seq.)
4. The struggle in France between Right and Left, reflected in this letter and others, had persisted after the Revolution of 1848 and the election of Louis-Napoléon Bonaparte as President in December of that year; and it culminated in the latter's coup d'état of December 1 and 2, 1851. In 1852 there would be no "presidential election": instead, Louis-Napoléon would be given supreme power, with the title of Emperor.
5. Perhaps one of the six volumes of Comte's *Cours de philosophie positive* (1839-42).

To HIS MOTHER

Constantinople, November 14, 1850.

. . .

P.S. . . . As to the idea that's worrying you, that I'll be bored on my return, rest easy. I have passed the age of boredom, and I left part of myself with it. Besides, I shall have too much work to do. Something new is germinating in me: a second manner, perhaps? But at some point I'll have to give birth. I am impatient to discover what I am capable of. Shall I be able to retrieve, for another piece of work, everything I invested—and lost—in *Saint Antoine???*

To LOUIS BOUILHET

Constantinople, November 14, 1850

. . .

About Constantinople, where I arrived yesterday morning, I'll tell you nothing today, except to say that I have been struck by Fourier's idea that some time in the future it will be the capital of the world. It is really fantastic as a human anthill. That feeling of being crushed and overwhelmed you had on your first visit to Paris: here one is penetrated by it, elbowing as one does so many unknown men, from the Persian and the Indian to the American and the

Englishman, so many separate individualities which in their frightening total humble one's own. And then, the city is immense. One gets lost in the streets, which seem to have no beginning or end. The cemeteries are forests in the midst of the city. From the top of the tower at Galata, looking out over all the houses and all the mosques (beside and between the Bosphorous and the Golden Horn, both full of ships), the houses too seem like ships—a motionless fleet, with the minarets as masts. (A rather tortuous sentence—skip it.) We walked through (no more than that) the street of the male brothels. I saw bardashes buying sugared almonds, doubtless with bugger-money—the anus thus about to provision the stomach instead of the usual other way round. I heard the sound of a scratchy violin coming from ground-floor rooms: they were dancing a Greek dance. These young boys are usually Greeks. They wear their hair long.

Tomorrow I'll have your name, *Loue Bouilhette* (Turkish pronunciation), written on a sheet of blue paper in gold letters—a present intended as a decoration for your room. When you are alone and look at it, it will remind you that I have had you much with me during my journey.

.   .   .

I want you to know, dear Sir, that in Beirut I picked up (I first noticed them at Rhodes, land of the dragon)[1] VII chancres, which eventually merged into two, then one. In that condition I rode my horse from Marmaris to Smyrna. Every night and morning I dressed my wretched prick. Finally it cured itself. In two or three days the scar will be closed. I'm being desperately careful about it. I suspect a Maronite woman of making me this gift, or perhaps it was a little Turkish lady. The Turk or the Christian? Which? *Problème!* Food for thought! That's an aspect of the "Eastern Question" the *Revue des Deux Mondes* doesn't dream of. We discovered this morning that Sassetti has the clap (from Smyrna), and last night Maxime discovered, even though it's six weeks since he did any fornicating, a double abrasion that looks to me very much like a two-headed chancre. If it is, that makes the third time he's caught the pox since we set out. There's nothing like travel for the health.

Where are you, with the muse? I expected to find a letter from you here, with some lines of verse . . . What are you reading? What are you doing? How I long to see you!

As for me, literarily speaking, I've lost my bearings. At times I feel annihilated (the word is weak); at other times my "aural" style (i.e. in the state of an aura, an imponderable fluid) passes and circulates within me with intoxicating heat. Then it dies down. I meditate very little, daydream occasionally. My observation is preponderantly of the moral kind. I should never have suspected this facet of travel. The psychological, human, comic side abounds. One meets splendid specimens—variegated, iridescent existences very lustrous to the eye, like tattered embroidered garments heavy with filth and gold braid. And underneath it all, the same old low-life, immutable, invincible. That's the basis. How much of it one sees! From time to time, in the towns, I open a newspaper. Things seem to be going at a dizzy rate. We are dancing not on a volcano, but on the rotten seat of a latrine. Before very long, society is going to drown in nineteen centuries of shit, and there'll be a lot of shouting. I am thinking seriously of "studying the question." If you'll forgive my presumption, I'd like to squeeze the whole thing in my hands, like a lemon, to acidulate my drink. After my return I want to immerse myself in the Socialists' theories, and do, in theatrical form, something very brutal, very farcical, and—of course—impartial. I have the words on the tip of my tongue and the tone at my fingertips. Many subjects for which I have more defined plans are less eager to be born than that one.[2]

As for subjects, I have three; perhaps they are all the same, a thought that galls me considerably. *One: Une Nuit de Don Juan,*[3] which I thought of in quarantine at Rhodes. *Two: Anubis,*[4] the story of the woman who wants to be laid by the God. This is the loftiest of the three, but full of atrocious difficulties. *Three:* my Flemish novel[5] about the young girl who dies a virgin and mystic after living with her father and mother in a small provincial town, at the end of a garden full of cabbages and fruit trees, beside a stream the size of the Robec. What torments me is the kinship of idea of these three projects. In the first, insatiable love in the two forms: earthly love and mystical love. In the second, the same story, only there is fornication in it, and the earthly love is less exalted because more precise. In the third they are combined in the same person, and the one leads to the other; only, my heroine dies of religious masturbation after indulging in digital masturbation. Alas! It seems to me that when one is as good as this at dissecting children yet to be born, one doesn't harden up enough to create them. My clear-cut metaphysics fills me with terrors. But I must get rid of them. I need to know my measure. In order to live in peace, I want to have an opinion of myself, a definite opinion that will regulate me in the use of my powers. I have to know the quality and extent of my land before beginning to plough. I am experiencing a need, with relation to my personal literary situation, which everyone of our age feels to some extent with relation to the life of society: I feel the need of "becoming established."

At Smyrna, during a rain that kept us indoors, I took Eugène Sue's *Arthur* from the reading-room. It's enough to make you vomit; there's no word to describe it. You have to read this book to realize the pitifulness of money, success, and the public. Literature has become consumptive. It spits and slobbers, covers its blisters with salves and sticking-plasters, and has grown bald from excessive hair-brushing. It would take Christs of art to cure this leper. To return to the Antique in literature has been done already. The Middle Ages, the same. Remains the present. But the ground is shaky: where lay the foundation? And yet there is no other way of constructing something vital and therefore durable. All this worries me so much that I have come to dislike being spoken to about it. I am irritated by it sometimes, like a released convict listening to a discussion of the penal system. Especially with Maxime, who strikes hard and isn't an encouraging fellow—and I badly need to be encouraged. On the other hand, my vanity is not yet resigned to being awarded encouragement prizes only!

I am about to reread the whole of the *Iliad*. In a fortnight we are to make a little trip to the Troad, and in January we shall be in Greece. I fret at my ignorance: if only I knew Greek! And I have lost so much time over it!

"La sérénité m'abandonne!"

The man who retains the same self-esteem while traveling that he had when he looked at himself every day in the mirror of his room at home is either a very great man or a very sturdy fool. I don't know why, but I'm becoming very humble.

Passing Abydos, I thought much about Byron. That is his Orient, the Turkish Orient, the Orient of the curved sword, the Albanian costume, and the barred window looking on the blue sea. I prefer the baked Orient of the Beduin and the desert, the vermilion depths of Africa, the crocodile, the camel, the giraffe.

I regret not getting to Persia (money! money!). I keep dreaming of Asiatic journeys, of going overland to China, of impossibilities—the Indies, or California, which always excites me on the human side. At other times I get so choked up with emotion that I could weep, thinking of my study at Croisset, of our Sundays. Ah, how I'll miss these days of travel, how I'll keep reliving them, how I'll repeat the eternal monologue: "Fool! You didn't enjoy it enough!"

. . . Why has Balzac's death "affected me strongly"? One is always saddened by the death of a man one admires. I had hoped to know him later, hoped he would like me. Yes, he was a stout fellow, one who had an extraordinary understanding of his age. He, who had studied women so well, died just after he married—and when the society he knew was approaching its end. With Louis-Philippe, something disappeared that we shall not see again. Now we must dance to a different tune.

Why have I a melancholy desire to return to Egypt, to go back up the Nile and see Kuchuk Hanem? All the same, it was a rare night I spent there, and I tasted it to the full. How I missed you!

. . . Good night. I must attend to that dressing.

1. A species of large lizard found on the island is known as "the dragon of Rhodes."

2. It would be born, twenty years later, in novelistic rather than dramatic form, in the definitive *Education Sentimentale*.

3. Flaubert's outline for *Une Nuit de Don Juan* exists. It consists chiefly of two dialogues: between the Don and Leporello, about the Don's way of life; and between the Don and a dead nun with whom he spends the night in her convent, about earthly and mystical love.

4. No outline for *Anubis* is known. From Flaubert's brief description, however, it must have been what Jean Bruneau suggests—a foreshadowing of *Salammbô*.

5. For the role of the projected "Flemish novel" in the genesis of *Madame Bovary*, see p. 144. In *Par les champs et par les grèves*, Flaubert notes his conception of a similar subject when in Blois with DuCamp in 1847. ("Flemish" here probably means, roughly, "realistic"—as in Flemish painting, with its "humbler" subjects drawn from daily life.)

The Robec was a small stream flowing through an old quarter of Rouen. It is mentioned in the first chapter of *Madame Bovary*.

December 15, 1850. Constantinople.

When is the wedding to be, you ask me, apropos of the news of Ernest Chevalier's marriage. When? Never, I hope. As far as man can answer for what he will do, I reply in the negative. Contact with the world—and I've been rubbing shoulders with it now for fourteen months—makes me feel more and more like returning to my shell. Uncle Parain, who claims that travel changes a man, is wrong as far as I am concerned. As I set out, so shall I return, except that there **are fewer hairs on my head and** considerably more landscapes within it. That is the only difference. As to the principles that guide me, I shall retain the ones I have always had until further notice. Besides, if I had to say how I feel deep down, and if it doesn't sound too presumptuous, I would say: "Too late, now. I'm too old to change." When one has lived, as I have, a completely inner life, full of turbulent analyses and repressed enthusiasms, when one has so frequently excited and calmed oneself by turns, and employed all one's youth in learning to manage one's soul, as a horseman manages his horse, making it gallop across fields at the touch of the spur, walk with short steps, jump ditches, trot, and amble, all simply for his own enjoyment and to learn more about such things—well, what I mean is, if one doesn't break one's neck at the outset, the chances are one won't break it later. I, too, am "established," in that I have found my seat, my center of gravity. And I don't imagine that any jolt from within could ever unseat me and throw me to the ground. For me, marriage would be an apostasy: the very thought terrifies me. Alfred's death has not erased the memory of how shocked I was by his marriage—as pious folk react to the news of a great scandal caused by their bishop. If a man, whether of low or high degree, wishes to meddle with God's works, he must begin, if only as a healthy precaution, by putting himself in a position where he cannot be made a fool of. You can depict wine, love, women and glory on the condition that you're not a drunkard, a lover, a husband, or a private in the ranks. If you participate actively in life, you don't see it clearly: you suffer from it too much or enjoy it too much. The artist, to my way of thinking, is a monstrosity, something outside nature. All the misfortunes Providence inflicts on him come from his stubbornness in denying that axiom. He suffers from that denial and makes others suffer. Ask women who have loved poets, or men who have loved actresses. So (and this is my conclusion) I am resigned to living as I have lived: alone, with my throng of great men as my only cronies—a bear, with my bear-rug as company. I care nothing for the world, for the future, for what people will say, for any kind of establishment, or even for literary renown, which in the past I used to lie awake so many nights dreaming about. That is what I am like; such is my character.

The devil take me if I know why I've written you these two pages of tirade, poor dear. No, no: when I think of your sweet face, so sad and loving, and of the joy I have in living with you, who are so full of serenity and such grave charm, I know very well that I shall never love another woman as I do you.

You will have no rival, never fear! The senses or a momentary fancy will not take the place of what lies locked in the fastness of a triple sanctuary . . .

Good old Ernest! There he is, married, established—and a magistrate to boot. What a perfect bourgeois and gentleman! How much more than ever he'll be the defender of order, family, property! But then he has followed the normal course. He too was an artist; he carried a hunting knife and dreamed of plots for plays. Then he was a student in the Latin Quarter; he had what he called his "mistress," a neighborhood grisette whom I scandalized with my talk when I went to see him in their sordid ménage. He danced the cancan at the Chaumière, drank punch at the Café Voltaire. Then he got his doctorate. Immediately there began the comedy of being serious, following what had been the serious business of living a comedy. He became very solemn; concealed his few wild oats; bought a watch (definitive step!), and "gave up imagination" (his own words). How painful that separation must have been! My heart bleeds to think of it. Now I'm sure that down where he is[1] he's thundering against Socialist doctrines, talking about the "edifice," the "basis," the "helm of State," the "hydra-headed monster." As a magistrate, he is reactionary; married, he'll be a cuckold; and so, spending his life between his female and his children on the one hand, and the turpitudes of his profession on the other, there he is, the perfect example of the man who has managed to attain everything life has to offer. Ouf! Let's talk about something else.

1. Ernest Chevalier was now assistant public attorney in Grenoble.

To Louis Bouilhet

Athens, in the Lazaretto at the Piraeus.
December 19, 1850. Thursday.

I have been here since yesterday—we are being kept in quarantine until Sunday. I'm reading Herodotus and Thirlwall.[1] The rain falls in torrents, but at least it's warmer here than in Constantinople, where these last few days the snow was covering the houses. I was truly happy yesterday when I caught sight of the Acropolis, shining white in the sun under a sky heavy with clouds.

.   .   .

We spent five weeks in Constantinople; one would have to stay there six months . . . I saw the mosques, the seraglio, Santa Sophia. In the seraglio, a dwarf, the sultan's dwarf, was playing with white eunuchs outside the throne room; the dwarf was hideous, expensively dressed in European style—gaiters, overcoat, watch-chain. As for eunuchs, I had no particular feeling about the black ones, the only ones I had seen until then. But the white! I wasn't prepared for them. They look like nasty old women. The sight of them makes you nervous, and torments the imagination. You find yourself devoured by curiosity, and at the same time the bourgeois in you makes you loathe them. The antinormality of their appearance is a shock to one's virility. Explain that to

133

me. No question, though, that they are one of the most curious products of the human hand. What wouldn't I have given, in the Orient, to become the friend of a eunuch! But they are unapproachable. Apropos of the dwarf, dear Sir, it goes without saying that he brought to mind your nice Caracoïdès.[2]

. . .

One day we went to a filthy whorehouse in the Galata quarter to fuck some negresses. They were so disgusting my heart failed me. I was about to walk out when the madam of the place signaled to my dragoman and I was ushered into a separate room, very clean. There, hidden behind curtains, in bed, was a very young girl, 16 or 17, white, a brunette, silk corsage tight at the waist, delicate hands and feet, face sweet and sulky. She was Madame's own daughter, reserved for special circumstances. She made objections; they forced her to stay with me. But when we were in bed together and my forefinger was already in her vagina, and my hand had slowly explored two lovely alabaster columns sheathed in satin (it was like a naughty Empire engraving), I heard her ask me in Italian to let her examine my tool, to make sure I wasn't sick. Well! Since on the lower part of my glans I still have an induration, and was afraid she would see it, I acted the Monsieur and jumped down from the bed, saying loudly that she was insulting me, that such behavior was revolting to a gentleman; and I left, very annoyed not to have fired such a pretty shot and thoroughly humiliated to think of myself as having a nonpresentable prick.

The law permitting private persons to correspond "by electricity"[3] has inspired me with strange thoughts. For me it is the clearest possible sign of imminent debacle. It shows how, thanks to "progress", all government is becoming impossible. It is wildly grotesque to see the law torturing itself almost to death in an attempt to keep up with the New that is breaking out everywhere . . . Don't you often think about balloons? The man of the future may have tremendous fun. He'll travel among the stars, with air-pills in his pocket. We—you and I and the rest of us—have come on the scene too early and too late. We'll have performed the most difficult and least glamorous of all tasks: transition.

To accomplish something lasting, one must have a solid foundation. The thought of the future torments us, and the past is holding us back. That is why the present is slipping from our grasp.

1. Connop Thirlwall, British author of a celebrated *History of Greece*, one volume of which had been translated into French. (J.B.)
2. A dwarf in Bouilhet's poem *Melaenis*.
3. The electric telegraph, then gradually replacing the aerial telegraph, and hitherto reserved for government use, was "put at the disposition of the public" by the law of November 29, 1850. (J.B.)

To Louis Bouilhet

. . .

What has become of you? What are you up to? I refer to the material aspect of your life. *Quid de Venere?*[1] It's a long time since I last heard about your "youthful exploits." As for me, my frightful chancres have finally closed. The induration is still hard, but seems to be disappearing. Something else that is disappearing, and faster, is my hair. Expect to see me with a skullcap. Bald, like an office clerk or a worse-for-wear notary—the stupidest kind of premature senility. I am depressed about it. Maxime makes fun of me; he may be right. It is a feminine feeling, unworthy of a man and a republican, I know. But I see this as the first symptom of a humiliating decline, and feel it keenly. I am getting fat and paunchy and repulsively common-looking, about to enter the category of those the whore finds it unappetizing to handle. Perhaps I'll soon be lamenting my youth—and my wasted time, like the grandmother in Béranger. Where are you, luxuriant locks of my eighteen summers, falling to my shoulders with such hopes and such pride![2]

Yes, I am growing old. I feel that I am no longer capable of coming up with anything good. I have a terror of everything to do with style. What am I going to write when I return? That is what I keep asking myself. These last days, in the saddle, I have thought a good deal about my *Nuit de Don Juan*. But it seems to me very commonplace, old stuff; it would be just another treatment of the nun theme. To carry it off would require an excessively strong style, without a single weak line. Add to all this the fact that it's raining, that we're in a filthy little inn where we have to wait several more days for the steamer, that my trip is over and that I'm depressed. I want to go back to Egypt. I keep thinking of India. What a foolish creature is man, and especially me!

Even after the Orient, Greece is beautiful. I was immensely moved by the Parthenon. It's as good as the Gothic, whatever anyone may say to the contrary; and above all, I think, it is harder to understand.

. . .

Nature did everything for the Greeks—language, landscape, anatomy, the sun; even the forms of the mountains, which are as though sculptured, with lines more architectural than anywhere else.

I saw the cave of Trophonius, visited by that Apollonius of Tyana of whom I once sang.[3]

The choice of Delphi as the abode of the Pythoness was a stroke of genius. The landscape is one to inspire religious terrors—a narrow valley between two nearly perpendicular mountains, its floor a forest of dark olive trees, the mountains red and green; precipices on all sides, the sea at the far end, and snow-capped peaks on the horizon.

We lost our way in the snows of Mt. Cithaeron and narrowly escaped spending the night there.

As we gazed at Parnassus, we thought of the exasperation the sight would have caused a Romantic poet of 1832, and the diatribe he would have hurled against it.

.   .   .

The Parthenon is the color of brick, with, in places, tones of bitumen and almost of ink.[4] The sun shines on it almost constantly, whatever the weather. It gleams gloriously. Birds come and perch on the dismantled cornice—falcons, crows. The wind blows between the columns; goats browse amid pieces of white marble, fragments that shift under your feet. Here and there, in holes, piles of human bones: reminders of the war. Small Turkish ruins amid the great Greek ruin; and then, in the distance and always, the sea!

Among the pieces of sculpture found on the Acropolis I noticed especially a bas-relief representing a woman fastening her shoe. There remains only a fragment of the torso, just the two breasts, from the base of the neck to above the navel. One of the breasts is draped, the other uncovered. What breasts! Good God! What a breast! It is apple-round, full, abundant, widely spaced from the other: you can feel the weight of it in your hand. Its fecund maternity and its love-sweetness make you swoon. The rain and sun have turned the white marble to yellow, a tawny color, almost like flesh. It is so calm, so noble! It seems about to swell; one feels that the lungs beneath it are about to expand and breathe. How well it wore its sheer pleated drapery! How one would have rolled on it, weeping! How one would have fallen on one's knees before it, hands joined! Standing in front of it, I felt the beauty of the expression *Stupet aeris.*[5] A little more and I'd have prayed . . .

1. "What about your love-life?" The first paragraph of this letter, and numerous passages in most of the letters to Louis Bouilhet, consist of Flaubert's comments on drafts of poems Bouilhet has sent him.

2. Two weeks later, in Naples, Flaubert would write to his mother: "I bought some razors, and now I no longer have my beard—my poor beard, bathed in the Nile, blown by desert winds, long perfumed by tobacco smoke! Underneath it I discovered a face enormously fatter than before. I am disgusting. I have a double chin and jowls." It seems that already, in his thirtieth year, Flaubert had begun to look as he does in the well known later photographs.

3. In *Saint Antoine.*

4. "What color is the Parthenon?" is a perennial question, the tones are so variegated and so changeable with the light. Perhaps everyone sees the building differently. Alberto Moravia greeted the present translator in Athens with the words: "Have you been to the Parthenon yet? It's like lobster meat."

5. Properly *Stupet Albius aere* ("Albius is in ecstasy before bronze statues.")(Horace, *Satires*, Book I, Satire IV, 1.28.)

To his mother

Rome, April 8, 1851.

This letter is the last, I think. It is the sixtieth . . .[1]

.   .   .

A thought came to me yesterday apropos of Michelangelo's *Last Judgment.* It is this: that there is nothing viler on earth than a bad artist, a poor wretch who all his life sails just offshore from beauty without ever landing and planting his flag. To go in for art as a way of making money, to flatter the public, to spin facetious or dismal yarns for reputation or cash—that is the most ignoble of prostitutions; whereas the true artist seems to me master among men. I would rather have painted the Sistine Chapel than won many a battle, even Marengo. The former will last longer, and was perhaps more difficult. And I consoled myself for my own inadequacy by the thought that at least I am sincere. Everybody can't be Pope. The lowliest barefoot itinerant Franciscan, with limited intellect and no understanding of the prayers he recites, is perhaps as worthy of respect as a cardinal, if he prays with conviction and does his work with ardor. It is true that at moments of discouragement the poor man can't take comfort in the sight of his own purple, or in the hope of some day setting his behind on the Holy See.

1. The sixtieth to his mother alone. Approximately one hundred letters written during the journey survive. Mme Flaubert was soon to join her son in Rome, whence they would return to France together via Tuscany, Venice, and Milan.

To Louis Bouilhet

Rome, April 9 [1851].

· · ·

The *Don Juan* goes ahead *piano;* from time to time a few ideas for it are "committed to writing."

But let's talk about Rome. You're waiting to hear about it, naturally. Well, I'm sorry to confess it, but my first impression was unfavorable. Like a bourgeois, I "experienced a disillusion." Seeking the Rome of Nero, I found only that of Sixtus V. The priest-ridden atmosphere casts a miasma of boredom over the city of the Caesars. The gown of the Jesuits has covered everything with a gloomy, seminarist murk. In vain I whipped myself on to continue the quest: invariably churches—churches and convents; and long streets, neither empty enough nor animated enough, bordered by high, blank walls; and Christianity so ever-encroaching, so omnipresent, as to swamp and overwhelm the antiquities that survive in its midst.

Antiquity does survive in the Campagna—fallow, empty, accursed as the desert, with its great stretches of aqueduct and its herds of large-horned cattle. That is truly beautiful, the antique beauty one has imagined. As for Rome itself, in this respect, I haven't yet recovered from my first impression, and must wait until it has subsided a little. What the wretches have done to the Colosseum! Stuck a cross in the center of the circus, and built twelve chapels around the arena! But for pictures, statues, the XVIth century, Rome is the most splendid museum in the world. The number of masterpieces in the city is dizzying. It is certainly the artists' city. One could spend one's life here in a completely *ideal* atmosphere—outside the world, above it. I am overwhelmed by Michelangelo's *Last Judgment.* It partakes of Goethe, Dante, Shakespeare, merged

137

into an art that is unique. It is beyond description. Even the word "sublime" seems to me inadequate: shrill and over-simple.

I have seen a *Virgin* by Murillo that haunts me like a perpetual hallucination, a *Rape of Europa* by Veronese that excites me enormously, and two or three other things one could say a great deal about. I have been in Rome a fortnight. I'll tell you more about it later. But Greece has made me exigent concerning ancient art. The Parthenon spoiled Roman art for me: it seems lumpish and trivial in comparison. Greece is so beautiful!

Ah, poor fellow, how I missed you at Pompeii! I enclose some flowers I picked in a lupanar whose door was marked with a phallus in a state of erection. There were more flowers in that house than in any other. Sperm from the pricks of the ancients had perhaps fertilized the ground. The sun was blazing on the gray walls.

I saw Pozzuoli, Lake Lucrinus, Baiae—each of them an earthly Paradise. The emperors had good taste. I melted with melancholy in those places.

Like a tourist, I climbed to the top of Vesuvius and arrived exhausted. The crater is strange. Sulphur has accumulated around the edges in weird growths, yellow and purplish-red. I have been to Paestum. I was set on going to Capri; and very nearly remained there—in the deep. Despite my prowess as a boatman, I thought my last hour had come, and I confess I was worried and even afeared, much afeared. I was within an inch of annihilation, like Rome at the worst moments of the Punic wars.

Naples is a charming city thanks to its great numbers of pimps and whores. One quarter is garrisoned with girls who stand in their doorways: it's like the antique world, a real Suburra. As you go down the street, they hoist their dresses up to their armpits and show you their behinds to earn a penny or two. They run after you in that state. We were in a carriage, and the coachman, holding his reins and slowing the horse, tried to flick the tip of his whip into the cunt of one of them. It was the rawest bit of prostitution and cynicism I've seen yet. When we reached the end of the street Maxime and I both let our heads fall to our chests and sighed, "Ce pauvre Bezet!"[1]

I did a certain amount of fornicating in Naples—quite pretty girls. Maxime caught the clap.

Naples is the place to come to for a bath in the fountain of youth and to fall in love with life all over again. The sun itself is enamored of the place. Everything is gay and easy. The ears of the horses are decked with bunches of peacock feathers.

The Chiaia is a long shorefront promenade, rows of live oaks arching overhead and the sea murmuring alongside. The newlyweds sitting there on moonlit nights warm their behinds on benches made of lava. The immemorial heat of the volcanos reaches their hearts by way of their buttocks: they squeeze each other's hands and choke with emotion. I envy them their sensations.

For almost a week I was tormented by desire for an actress (a French girl! and a vaudeville actress, at that!), and since I had neither enough money to pay her, nor enough nerve to accost her with empty purse, nor enough patience to woo her, I gave up. That cost me a pang. By dint of watching her in the theatre, I got over my temptation, and now think of her no longer. So much for passion.

. . .

As for my moral state, it is a strange one. *I feel the need of a success.* That would restore me, give me new strength, purge me a little . . .

1. Bouilhet's nickname—his name as pronounced by Flaubert's infant niece Caroline.

So it was that, as the traveling approached its end, Flaubert's earlier, hesitant "Unless some excessively literary wind begins to blow in a few years, I am resolved not to 'make the presses groan' with any elucubration of my brain" gave way, in that last letter to Louis Bouilhet from Rome, to the outright "I feel the need of a success."

The "excessively literary wind" probably referred less to a national upsurge of splendid writing than to impulses within Flaubert's own spirit; and the reader of the letters has seen such impulses intensifying. The remark on the death of Balzac—"I had hoped to know him later, hoped he would like me"—is itself eloquent of ambition and self-confidence: for why might Balzac have later "liked" Gustave Flaubert if not for some future writing? And now Balzac's own place was empty . . .

VI

Louise Colet II
Madame Bovary
1851-1855

IN A MEMENTO dated June 16, 1851, Louise Colet, recently widowed, records her great emotion on having learned the previous evening that Flaubert was in Paris, arrived there a few days earlier with his mother on the way back to Croisset after his long trip to the East. Promptly the next morning she had a note delivered to his hotel, suggesting that they meet, only to have it brought back with word that he was not there. After sending someone to inquire of Maxime DuCamp (who told her messenger "He won't see her"), she learned that Flaubert had already left the city; and she sent either the same letter, or a copy, or a different letter, to Croisset. (The draft of a second letter exists, teeming with reproaches, guaranteed to antagonize.) A week passed without an answer; she determined to see him. "On Thursday I will go to Rouen," she promised herself in her Memento of the 23rd, "and I will bring him this letter:

> 'I am in Rouen, and shall soon be going on quite a long journey. I come to bring you some news that I think will interest you. My visit will be short, and I hope may be well received. I could not accept even a half-day's hospitality. But I shall be happy to offer my respects to your mother, if she has not entirely forgotten having met me,[1] and I shall be happy to talk with you. Life passes so swiftly, its joys and vanities are so fleeting, that we should be kind to one another. That is the feeling I shall count on for an hour. Votre dévouée. L.C.' "

The morning of Thursday the 26th, as she was preparing to leave for Rouen, an answer from Flaubert arrived. It has not been preserved. Evidently it was anything but cordial; but it did not deter Louise.

She boarded a train to Rouen (so she records in her Memento of the 27th), took a room there at the Hôtel d'Angleterre, wrote Flaubert a note probably similar to the one she had planned, hired a river-boatman, and, taking the note with her, had herself rowed downstream to Croisset. About half-past six she found herself before "a charming two-story house in the English style beside the Seine, standing in the midst of a green lawn with flower-beds, and separated from the river only by the road and an iron grille." Passing through a gate, she walked around to a farm-like courtyard, and asked an employee to take her note in to Monsieur Flaubert. The servant returned: " 'Monsieur cannot see you; he will write to you.' " A maid came out of the house: " 'Monsieur is dining with guests. If Madame will give me her address in Rouen, he will write to Madame.'

"I replied that I was returning to Paris that same evening, and would like to speak with him here for a moment.

"The maid went in and returned: 'Monsieur will meet Madame this evening at eight o'clock if Madame will give her address. It is impossible for Monsieur to see Madame here.' "

"Wounded to the heart," Louise walked away.

She lingered on the quai, however, and as she stared wistfully at the "elegant white house . . . where my own image had dwelled so long, where he had written me such tender, beautiful letters," the front gate opened and Flaubert appeared.

" 'What do you want with me, Madame?' he said rudely, perhaps making an effort to be rude.

" 'I would like to speak with you.'

" 'That is really impossible, here.'

" 'You send me away? You think a visit from me would dishonor your mother?'

" 'Not at all, but it is impossible.' "

After a few moments:

" 'Madame, I will meet you in Rouen at eight o'clock, if you wish . . . Yes or no?'

" 'Yes.'

" 'At eight o'clock I will be at the Hôtel d'Angleterre.' "

"Mortified," Louise was rowed back to Rouen.

At the hotel, Flaubert was at first harsh and sarcastic, reproaching her for her intrusion. "He told me that what he found offensive about me was his knowing that I was capable of just such rash acts as this—coming and asking for him at Croisset." She spoke of her "difficult situation" (by which she meant chiefly her poverty, her reluctant financial dependence on Victor Cousin for the expenses of her daughter's upbringing), and of her continuing love for him, Flaubert.

"Marry the Philosopher," was his only reply.

" 'Shall I never, never, be in your arms again?'

" 'Marry the Philosopher,' he said, laughing, 'and then you and I will see each other.' "

She was revolted by the cynicism: " 'Oh! Profanation de l'amour!' "

But she made herself as seductive as she could—"I tried to assume his tone, and joked a bit"; she knew she was still pretty; and after some kissing Flaubert promised to meet her later, in Paris. They walked in the Rouen streets, "the night was splendid, the stars were shining, the air smelled sweet." Several times they were about to separate, but each time Louise said, "Just to the next street-light"; finally, after more kissing, they parted, saying "Au revoir."

"I returned to the hotel. As I walked, the thought of Croisset, closed against me, against *me*, rose up in my heart like an affront, like a poignant pain. As long as he had been with me, I had thought only of loving him, of awakening in him the memory of the past."

She took the midnight train back to Paris.

She went to England, sent him a letter, enclosing a flower from Windsor Park.

A month after their meeting, he wrote her.

1. "Met" in the sense of encountering by chance, probably at some time several years before when Flaubert was escorting his mother in Paris. As will be seen, despite Louise's best efforts she and Mme Flaubert never formally "met."

To Louise Colet

Croisset, July 26 [1851]

I write you because "my heart prompts me to speak to you kindly,"[1] pauvre amie. If I could make you happy, I would do so with joy: it would be only fair. The thought that I have made you suffer so much weighs on me heavily: you know that, don't you? But for this and for the rest neither you nor I are, or ever were, to blame: everything was inherent in the circumstances.

You must have found me very cold the other day in Rouen. But I was as little cold as I possibly could be. I made every effort to be kind. Tender, no: that would have been dishonorable, hypocritical, an insult to your sincerity.

Read. Do not brood. Immerse yourself in long study: only the habit of persistent work can make one continually content; it produces an opium that numbs the soul. I have lived through periods of atrocious ennui, spinning in a void, bored to distraction. One preserves oneself by dint of steadiness and pride. Try it.

I wish you were in such a state that we could see each other calmly. I love your company when it is not tempestuous. The storms one so enjoys in youth are tiring in maturity. It is like riding: there was a time when I loved to gallop: now I let my horse walk, and the reins lie loose. I am growing very old; every jolt upsets me, and feeling is as repugnant to me as action.

You tell me nothing about what would interest me most: your plans. I sense that you have not yet reached any decision. The opinion I gave you was good: as Phidias used to say, you must always have mutton and beef on the table.[2]

I will see you soon in Paris, if you are there. (Weren't you to stay in England a month?) I expect to be in Paris at the end of next week. I shall go to England toward the end of August: my mother wants me to take her there.[3] I dislike the interruption, but . . . If you are still there I will come to see you. We'll try to be happy together.

In Paris, I will leave at your house the two manuscripts you left with me. Also, I want to return, but personally, into your own hands, a bronze medal I was weak enough to accept long ago. I must not keep it: it belongs to your daughter.

Farewell. God bless you, poor child.[4]

1. "Mon coeur me porte à vous dire quelque bonne parole." Perhaps Flaubert is quoting words Louise herself had once used. (J.B.)
2. That is, in Louise's case, more than one project, or the possibility of choice.
3. To see the Great Exhibition at the Crystal Palace.
4. In English in the original.

A few days earlier, on July 21, Maxime DuCamp had written to Flaubert from Paris: "What are you up to? . . . Is it still Don Juan? Or is it the story of Mme Delamare, a splendid subject?"

What seems to have happened is that Flaubert had learned from his mother, after his return, or from Louis Bouilhet, of the death, during his absence, of a Norman country doctor whom the Flauberts had known, named Eugène Delamare, and that this brought to mind certain country gossip. Delamare had been an impecunious and mediocre medical student under Dr. Flaubert at the Hôtel-Dieu. He never passed all his examinations, and became not an M.D. but an *officier de santé*—a licensed "health officer," practising in a small town near Rouen. His second wife, Delphine, who had died before him, had been the subject of scandalous local talk: the details, unknown today, were apparently such as to make both DuCamp and Bouilhet urge Flaubert to make use of them.

With extraordinary rapidity, thus encouraged by his friends, Flaubert abandoned two of the three subjects he had considered, the exotic *Une Nuit de Don Juan* and the even more exotic *Anubis*, in favor of one from modern life; and he saw that for him, elements of the Delamare story held more promise than that earlier contemporary project, the "Flemish" novel about the virgin mystic.[1]

He made outlines.

In preparation for his trip to London with his mother, he went to Paris. He and Louise Colet were reunited.[2]

Then, just after leaving her and before going to London, he took the first steps in his narrative.

1. Flaubert seems to have first thought of the name "Emma Bovary" for the heroine of the earlier, "Flemish" project, and then used it in the new novel. DuCamp says in his memoirs that the name first came to Flaubert in Egypt. (One of their Cairo hotel-keepers was a former French actor named Bouvaret.)

After the publication of *Madame Bovary*, Flaubert wrote to his faithful correspondent Mlle Leroyer de Chantepie: 'The first idea I had was to make my heroine a virgin, living in the depths of the provinces, growing old in her sadness and so reaching the ultimate stages of mysticism and imagined passion. Of this plan I retained the setting (landscapes and characters quite somber)—the color, in short. However, to make the story more comprehensible

144

and entertaining (in the good sense of that word), I invented a more human heroine, a woman of a kind more often seen. Besides, I foresaw such difficulties in the execution of the earlier plan that I didn't dare go ahead with it."

2. Louise Colet's Memento of Monday, September 15, 1851:

" . . . He came for me on Saturday at four o'clock. We went to Fleury and Meudon via the Bois and the other woods, dined chez Michel, and thence to Saint-Cloud on foot . . . No constraint, very expansive. On his part, sweetness, kindness, but no deep feeling. Returned in a carriage from Saint-Cloud. The same violent emotions, even in the carriage, but always controlling himself; renunciation of everything he likes. The evening at my house; but there is always that bitter sadness at possessing him so little and having so little influence on his character. We said goodbye without speaking of my material situation—not that I would have accepted anything from him. Distressing of him, for his indifference to my poverty makes me realize how shallow his love is. And yet he is kind-hearted, generous (that is, an easy spender). Still, for all that, he is untroubled by the humiliations torturing the woman he presses so passionately in his arms. I have exactly ten francs in the house to keep me going until the October quarter." (The reference is probably to the next quarterly installment of her pension.)

TO LOUISE COLET

Croisset, Saturday night [September 20, 1851]

Ma chère amie, I leave for London next Thursday.

. . . Last night I began my novel. Now I foresee difficulties of style, and they terrify me. It is no small thing to be simple. I am afraid of becoming another Paul de Kock[1] or producing a kind of chateaubriandized Balzac.

I have had a sore throat since my return. My vanity likes to think that this is not due to fatigue, and I think my vanity is right. And you? How are you?

I am very busy at the moment on a temporary task I will tell you about later.

Adieu, chère Louise; I kiss your white neck. A long kiss[2] . . .

1. The author of best-selling humorous novels about the French bourgeoisie.
2. From Louise Colet's Memento of September 22, 1851:
"At last a note from Gustave. What a personality! The wretchedness of my poor life can expect nothing from such an affection as his. What I need is continuous hard work and unshakeable moral courage. All in all, it is better to have him back: even the palest gleam of light is better than total darkness."

Soon after his return from the East, Maxime DuCamp had bought, with a few friends, the title of a defunct magazine, the *Revue de Paris*, and had revived it, planning to publish fiction, poetry, and articles on literature and the social scene. The first issue, which included a story by DuCamp himself, "Tagahor, a Hindu Tale," appeared on October 1, 1851, and was generally well received. DuCamp was looking for new talent and, despite some opposition from his fellow editors (Théophile Gautier was one of them), who found its 2400 lines excessive, he decided to publish in an early issue Louis Bouilhet's *Melaenis*, the poem about the dancer in old Rome. It would be Bouilhet's debut.

DuCamp invited Flaubert, too, to contribute to the *Revue*, and reminded him that it was time to think of publication. Just launched on the hazardous adventure of a long novel about the bourgeoisie (which at that time he thought would take him "a year, at least"), Flaubert hesitated: all he had to offer the magazine were his chapters from *Par les champs et par les grèves*—and *Saint Antoine*, which DuCamp, along with Bouilhet, had declared unpublishable. DuCamp, a year his junior, had already published stories, articles, and a travel book; and now Bouilhet, who had had none of Flaubert's freedom, most of whose time had been spent in necessary drudgery, was about to achieve public notice. Perhaps *parts* of *Saint Antoine* could be printed?

Several documents—two Mementos by Louise Colet, and an exchange of letters between Flaubert and DuCamp—paint a somewhat confused picture; with DuCamp, if Louise is to be believed, not always telling the same story.

> *Memento of Saturday, October 4, 1851* . . . In the evening, visit from DuCamp. What he tells me about Gustave. He is fed up with him, and thinks there is nothing worthwhile in his heart or his intelligence, that he has no literary future, no center. Perhaps he is right. That tremendous personality of his will have its punishment; and yet I still think he has talent. Perhaps the memories of my love mislead me, but his imagination seems magnetic to me, like his eyes. We must judge him by his first published work. I have just read DuCamp's story in the *Revue de Paris:* it is quite boring. It does show, however, a genuine gift for style and a grasp of Hindu archaeology. But even the slightest wisp of sensibility would be more appreciated by the reader.

> *Saturday, October 18, 1851* . . . Gustave came at half-past eight. He arrived [from England] only last evening, he told me. I found him changed, deteriorated in looks. He had a cold, and said he was more disgusted with life than ever, that Gautier and DuCamp were advising him to publish fragments of his *Saint Antoine*, and that the idea was worrying him. Is it he, or DuCamp, who is not being sincere? The latter told me that *Saint Antoine* was worthless, and that he would be distressed if Gustave wanted to publish it in the *Revue*. Gustave told me that his friend was enchanted by the outline of the novel he is going to work on, whereas DuCamp told me in so many words that it would be a "tremendous fiasco." So who is being honest? I am not in a position to tell Gustave the truth; he does not love me enough . . . Despite what DuCamp says about him, I do not find that his imagination has become dulled; he has a highly developed, very sure literary sense . . .

It is clear from DuCamp's letter to Flaubert printed as Appendix III in the present volume that DuCamp was against publishing anything from *Saint Antoine* in the *Revue*. But perhaps he had not yet told Flaubert this. Théophile Gautier may have felt differently; as we shall see, he would later publish several sections from it in another magazine.

Meanwhile, Flaubert expressed agonies of indecision.

.   .   .

I am very impatient for you to come here for a long, detailed talk, so that I can reach some decision. Last Sunday, with Bouilhet, we read over parts of *Saint Antoine:* Apollonius of Tyana, some of the gods, and the second half of the second part—that is, the Courtesan, Thamar, Nebuchadnezzar, the Sphinx, the Chimera, and all the animals. It would be very difficult to publish excerpts: you'll see. There are some very good things, but—but—but! They are not satisfying in themselves, and "curious," I think, would be the verdict of the most indulgent readers, indeed the most intelligent. It is true that I would have on my side a lot of worthies who wouldn't understand a word and would admire it for fear their neighbors might understand it better. Bouilhet's objection to publication is that I have put into this all my defects and only a few of my good qualities. According to him, it diminishes me as a man. Next Sunday we shall read all the speeches of the gods; perhaps that would be the best single section. I have no more feelings of my own about this matter of choice than about the main question of publication. I don't know what to think. My position is exactly in the middle. So far, no one has ever reproached me for lacking individual traits, nor for being insensitive to the demands of my own little person. Well, in this question, perhaps the most important in the life of an artist, I completely lack all that. I cancel out. My very self is dissolved, with no effort on my part, alas: indeed I do everything I can to have some sort of opinion, but find myself utterly without one. The arguments for and against seem to me equally valid. If I were to toss a coin for it, I wouldn't regret the result, whichever it might be.

If I do publish, it will be for the stupidest of reasons—because I am told to, because I choose to emulate or obey others, not from any initiative of my own. I feel neither the need nor the desire to publish. And don't you think that we should do only as our hearts prompt us? The idiot who goes to a duel because his friends urge him to and tell him that he must, even though he himself has no desire to go and thinks it stupid, etc., is, at bottom, much more miserable than the self-confessed coward who swallows the insult without even noticing it and stays calmly at home. Yes, I repeat: what I dislike is that the idea comes not from me but from someone else, from others—proof, perhaps, that I am wrong.

And then, let's look further: if I publish, I'll publish; and it won't be by halves. When one does a thing one must do it well. I'll go to Paris for the winter. I'll be a man like other men. I'll lead a life given over to love affairs and scheming. I'll have to do many things that will revolt me and that I find lamentable in advance. Now: am I made for all that? As you well know, I am a man given to great élans and deep discouragements. If you knew all the invisible nets that keep me physically inactive, all the mists that float in my brain! Often, when I am faced with doing no matter what, I am overwhelmed by weariness and am ready to die of boredom; and I grasp even the most straightforward idea only by dint of great effort. My youth (you knew only its latter phase) steeped me in an opiate of boredom, sufficient for the remainder of my days. I hate life. There: I have said it; I'll not take it back. Yes, life; and everything that reminds me that life must be borne.[1] It bores me to eat, to dress, to stand on my feet, etc. I have dragged this hatred everywhere, wherever I have been: at school, in Rouen, in Paris, on the Nile. You, with your clear-cut, forthright nature, always rebelled against these vague Normandisms. In my clumsy way I used to excuse them, and that brought harsh words from you, Maxime, which were often bitter to swallow. I always put them out of my mind, but they were painful at the time.

Do you think it has been out of mere perversity, without long deliberation, that I have lived to the age of thirty in this way you scold me for? Why have I not had mistresses? Why have I preached chastity? Why have I stayed in this provincial backwater? Do you think I don't have erections like other men, and that I wouldn't enjoy cutting a fine figure in Paris? Indeed, I'd enjoy that considerably. But take a good look at me and tell me whether it's possible. I am no more cut out for that sort of thing than to be a fine waltzer. Few men have had fewer women than I (that is the punishment for my cult of "plastic beauty," so admired by Theo), and if I remain unpublished, that will be the punishment for all my youthful dreams of glory. Must one not follow one's own path? If I find it repugnant to move about, maybe I am right not to. Sometimes I even think it wrong of me to want to write a rational book, instead of letting myself indulge in all the lyricism, all the bombast, all the fantastic philosophical extravagance that might enter my head. Who can tell? Some day I may give birth to a work that will be my own, at least.

Suppose I do publish. Will I be able to stand up against the consequences? They have been the ruin of stronger men than I. Who can tell whether in four years I might not become an ignoble fool? Am I really to have a goal other than Art itself? It alone has been sufficient for me until now; and if I need something more, that is proof that I am deteriorating. And if I *enjoy* the additional something, that is proof that I have deteriorated already.

Only the fear lest I be giving voice to the demon of pride keeps me from saying immediately, "No! A thousand times no!" Like a snail afraid of touching something unclean on the sand or of being crushed underfoot, I retreat into my shell. I don't say I am incapable of activity of any kind. I plunged into the fray on two occasions, to help Achille and to help you,[2] and both times I was successful. It has to be of short duration and something that I enjoy. I have the physical strength for it, but not the patience, and patience is everything. Were I a strong man at a fair, I could lift the weights perfectly well, but not walk about brandishing them in my fists. Brashness, dissembling, the necessary tact, knowing how to get on in the world—all that's a closed book to me, and I'd make many blunders. The two deletions you made in your story, *Tagahor*— "urine" and "women who love other women"—shocked me as being humiliating concessions. That offended me, and I am not sure I forgive you even now. You see what I am like.

The Muse[3] reproaches me for being tied to my mother's apron strings. Just now I followed those apron strings to London; before that, they met me in Rome; and they might well come with me to Paris. Ah, if you could rid me of my brother-in-law and my sister-in-law,[4] how little the apron strings would bother me! Yesterday I had a long talk about all this business with my mother. Like me, she came to no conclusion. Her final word was: "If you have written something you think good, publish it." How far that gets me!

So there you are, old fellow. I assign you all the foregoing as a theme for meditation. Only, do meditate—and consider my whole self. Despite what I wrote in the *Education*—that even in the most intimate confidences there is something that remains unsaid—I have told you everything, insofar as a man can be honest with himself. It seems to me that I am that. I am showing you my very entrails. I am putting my trust in you—in you, my dear, old friend; in your instinct, which I sense is sure, and in your intelligence, which is keen when not outweighed by extraneous considerations. I will do whatever you wish, whatever you tell me. I entrust my *self* to you: I am weary of it. I had no idea, when I began my letter, that I was going to write all this. It came of itself; let it go off to you. It may make things easier when we have our discussion two weeks from now. Adieu: je t'embrasse with all manner of feelings.

1. A passage often cited, usually by those who dislike Flaubert the writer because of his famous self-styled "impersonality"—his abstaining from expressing his own feelings concerning his characters (an abstinence which was, however, far from total). Taking Flaubert's words *au pied de la lettre*, not seeking any deeper meaning, such critics point to this outburst as constituting a fatal handicap, a disqualification, for a novelist.
   2. For the help to Achille, see p. 38, n.1. DuCamp had apparently been aided by Flaubert in a financial crisis. (J.B.)
   3. As Louise Colet was called by Flaubert, DuCamp, and Bouilhet among themselves.
   4. Hamard, who was still making trouble, and Achille's wife, Anathalie-Julie, never a favorite.

If the "discussion" mentioned by Flaubert took place, Louis Bouilhet was probably one of the participants. In any case, on October 29-30, 1851, Maxime DuCamp—without waiting for the two weeks to elapse—sent Flaubert the long reply printed as Appendix III in the present volume.

Meanwhile, in letters usually written—like his earlier messages to her—late at night, after the day's work was done, Flaubert was beginning to cast Louise Colet in the role for which she has come to be chiefly known—his epistolary confidante concerning the progress of *Madame Bovary*. The passages translated from this second series of Flaubert's letters to Louise have been chosen primarily to chronicle that progress, and to reveal some of the ideas that occupied Flaubert while he was writing his novel. The uneven course of the renewed liaison is charted, but it takes second place to the drama of the novel itself. Louise constantly sent Flaubert drafts of the poems she was writing in competition for the cash prizes awarded by the French Academy; and in his letters he returned detailed suggestions, often in collaboration with Bouilhet. These have almost invariably been omitted here

To LOUISE COLET

[Croisset,] Thursday night, 1 A.M. [October 23, 1851]

Poor child! So will you always refuse to understand things as they are said? Really, that remark you find so harsh requires no apology or commentary. And if it tastes bitter to anyone, it can only be to me. Yes: I do wish that you did not love me, and that you had never known me; and in so wishing I think I express a regret that concerns your happiness.[1] Just as I wish I were not loved by my mother, did not love her or anyone in the world, so I wish there were nothing in my heart that reached out to others, and nothing in the hearts of others that reached out to me. The more one lives, the more one suffers. To make existence bearable, haven't there been inventions ever since the world began—imaginary worlds, opium, tobacco, strong drink, ether? Blessed be he who invented chloroform. The doctors object that one can die of it. But that is the very point! You lack sufficient hatred of life and of everything connected with it. You would understand me better if you were inside my skin: what you now consider unwarranted harshness you would see to be heartfelt compassion, something tender and generous, it seems to me. You believe I am wicked, or at least selfish, that I think only of myself, love only myself. Surely that is no more true of me than of anyone else: less, perhaps, if one may sing one's own praises. In any case, you will grant me the merit of always speaking the truth. Perhaps I feel more than I say, for I have relegated all my emphasis to my written style; there it stays, and doesn't budge. Each of us can only do what he is capable of. A man steeped for years, as I was, in all the excesses of solitude, nervous to the point of losing consciousness, agitated by repressed passions, racked by doubts from within and without: that is not the man for you to love. I love you as best I can; badly, not enough, I know it, I know it, oh God! Who is to blame? Chance! Fatality—that old ironic fatality, which joins things together for the greatest harmony of the whole and the greatest disharmony between the parts. Individuals meet only to collide; and each, bearing his torn entrails in his hands, accuses the other—who is gathering up his own. Still, there are some good days, some delicious moments. I love your company, I love your body, yes, your body, poor Louise, when you lean on my left arm and bend back your head and I kiss your neck. Stop weeping; think not about past or future, but about today. "What is your duty? Whatever each day requires," Goethe said. Submit to that requirement and you will have a tranquil heart.

Look at life from a loftier viewpoint, stand high on a tower (even though the foundation may crack, have faith in its solidity); then around you you will see only the blue ether. Sometimes the blue will change to mist: what matter, if everything disappears, drowned in placid vapor?

One must esteem a woman, to write her such things as these.

I am finding it very hard to get my novel started. I suffer from stylistic abscesses; and sentences keep itching without coming to a head. I am fretting, scratching. What a heavy oar the pen is, and what a strong current ideas are to row in! This makes me so desperate that I enjoy it considerably. In this state I spent a good day today, with the window open, the sun on the river, and the greatest serenity in the world. I wrote one page and sketched three more. A fortnight from now I hope to be in gear, but the colors I am working with are so new to me that I keep staring at them in astonishment.[2]

My cold is ending; I feel well. The middle of next month I shall come to Paris for two or three days. Work, think of me, and if you see me in your mind, avoid dark colors; let my image evoke happy memories. After all, we have to laugh. *Vive la joie!* Adieu. One more kiss . . .

1. From Louise Colet's Memento of October 18, 1851:
". . . We talked amicably for an hour and a half. His personality is very hard. He said, 'I would like you to find me disagreeable, so that you would stop loving me, for I see how it makes you suffer.' I replied that those words demonstrated a total absence of love, and tears came to my eyes. Then he wanted to embrace me and to kiss my eyes—the eyes, he said, that were shedding tears because of him."

2. It is easy to picture Flaubert's astonishment at finding himself using the colors of the everyday Norman lives and places he was describing with deliberate objectivity in *Madame Bovary*, "so new" as contrasted with the Eastern and Mediterranean pictures he had been painting in recent letters, with the fantasmagoria of *Saint Antoine*—and, especially, with the emotional, confessional tones of his earlier work.

We ourselves are tempted to feel a certain astonishment at the mastery rapidly displayed by Flaubert in working with these "new" colors—which characterize the novel, as we know it, from its very opening; even though preliminary drafts, many extant and published in a variorum edition, testify to his difficulty in getting started. However, the correspondence has already revealed the constant coexistence, in Flaubert, of these "new" colors along with the old; and especially the most prominent of the "new" colors—detachment. One has only to reread the account of the night spent with Kuchuk Hanem: the bedbugs on the wall exemplify elements in the picture as striking as the exoticism.

Following the exchange of letters with DuCamp, and perhaps as an aftermath of the "discussion," the question of Flaubert's publishing parts of *Saint Antoine*—or anything else[1]—in the *Revue de Paris* at present was dropped, and he devoted himself entirely to his novel. Louis Bouilhet, coming to Croisset almost every Saturday or Sunday, hearing the week's work read aloud, became his dearest friend, his mentor.

Flaubert called Bouilhet something more—his "midwife." As such, Bouilhet neither conceived nor bore the child (his own poetry reveals no great creative power), but his assistance was devoted and invaluable; he was a gifted, highly sensitive reader and editor. The varying existing drafts of sections of *Madame Bovary*, especially its earlier parts, are suggestive of Bouilhet's role—tantalizing hints of unrecorded conversations between author and editor.

1. In his memoirs, Maxime DuCamp (who several years before had published an account of his earlier trip to the "Orient") says that he had made Flaubert an alternative suggestion: "I

had urged him to write up the Greek portion of our journey; it could make a short, interesting book, excellent for a debut in letters. He rejected my advice, saying that travel, like the humanities, should serve only to 'enliven one's style,' and that incidents gleaned abroad might be used in a novel, but not in a straight account. Travel writings were to him the same as news items, he said, a low form of literature, and he had higher aspirations."

To Louise Colet

[Croisset,] Monday night. [November 3, 1851]

.   .   .

It is splendid to be a great writer, to put men into the frying pan of your words and make them pop like chestnuts. There must be a delirious pride in the feeling that you are bringing the full weight of your ideas to bear on mankind. But for that you must have something to say. Now, I will confess to you it seems to me I have nothing that everyone else doesn't have, or that hasn't been said equally well, or that can't be said better. In the life you preach to me,[1] I would lose the little I do have; I would take on the passions of the crowd, in order to please it, and would descend to its level. Rather sit by the fire and make Art for oneself, the way one plays ninepins. When all is said and done, Art is perhaps no more serious than a game of ninepins. Perhaps everything is an immense bluff. I am afraid of that. And when we turn the page we may be very surprised to find that the answer to the riddle is so simple.

In the midst of all this I am advancing painfully with my book. I spoil a considerable quantity of paper. So many deletions! Sentences are very slow in coming. What a devilish style I have adopted! A curse on simple subjects! If you knew how I was torturing myself you'd be sorry for me. I'm certainly saddled with this book for a year, at least. Once under way, I'll enjoy it, but it is hard. I have also resumed a little Greek and Shakespeare.

I was forgetting to tell you that the governess arrived ten days ago. Her "physique," incidentally, does not impress me. I have never felt less venereal . . .

1. Despite his self-doubts as he tries to get his novel under way, Flaubert is resisting Louise's renewed urging that he come and lead the literary life in Paris.

Caroline's new governess, her second, was an Englishwoman, Isabel Hutton, called by the Flauberts "Miss Isabel." (Her predecessor, "Miss Jane," also English, had left to be married, and will be met later as Mrs. Farmer.) The mention of Miss Isabel's "physique," in that last letter of Flaubert's, suggests that Louise had already made some remark about her possible charms. Despite Flaubert's denial of them, it would seem that the thought of the young woman's presence in the house at Croisset inspired the jealousy now recorded by Louise and the murderous gesture she—who had already shown herself physically violent with Alphonse Karr—now contemplated.

Memento of Friday night, November 21, 1851. Horrible night, Sunday-Monday—the thought of killing him rather than see him take up with another woman. Until four in the morning, in bed, revolving the most sinister projects. Arranged to be alone to receive him—sent my daughter to spend the night with her teacher. Put on my velvet gown; the dagger. Finally he rings—nine o'clock. I collect myself: what's the use? DuCamp is right, he is a being apart, perhaps a non-being. I had guessed right instinctively: the solemn decision he had come to discuss was whether or not he should publish something and whether or not he should come to Paris.

The decision is put off for a year. Meanwhile, he will work. He was kind and sweet with me, but as for solicitude, devotion—no hope of that.

He came again Tuesday night. On Wednesday we walked in the Bois. About four o'clock. (Pale sun setting behind Mont Valérien.) He was depressed, out of sorts. He showed me the dregs of his heart —that sediment that life precipitates in all of us. We must keep it down and let it harden, I told him, to prevent its nauseating us— whereas he keeps stirring up its stench. I said profound, tender things that moved him . . . Everyone has his own anguish, believe me (I said); and some have the additional affliction of being poor, etc. etc. If you haven't determined to die, then have the strength to live and not suffer too much nor cause suffering to those who love you. He was affected: "Oh, bonne Louise!" he said. "Si tu savais quelles bénédictions je te donne devant Dieu!" We embraced.

When he left he seemed revived. Yesterday we spent a last evening together, he was more passionate than ever, told me he had never loved me more, that he would come back in three weeks. His ideas about the bliss of being a priest—(career)—the stationary brain. I am eager to read a complete work by him. He said he would send me his manuscripts[1] . . . All in all, the feeling that even as he is, he is preferable to the others;[2] he will stimulate me to work.

Still without funds! I need 500 francs. Where to turn. He is going to write to England for that album.[3] Think of his not having the idea of helping me in this way, delicately, without my knowing about it. Strange! If I had a million, I would give it to him! . . .

---

1. Flaubert sent Louise three of his manuscripts, on all of which she commented in her Memoranda.

Novembre: ". . . weak, mediocre, except for the dramatic part, the woman's story; I wrote him 12 pages about it today."

L'Education Sentimentale (version of 1843-1844): "Admirable pages about art. He is a great artist."

Saint Antoine (earliest version): "I admire his *Saint Antoine* tremendously, and was greatly surprised by it. He is a genius."

2. There had been several "others" during the past two years.

3. Louise had given Flaubert her autograph album, asking him to "try to sell it in England." He had done just that, leaving it there with a friend in the hope a buyer might turn up. Louise would always resent his not taking the hint and quietly buying it himself.

To Louise Colet

[Croisset,] Friday night. [January 16, 1852]

. . .

There are in me, literarily speaking, two distinct persons: one who is infatuated with bombast, lyricism, eagle flights, sonorities of phrase and lofty ideas; and another who digs and burrows into the truth as deeply as he can, who likes to treat a humble fact as respectfully as a big one, who would like to make you feel almost *physically* the things he reproduces. The former likes to laugh, and enjoys the animal side of man.

. . .

[In *Saint Antoine*,] having taken a subject which left me completely free as to lyricism, emotions, excesses of all kinds, I felt in my element, and had only to let myself go. Never will I rediscover such recklessness of style as I indulged in during those eighteen long months. How passionately I carved the beads of my necklace! I forgot only one thing—the string . . .

What seems beautiful to me, what I should like to write, is a book about nothing, a book dependent on nothing external, which would be held together by the internal strength of its style, just as the earth, suspended in the void, depends on nothing external for its support; a book which would have almost no subject, or at least in which the subject would be almost invisible, if such a thing is possible. The finest works are those that contain the least matter; the closer expression comes to thought, the closer language comes to coinciding and merging with it, the finer the result. I believe the future of Art lies in this direction. I see it, as it has developed from its beginnings, growing progressively more ethereal, from Egyptian pylons to Gothic lancets, from the 20,000-line Hindu poems to the effusions of Byron. Form, in becoming more skillful, becomes attenuated; it leaves behind all liturgy, rule, measure; the epic is discarded in favor of the novel, verse in favor of prose; there is no longer any orthodoxy, and form is as free as the will of its creator. This progressive shedding of the burden of tradition can be observed everywhere: governments have gone through similar evolution, from oriental despotisms to the socialisms of the future.

It is for this reason that there are no noble subjects or ignoble subjects; from the standpoint of pure Art one might almost establish the axiom that there is no such thing as subject—style in itself being an absolute manner of seeing things.

I should need an entire book to develop what I want to say. I'll write about all that in my old age, when I'll have nothing better to scribble. Meanwhile, I'm working hard on my novel. Will the great days of *Saint Antoine* return? May the result be different, Lord God! I go slowly: in four days I have done five pages, but so far I find it good fun. It brings me some peace of mind. The weather is ghastly, the river like an ocean; not a cat passes under my windows. I keep a big fire going . . .

[Croisset, February 8, 1852]

So you are decidedly an enthusiast for *Saint Antoine*. At last! I'll at least have had *one!* That's something. Though I don't accept all you say about it, I think my friends were unwilling to see everything that is there. It was lightly judged; I don't say unjustly, but lightly. As for the correction you suggest, we'll talk about it; it is *splendid*. It is repugnant to me to re-enter a sphere of ideas I have moved away from, and that is what I would have to do in order to make corrections in the tone of the rest. To do my saint over would give me a great deal of trouble: long absorption would be needed to enable me to invent something. I don't say I won't try, but it will not be right away.

Now I am in an entirely different world, that of close observation of the most trivial details. My attention is fixed on the mouldy mosses of the soul. It is a long way from the mythological and theological extravagances of *Saint Antoine*. And just as the subject is different, so I am writing in an entirely different way. I do not want my book to contain a *single* subjective reaction, nor a *single* reflection by the author. I think it will be less lofty than *Saint Antoine* as to *ideas* (which I don't think very important), but it will perhaps be stronger and more extraordinary, without seeming so.

But let's not talk any more about *Saint Antoine*. It disturbs me to do so—my mind becomes filled with the subject and I waste time thinking about it. If it is good, so much the better; if bad, too bad. In the former case, what difference does it make *when* it is published? In the latter, since it is destined to perish, why speak of it?

.   .   .

Yes, for me you are a diversion, but one of the best, the most complete kind. You relieve me emotionally, for the thought of you fills me with tenderness, and my heart reposes on this thought, just as when I lie on you. You loved me very much, pauvre chère femme, and now you admire me very much, and you love me still. Thank you for all that. You have given me more than I have given you, for what is noblest in the soul is the enthusiasm it radiates.

Adieu, chère et bonne Louise . . .

[Croisset,] Wednesday night, 1 a.m. [March 3, 1852]

.   .   .

I have just been rereading a number of children's books for my novel.[1] I am half crazy tonight, after all the things I looked at today—from old keepsakes to tales of shipwrecks and buccaneers. I came upon old engravings that I colored when I was seven or eight and hadn't seen since. There are rocks painted in blue, and trees in green. Some of them, a wintry scene showing people stranded on Ice floes, for instance, made me re-experience the terrors I felt when I was a child. I wish I had something to distract me; I'm almost afraid to go to bed. There is a story about Dutch sailors in the icy sea, with bears attacking them in their hut (this picture used to keep me awake), and one about Chinese pirates sacking a temple full of golden idols. Tonight my travels and my childhood memories are all coloring off from each other; they keep following one after the other and spiraling upward in a prodigious flamboyant dance . . .

For two days now I have been trying to enter into the dreams of young girls, and for this have been navigating in the milky oceans of books about castles, and troubadours in white-plumed velvet hats. Remind me to speak to you about this. You can give me exact details I need. So: adieu until soon. If I am not with you by ten o'clock on Monday, it will be for Tuesday. A thousand kisses.

1. *Madame Bovary*, Part I, Chapter 6.

Louise Colet has left a record of the time Flaubert spent with her—and, one evening, with two of her friends—the following week:

> *Memento of Sunday night, March 14, 1852.* How boring everyone has seemed whom I saw today, after the splendid, marvelous day spent with him yesterday! His arrival at half-past two, our reading my poems and those of Mme Valmore, his telling me the outline of his novel *Bovaris* [*sic*]; our embraces, his passion, his tender words; our dinner at the Restaurant Durant, Place de la Madeleine—like our first days, long ago! Our return in a carriage—Place de la Concorde, Champs Elysées as far as the Rond-Point, our reading the *Dialogue de Sylla*,[1] our two hours of bliss. This morning I found his handkerchief in my bed! He left me his Egyptian ring! What a splendid week! Monday, Tuesday, Wednesday—short visits; then Thursday, full fête! Bouilhet's arrival; dinner, the evening, Babinet, the Captain. Gustave took Bouilhet away and they spent the night at the Café Anglais discussing art and feelings; at six o'clock they went to watch the sunrise from the Place de la Concorde; then Bouilhet left. The next day Gustave talked happily with me about that evening—he thanked me, kissed me, he loves me; I think he can no longer do without me, as I cannot do without him. We are at a level where we should understand one another, and we are alone enough to feel that we are necessary to each other . . . For me there is nothing but Gustave and work. I would like to shut the doors of my house and wall myself up in work, like him, but with my daughter this is very difficult. Then the complication of being poor. He never thinks of saying a word to me about that, of using the pretext of the album to oblige me—that seems to me ever more strange. He has all the essential intellectual virtues; he should also have those of the heart. Such as he is, he is superior to anyone I have ever known. I love him; he lifts my spirits. I am going to resume hard work.

FLAUBERT AT AGE TEN
by E. Langlois

FLAUBERT IN ADOLESCENCE
by Delaunay

LOUISE COLET
by Winterhalter

FLAUBERT IN HIS TWENTIES
by Desandré

Maxime DuCamp, "the man who is excessively thin,"
caricature by E. Giraud

FLAUBERT DISSECTING EMMA BOVARY
caricature by Lemot

LOUISE COLET
(anonymous; authenticated by V. Sardou)

Tonight I am sunk in lassitude and depression. The flight of time is heart-rending. Never, never, can one stop the hours; the happy ones speed by, reminding us of our nothingness. Yesterday I was in his arms, today he is far away! And now, two months of absence. To work! To work!

1. Montesquieu's *Dialogue de Sylla et d'Eucrate*.

Flaubert wrote her a few days after his return to Croisset.

To Louise Colet
[Croisset,] Saturday night, 1 A.M. [March 20, 1852]

I did nothing for two days—very bored, very idle, very drowsy. Then I gave my clock a mighty winding, and now my life has resumed the tic-tac of its pendulum. I have gone back to my eternal Greek, and will master it in a few months, because that is what I have sworn to do; and to my novel—which will be finished God knows when. There is nothing at once so frightening and so consoling as having a long task ahead. There are so many obstacles to overcome, the hours one devotes to it are so satisfying. For the moment, I am up to my neck in a young girl's dreams . . . The entire value of my book, if it has any, will consist of my having known how to walk straight ahead on a hair, balanced above the two abysses of lyricism and vulgarity (which I want to fuse in a narrative analysis). When I think of what it can be, I am dazzled. But then, when I reflect that so much beauty has been entrusted to me—to *me*—I am so terrified that I am seized with cramps and long to rush off and hide, no matter where. I have been working like a mule for fifteen long years. All my life I have lived in this maniacal stubbornness, keeping all my other passions locked up in cages and visiting them only now and then, for diversion. Oh, if I ever produce a good book I'll have earned it! Would to God that Buffon's blasphemous words were true.[1] I should certainly be among the foremost.

   .   .   .

1. See p. 66, n.2.

To Louise Colet
[Croisset,] Saturday night, half-past midnight. [March 27, 1852]

   .   .   .

Tonight I finished scribbling the first draft of my young girl's dreams. I'll spend another fortnight sailing on these blue lakes, after which I'll go to a ball and then spend a rainy winter, which I'll end with a pregnancy, and about a third of my book will be done.

   .   .   .

[Croisset,] Saturday night [April 24, 1852]

.   .   .

If I haven't written sooner in reply to your sad, discouraged letter, it's because I have been in a great fit of work. The day before yesterday I went to bed at five in the morning and yesterday at three. Since last Monday I have put everything else aside, and have done nothing all week but sweat over my *Bovary*, disgruntled at making such slow progress. I have now reached my ball, which I will begin Monday. I hope that may go better. Since you last saw me I have written 25 pages in all (25 pages in six weeks). They were rough going. Tomorrow I shall read them to Bouilhet. I have gone over them so much myself, copied them, changed them, shuffled them, that for the time being I see them very confusedly. But I think they will stand up. You speak of your discouragements: if you could see mine! Sometimes I don't understand why my arms don't drop from my body with fatigue, why my brain doesn't melt away. I am leading an austere life, stripped of all external pleasure, and am sustained only by a kind of permanent frenzy, which sometimes makes me weep tears of impotence but never abates. I love my work with a love that is frantic and perverted, as an ascetic loves the hair shirt that scratches his belly.

Sometimes, when I am empty, when words don't come, when I find I haven't written a single sentence after scribbling whole pages, I collapse on my couch and lie there dazed, bogged in a swamp of despair, hating myself and blaming myself for this demented pride that makes me pant after a chimera. A quarter of an hour later, everything has changed; my heart is pounding with joy. Last Wednesday I had to get up and fetch my handkerchief; tears were streaming down my face. I had been moved by my own writing: the emotion I had conceived, the phrase that rendered it, and the satisfaction of having found the phrase—all were causing me the most exquisite pleasure. At least I think that all those elements were present in this emotion, which after all was predominantly a matter of nerves. There exist even higher emotions of this same kind: those which are devoid of the sensory element. These are superior, in moral beauty, to virtue—so independent are they of any personal factor, of any human implication. Occasionally (at great moments of illumination) I have had glimpses, in the glow of an enthusiasm that made me thrill from head to foot, of such a state of mind, superior to life itself, a state in which fame counts for nothing and even happiness is superfluous. If everything around us, instead of permanently conspiring to drown us in a slough of mud, contributed rather to keep our spirits healthy, who can tell whether we might not be able to do for aesthetics what stoicism did for morals? Greek art was not an art; it was the very constitution of an entire people, of an entire race, of the country itself. In Greece the profile of the mountains was different from elsewhere, and they were made of marble, for sculptors, etc.

The time for beauty is over. Mankind may return to it, but it has no use for it at present. The more Art develops, the more scientific it will be, just as science will become artistic. Separated in their early stages, the two will become one again when both reach their culmination. It is beyond the power of human thought today to foresee in what a dazzling intellectual light the works of the future will flower. Meanwhile we are in a shadowy corridor, groping in the dark. We are without a lever; the ground is slipping under our feet; we all lack a basis—literati and scribblers that we are. What's the good of it all? Is our chatter the answer to any need? Between the crowd and ourselves, no bond exists. Alas for the crowd; alas for us, especially. But since there is a reason for everything, and since the fancy of one individual seems to me just as valid as the appetite of a million men, and can occupy an equal place in the world, we must (regardless of material things and of mankind, which disavows us) live for our vocation, climb up our ivory tower, and there, like a bayadere with her perfumes, dwell alone with our dreams. At times I have feelings of great despair and emptiness—doubts that taunt me in the midst of my simplest satisfactions. And yet I would not exchange all this for anything, because my conscience tells me that I am fulfilling my duty, obeying a decree of fate—that I am doing what is Good, that I am in the Right.

.   .   .

. . . I envision a style: a style that would be beautiful, that someone will invent some day, ten years or ten centuries from now, one that would be rhythmic as verse, precise as the language of the sciences, undulant, deep-voiced as a cello, tipped with flame: a style that would pierce your idea like a dagger, and on which your thought would sail easily ahead over a smooth surface, like a skiff before a good tail wind. Prose was born yesterday: you have to keep that in mind. Verse is the form par excellence of ancient literatures. All possible prosodic variations have been discovered; but that is far from being the case with prose.

To Louise Colet

[Croisset,] Saturday night [May 29, 1852]

.   .   .

Since my humor is particularly bad today (and frankly my heart is heavy with it), I'll drain it to the last drop. You talk about your "days of pride," when "people seek you out, flatter you," etc. Come! Those are days of weakness, days you should blush for. I'll tell you which are your days of pride. When you're at home at night in your oldest dressing-gown, with Henriette getting on your nerves, the fire smoking and money worries and other troubles looming large, and you get ready for bed with heavy heart and weary mind; when you walk restlessly up and down your room, or sit staring at the fire, telling yourself you have nothing to back you up, that there isn't a soul you can count on, that you have been abandoned by all; and then—somewhere underneath your dejection as a woman you feel the stirring of the muse, deep within you something begins to sing, to sing something joyous and solemn, like a battle-hymn, a challenge flung in the face of life, a surge of confidence in your own strength, the flaring-up of works to come. The days when *that* happens to you are your days of pride. Don't talk to me about other kinds of pride. Leave those to weaklings—to the great Enault,[1] flattered to be published in the *Revue de Paris*, to DuCamp, enchanted to be received chez Mme Delessert,[2] to all who honor themselves so little that they can be "honored" by others. To have talent, you must be convinced that you possess it; and to keep your conscience pure you must set it above everybody else's. The way to live serenely, in clean, fresh air, is to install yourself atop some pyramid, no matter which, provided it be lofty and have a solid foundation. Ah! It isn't always "amusing" up there, and you are utterly alone; but there is consolation to be taken in spitting from so high a place.

.   .   .

1. Louis Énault (1824-1900), lawyer, journalist, author of novels and travel books.
2. Valentine, née de Laborde, the elegant wife of Gabriel Delessert, ex-Prefect of Police and son of a wealthy banker, presided over a fashionable Paris salon. She had become DuCamp's mistress the year before. One of her earlier lovers had been Prosper Mérimée. DuCamp wrote Flaubert the most precise details of this amatory victory.
Relations between Flaubert and DuCamp were beginning to sour. In letters now lost, DuCamp was again reproaching Flaubert for his way of life and urging him to live in Paris.

To Louise Colet

[Croisset,] Sunday, 11 P.M. [June 13, 1852]

.   .   .

I like clear, sharp sentences, sentences which stand erect, erect while running —almost an impossibility. The ideal of prose has reached an unheard-of degree of difficulty: there must be no more archaisms, clichés; contemporary ideas must be expressed using the appropriate crude terms; everything must be as clear as Voltaire, as abrim with substance as Montaigne, as vigorous as La Bruyère, and always streaming with color.

.   .   .

To Maxime DuCamp

[Croisset, June 26, 1852]

Mon cher ami

It seems to me that where I am concerned you suffer from a tic, or an incurable lack of comprehension that vitiates your judgment. It does not bother me—have no fear of that. I have long since made up my mind on the matters you mention.

I shall merely tell you that all the words you use—"hurry," "this is the moment," "it is high time," "your place will be taken," "become established," "inadmissible"—are for me a vocabulary devoid of sense. It is as though you were talking to an Algonquin. I don't understand.

"Get somewhere"—where? To the position of MM. Murger, Feuillet, Monselet, Arsène Houssaye, Taxile Delord, Hippolyte Lucas, and six dozen others? Thank you.[1]

"To be known" is not my chief concern: that can give complete gratification only to very mediocre vanities. Besides, is there ever any certainty about this? Even the greatest fame leaves one longing for more, and seldom does anyone but a fool die sure of his reputation. Fame, therefore, can no more serve you as a gauge of your own worth than obscurity.

I am aiming at something better—to please myself. Success seems to me a result, not the goal. Now it is this goal that I am trying to attain; and it seems to me that for a long time I have not strayed an inch from the path, whether to make love to the ladies or to take a nap on the grass. If I must chase will-o'-the-wisps I may as well chase the most exalted.

Perish the United States, rather than a principle! May I die like a dog rather than hurry by a single second a sentence that isn't ripe!

I have conceived a manner of writing and a nobility of language that I want to attain. When I think that I have harvested my fruit I shan't refuse to sell it, nor shall I forbid hand-clapping if it is good. In the meantime I do not wish to fleece the public. That's all there is to it.

If by that time it is too late and nobody wants it, too bad. I assure you I wish I had much greater facility, much less toil, and larger profits. But I see no remedy for this.

It may well be that from a commercial point of view there are "favorable moments," a ready market for one kind of article or another, a passing public taste which raises the price of rubber or cotton. Let those who wish to manufacture those things hasten to set up their factories: I well understand that they should. But if your work of art is good, if it is authentic, its echo will be heard, it will find its place—in six months, six years, or after you're gone. What difference does it make?

You tell me that it is only in Paris that one breathes "the breath of life." In my opinion your Parisian "breath of life" often has the odor of rotten teeth. In that Parnassus to which you invite me one is visited more often by a miasma than by divine madness, and you will agree that the laurels gathered there are apt to be somewhat spattered with shit.

I am sorry to see a man like you go one better than the marquise d'Escarbagnas,[2] who thought that "outside Paris there was no salvation for gentlefolk." That judgment seems to me itself provincial, that is, narrow. Humanity exists everywhere, my dear Sir, but in Paris nonsense is more prevalent than elsewhere, I agree.

And there is unquestionably one thing that you do acquire in Paris—and that is impertinence; but at the cost of losing a bit of your lion's mane.

Anyone raised in Paris who nevertheless becomes a man of real consequence was born a demigod. He grew up straitjacketed and with heavy burdens on his head; whereas one must be born destitute of natural originality if solitude, concentration, and persistent work fail in the end to create in you something comparable.

As for deploring so bitterly my "ineffectual" way of life, it is as though you were to reproach a shoemaker for making shoes or a blacksmith for striking his iron or a painter for living in his studio. Since I work every day from one in the afternoon until one in the morning, except from six o'clock to eight, I scarcely see how I can make use of the remaining time. If I led a genuinely provincial or rural existence, devoting myself to dominoes or raising melons, I could understand the reproach. But, if I am becoming stultified, you will have to lay the blame on Lucian, Shakespeare, and writing a novel.

I told you I shall move to Paris when my book is done, and that I shall publish it if I am satisfied with it. My resolution has not changed in the slightest. That is all I can say, and nothing more.

And believe me, my friend, you would do well not to fret about me. As for the waxing and waning of literary quarrels, I don't give a damn. As to whether or not Augier has a success I don't give a double damn. And as to whether Vacquerie and Ponsard so inflate themselves as to occupy the place that should be mine, I don't give a triple damn, and I have no intention of troubling them to give it back to me.[3]

Whereupon je t'embrasse.

1. The present obscurity of these names speaks for itself.
2. The comtesse d'Escarbagnas, in Molière's one-act comedy of that name.
3. Flaubert wrote to Louise Colet that same night:
"Apropos of Ponsard's *Ulysse* [a play], Monsieur DuCamp has written me very bluntly. Once again he deplores—'bitterly' is his word—my not being in Paris, where my place is between Ponsard and Vacquerie. It is only in Paris that one really lives, etc. I lead an 'ineffectual' life. I have sent him a severe, concise reply on this subject. I think he won't return to it, or show my letter to anyone."

To Maxime DuCamp

[Croisset, early July, 1852]

Mon cher bonhomme

It pains me to see you so sensitive. Far from intending to make my letter wounding, I tried to make it the opposite. To the extent that I could, I kept within the limits of the subject, as they say in rhetoric.

But why begin the same old story all over again? Are you forever going to preach diet to a man who insists he is in good health? I find your distress on my account comical, that's all. Do I reproach you for living in Paris, for having published, etc.? Even when you wanted, once, to move into Hamard's house, did I applaud that project? Have I ever advised you to lead a life like mine? Have I ever tried to put leading-strings on your talent, saying "Baby mustn't eat that," "Come here, baby," or "You mustn't dress like that, darling"? To each what suits him. All plants don't require the same cultivation. And besides, if destiny is not with us, you will strive in vain in Paris and I here; if we haven't the vocation, nothing will come of our efforts; and if, on the contrary, we have it, why worry ourselves about other things?

Everything you can tell me, I assure you, I have already told myself, whether it be blame or praise, bad or good. Everything added by you will be merely a repetition of many a monologue I know by heart.

One thing more, however. I deny the existence of the literary renascence which you proclaim. So far, I see no new writer, no original book, no idea that isn't outworn. (Everyone is trailing at the backside of the masters, as in the past.) The same old humanitarian or aesthetic saws are repeated over and over again. I don't deny the good intentions of the young men of today who want to create a new school, but I challenge them to do it. Glad if I find myself mistaken: I'll profit from the discovery.

As for my "post" as man of letters, I gladly relinquish it to you. I abandon the sentry-box—walk away from it with my gun under my arm. I disown the honor of such a title and such a mission. I am simply a bourgeois living retired in the country, occupying myself with literature, and asking nothing of others, neither consideration nor honor nor even esteem. So they will get along without my bright lights. All I ask in return is that they not poison me with the reek of their kitchen-candles. That is why I keep my distance.

As for "helping" them, I will never refuse assistance in any cause. I would plunge into the water to save a good line of verse or a good sentence, no matter by whom. But I don't think that humanity needs me for that, or vice versa.

And correct this idea of yours: that as long as I am alone "I shall never be satisfied with myself." On the contrary, it's when I become satisfied with myself that I'll emerge from this retreat, where no one is spoiling me with encouragement. If you could see deep into my brain, you would think that sentence you wrote a monstrosity.

If your conscience prompted you to give me advice, you did the proper thing, and I thank you for your intention. But I think that you extend that conscience of yours to include others, and that our friend Louis [de Cormenin] and good old Théo [Théophile Gautier], who, you say, share your wish to fashion a little wig to cover my baldness, don't really give a shit about my way of life, or at least never think about it. They may be convinced that "poor Flaubert has gone bald," but "distressed" about it I doubt. Try to be like them, resign yourself to my premature baldness, to my having become an incurable stick-in-the-mud. That mud clings to me like scales: you'll break your nails on it. Save them for lighter work.

You and I are no longer following the same road; we are no longer sailing in the same skiff. May God lead each of us to where each of us wants to go! As for me, I am not seeking port, but the high seas. If I am shipwrecked, I absolve you from mourning[1] . . .

1. The assured, uncompromising tone of these letters from Flaubert to DuCamp strikes us in retrospect as triumphantly right, and even inspired—knowing, as we do, that his confidence in his course was vindicated. It is a kind of assurance that can be compared to the rev-

eling of the Allied officers at the Duchess of Richmond's ball in Brussels on the eve of Waterloo: their defiance seems to us superb—since we know they won the ensuing battle; had they lost, we might condemn their bravado.

Flaubert wrote to Louise: "DuCamp's reply was 'benevolent' and aggrieved. I have sent him another letter from the same barrel (of vinegar) as my first. I think he'll be reeling for some time from such a blow, and that he will now keep quiet. I am a very peaceable fellow up to a certain point—up to a certain frontier (that of my freedom), which no one is to pass. So, since he chose to trespass on my most personal territory, I knocked him back into his corner."

In a Memento dated the previous February 12 (1852), Louise had written: "Oh, what a joy to have Gustave back. I love him more than anyone else: he appreciates me; and then, all those affairs ending with a break are hurtful and humiliating." But Louise continued to court hurt and humiliation. Several of Flaubert's letters written during the summer of 1852 refer to a flirtation on which she now embarked with Alfred de Musset, who, as a member of the French Academy, might help advance her career. The details, confided to her Memoranda and to Flaubert, included her leap, one moonlight night, from a speeding fiacre in which the drunken Musset had become "insulting." Flaubert expressed indignation against Musset, and concern for the bruises Louise suffered on the pavement of the Place de la Concorde, but he pointed out: "Instead of jumping from the cab, you had only to order the driver to stop, and tell him: 'Please throw out M. Alfred de Musset: he is insulting me.' " However, Flaubert's chief reactions to what she told him about Musset were literary ones.

To Louise Colet
[Croisset,] Tuesday [July 6, 1852]

. . .

Convention has it that one doesn't go for a moonlight drive with a man for the purpose of admiring the moon, and milord de Musset is devilishly conventional: his vanity bespeaks bourgeois blood. I do not share your belief that what means most to him are works of art. What means most to him are his own passions. Musset is more poet than artist, and now much more man than poet—and a poor kind of man at that.

Musset has never distinguished between poetry and the feelings it supplements. Music, according to him, was made for serenades, painting for portraits, and poetry for consolations of the heart. When you undertake in that way to put the sun in your breeches, you burn your breeches and piss on the sun. That is what happened to him. Nerves, magnetism: *voilà la poésie!* No: poetry is built upon a more settled foundation. If having sensitive nerves were sufficient qualification for being a poet, I would be better than Shakespeare—or than Homer, who, I take it, was far from nervous. Such confusion is ungodly. I am qualified to speak of such things, for I have been known to hear what people were saying in low voices beyond closed doors thirty paces away; I have watched the viscera quiver beneath my skin; and sometimes, within the space of a single second, I have been aware of a thousand thoughts, images and associations of all kinds illuminating my brain like so many brilliant fireworks. Such displays are excellent subjects for conversation, and people find them quite moving.

Poetry is not a sort of spiritual languor, whereas those nervous susceptibilities are precisely that. Abnormally keen feeling is a weakness. Let me explain.

Had my brain been sounder, I would not have fallen sick from studying law and being bored. I would have turned those circumstances to my advantage, instead of being hurt by them. My unhappiness, instead of remaining confined within my mind, overflowed into the rest of my body and sent it into convulsions. It was a "deviation." There are many children who are upset by music: they are immensely gifted, remember songs after hearing them only once, get overexcited when they play the piano, their hearts pound, they grow thin and pale, fall sick, and their poor nerves, like the nerves of a dog, quiver with pain at the sound of the notes. These children are not future Mozarts. Their vocation has been displaced; the idea has been misdirected to the flesh; once there, it remains sterile, while the flesh perishes; the result is neither genius nor health.

The same in art. Passion does not make verses; and the more personal you are, the weaker. I myself always sinned in that respect: I always put myself into everything I did. Instead of Saint Anthony, for example, *I* was in that book; my *Tentation* was written for myself, not for the reader. The less you feel a thing, *the more capable you are of expressing it as it is* (as it *always* is, in itself, in its universality, freed from all ephemeral contingencies). But one must be able to *make oneself feel it*. This faculty is, simply, genius: the ability to *see*, to have the model posing there before you.

That is why I abhor rhetorical poetry, pompous poetry. To express things that are beyond words, a look is enough. Exhalations of the soul, lyricism, descriptions—I want all that to be in the *style.* Elsewhere, it is a prostitution of art and of feeling itself.

It is that constraint that has always prevented me from paying court to a woman. I would have been afraid, had I uttered the "poetical" phrases that sprang to my lips, that she might say to herself "What a charlatan!"; and the fear of actually being one held me back.

.   .   .

What beautiful weather, Louise; how the sun is shining! All my shutters are closed; I am writing you in the shade. We have had two or three lovely nights. Such moonlight! I am well physically and spiritually, and I hope that my *Bovary* will begin to move ahead again, a little. Heat affects me like brandy: it dries out the fibers and excites me . . .

165

To Louise Colet

I am in the midst of copying and correcting (with much scratching out) all my first part of *Bovary*.[1] My eyes are smarting. I should like to be able to read these one hundred and fifty-eight [manuscript] pages at a single glance and grasp them with all their details in a single thought. A week from Sunday I shall reread the whole thing to Bouilhet; and the next day, or the day after, you will see me. What a bitch of a thing prose is! It is never finished; there is always something to be done over. However, I think it can be given the consistency of verse. A good prose sentence should be like a good line of poetry—*unchangeable*, just as rhythmic, just as sonorous. Such, at least, is my ambition (one thing I am sure of: no one has ever conceived a more perfect type of prose than I; but as to the execution, how many weaknesses, how many weaknesses, oh God!) Nor does it seem to me impossible to give psychological analysis the swiftness, clarity, and impetus of a purely dramatic narrative. This has never been attempted, and it would be beautiful. Have I succeeded a little in this? I have no idea. As of this moment I have no clear opinion about my work.

    . . . In a fortnight, dear Louise, I hope to be beside you (and on top of you). I need that. The end of this part of my novel has left me a little tired. I am becoming aware of it, now that the oven is beginning to cool . . .

1. Ending with Emma Bovary's pregnancy and the move to Yonville. The shortest of the novel's three parts.

To Louise Colet

[Croisset,] Monday night, 1 A.M. [July 26, 1852]

. . .

Yes, it is a strange thing, the relation between one's writing and one's personality. Is there anyone who loves antiquity more than I, anyone more haunted by it, anyone who has made a greater effort to understand it? And yet in my books I am as far as possible from being a man of the antique world. From my appearance one would think I should be a writer of epic, of drama, of brutally factual narrative; whereas actually I feel at home only in analysis—in anatomy, if I may call it such. Fundamentally I am the man of the mists; and it is only by patience and study that I have rid myself of all the whitish fat that clogged my muscles. The books I am most eager to write are precisely those for which I am least endowed. *Bovary*, in this respect, will have been an unprecedented tour de force (a fact of which I alone shall ever be aware): its subject, characters, effects, etc.—all are alien to me. It should make it possible for me to take a great step forward later. Writing this book I am like a man playing the piano with lead balls attached to his knuckles. But once I have mastered my fingering, and find a piece that's to my taste and that I can play with my sleeves rolled up, the result will perhaps be good. In any case, I think I am doing the right thing. What one does is not for oneself, but for others. Art is not interested in the personality of the artist. So much the worse for him if he doesn't like red or green or yellow: all colors are beautiful, and his task is to use them.

Have you read *The Golden Ass?* Try to read it before I come, and we'll talk about it a little. I will bring you Cyrano.[1] There's a fantasist for you, that fellow! And a real one, for a change. I have read the Gautier volume:[2] lamentable! Here and there a fine strophe, but not a single good poem. It is strained, contrived; he has pulled all the old strings. One feels it's a mind that has taken Spanish fly. An inferior kind of erection—the erection of a weakling. Ah, all these great men are old; they are old; they drool. And as for the state they're in, they have done all they could to bring it on themselves.

                    .   .   .

1. Flaubert had written to Louise of Cyrano de Bergerac's *Les Estats et Empires du Soleil* (1662): "I recommend the fighting 'Icicle Animal' and the Kingdom of the Trees. I find it marvelously poetic."
2. *Émaux et Camées.*

According to Louise Colet's Memento of August 15, 1852, Flaubert arrived in Paris for one of his periodic visits on August 3. He saw Louise several times; he and Louis Bouilhet spent an afternoon with her, choosing from among her poems those to be included in a volume. On Monday the 9th, he and Louise dined with a friend. Louise records what happened later that night:

> His seizure at the hotel. My terror. He begs me not to call anyone. His convulsions, his *râle*. He foams at the mouth: my arm is bruised by his clenched hands and nails. In about ten minutes he comes to himself. Vomiting. I assure him the attack lasted only a few seconds, and that there was no foaming. Deep sympathy for him on my part, great tenderness. I return home at one o'clock, exhausted by fatigue and sadness. He spends the entire next day with me, more amorous, more passionate, than ever; tired, but looking very well.

It was apparently Louise's first view of the kind of attack to which Flaubert had been subject since the onset of epilepsy during his New Year vacation from the Law School in 1844. Flaubert sometimes said that during these attacks he was never fully unconscious (see p. 22, n.1).

To Louise Colet

[Croisset,] Wednesday, midnight. [September 1, 1852]

                    .   .   .

You speak about women's sufferings: I am in the midst of them. You will see that I have had to descend deeply into the well of feelings. If my book is good, it will gently caress many a feminine wound: more than one woman will smile as she recognizes herself in it. Oh, I'll be well acquainted with what they go through, poor unsung souls! And with the secret sadness that oozes from them, like the moss on the walls of their provincial backyards[1] . . .

1. The original is an apostrophe à la Chateaubriand: "J'aurai connu vos douleurs, pauvres âmes obscures, humides de mélancolie renfermée, comme vos arrière-cours de province, dont les murs ont de la mousse." Flaubert was "letting himself go" in writing *about* his current work, from which he was rigorously excluding any such effusions.

To Louise Colet
[Croisset,] Saturday, 5 o'clock. [September 4, 1852]

. . .

Since we last saw each other, I have written eight pages of my second part—the topographical description of a village. Now I am going to begin a long inn scene,[1] which worries me considerably. How I wish it were five or six months from now! I would be over the worst—the parts where I find myself least productive: that is, where the idea must be struck most persistently in order to force it to yield a return.

Your letter of this morning makes me sad. Poor darling, how I love you! Why are you hurt by a sentence that was, on the contrary, an expression of the strongest love one human being can offer another? Oh Woman! Woman, be less so! Be so only in bed! Doesn't your body set me afire when I am there? Haven't you seen me stare at you, entranced, while my hands rapturously stroke your skin? The very thought of your body always excites me: and if I don't dream of you more often, it is because one doesn't dream of what one desires.[2] Breathe deeply of the woodland air this week, and look closely at the leaves for what they are: to understand nature we must be calm, like nature itself.

Let nothing distress us: to complain of everything that grieves or annoys us is to complain of the very nature of life. You and I were created to depict it, and nothing more. Let us be religious. As for myself, everything disagreeable that happens to me, whether large or small, makes me hold the faster to my one great concern. I grasp it tightly, with both hands, and close both eyes. I keep calling for Grace until it comes. God is merciful to the meek, and the sun always shines for the strong-hearted, who survey the world from the top of their mountain.

I am turning toward a kind of aesthetic mysticism (if those two words can go together), and I wish it were more intense. When you are given no encouragement by others, when the outside world disgusts, weakens, corrupts, and stupefies you, so-called "decent" and "sensitive" people are forced to seek somewhere within themselves a more suitable place to live. If society continues on its present path, I think we shall once again see mystics, such as existed in all dark ages. Unable to expand, the soul will concentrate on itself. The time is not far off when there will be a resurgence of melancholy fantasies, the expectation of a Messiah, beliefs in the approaching end of the world. But lacking any theological foundation, what will be the basis of this fervor? (It will certainly be ignorant concerning itself.) Some will seek it in the flesh, others in the ancient religions, still others in Art; and Mankind, like the Jews in the desert, will adore all kinds of idols. People like us were born a little too soon. Twenty-five years from now, the point of intersection of all these quests will provide superb subjects for a master. Then prose—prose especially, the younger form —may serve to orchestrate a symphony with an extraordinarily rich human content. We may once again have books like the *Satyricon* and *The Golden Ass*, but bubbling over with intellect as those bubble over with sensuality.

This is the very thing that the socialists of the world, with their incessant materialistic preaching, refuse to see. They have denied suffering; they have blasphemed three-quarters of modern poetry, the blood of Christ that stirs within us. Nothing will extirpate suffering, nothing will eliminate it. Our purpose is not to dry it up, but to create outlets for it. If the sense of man's imperfection, of the meaninglessness of life, were to perish—as would follow from their premise—we would be more stupid than birds, who at least perch on trees. The human soul is at present sleeping, drunk with the words it has heard; but some day it will awake in a frenzy and give itself over to a freedman's pleasures; for there will no longer be anything to restrain it, neither government, nor religion, nor any formula. Republicans of every stripe seem to me the most primitive pedagogues in the world—they dream of organization, legislation, a society like that of a monastery. I believe, on the contrary, that all rules are on their way out, that barriers are crumbling, that all is being reduced to the same level. This great confusion will perhaps bring freedom in its train. At least Art, which is always in the van, has followed this course. What poetics survives today? Plastic form itself is becoming increasingly impossible as our languages become increasingly limited and precise, and our ideas vague, confused, and elusive. All we can do, then, is to use our brains; we must tighten the frayed strings of our guitars, and above all we must become virtuosos, since in the present age naiveté is a chimera. Moreover, the picturesque has almost disappeared. Even so, poetry will not die; but what will be its fate in the future? I cannot conceive. Who can tell? Beauty will perhaps become a feeling useless to mankind, and Art something halfway between algebra and music.

Since I cannot see tomorrow, I wish I might have seen yesterday. Why didn't I at least live under Louis XIV, with a great wig, smooth stockings, and the company of M. Descartes! Why didn't I live at the time of Ronsard! Or Nero! How I would have talked with the Greek rhetors! How I would have traveled in great chariots over the Roman roads, and slept at night in the hostelries with the itinerant priests of Cybele! Why, above all, didn't I live at the time of Pericles, to sup with violet-crowned Aspasia and sing verses in white marble halls? Ah! All that is past: it is a dream, never to return. I certainly did live in all those places in some former existence. I am sure that in the Roman Empire I was the leader of a troupe of strolling players, one of those who went to Sicily to buy women to make actresses of them, and who were at once professor, pimp, and performer. They are great characters, those rogues in Plautus's plays, and when I read about them they seem to evoke memories in me. Have you occasionally experienced something like that—the shiver of history?

Adieu, je t'embrasse, tout à toi, partout.

1. *Madame Bovary*, Part II, Chapters 1 and 2.
2. Flaubert had apparently told Louise that he seldom dreamed about her.

To Louise Colet
[Croisset,] Sunday, 11 p.m. [September 19, 1852]

. . .

What trouble my *Bovary* is giving me! Still, I am beginning to see my way a little. Never in my life have I written anything more difficult than what I am doing now—trivial dialogue. This inn scene will perhaps take me three months, I can't tell. There are moments when I want to weep, I feel so powerless. But I'll die rather than botch it. I have to portray, simultaneously and in the same conversation, five or six characters (who speak), several others (who are spoken about), the setting itself, and the entire town, giving physical descriptions of people and objects; and in the midst of all that I have to show a man and a woman who are beginning (through a similarity in tastes) to be a little taken with each other. If only I had space! But the whole thing has to move quickly without being dry, and it requires a certain development without being spread thin; and many details which would be more striking here I have to keep in reserve for use later. I am going to put everything down quickly, proceeding by a series of sketches of the ensemble. By repeated revision I can perhaps pull it together. The language itself is a great stumbling-block. My characters are completely commonplace, but they have to speak in a literary style, and the politeness of the language takes away so much picturesqueness from their way of expressing themselves!

Once again, poor dear Louise, you talk to me about fame, the future, applause. That old dream no longer obsesses me, because it did so too much in the past. I am not showing false modesty here: no, I believe in nothing. I doubt everything, and why shouldn't I? I am quite resigned to working all my life like a nigger with no hope whatever of reward. It is a sore that I keep scratching, that's all. I have more books in my head than I'll have time to write between now and the day of my death, especially considering my pace. I'll never lack occupation (and that's the important thing) . . . And then, even admitting the hypothesis of success, what certainty can we derive from it? Unless one is a moron, one always dies unsure of one's own value and that of one's works. Virgil himself, as he lay dying, wanted the Aeneid burned. When you compare yourself to what surrounds you, you find yourself admirable; but when you lift your eyes, toward the masters, toward the absolute, toward your dream, how you despise yourself! These last days I have been reading something good, the life of Carême, the cook.[1] Some association of ideas led me to think of that famous inventor of sauces, and I looked up his name in the *Biographie universelle*. His is a magnificent example of the life of an enthusiastic artist: it would be the envy of more than one poet. Here is what he said when he was urged not to work so hard, to take care of his health: "Coal gas kills, but what of it? Shorter life and longer fame." And in one of his books, admitting that he was a glutton: ". . . but I had such a sense of my vocation that I didn't stop eating." That "didn't stop eating" is marvelous, coming from a man for whom eating was his art . . .

1. Marie-Antoine Carême (1784-1833), "chef de bouche" of Talleyrand and of the emperors of Russia and Austria.

To Louise Colet

[Croisset,] Saturday night [September 25, 1852]

. . .

What is characteristic of great geniuses is their faculty of generalizing and their power of creation. They create types, each of which epitomizes a class, and by doing so they enrich the consciousness of mankind. Don't we believe that Don Quixote is as real as Caesar? Shakespeare is formidable in this regard. He was not a man, he was a continent; he contained whole crowds of great men, entire landscapes. Writers like him do not worry about *style:* they are powerful in spite of all their faults and because of them. When it comes to us, the little men, our value depends on finished execution. Hugo, in this century, will rout all his contemporaries, even though he is full of bad things: but what lung-power! What inspiration! I will risk a proposition here that I wouldn't dare utter to anyone else: that very great men often write very badly—and bravo for them. To discover the art of form, one should go not to them but to writers of the second class (Horace, La Bruyère). It is essential to memorize the masters, idolize them, try to think like them, and then put them aside once and for all. To learn technique, it is more profitable to go to the erudite, the skillful. Adieu—I have been constantly interrupted while writing the above—it must lack common sense . . .

To Louise Colet

[Croisset,] Saturday, 1 A.M. [October 9, 1852]

. . .

Things have been going well for two or three days. I am doing a conversation between a young man and a young woman about literature, the sea, the mountains, music—all the poetical subjects.[1] It is something that could be taken seriously, and yet I fully intend it as grotesque. This will be the first time, I think, that a book makes fun of its leading lady and its leading man.

The irony does not detract from the pathetic aspect, but rather intensifies it. In my third part, which will be full of farcical things, I want my readers to weep.

·　　·　　·

1. *Madame Bovary*, Part II, Chapter 2.

To Louise Colet

[Croisset,] Tuesday night. [October 26, 1852]

·　　·　　·

On Sunday I read to Bouilhet the twenty-seven pages (just about finished) that are the work of two long months. He didn't dislike them at all, and that means much, as I was afraid they might be execrable. I was no longer able to see them clearly, and then the material lent itself so little to any stylistic effect. Perhaps it is an achievement to have made this part passable. Now I am coming to things that will be more entertaining to do. Forty or fifty pages more and I'll reach the climax of adultery. That's when all of us will have a romp, including my little lady.

·　　·　　·

To Louise Colet

[Croisset,] Monday night. [November 22, 1852]

·　　·　　·

I am going to read *Uncle Tom* in English. I admit I'm prejudiced against it. Literary merit alone doesn't bring that kind of success. A writer can go far if he combines a certain talent for dramatization and a facility for speaking everybody's language, with the art of exploiting the passions of the day, the concerns of the moment. Do you know what books sell best year after year? *Faublas* and *L'Amour conjugal*,[1] two inept productions. If Tacitus were to return to earth he would sell less well than M. Thiers. The public respects monuments, but has little love for them. They are given conventional admiration and no more. The bourgeoisie (which today comprises all of mankind, including the "people") has the same attitude toward the classics as toward religion: it knows that they exist, would be sorry if they didn't, realizes that they serve some vague purpose, but makes no use of them and finds them very boring.

I have had *La Chartreuse de Parme* brought to me from the lending library and shall read it carefully. I know *Le Rouge et le noir*, which I find badly written and incomprehensible as regards characters and intentions. I am quite aware that people of taste are not of my opinion; but people of taste are a queer caste: they have little saints of their own whom nobody knows. It was our friend Sainte-Beuve who launched this fashion. People swoon with admiration before parlor wits, before talents whose only recommendation is that they are obscure. As for Beyle, after reading *Le Rouge et le noir* I failed completely to understand Balzac's enthusiasm for such a writer. Speaking of reading, I read Rabelais and *Don Quixote* every Sunday with Bouilhet and never tire of them. What overwhelming books! The more one contemplates them the bigger they grow, like the pyramids, and in the end they almost frighten you. What is prodigious about *Don Quixote* is the absence of art, and that perpetual fusion of illusion and reality which makes the book so comic and so poetic. All others are such dwarfs beside it! How small one feels, oh Lord, how small one feels!

I am working quite well, I mean with plenty of energy, but it is difficult to give adequate expression to something one has never felt: long preparations are necessary, and one must devilishly rack one's brains to achieve one's aim without going too far. The gradual development of my character's emotional life is giving me a lot of trouble; and everything in this novel depends on it: for in my opinion ideas can be as entertaining as actions, but in order to be so they must flow one from the other like a series of cascades, carrying the reader along amid the throbbing of sentences and the seething of metaphors. When we next see each other, I shall have made a great step ahead: I'll be plunged into love, the core of my subject, and the fate of my book will be decided; but I think that just now I'm in a dangerous pass.

. . .

1. *Tableau de l'amour conjugal,* by Dr. Nicolas Venette (1686) and *Amours du Chevalier Faublas,* by J. B. Louvet de Couvray (one of the three parts of his novel, *Les Aventures du Chevalier Faublas,* 1787-1789).

To Louise Colet

[Croisset,] Thursday, 1 p.m. [December 9, 1852]

. . .

The author's comments [in *Uncle Tom's Cabin*] irritated me continually. Does one have to make observations about slavery? Depict it: that's enough. That is what has always seemed powerful to me in *Le Dernier jour d'un condamné.*[1] No observations concerning the death penalty (it is true that the preface spoils the book, if that book could be spoiled). Look at *The Merchant of Venice* and see whether anyone declaims against usury. But the dramatic form has that virtue—of eliminating the author. Balzac was not free of this defect: he is legitimist, Catholic, aristocrat. An author in his book must be like God in the universe, present everywhere and visible nowhere. Art being a second Nature, the creator of that Nature must behave similarly. In all its atoms, in all its aspects, let there be sensed a hidden, infinite impassivity. The effect for the spectator must be a kind of amazement. "How is all that done?" one must ask; and one must feel overwhelmed without knowing why. Greek art followed that principle, and to achieve its effects more quickly it chose characters in exceptional social conditions—kings, gods, demigods. You were not encouraged to identify with the dramatis personae: the *divine* was the dramatist's goal.

Adieu. It is late. Too bad! I was in a mood to chat. A thousand and a thousand kisses. And—my God!—see that *it* happens![2]

1. By Victor Hugo.
2. See the following letter.

To Louise Colet

[Croisset,] Saturday, 1 o'clock [December 11, 1852]

I begin by devouring you with kisses, I am so happy. Your letter of this morning lifted a terrible weight from my heart. It was high time. Yesterday I could not work all day. Every time I moved (literally), my brain throbbed in my skull, and I had to go to bed at 11 o'clock. I was feverish and completely despondent. For these past three weeks I have suffered from horrible apprehensions: I never stopped thinking of you, but in a way that was scarcely pleasant. Yes, the thought tortured me; once or twice I actually saw stars before my eyes—on Thursday, among other days. The idea of bringing someone into this world fills me with *horror*. I would curse myself if I were to become a father. A son! Oh, no, no, no! May my flesh perish utterly! May I never transmit to anyone the boredom and the ignominies of existence! My soul rebelled against this hypothesis; and then, and then . . . Well, now there is nothing to fear, thank God. Blessed be the Redcoats.

I also had a superstitious idea: tomorrow I shall be 31. I shall have passed that fatal age of thirty, which *ranks* a man. That is the age at which you assume your future shape, take your place in society, embrace a profession. There are few people who do not become bourgeois at 30. Paternity would have relegated me to the ordinary condition of life. My innocence in relation to the world would have been destroyed, and that would have cast me into the pit of common miseries. Well, today I am overflowing with serenity. I feel calm and radiant. My entire youth has passed unmarred, unsapped by weakness. From my childhood to this very hour it has followed a single straight line. And since I have sacrificed nothing to the passions, have never said "Youth must end," youth will not end. I am still full of freshness; I am like a springtime. I have a great, flowing river in me, something that keeps churning and never ceases. My style and my muscles are still supple; and if the hair is gone from my brow, I think there is still many a plume in my mane. One more year, poor dear Louise, ma bonne femme aimée, and we will spend long days together.

Why did you wish that bond? Oh, no! You do not have to reassume woman's lot, to be loved by me. On the contrary, I love you because you have so little femininity—you lack woman's social hypocrisy, her weakness of intellect. Don't you feel that between us there is an attachment superior to that of the flesh? Independent, even, of love's tenderness? Do not spoil any of this for me. One is always punished if one strays from one's true road. So let us remain in our own private path: that separate path which is for us alone. The less one's feelings have in common with those of the world, the less they partake of the world's fragility. Time will not affect my love, because it is not a love "such as love should be." And I am going to say something that will seem strange to you. It does not seem to me that you are my mistress. Never does that banal term enter my mind when I think of you. In me you have a special place, which has never been occupied by anyone. If you were absent, it would remain empty; and yet my flesh loves your flesh, and when I see myself naked it seems to me that every pore of my skin is yearning for you; and what rapture there is in our embraces!

I am not talking literature; I am only now recovering from my long worry, and my heart is expanding. I breathe: it is a beautiful day, the sun sparkles on the river, at this moment a brig is passing in full sail; my window is open and my fire burning. Adieu, I love you more than ever, I stifle you with kisses, for my birthday.

Adieu, chère amour, mille tendresses. Encore à toi.

To Louise Colet

[Croisset,] Thursday night, 1 A.M. [December 16, 1852]

What is wrong with your health, pauvre chérie? What are all these vomitings, stomach pains, etc.? I am sure that you came close to doing something foolish. I should like to hear that you were well again—completely. No matter: I'll not hide from you that the landing of the Redcoats was a tremendous relief for me. May the god of coitus grant that I never again go through such agony . . . But the joy I subsequently felt has been profitable for me, I think.[1]

.   .   .

Have you noticed that I'm becoming a moralist? Is it a sign of old age? But I am certainly turning toward high comedy. Sometimes I have an itch to lash out at my fellow humans, and some day I will, ten years from now,[2] in a long novel with wide range. Meanwhile an old idea has come back to me—that of my *Dictionary of Accepted Opinions*[3] (do you know what it is?) The preface, especially, greatly excites me, and in the way I conceive it (it would be a book in itself) no law could touch me although I would attack everything.[4] It would be the historical glorification of everything generally approved. I would demonstrate that majorities have always been right, minorities always wrong. I would immolate the great men on the altars of the fools, deliver the martyrs to the executioners—and that in a style pushed to the extreme, with all possible fireworks. For example: I would show that in literature, mediocrity, being within the reach of everyone, is alone legitimate, and that consequently every kind of originality must be denounced as dangerous, ridiculous, etc. I would declare that this apologia for human vulgarity in all its aspects—and it would be raucous and ironic from beginning to end, full of quotations, proofs (which would prove the opposite), frightening texts (easily found)—was aimed at doing away, once and for all, with all eccentricities, whatever they might be. That would lead to the modern democratic idea of equality, using Fourier's remark that "great men won't be needed"; and it is for this purpose, I would say, that the book is written. It would include, in alphabetical order and covering all possible subjects, "everything one should say if one is to be considered a decent and likeable member of society."

For example:

Artists: never interested in money.
Crayfish: the female of the lobster.
France: must be ruled with an iron hand.
Bossuet: "the eagle of Meaux".
Fénélon: "the swan of Cambrai."
Negresses: hotter than white women.
Erection: must be said only when speaking of monuments, etc.

I think that as a whole it would deliver a strong punch. There would not be a single word invented by me in the book. If properly done, anyone who read it would never dare open his mouth again, for fear of spontaneously uttering one of its pronouncements. Furthermore, certain items could be gone into in quite splendid detail, for example MAN, WOMAN, FRIEND, POLITICS, MORES, JUDGE. And a concisely written list of types could be included, to show not only what one should *say*, but what one should *seem to be*.

· · ·

Poetry has to be disguised, in France: the French hate it, and of all our writers perhaps only Ronsard was quite simply a poet, what a poet was in antiquity and is today in other countries.

Perhaps all plastic forms have been done and redone: that was the work of the earlier masters. What remains to us is the exterior[5] of man—more complex, but far less subject to the conditions of "form." And so I think that the novel has only just been born: it awaits its Homer. What a man Balzac would have been, had he known how to write! But that was the only thing he lacked. An artist, after all, would not have done so much, would not have had that amplitude.

· · ·

Just now a frightful wind is blowing; the trees and the river are roaring. This evening I was writing a summer scene, with midges, sun on the grass, etc.[6] (The greater the contrast between what I am writing and my actual surroundings, the better I see my subject.) The high wind has been fascinating me all evening—it is both soothing and distracting. At ten o'clock, when my mother came into my study to say good-night, my nerves were so taut that I frightened her by giving a great shout of terror. This set my heart pounding, and it took me a quarter of an hour to calm down. Such is my absorption when I am working . . . What a poor machine is ours! And all that because a little man was shaping a sentence!

· · ·

176

1. Meaning, no doubt, "good for my work"?

2. Not ten years later, but eleven, Flaubert would keep his word and begin the definitive version of *L'Education Sentimentale*.

3. See p. 127, and p. 128, n.3.

4. This is Flaubert's first reference to the heavy press censorship that marked the early Second Empire—a censorship from which he himself was to suffer with *Madame Bovary*.

Soon, on February 23, 1853, he was to write to Louise from Croisset:

"We have here, since Monday, an old lady, a friend of my mother's (wife of a former consul in the Orient), with her daughter. Her son, who was one of my school friends, is at this moment in Sainte-Pélagie [a place of detention for political prisoners, especially dissenting writers] for a year (plus 500 francs fine) for distributing copies of *Napoléon le Petit* [by the exiled Victor Hugo]. Watch out! No one has news of him."

As we shall see, Flaubert and Louise were themselves in touch with Hugo. Flaubert's imprisoned school friend was Emmanuel Vasse, the student of Cretan history (see p. 23). He had borrowed books for Flaubert from the Bibliothèque Royale in Paris (today the Bibliothèque Nationale) when Flaubert was reading for his oriental tale and *Saint Antoine*.

5. Flaubert wrote "exterior" here. Some scholars have believed he intended the opposite.

6. *Madame Bovary*, Part II, Chapter 3.

To Louise Colet

[Croisset,] Monday, 5 o'clock. [December 27, 1852]

At this moment I am as though in the grip of a ghastly terror, and if I am writing you it is perhaps to avoid being alone with myself, the way one lights one's lamp at night when one is afraid. I don't know whether you are going to understand me, but it is very strange. Have you read a book by Balzac called *Louis Lambert?* I finished it five minutes ago: I am thunderstruck by it. It is the story of a man who goes mad from thinking about intangible things. I cannot shake it off: it has grappled itself on to me in a thousand places. This Lambert is, in all but a few particulars, my poor Alfred. I have found some of *our* sentences (from years ago) almost word for word: the conversations between the two school friends are our conversations, or analogous. There is a story about a manuscript stolen by the two of them, and remarks made by the schoolmaster—*all of which happened to me*, etc. etc. Do you remember my speaking to you about a metaphysical novel (in outline) in which a man thinks himself into hallucinations that culminate in the ghost of his friend appearing to him and drawing the (ideal, absolute) conclusion from his (worldly, tangible) premises? Well, this idea is suggested in *Louis Lambert:* the entire novel is the preface to it. At the end, the hero wants to castrate himself, in a kind of mystical madness. During my wretchedness in Paris, when I was nineteen, I had that same wish. I will show you where I stopped in front of a shop in the rue Vivienne one night, intensely, imperiously gripped by this idea, and later I spent two entire years without touching a woman. (Last year, when I told you about my idea of entering a monastery,[1] it was my old leaven rising in me again.) There comes a moment when one needs to make oneself suffer, needs to loathe one's flesh, to fling mud in its face, so hideous does it seem. Without my love of form, I would perhaps have been a great mystic. Add to that my nervous attacks, which merely mark moments when, without my being able to do anything about it, ideas and images begin to fade. At such moments the psychic element is leaping above and beyond me, and self-awareness is disappearing, along with all sensation of life. I am sure I know what dying is. I have often distinctly felt my soul was escaping, as one feels blood flowing from the incision when one is being bled. This devilish book made me dream of Alfred all night.

. . .

Another case of similarity: my mother showed me a scene in Balzac's *Un Médecin de campagne* (she discovered it yesterday) *exactly the same* as one in my *Bovary:* a visit to a wet nurse. (I had never read that book, any more than I had *Louis Lambert.*) There are *the same details,* the same effects, the same meaning. One would think I had copied it, if it weren't that my page is infinitely better written, no boasting intended. If DuCamp knew all this, he would say I am comparing myself to Balzac, as [he said] I did to Goethe.[2] In the past, I was annoyed by people who thought I looked like this person or that; now it is worse, it is my soul. I find it everywhere: everything reminds me of it. Why, I wonder?

Louis Lambert begins, like *Bovary,* with a first day at school, and there is one sentence *the same* as one of mine . . .

I think that *Bovary* will move along, but I am bothered by my tendency to metaphor, decidedly excessive. I am devoured by comparisons as one is by lice, and I spend my time doing nothing but squashing them: my sentences swarm with them.

Adieu . . .

1. Compare Louise Colet's Memento on p. 153: "the bliss of being a priest."
2. Probably in connection with *Saint Antoine.*

Flaubert's next letter to Louise, dated December 29, 1852, was devoted almost entirely to suggestions concerning a long poem she was writing, entitled *La Paysanne.* It is a letter of minimal interest to anyone else, but it was of a kind to delight Louise, and it was probably what inspired part of her Memento of Saturday, January 1, 1853: "This past year has been the sweetest and best in my life. Gustave has truly loved me, and through him I have tasted art and love more fully than ever before . . . What a good letter he wrote me yesterday morning; I wept with joy on reading it."

A few months later, in her Memento of April 7, Louise was writing differently: "In his letters, Gustave never speaks to me of anything except art—or himself."

But this is somewhat misleading. For the "art" to which many of Flaubert's letters refer during these months was the "art" which he felt would improve the poems she sent him for comment—comment which she demanded, resented, resisted, and often repudiated. Her next poem after *La Paysanne* was *L'Acro-*

pole d'Athènes, that having beeen announced by the Académie Française as the subject for its 1853 prize contest. (The contest was to be postponed for a year, and Louise would win it.) These letters about Louise's work are omitted from the present volume.

To Louise Colet

[Croisset,] Wednesday, 1 a.m. [January 12, 1853]

I am hideously worried, mortally depressed. My accursed *Bovary* is torturing me and driving me mad. Last Sunday Bouilhet raised some objections to one of my characters and to the plan. I can do nothing about it: though there is some truth in what he says, I feel the opposite is true also. Ah, I am very tired and very discouraged! You call me Master. What a wretched Master!

No—perhaps the whole thing hasn't had enough spadework, for distinctions between thought and style are a sophism. Everything depends on the conception. So much the worse! I am going to push on, and as fast as I can, in order to have a complete picture. There are moments when all this makes me want to croak. Ah! I'll be well acquainted with them, the agonies of Art![1]

. . .

1. Such, at least, would seem to be the least inadequate translation of Flaubert's famous phrase "les affres de l'Art."

To Louise Colet

[Croisset,] Saturday night, 3 o'clock. [January 15, 1853]

. . .

Last week I spent *five days writing one page*, and I dropped everything else for it—my Greek, my English; I gave myself up to it entirely. What worries me in my book is the element of *entertainment*. That side is weak; there is not enough action. I maintain, however, that *ideas* are action. It is more difficult to hold the reader's interest with them, I know, but if the style is right it can be done. I now have fifty pages in a row without a single event. It is an uninterrupted portrayal of a bourgeois existence and of a love that remains inactive[1] —a love all the more difficult to depict because it is both timid and deep, but alas! lacking in inner turbulence, because my gentleman is of a sober temperament. I had something similar in the first part: the husband loves his wife somewhat after the same fashion as her lover. Here are two mediocrities in the same milieu, and I must differentiate between them. If I bring it off, it will be a great achievement, I think, for it will be like painting in monotone without contrasts—not easy. But I fear all these subtleties will be wearisome, and that the reader will long for more movement. Still, one must be loyal to one's concept. If I tried to insert action, I would be following a rule, and would spoil everything. One must sing with one's own voice, and mine will never be dra-

179

matic or attractive. Besides, I am convinced that everything is a question of style, or rather of form, of presentation.

A bit of news: our young friend DuCamp has been promoted to *officier* in the Légion d'Honneur! How pleased he must be! When he compares himself with me and surveys the distance he has traveled since leaving me, he must certainly think that I am very far behind him indeed, and that he has done very well for himself (externally). You'll see: he'll end by getting himself a good post and turning his back on literature.[2] He makes no distinctions: women, decorations, art, fashion—for him all these things are on the same level, and whatever advances his career is important. These are fine times we are living in (curious symbolisms, as old Michelet would say)—we decorate photographers and exile poets;[3] how many good pictures do you suppose a painter would have to produce to be made an *officier?* Of all the writers in the Légion d'Honneur only one has the rank of *commandeur*, and that is Monsieur Scribe! How immensely ironic it all is! And how honors swarm where there is no honor!

1. Part II, Chapter 3 et seq. Léon and Emma.
2. Maxime DuCamp never held a post (on one occasion he was an unsuccessful candidate for the Senate); he always remained what we would call today a "free-lance writer." From the point of view of a writer of genius, such as Flaubert, he did "turn his back on literature," in the sense that his later work consisted chiefly of factual books on social questions—Parisian life, the Commune, and so on.
3. The reference is to Victor Hugo, in exile on Jersey, and to DuCamp, whose book of Egyptian photographs had been published in splendid format. The photographs are excellent, and the collection is prized today as an example of early photography and as a record of Egyptian monuments as they were at the time. But the contrast made by Flaubert can scarcely be faulted.

To Louise Colet

[Croisset,] Sunday night, 1.30 a.m. [February 27, 1853]

.   .   .

We must be on our guard against that feverish state called inspiration, which is often a matter of nerves rather than muscle. At this very moment, for example, I am keyed up to a high pitch—my brow is burning, sentences keep rushing into my head; for the past two hours I have been wanting to write to you and haven't been able to wrench myself away from work for an instant. Instead of one idea I have six, and where the most simple exposition is called for I am tempted to elaborate. I am sure I could keep going until tomorrow noon without fatigue. But I know these masked balls of the imagination! You come away from them exhausted and depressed, having seen only falsity and spouted nonsense. Everything should be done coldly, with poise.

.   .   .

To Louise Colet

[Croisset,] Easter Sunday, 4 o'clock. [March 27, 1853]

.   .   .

The impression my travel notes make on you has inspired me with some strange reflections, dear Muse, concerning a man's heart and a woman's. Decidedly, they are not the same, whatever people may say.

We, on our side, are frank, if not delicate. We are wrong, however, for our frankness is a harshness. If I had omitted my impressions of women, nothing would have wounded you! Women, on the other hand, keep everything hidden. Their confidences are never the whole story. The most they do is let you guess; and when they tell you things, everything is so covered over with sauce that the meat of the matter disappears. But if we admit to two or three mediocre lays, in which our heart wasn't even involved, just listen to their moans! Strange! Strange! I rack my brain trying to understand it all, and yet I have thought about it much of my life.

.   .   .

As for Kuchuk Hanem,[1] ah! Set your mind at rest, and at the same time correct your ideas about the Orient. You may be sure that she felt nothing at all: emotionally, I guarantee; and even physically, I strongly suspect. She found us very good *cawadjas* (seigneurs), because we left a goodly number of piastres behind, that's all. Bouilhet's piece is very fine, but it is poetry and nothing else. The oriental woman is no more than a machine: she makes no distinction between one man and another. Smoking, going to the baths, painting her eyelids and drinking coffee—such is the circle of occupations within which her existence is confined. As for physical pleasure, it must be very slight, since the famous button, the seat thereof, is sliced off at an early age. What makes this woman, in a sense, so poetic, is that she relapses into the state of nature.

. . . You tell me that Kuchuk's bedbugs degrade her in your eyes; for me they were the most enchanting touch of all. Their nauseating odor mingled with the scent of her skin, which was dripping with sandalwood oil. I want a bitter undertaste in everything—always a jeer in the midst of our triumphs, desolation in the very midst of enthusiasm.

. . . To go back to Kuchuk. You and I are thinking of her, but she is certainly not thinking of us. We are weaving an aesthetic around her, whereas this particular very interesting tourist who was vouchsafed the honors of her couch has vanished from her memory completely, like many others. Ah! Travel makes one modest: one sees what a tiny place one occupies in the world.

.   .   .

As for me, the more I realize the difficulties of writing, the more daring I become; this is what keeps me from pedantry, into which I would otherwise doubtless fall. I have plans for writing that will keep me busy till the end of my life, and though I sometimes have bitter moments that make me almost scream with rage (so acutely do I feel my own impotence and weakness), I have others when I can scarcely contain myself for joy. Something deep and ultra-voluptuous gushes out of me, like an ejaculation of the soul. I feel transported, drunk with my own thought, as though a hot gust of perfume were being wafted to me through some inner conduit. I shall never go very far: I know my limitations. But the goal I have set for myself will be achieved by others: thanks to me, someone more talented, more instinctive, will be set on the right path. It is perhaps absurd to want to give prose the rhythm of verse (keeping it distinctly prose, however), and to write of ordinary life as one writes history or epic (but without falsifying the subject). I often wonder about this. But on the other hand it is perhaps a great experiment, and very original. I know where I fail. (Ah, if only I were fifteen!) No matter: I shall always be given some credit for my stubbornness. And then, who can tell? Some day I may find a good motif, a melody completely suited to my voice, neither too high nor too low. In any case, I shall have lived nobly and often delightfully.

There is a saying by La Bruyère that serves me as a guide: "A good author likes to think that he writes reasonably."[2] That is what I ask—to write reasonably; and it's asking a good deal. Still, one thing is depressing, and that is to see how easily the great men achieve their effects by means extraneous to Art. What is more badly put together than much of Rabelais, Cervantes, Molière and Hugo? But such quick punches! Such power in a single word! We have to pile up a mass of little pebbles to build our pyramids; theirs, a hundred times greater, are hewn in monoliths. But to seek to imitate the methods of those geniuses would be fatal. They are great for the very reason that they have no methods.

. . .

1. Flaubert had allowed Louise to see his travel notes, which he had transcribed and expanded from the jottings in the notebooks he had carried with him. Bouilhet's poem, "Kuchiuk-Hanem: Souvenir," dedicated to Flaubert, was based on Flaubert's letter of March 13, 1850 (see pp. 161-162). Bouilhet depicted the almeh as brooding, "sad as a widow," after her visitors' departure.
2. La Bruyère's words: "Un esprit médiocre croit écrire divinement, un bon esprit croit écrire raisonnablement."

To Louise Colet

[Croisset,] Thursday, half past four [March 31, 1853]

I am just back from Rouen, where I went to have a tooth pulled. It was not pulled: my dentist urged me to wait. However, I think that very soon I shall indeed have to part with one of my dominoes. I am aging: there go the teeth, and soon I shall be quite hairless. Well, provided one keeps one's brain: that's the main thing. How annihilation stalks us! No sooner are we born than putrefaction sets in, and life is nothing but a long battle it wages against us, ever more triumphantly until the end—death—when its reign becomes absolute. There were only two or three years in my life (approximately from seventeen to nineteen) when I was *entire*. I was splendid—I can say it now: sufficiently so to attract the attention of an entire theatre audience—it was in Rouen, the first night of *Ruy Blas.* But since then I have deteriorated shockingly. There are mornings when I am afraid of myself, I am so wrinkled and worn. Ah! It was then that you should have come into my life, poor Muse. But such a love would have driven me mad; or worse—it would have made me vain to the point of idiocy. If I still have a warm heart, it is because for many years I conserved my fire: what I have not spent, I can put to use. There is enough heat in me to feed all my books. No, I regret none of my youth. I was hideously depressed; I contemplated suicide; I was prey to every possible kind of melancholy. My nervous sickness was beneficial, in that it converted all those feelings into physical symptoms, leaving me with a cooler head; and furthermore it made me acquainted with peculiar psychological phenomena that no one has any idea of, or rather that no one has ever experienced. Some day I will have my revenge, in a book (that metaphysical novel with ghosts I spoke to you about).[1] But that subject frightens me, speaking from the medical point of view. I must wait until I'm sufficiently distant from such impressions to be capable of using them factitiously, as symbols, ideal projections, without danger to myself or the book.

Here is my opinion about your idea of a Review:[2]

All the Reviews in the world began with the intention of being virtuous: none has been. The *Revue de Paris* itself (when a project) had the ideas you express, and was very determined to follow them.[3] One swears to be chaste; one is, for a day, two days; and then . . . then . . . Nature! Secondary considerations! Friends! Enemies! Don't you have to boost some, bury others? Admitting that for a time you do stick to the program: the public gets bored, subscriptions don't come in. Then people give you advice outside the lines you set for yourself, you follow it as an experiment, and it becomes a habit. In fact, there is nothing more pernicious than being able to say everything and having a convenient outlet.[4] You become very indulgent with yourself; and your friends are the same with you, in order that you may be so with them. And there you are, fallen into the trap out of pure naiveté. A model Review would be a splendid thing, and would require nothing less than the full time of a man of genius. The directorship of a Review should be a post for a patriarch; he should be dictator, with great *moral* authority acquired through his own writings. The authority cannot possibly be shared, for then immediate muddle is unavoidable. You talk a lot and spend all your talent skimming pennies on the river, whereas with greater economy you could in time buy fine farms and excellent châteaux.

What you say, DuCamp used to say: and see what he and his friends have done! Let's not think ourselves stronger than they; for they failed, as we would fail, from being carried away, and because of the slippery slope of the thing itself. After all, a magazine is a shop. And being a shop, . . . sooner or later the question of pleasing the customers comes to dominate all others. I well know that it is impossible to publish anywhere these days, and that all existing reviews are squalid whores acting like coquettes. Rotten to the marrow of their bones with the pox, they grimace with distaste at the thought of opening their thighs to healthy creatlons which badly need to get in. So, do as you've been doing: publish your work in book form—it's more intrepid; and be on your own. Who needs to hitch himself up as one of a team dragging an omnibus when he can still be a *cheval de tilbury?* As for me, I should be very glad if your ideas could be realized. But as to actually participating in anything at all in this world, no! no! a thousand times no! I no more want to be associated with a review, or to be a member of a society, a club, or an academy, than to be a city councillor or an officer in the national guard.

. . .

We marvel at the men of the age of Louis XIV, and yet they were not men of enormous genius. Reading them we experience none of that awe which makes us feel that Homer, Rabelais, and above all Shakespeare were more than human; certainly not. But what conscientious workmen! How they strained to find the exact expression for their thoughts! Such labor! Such tireless revision! How they sought one another's advice! How well they knew Latin! How attentively they read! That is why we have their thought in its entirety, why their form is so full, charged with substance to bursting-point. Well, *there are no degrees: all good things are of equal value.* LaFontaine will live as long as Dante, and Boileau as long as Bossuet or even Hugo.

. . .

1. The novel mentioned on page 177 as being "in outline." Never written, it was to have been called *La Spirale.*
2. Louise Colet had thought of starting a magazine to be called *La Revue Française.* Nothing came of it. (J.B.)
3. The first issue of the *Revue de Paris* had contained a manifesto, called "Liminaire"— "Introduction"—signed by Théophile Gautier, which was to be one of the ironic elements in the story of the publication of *Madame Bovary.* It reads, in part:
"We have but one literary principle: absolute liberty . . . We shall refuse manuscripts, but we will not deface them . . . Those who write for the *Revue* will feel no need even to exercise that preliminary self-censorship which forestalls correction . . . Let the poet spread the wings of his strophe to their fullest: we will not clip them . . .
"What we desire above all is to have every author, obscure or famous, in his own idiosyncratic form, in his most characteristic originality, in his own frank and free nature, without timidity or reticence, with his own bitter or sweet savor . . . as though he were writing, for himself and in solitude, a work which was never to see the light . . . We desire the anarchy and the autonomy of art."
4. "Un déversoir commode": could there be a better description of the role in which Flaubert cast Louise?

To Louise Colet
[Croisset,] Wednesday, half after midnight. [April 13, 1853]

. . .

Finally I am beginning to see a little light in my accursed dialogue with the curé.[1] But frankly, there are moments when I almost feel like vomiting *physically*, the whole thing is so low. I want to express the following situation: my little lady, in an access of religiosity, goes to church; at the door she finds the curé, who, in a dialogue (on no definite subject) shows himself to be so stupid, trivial, inept, sordid, that she goes away disgusted and undevout. And my curé is a very good man, indeed an excellent fellow, but he thinks only of the physical side (the sufferings of the poor, no bread, no firewood), and has no inkling of my lady's moral lapses or her vague mystical aspirations; he is very chaste, faithfully performs all his duties. This must have six or seven pages at the most, and must contain no comment, no analysis (it will all be in direct dialogue). Furthermore, since I consider it very cheap to write dialogue substituting dashes for "he said" and "he answered," you can imagine it isn't easy to avoid repetitions of the same turns of phrase. So: you are thus initiated into the torture I have been undergoing for a fortnight. By the end of next week, however, I hope it will all be off my hands. Then, after ten more pages (two long passages), I'll have finished the first section of my Part Two. My lovers are ready for adultery: soon they will be committing it. (I too, I hope.) . . .

1. *Madame Bovary*, Part II, Chapter 6.

To Louise Colet

[Croisset,] Tuesday night, 1 a.m. [April 26, 1853]

. . . .

At the present moment I believe that a thinker (and what is an artist if not a triple thinker?) should have neither religion, country, nor even any social conviction.[1] Absolute doubt now seems to me so completely substantiated that it would be almost silly to seek to formulate it. Bouilhet told me the other day that he felt the need to proclaim himself publicly, in writing, setting down all his reasons, an apostate Christian and an apostate Frenchman. And then to leave Europe and if possible never hear of it again. Yes, it would be a relief to vomit out all the immense contempt that fills the heart to overflowing. What good cause is there these days to arouse one's interest, let alone one's enthusiasm? . . .

I am reading Montaigne in bed, now. I know of no more soothing book, none more conducive to peace of mind. It is so healthy, so down to earth! If you have a copy, read the chapter on Democritus and Heraclitus. And reflect on the last paragraph.[2] One has to become a stoic when one lives in such sad times as ours . . .

1. Seventy years later, Marcel Proust was to make a similar assertion, with particular reference to the work of Flaubert, when he wrote that the artist can serve the glory of his country "only by being an artist, or, in other words, on condition that when he is studying the laws of Art, making his experiments and his discoveries, as delicate as those of Science, he think of nothing—not even his country—except the truth that is before him . . . It was not out of the kindness of his virtuous heart—and he was very kind—that Choderlos de Laclos wrote *Les Liaisons Dangereuses*, nor because of his liking for the *petite bourgeoisie*—or the *grande*, either—that Flaubert selected for subjects those of *Madame Bovary* and *L'Education Sentimentale*." (*The Past Recaptured*, translation by Frederick A. Blossom.)

In this connection, Oscar Wilde, who in a letter to W. E. Henley [?December 1888], had announced "Flaubert is my master," wrote in a subsequent letter to Henley: "Flaubert did not write French prose, but the prose of a great artist who happened to be French." (*The Letters of Oscar Wilde*, ed. Rupert Hart-Davis. London: Rupert Hart-Davis, 1962.)

2. "Of the same stampe was the answer of Statilius, to whom Brutus spake to win him to take part, and adhere to the conspiracie against Caesar. He allowed the enterprize to be very just, but disallowed of the men that should perform the same, as unworthy that any man should put himself in any adventure for them. Conformable to the discipline of Hegesias, who said, 'That a wise man ought never to do anything, but for himself; forasmuch as he alone is worthy to have any action performed for him'; and to that of Theodorus, who thought it an injustice, that a wise man should in any case hazard himself for the good and benefit of his country, or to endanger his wisdom for fooles.

"Our own condition is as ridiculous as risible."

(John Florio translation.)

To LOUISE COLET

[Croisset,] Wednesday midnight. [June 1, 1853]

I have just written to the great man[1] (the letter will go off tomorrow at the latest). It wasn't easy, because of the moderate tone I wanted to employ. He has been guilty of too many abominations for me to express my admiration without reserve (his encouragement of mediocrities, the Academy, his political ambition, etc.). On the other hand, he has afforded me so many fine hours of enthusiasm, given me so many splendid erections (if one may put it that way), that it was hard for me to strike a balance between constraint and adulation. However, I think I was both polite and sincere (a rarity).

.   .   .

I am not inveighing against our good friend de Lisle,[2] but I do say that to me he seems a little *ordinary* in his passions. The true poet, for me, is a priest. As soon as he dons the cassock he must leave his family . . .

There is another thing that seemed to me slightly bourgeois in this same individual: his saying "I have never been able to go with a whore."

Well, let me declare that *I* have, and often! Speaking of disgust, all these disgusted people disgust me profoundly. Did he think he wasn't wallowing in prostitution when he wiped from his body the leavings of the husband? The little lady doubtless had a third, and, in the arms of all three, was thinking of a fourth. Oh the irony of love-making! Still, since she carried no card,[3] our nice de Lisle could "go with" her.

Let me say that that theory makes me gag. There are certain things that tell me immediately with what manner of man I have to deal: (1) admiration for Béranger; (2) dislike of perfumes; (3) liking for thick cloth; (4) a fringe beard; (5) aversion to brothels. How many nice young men I have known who had a pious horror of "houses" and yet picked up the most beautiful cases of clap you can imagine from their so-called mistresses. The Latin Quarter is full of this doctrine and such occurrences. It is perhaps a perverse taste, but I like prostitution—and for its own sake, independently of what lies underneath. My heart has never failed to pound at the sight of one of those provocatively dressed women walking in the rain under the gas lamps, just as the sight of monks in their robes and knotted girdles touches some ascetic, hidden corner of my soul. Prostitution is a meeting-point of so many elements—lechery, frustration, total lack of any human relation, physical frenzy, the clink of gold—that a glance into its depths makes one giddy and teaches one all manner of things. It fills you with such sadness! And makes you dream so of love! Ah, elegy-makers, it is not on ruins that you should lean, but on the breasts of these light women.

Yes, that man has missed something who has never awakened in an anonymous bed beside a face he will never see again, and who has never left a brothel at sunrise feeling like throwing himself into the river out of pure disgust for life. And just their shameless way of dressing—the temptation of the chimera—the aura of the unknown, of the *maudit*—the old poetry of corruption and venality! During my first years in Paris, I used to sit in front of Tortoni's on hot summer evenings and watch the streetwalkers stroll by in the last rays of the sun. At such moments I ate my heart out with biblical poetry. I thought of Isaiah, of "fornication in high places," and I walked back along the rue de la Harpe saying to myself: "And her mouth is smoother than oil."[4] I swear I was never more chaste. My only complaint about prostitution is that it is a myth. The kept woman has invaded the field of debauchery, just as the journalist has invaded poetry; everything is becoming mongrelized. There are no more courtesans, just as there are no more saints; there are only "soupeuses" and "lorettes"—even more sordid than grisettes . . .

1. Victor Hugo. (See the following letter.) Flaubert was helping the exiled Hugo correspond surreptitiously with friends in France, including colleagues in the French Academy who might vote for Louise in the 1854 poetry contest.
2. Louise had introduced Flaubert to Charles-Marie-René Leconte de Lisle (1818-94), whose first volume of "Parnassian" poetry, *Poèmes antiques*, had been published the previous year. Flaubert liked him, but found him and his poetry somewhat pallid. Both Flaubert and Louise vary in the spelling of his name.
3. That is, the married woman in question (she is not identified) was not licensed as a prostitute.
4. Flaubert is possibly thinking of Jeremiah 3:6 or 13:27, and of Proverbs 5:3.

To Victor Hugo

Croisset, June 2, 1853

I think, Monsieur, that I should warn you about the following:

Your communication dated April 27 arrived here badly damaged. The outer envelope was torn in several places and a few words in your handwriting were exposed. The inner envelope (addressed to Mme C.) had been torn along the edges, and portions of its contents were visible—two other letters and a printed sheet.

Was it the Customs that opened the envelope, hoping to find a bit of lace? It would be naive, I think, to suppose that; the indiscretion must be laid at the door of the saviors of society. If you have something of importance to transmit to me, Monsieur, I think that the following procedure would be the most secure: you could address your letters from Jersey to a family of honest merchants I know in London; they would open the outer envelope and re-enclose the inner (addressed to me) in one which would thus bear their English handwriting and a London postmark. Communications *from* Mme C. would be forwarded by me via the same route.

Your later envelope, dated May (via Le Havre) arrived here intact.

However, please allow me, Monsieur, to thank you for all your thanks and to accept none of them. The man who in my restricted life has occupied the greatest place, and the best, may indeed expect some service of me, since you call it service!

The diffidence one feels in declaring any true passion inhibits me, despite your exile, from telling you what underlies my attachment to you. It is my gratitude for all the enthusiasm you have aroused in me. But I do not wish to become entangled in sentences which would serve but poorly to specify its extent.

I have already seen you "in person." We have met several times—you unaware of me, I gazing eagerly at you. It was in the winter of 1844, in the studio of poor Pradier, of happy memory. There were five or six of us; we drank tea and played "the game of the goose"; I even remember your large gold ring, with its engraved lion rampant, which we used as a stake.

Since then you have played for higher stakes, and in more fearsome games; but in whatever you do, the lion rampant plays its part. *He*[1] bears on his brow the mark of its claws, and when he passes into history, the centuries will know him by that red scar.

As for you—who knows? Future makers of aesthetic will perhaps thank Providence for this atrocity, this consecration. For is it not by martyrdom that virtue is brought to perfection? Is it not by outrage that grandeur is rendered yet more grand? And in you there is no lack either of inherent grandeur or of that conferred by circumstances.

I send you, Monsieur, together with all my admiration for your genius, the assurance of my entire devotion to your person.

Gust. Flaubert.

(Mme Farmer, Upper Holloway Manor Road, No. 5, London.)[2]

1. Napoleon III, excoriated by Hugo in *Napoléon le Petit.*
2. Mrs. Richard Farmer was Caroline's former governess, "Miss Jane." The envelopes to her would be addressed in the hand of the present governess, "Miss Isabel" (soon, however, to be discharged: see p. 191).

To Louise Colet

[Croisset,] Saturday night, 1 o'clock. [June 25, 1853]

Only now have I finished my first section of Part Two,[1] the very section I had planned to have ready before our last meeting in Mantes. You see how slow I have been. I'll spend a few more days reading it over and recopying it, and a week from tomorrow will spill it all out to the Hon. Bouilhet. If it passes the test, that will be one great worry the less—and a good thing, too, believe me, for the substructure was very flimsy. Apart from that, I think the book will have a big defect, namely faulty proportions in regard to length. I already have two hundred sixty pages which are merely preliminary to the action, containing more or less disguised descriptions of character, . . . of landscapes, of places. My conclusion, which will be my little lady's death, her burial and her husband's subsequent grief, will be at least sixty pages. That leaves, for the body of the action itself, one hundred twenty to one hundred sixty pages at the most. Isn't that a great flaw? What reassures me (though only moderately) is that the book is a biography rather than a story with a complicated plot. The drama plays only a small part in it, and if this dramatic element is skillfully blended with the rest, so that a uniform, overall tonality is achieved, then perhaps the lack of harmonious development of the various phases will pass unnoticed. Besides, I think that this is rather characteristic of life itself. The sexual act may last only a minute, though it has been anticipated for months! Our passions are like volcanoes: they are always rumbling, but eruption is only intermittent.

Unfortunately the French spirit is mad for entertainment. It demands so much that is showy. It takes so little pleasure in what for me is the essence of poetry, namely exposition, whether our treatment of it is descriptive or moral, whether we stress picturesque aspects or psychological analysis . . . I would like to produce books which would entail only the writing of sentences (if I may put it that way), just as in order to live it is enough to breathe. What I dislike are the tricks inherent in the making of an outline, the arranging of effects, all the underlying calculations—which are, however, Art, for they and they alone account for the stylistic effect.

.   .   .   .

If the book I am writing with such difficulty turns out well, I'll have established, by the very fact of having written it, these two truths, which for me are axiomatic, namely: (1) that poetry is purely subjective, that in literature there are no such things as beautiful subjects, and that therefore Yvetot is the equal of Constantinople; and (2) that consequently one can write about any one thing equally well as about any other. The artist must raise everything to a higher level: he is like a pump; he has inside him a great pipe that reaches down into the entrails of things, the deepest layers. He sucks up what was lying there below, dim and unnoticed, and brings it out in great jets to the sunlight.

1. *Madame Bovary*, Part II. Chapters 1-7. From the Bovarys' arrival in Yonville to the first appearance of Rodolphe.

To Louise Colet

. . .

I find Musset's remarks about *Hamlet* utterly bourgeois, and this is why. He criticizes this "inconsistency": that Hamlet is skeptical even after seeing his father's soul with his own eyes. But in the first place it was not the soul that he saw. He saw a ghost, a shade, a *thing*, a material living thing, which was in no way popularly or poetically related, at that period, to the abstract idea of the soul. It is we, metaphysicians and moderns, who use that language. And Hamlet does not *doubt* at all, in the philosophical sense; rather, he *wonders*.

I think that Musset's observation is not original with him; that he took it from Mallefille's preface to his *Don Juan*.[1] In my opinion it is superficial. A peasant of our own day may perfectly well still see a ghost, and next morning, in the crude light of day, think coolly about life and death, but not about the flesh and the soul. Hamlet thinks in terms not of scholastic concepts, but of human attitudes. On the contrary, his perpetual state of fluctuation, his constant uncertainty, his irresolution, and his inability to resolve his thoughts— these are what make the play sublime. But our clever friends want characters to be all of a piece, consistent—as they are in books only. The truth is that Shakespeare's conception of Hamlet reaches into the remotest corners of the human soul. Ulysses is perhaps the greatest type in all ancient literature, and Hamlet in all modern.

If I weren't so weary, I would develop my ideas at greater length. It is so easy to chatter about the Beautiful. But it takes more genius to say, in proper style: "close the door," or "he wanted to sleep," than to give all the literature courses in the world.

Criticism occupies the lowest place in the literary hierarchy: as regards form, almost always; and as regards "moral value," incontestably. It comes after rhyming games and acrostics, which at least require a certain inventiveness.

Allons, adieu. Mille bons baisers. À toi, coeur sur coeur.

1. Félicien Mallefille (1813-1868), playwright and novelist. As delegate of the provisional government in 1848, he is credited with saving the museum of Versailles from incendiarists.

To Louise Colet

Croisset, Saturday midnight. [July 2, 1853]

. . .

Tomorrow I shall read to Bouilhet 114 [*sic*] pages of *Bovary*, pages 139 to 251. That is what I have done since last September—in ten months! This afternoon I finally stopped making corrections, not being able to see straight any longer: continuous concentration on a piece of writing results in your being dazed; what seems a mistake now, five minutes later no longer seems so; it's a never-ending series of corrections and of recorrections of corrections. Eventually one begins to function badly, and it's more sensible to stop. The entire week has been rather tedious, and today I feel a great relief in the thought that I've got something finished, or almost; but I have had to remove a lot of cement that was oozing out from between the stones, and the stones had to be reset so that the joints wouldn't show. Prose must stand upright, from one end to the other, like a wall whose ornamentation continues down to its very base: seen in perspective, it must make a long continuous line. Oh! If I wrote the way I know one has to write, I'd write so well! Still, it seems to me that among these 114 pages there are a good many strong ones, and that the whole thing, though not dramatic, moves at a lively pace.[1] Also, I have been musing on what's to follow. I have a fornication coming up that worries me considerably, and which I mustn't shirk, although I want to make it chaste—that is, literary, without gross details or lascivious images: the carnality must be in the emotion.

. . .

I never talk to you about domestic matters, in fact they are usually quite boring: however, some can be interesting as examples of the grotesque. (1) My mother has just discovered that the gardener is swindling us. Only we, in all the village, have no vegetables, because the village lives somewhat at our expense. Our flowers are sold in Rouen: bunches of them are taken there by steamer. Can't you picture the gardener "making his gravy" by cheating the boss, and the boss not being happy about it? (2) The governess has been so arrogant, so capricious and rude, and was so mistreating the little girl, that we told her she was no longer needed, and she is leaving. (3) We have discovered by chance that last winter my brother gave a soirée for "important people" without telling us, so as not to have to invite us. (He and his wife come here every Sunday.) Nice, isn't it? You can gauge from that the degree of warmth and cordiality that surrounds us, my mother and me. But these worthies (not so worthy), who are banality itself, can barely understand—and consequently do not like—anyone out of the ordinary. However that may be, you see how little consideration I enjoy on my native heath and in my family! You'll find the same thing in any life: it's the norm.

1. A few days later, Flaubert wrote to Louise:
"I don't know whether Bouilhet has written you. If so, he must have told you he was pleased with what I had done; and so was I, frankly. As a difficulty overcome, it seems to me excellent, but that is all. The subject in itself (so far, at least) precludes the great outbursts of style that ravish me in other writers and which I think I am suited to. The good thing about *Bovary* is that it will have been a splendid exercise. I shall have produced written reality, which is rare. But I will take my revenge: just let me find a subject suited to my voice, and I'll go far." The first rumble of *Salammbô*.

To VICTOR HUGO

How am I to thank you, Monsieur, for your magnificent gift?[1] What am I to say—unless perhaps I echo the dying Talleyrand when visited by Louis-Philippe: "This is the greatest honor ever conferred upon my house!"? But there the parallel ends, for any number of reasons.

I will not hide from you that you have profoundly "Chatouillé de mon coeur l'orgueilleuse faiblesse" as good old Racine would have said.[2] A true poet! And how many monsters he would find now to depict, different from his dragon-bull and a hundred times worse!

Exile at least spares you the sight of them. Ah, if you knew into what filth we are plunged! Private infamies proceed from political turpitude, and it is impossible to take a step without treading on something unclean. The atmosphere is heavy with nauseous vapors. Air! Air! For that, I open my window and turn toward you. I hear the great wings of your Muse as she passes, and I breathe, as one might breathe the fragrance of the forests, the exhalations that rise from the depths of your style.

And in addition, Monsieur, you have been a charming obsession in my life, a long love that has never weakened. I have read you during awesome nights spent beside the dead, and on soft beaches by the sea in the full sunshine of summer. I carried you with me to Palestine, and it was you who comforted me, ten years ago, when I was dying of ennui in the Latin Quarter. Your poetry became a part of me, like my nurse's milk. Many of your lines will remain in my memory forever, unforgettable as a momentous exploit.

Here I stop. But if anything is sincere, it is what I have just said. From now on, I shall importune you no longer with my person, and you may make use of the correspondent without fear of his correspondence.

But since you extend your hand to me across the ocean, I take and grasp it. I grasp it proudly, the hand that wrote *Notre-Dame* and *Napoléon le Petit*, the hand that has hewn colossi and fashioned bitter cups for traitors, that has culled the most glorious delights from the loftiest reaches of the intellect, and that now, like the hand of the biblical Hercules,[3] alone stays raised amid the twofold ruins of Art and of Liberty!

I am, Monsieur, yours, with once again a thousand thanks.

Ex imo.

1. Hugo's note accompanying the gift (a photograph of himself) had said, in part: "Allow me to send . . . you my portrait: it is the work of my son, done in collaboration with the sun." See the following letter for Flaubert's comment on his present reply to the great man, which reads like an embarrassing parody of Hugo's own grandiose epistolary style.

2. Agamemnon, in Racine's *Iphigénie:* "Ces noms de roi des rois, et chef de la Grèce,/Chatouillaient de mon coeur l'orgueilleuse faiblesse."

3. "The biblical Hercules" is, of course, Samson.

[Croisset,] Friday night, 1 o'clock. [July 15, 1853]

.   .   .

What artists we would be if we had never read, seen, or loved anything that was not beautiful; if from the outset some guardian angel of the purity of our pens had kept us from all contamination; if we had never associated with fools[1] or read newspapers! The Greeks were like that. As regards plastic form, they lived in conditions that will never return. But to want to wear their shoes is madness. What we in the North need are not chlamyses but fur coats. Classic form is insufficient for our needs, and our voices are not created to sing those simple tunes. Let us, if we can, be as dedicated to art as they were, but differently. The human consciousness has broadened since Homer. Sancho Panza's belly has burst the seams of Venus's girdle. Rather than persist in emulating old styles, we must exert ourselves to invent new ones. I think de Lisle is unaware of this. He has no instinct for modern life; he lacks heart. By this I do not mean personal or even humanitarian feelings, no—but *heart*, almost in the medical sense of the word. His ink is pale; his muse suffers from lack of fresh air. Thoroughbred horses and thoroughbred styles have plenty of blood in their veins, and it can be seen pulsing everywhere in them, under the skin and the words. Life! Life! To have erections! That is everything, the only thing that counts! That is why I so love lyricism. It seems to me the most natural form of poetry —poetry in all its nakedness and freedom. All the power of a work of art lies in this mystery, and it is this primordial quality, this *motus animi continuus* (vibration, continual movement of the mind—Cicero's definition of eloquence), which results in conciseness, relief, form, energy, rhythm, diversity. It doesn't require much brain to be a critic: you can judge the excellence of a book by the strength of the punches it has given you and the time it takes you to recover from them. And then, how dauntless are the great masters! They pursue an idea to its furthermost limits. In Molière's *Monsieur de Pourceaugnac* there is a question of giving a man an enema. Not just *one* enema is brought in: a whole troupe of actors carrying syringes pour down the aisles of the theatre! Michelangelo's figures have cables rather than muscles; in Rubens's bacchanalian scenes men piss on the ground; and think of everything in Shakespeare, etc., etc., and the most recent member of the family, old Hugo. What a beautiful thing *Notre Dame* is! I lately reread three chapters in it, including the sack of the church by the beggars. That's the sort of thing that's *strong!* I think the greatest characteristic of genius is, above all, *power*. Hence, what I detest most of all in the arts, what sets me on edge, is the *ingenious*, the clever. This is not at all the same as bad taste, which is a good quality gone astray. In order to have what is called bad taste, you must have a sense for poetry; whereas cleverness, on the contrary, is incompatible with genuine poetry. Who was cleverer than Voltaire, and who less a poet? In our beloved France, the public will accept poetry only if it is disguised. If it is given to them straight, they protest: they must be treated like the horses of Abbas-Pasha, which are fed a tonic of meatballs masked in flour. That's what Art is: knowing how to disguise! But never fear: if you offer this sort of flour to lions, to real carnivores, they will smell the meat twenty paces away and spring at it.

I have written a monumental letter to the Grand Crocodile. I won't pretend it didn't give me trouble (but I think it quite high-styled, excessively, perhaps); in fact it gave me so much that now I know it by heart. If I still remember it when we meet, I will repeat it to you. The parcel leaves tomorrow.

I have been in excellent form this week. I have written eight pages, all of which I think can stand pretty much as they are. Tonight I have just sketched my entire big scene of the Agricultural Show.[2] It will be enormous—thirty pages at least. Against the background of this rustico-municipal celebration, with all its details (all my secondary characters will be shown talking and in action), there must be continuous dialogue between a gentleman and the lady he is "warming up." Moreover, somewhere in the middle I have a solemn speech by a councillor from the Prefecture, and at the end (this I have already done) a newspaper article written by my pharmacist, who gives an account of the celebration in fine philosophical, poetical, progressive style. You see it is no small chore. I am sure of my local color and of many of my effects; but it's a devilish job to keep it from getting too long. And yet this kind of thing must be full and ample. Once this is behind me, I shall soon reach my fornication in the autumn woods, with the lovers' horses cropping the leaves beside them; and then I think I'll have clear sailing—I'll have passed Charybdis, at least, even though Scylla may remain to be negotiated.

· · ·

1. In a recent letter to Louise, Flaubert had written: "Another law of mathematics to be discovered is: How many imbeciles do you have to know before wanting to cut your throat?"
2. *Madame Bovary*, Part II, Chapter 8.

To Louise Colet

[Croisset,] Friday night, one o'clock. [July 22, 1853]

· · ·

Today I had a great success. You know that yesterday "we" had the "pleasure" of having Monsieur Saint-Arnaud.[1] Well, in this morning's *Journal de Rouen* I came on a sentence in the Mayor's speech—a sentence which, the day before, I had written *word for word* in my *Bovary* (in the Prefect's speech at the Agricultural Show). Not only the same idea, the same words, but the same assonances of style. I don't mind telling you that this is the sort of thing I enjoy. When literature attains the precision of an exact science, that's something!

· · ·

1. Maréchal de Saint-Arnaud, Minister for War. Replying to a speech by the Mayor of Rouen, he assured the citizens that the Emperor intended to help the farmers of the region, whose crops had been largely destroyed by a recent heavy hailstorm.

About the storm, Flaubert had written to Louise:

"It wasn't without a certain pleasure that I surveyed my ruined espaliers, all my flowers torn to pieces, the disheveled vegetable garden. As I contemplated all these factitious little man-made arrangements which five minutes of nature had sufficed to destroy, I admired the way the true order had reimposed itself on the false. These things so tormented by us—trees pruned and shaped, flowers growing where they don't want to, vegetables brought from other countries—they all found a kind of revenge in this atmospheric rebuke . . . It is too generally believed that the sun has no other function here below than to help the cabbages along. Now and then we must restore God to his pedestal."

To Louise Colet

[Trouville,][1] Sunday 14, 4 o'clock. [August 14, 1853]

. . .

I spent an hour yesterday watching the ladies bathe. What a sight! What a hideous sight! The two sexes used to bathe together here. But now they are kept separate by means of signposts, wire netting, and a uniformed inspector: (what an atrociously lugubrious object, this grotesque figure!) And so, yesterday, from the place where I was standing in the sun, with my spectacles on my nose, I could contemplate the bathing beauties at my leisure. The human race must indeed have become completely moronic to have lost all sense of elegance to this degree. Nothing is more pitiful than these bags in which women encase their bodies, and these oilcloth caps! What faces! And how they walk! Such feet! Red, scrawny, covered with corns and bunions, deformed by shoes, long as shuttles or wide as washerwomen's paddles. And in the midst of it all, scrofulous brats screaming and crying. Farther off, grandmas knitting and respectable old gentlemen with gold-rimmed spectacles reading newspapers, looking up from time to time between the lines to survey the vastness of the horizon with an air of approval. The whole thing made me long all afternoon to escape from Europe and go to live in the Sandwich Islands[2] or the forests of Brazil. There, at least, the beaches are not polluted by such ugly feet, by such foul-looking specimens of humanity.

The day before yesterday, in the woods near Touques, in a charming spot beside a spring, I found old cigar butts and scraps of pâté. People had been picnicking. I described such a scene in *Novembre*, eleven years ago: there it was entirely imagined, and the other day it was experienced. Everything one invents is true, you may be sure. Poetry is as precise as geometry. Induction is as good as deduction; and besides, after reaching a certain point one no longer errs about matters of the soul. My poor Bovary, without a doubt, is suffering and weeping at this very hour in twenty villages of France.

The other day I saw something that moved me—something not having to do with myself. We were a league from here, at the Château de Lassay (built in six weeks for Mme Dubarry, who used to come to this coast for sea-bathing). All that remains is a staircase—a great Louis XV staircase, a few empty windows, a wall, and wind, wind. It is on a plateau, visible from the sea. Beside it stands a peasant's hovel. We went in to get some milk for Liline, who was thirsty. In

195

the tiny garden there were fine hollyhocks as high as the roof, string beans, and a cauldron full of dirty water. Nearby a pig was grunting . . . and farther off, beyond the wall, free-running colts were grazing and neighing, their long manes blowing in the sea wind. Inside, on the walls of the cottage hung a picture of the Emperor and another of Badinguet.[3] I would probably have made some joke, when I saw, sitting half-paralyzed in a corner by the fireplace, a gaunt old man with a two-weeks' growth of beard. Above his armchair, attached to the wall, were two gold epaulettes! The poor old fellow was so feeble that he had trouble taking his pinch of snuff. No one paid any attention to him. He sat there regurgitating, groaning, eating from a bowl of white beans. The glint of the sun on the metal bands around the pails was making him blink. The cat was lapping milk from an earthenware dish on the floor. And that was all. I thought that in the perpetual half-sleep of old age (which precedes the other sleep, and is like a transition from life to oblivion), the old fellow was probably having visions of the snows of Russia or the sands of Egypt. What other visions were floating before those dulled eyes? And the jacket he was wearing—so patched, so clean! The woman who served us (his daughter, I think) was a dame of fifty, in short skirts and a cotton cap, with wrists like the balustrades of the Place Louis XV.[4] She bustled about the room in her blue stockings and heavy petticoat; and Badinguet, splendid amid it all, was there on his rearing yellow horse, tricorne in hand, saluting a cohort of disabled veterans, all their wooden legs neatly in line. The last time I visited the Château de Lassay was with Alfred. I still remember the conversation we had, the poetry we recited, the plans we made.

How little Nature cares about us! And how impassive the look of the trees, the grass, the waves! (The bell on the steamer for Le Havre is ringing so fiercely that I must break off here.) What a din industry makes in the world! What a clackety thing the machine is! Speaking of industry, have you sometimes thought of the quantity of stupid professions it begets, and the vast amount of stupidity that must inevitably accrue from them over the years? Such a statistic could be frightening! What can be expected of a population like that of Manchester, which spends its life making pins? And the manufacture of a pin involves five or six different specialties! As work is broken down into compartments, men-machines take their places beside the machines themselves. Think of spending one's life selling tickets in a railway station, or pasting on labels in a printing shop, etc., etc. Yes, mankind is becoming increasingly brutish. Leconte is right: he formulated that in a way I shall never forget.[5] The "dreamers" of the Middle Ages were a different breed from the "men of action" of modern times.

Mankind hates us: we serve none of its purposes; and we hate it, because it injures us. So let us love one another "in Art," as mystics love one another "in God." Let everything else pale before this love. May all life's kitchen-candles (every one of which reeks) disappear in the light of that great sun. In periods when every common bond is broken, and when Society is but one vast banditry (governmental term), more or less well organized, when the values of the flesh and those of the mind are far apart, howling at each other from a distance, like wolves, we must, like the rest of the world, fashion ourselves an egoism (but one that is nobler), and live inside our den. Each day I feel a greater distance between myself and my fellow men; and I am glad of it, for my ability to recognize what is sympathetic to me increases thanks to this very distance.

.   .   .

1. Flaubert was spending a few weeks in Trouville with his mother and Caroline, "Liline." In this letter and in others from Trouville he evokes his adolescent days there and the birth of his passion for Elise Schlesinger, causing Louise to write him jealously about his obsession with "Trouville ghosts."
2. The Hawaiian Islands. The "unpolluted beaches" alluded to by Flaubert are therefore such present-day fun-fairs as Waikiki.
3. Napoleon and Napoleon III. Flaubert tended to sentimentalize about the first Empire. In 1853 he still considered his own Emperor a shoddy figure, and was glad to use the popular, comic-sounding nickname, which had originated in a satirical cartoon by Gavarni.
4. One of the earlier names of the Place de la Concorde, but still in common use.
5. "Since Homer and Aeschylus, who represent poetry as it was at its most vital, in its greatest fullness and harmony, decadence and barbarism have buried the human spirit." (Leconte de Lisle, preface to *Poèmes antiques*, 1852.) (J.B.)

To Louise Colet
                              [Trouville,] Sunday, 11 o'clock [August 21, 1853]

.   .   .

Yes, I maintain (and in my opinion this ought to be a practical dogma in the artist's life) that you should divide your existence into two parts: live like a bourgeois, and think like a demigod. Physical and intellectual satisfactions have nothing in common. If they happen to be combined, seize hold of them and never let go. But do not *seek* the combination, for that would be artificial. Incidentally, that idea of "happiness" is the cause, almost single-handed, of all human misfortunes . . .

If you seek happiness and beauty at the same time, you will find neither the one nor the other, for the latter is attained only by sacrifice. Art, like the God of the Jews, feasts on holocausts.

.   .   .

To Louis Bouilhet
                              [Trouville,] Wednesday, 1 o'clock. [August 24, 1853]

.   .   .

How eager I am to finish *Bovary, Anubis,* and my three prefaces,[1] so that I can enter on a new period and revel in pure beauty. My idleness of these past few weeks has given me a burning desire to transform, by art, everything that originates in myself, everything I have ever felt. I have not the slightest urge to

197

write my memoirs. I find my own personality repugnant, and everything around me hideous or stupid, I am so fed up with it all. In my desperation I take refuge in fantasy. I see the fishing boats here as feluccas; I strip the sailors as they pass by, and turn them into savages striding naked on vermilion strands. I think of India, of your China,[2] of my oriental story (ideas for bits of it keep coming to me); I feel the need for gigantic epics. It is you, *cher bougre*, who fill me with this tail wind, from afar.

But life is so short! I want to cut my throat when I think that I shall never write the way I want, or set down a quarter of what I dream. All this energy we feel ourselves choking on: we are fated to die with it still in us, unexpended. It is like those sudden cravings for a lay. In imagination we lift up every passing petticoat; but after the fifth discharge no sperm is left. Blood comes to the glans, but our lust is confined to our hearts.

It is six years since I was last here. Where will I be six years from now?[3] And what will I have accomplished?

.   .   .

1. For *Anubis*, see pp. 130 and 131, n.4. Of the "three prefaces," mentioned as projects in other letters to Louise, one, an introduction to the works of Pierre Ronsard, was never written; another, a foreword to a volume of poems by Louis Bouilhet, would be written only after Bouilhet's death; and the third, a preface to the *Dictionary of Accepted Opinions* (see pp. 127, 128, n.3., and 175), would be absorbed in *Bouvard et Pécuchet*.

2. Bouilhet was studying Chinese.

3. He would be at Croisset, writing his second published novel, *Salammbô*—satisfying his "need for gigantic epics."

To LOUISE COLET

[Trouville,] Friday night, 11 o'clock. [August 26, 1853]

.   .   .

What seems to me the highest and most difficult achievement of Art is not to make us laugh or cry, nor to arouse our lust or rage, but to do what nature does—that is, to set us dreaming. The most beautiful works have this quality. They are serene in aspect, inscrutable. The means by which they act on us are various: they are as motionless as cliffs, stormy as the ocean, leafy, green and murmurous as forests, forlorn as the desert, blue as the sky. Homer, Rabelais, Michelangelo, Shakespeare and Goethe seem to me *pitiless*. They are unfathomable, infinite, manifold. Through small apertures we glimpse abysses whose sombre depths turn us faint. And yet over the whole there hovers an extraordinary tenderness. It is like the brilliance of light, the smile of the sun; and it is calm, calm and strong.

.   .   .

[Croisset,] Wednesday, midnight. [October 12, 1853]

My head is on fire, as it used to be after a long day on horseback. Today it's my pen that I've been riding—and hard. I have been writing since half-past noon without stopping, except for an occasional five minutes to smoke my pipe, and just now an hour for dinner. My agricultural show[1] was giving me such trouble that I decided to put aside Greek and Latin until it was finished, and beginning today I am devoting myself to it exclusively. It is taking too long! Sometimes I think it will be the death of me, and I want to come and see you.

Bouilhet says it will be the best scene in the book. What I am sure of is that it will be new, and that I am aiming at something good. If the effects of a symphony have ever been conveyed in a book, it will be in these pages. I want the reader to hear everything together, like one great roar—the bellowing of bulls, the sighing of lovers, the bombast of official oratory. The sun shines down on it all, and there are gusts of wind that threaten to blow off the women's big bonnets. The most arduous passages in *Saint Antoine* were child's play in comparison. I achieve dramatic effect simply by the interweaving of dialogue and by contrasts of character. I am in the midst of it now. In less than a week I'll have tied the knot on which all the rest depends. I keep feeling that my brain is too small to encompass this complex situation in a single glance. I write ten pages at a time, dashing from one sentence to another. However, one of these days I must write to the Crocodile. He has lost Mrs. Farmer's address, and would have to send letters directly to us from Jersey, which is to be avoided if at all possible.   .   .   .

What a strange creature you are, dear Louise, sending me more "diatribes," as my pharmacist would say. You ask me a favor, I say yes, I promise again, and you still scold! Well, since you hide nothing from me (a habit I approve of), I won't hide from you that this idea strikes me as one of your obsessions. You want to link two very different kinds of affection, and I don't see the sense of it, much less the use. I fail completely to understand how your hospitality to me in Paris puts my mother under the slightest obligation. For three years I went continually to the Schlesingers', where she never once set foot. Similarly, Bouilhet has been spending the night at our house and having Sunday lunch and dinner here for eight years, without our having had a single glimpse of his mother, who comes to Rouen almost every month. I assure you that doesn't shock my mother in the slightest. However, it shall be as you wish. I promise, I swear, that I will explain your reasons to her and ask her to arrange a meeting. As for what happens then, with the best will in the world I can do nothing. Perhaps you will get along very well, perhaps you will dislike each other intensely. The good lady tends to be standoffish. She has stopped seeing not only all her old acquaintances, but her friends as well. She has only one that I know of, and that one doesn't live in Croisset.   .   .   .

---

1. *Madame Bovary*, Part II, Chapter 8.

[Croisset,] Tuesday night, midnight. [October 25, 1853]

. . .

You are lucky, you poets: you have an outlet in your verse. When something troubles you, you spit out a sonnet, and that relieves you. But we poor devils, writers of prose, who are forbidden (myself in particular) any expression of personal feelings—think of all the bitterness that remains in our souls, all the moral mucus we gag on!

There is something faulty in my character and in my vocation. I was born a lyricist and I write no poetry. I want to shower good on those I love, and I make them weep. Look at Bouilhet: there's a man for you! Such a complete nature! If I were capable of being jealous of anyone, it would be of him. With the stultifying life he has had and the misfortunes that have befallen him, I would certainly be an imbecile by now, or deported, or hanged by my own hand. The buffetings he has suffered have only improved him. That is what happens to forests of tall trees: they keep growing ever higher in the wind, and they force their roots through silex and granite; whereas espaliers, with all their fertilizer and their straw matting, die against the wall that supports them, in full sun. Be fond of him—that is all I can say to you about him—and never doubt him for an instant.

Do you know what I talked about with my mother all last evening? About you. I told her many things she didn't know, or which she had at most half guessed. She appreciates you, and I am sure that this winter she will be glad to see you. So that question is settled.

Bovary is marching ahead again. Bouilhet was pleased on Sunday. But he was in such high spirits, and so preoccupied with Eros (not that I was the object of his passion), that perhaps he judged too favorably. I am waiting for his second reading, to be sure I am on the right track. I can't be far off it, however. This agricultural show will take me another full six weeks (a good month after my return from Paris). But the difficulties that remain are mostly in the execution. Then I will have to go over the whole thing, as the style is a little choppy. Some passages will have to be rewritten, others eliminated. So it will have taken me from July to the end of November to write *one scene!* If at least I enjoyed doing it! But I will never like this book, no matter how successfully I may bring it off. Now that I have a clear view of it as a whole, it disgusts me. But at least it will have been good training. I'll have learned how to do dialogue and portraits. I will write other books! The pleasure of criticism surely has a charm of its own, and if a fault you find in your work leads you to conceive a greater beauty, isn't this conception alone a delight in itself, almost a promise?

Adieu, à bientôt. Mille baisers.

A few months after the appearance of Louis Bouilhet's first published poem, *Melaenis*, in the *Revue de Paris*, Louise Colet had given a reception in his honor, in the course of which an attractive Parisienne, Mme Edma Roger des Genettes, read a portion of the poem to the assembled guests. Poet and *diseuse* were soon on the best of terms, and they continued to see each other from time to time. Now, in the autumn of 1853, Bouilhet was taking the risk of giving up his tutoring, borrowing money, and moving to Paris, hoping to profit from the favorable impression created in literary circles there by *Melaenis*. He was finishing a second long work, a "scientific" poem to be called *Les Fossiles*, and was planning a play. It was perhaps the prospect of being reunited more regularly with Edma that caused him, on that Sunday, October 23, 1853, to be "preoccupied with Eros."

With Bouilhet in Paris, recommended to her anew by Flaubert, Louise Colet did her best to use him as go-between, as she had earlier tried to use DuCamp. But as usual she followed, with Flaubert, a course little calculated to further her interests: few things could have irritated him more than her insistence on meeting his mother—to which she added the bizarre grievance that he had never brought about a meeting between her daughter Henriette (now thirteen) and his niece Caroline (ten). Writing his novel, Flaubert was portraying his heroine ever more fully; and his depiction of one trait increasingly displayed by Emma Bovary—vehemence—was doubtless nourished somewhat by Louise's shrill demands.

Even at this late date, neither of the lovers ceased attempting to reform the other. One of the causes for conflict at this time was an intolerable literary crime committed by Louise—her newest, very feminist poem, *La Servante*, over two thousand lines long, didactic, sentimental, flat, infelicitous, in which she insisted on retaining, despite Flaubert's strongest pleas, the vengeful portrait of a drunken, decayed poet-seducer, blatantly modeled on Alfred de Musset. Other lines depict actresses as being little more than prostitutes, "protected" by rich, coarse businessmen. Flaubert continued to use literary objection as a vehicle for broader reproof.

To Louise Colet

[Croisset,] Friday night, 1 o'clock. [November 25, 1853]

. . .

Must I speak to you about art?[1] Won't you accuse me of passing quickly over affairs of the heart? But in fact everything is bound up together, and what distorts your life is also distorting your style. For you continually alloy your concepts with your passions, and this weakens the first and prevents you from enjoying the second. Oh, if I could make you what I dream of! What a woman, what a human being, you would be! And first and foremost, how happy you would be!

. . . You are a poet shackled to a woman, just as Hugo is a poet shackled to an orator . . . Do not imagine you can exorcise what oppresses you in life by giving vent to it in art. No. The heart's dross does not find its way on to paper: all you pour out there is ink, and no sooner do you voice your sorrows than they return to the soul through the ear, louder, reaching deeper than ever. Nothing has been gained . . . Only in the Absolute are we well off. Let us hold fast to that; let us keep climbing.

And so, let nothing—me, above all—disturb your sleep. Rest assured that you are, and always will be, the woman for whom I have had the greatest, the most complete affection. But I am all frayed at the edges, and you must have consideration for my tics, for my upbringing, and for my nerves. Next year, even if *Bovary* isn't finished, I will come. I will take lodgings. I will stay at least four consecutive months each year, and the rest of the time will come to Paris more often than I ever did. Meanwhile, I will see you every two months, as I promised.

As for your work, you will write beautiful things, very beautiful, and you will succeed materially, provided you confine yourself to your subjects, make outlines, and offer the public what it can conceivably accept. I am not telling you to be in tow to public taste. But in our beloved France one's form must be disguised. Whereas you flaunt your form. For *La Servante* you would have been tried, jailed, and perhaps physically assaulted by actresses.[2]

This letter is not long, but I beg you, for the love I bear you, to weigh its every line. It is pregnant with truths. Do not be upset. The sweet things I might have written you instead of this would have carried less affection.

1. The reference is to Louise's insistence on discussing *La Servante*.
2. Nevertheless, in *La Servante* Louise persisted in portraying actresses, as a class, in the guise of near-prostitutes—courtesans with crude, coarse "protectors." In another letter about *La Servante*, Flaubert wrote: "You have made Art an outlet for passions, a kind of chamber-pot to catch the overflow of I don't know what. It doesn't smell good! It smells of hate!"

To Louis Bouilhet
                              [Croisset,] Thursday, 11 o'clock. [December 8, 1853]

                              .   .   .

She makes me very sad, our poor Muse. I don't know what to do about her. I assure you that this grieves me in all kinds of ways. How do you think things will end? I suspect her of being thoroughly tired of me. And for her own peace of mind it would be best if she broke with me. She is a girl of twenty as far as feelings are concerned, and I am a sexagenarian. (Surely you yourself must have interesting things to say on this subject.) In her letter of today she tells me she is sick. If she were *really* sick, I would count on you to tell me and would come running. In two weeks my mother will be passing through Paris again. I hesitate to have her call on the Muse. It would be a kind action, I think, and one should try to be as kind as possible. But . . . but . . . *quid?* Not a word to her about this, needless to say . . .

Smarting under Flaubert's repeated warnings that to publish *La Servante* as it stood would be an indignity and a dangerous folly, and exasperated by his total behavior, Louise made a resolution (in her Memento of December 9, 1853): "I am giving up writing to him. DeLisle is right. It is beneath my dignity to complain. Silence or short letters. If he is going to change, he will do so of his own accord. Complaining weakens my position. Oh! mon Dieu, how I am suffering! Never a great and noble heart."

To Louise Colet

[Croisset,] Friday night, 2 o'clock. [December 23, 1853]

I must love you to write you tonight, for I am *exhausted.* My skull feels encased in an iron helmet. Since two o'clock yesterday afternoon (except for about twenty-five minutes for dinner), I have been writing *Bovary.* I am in full fornication, in the very midst of it: my lovers are sweating and gasping. This has been one of the rare days of my life passed completely in illusion, from beginning to end. At six o'clock tonight, as I was writing the word "hysterics," I was so swept away, was bellowing so loudly[1] and feeling so deeply what my little Bovary was going through, that I was afraid of having hysterics myself. I got up from my table and opened the window to calm myself. My head was spinning. Now I have great pains in my knees, in my back, and in my head. I feel like a man who has been fucking too much (forgive the expression) —a kind of rapturous lassitude. And since I am in the midst of love it is only proper that I should not fall asleep before sending you a caress, a kiss, and whatever thoughts are left in me.

Will what I have written be good? I have no idea—I am hurrying a little, to be able to show Bouilhet a complete section when he comes. What is certain is that my book has been going at a lively rate for the past week. May it continue so, for I am weary of my usual snail's pace. But I fear the awakening, the disillusion that may come when the pages are copied. No matter: for better or worse, it is a delicious thing to write, to be no longer yourself but to move in an entire universe of your own creating. Today, for instance, as man and woman, both lover and mistress, I rode in a forest on an autumn afternoon under the yellow leaves, and I was also the horses, the leaves, the wind, the words my people uttered, even the red sun that made them almost close their love-drowned eyes.[2]

Is this pride or piety? Is it a foolish overflow of exaggerated self-satisfaction, or is it really a vague and noble religious instinct? But when I brood over these marvelous pleasures I have enjoyed, I would be tempted to offer God a prayer of thanks if I knew he could hear me. Praised may he be for not creating me a cotton merchant, a vaudevillian, a wit, etc.! Let us sing to Apollo as in ancient days, and breathe deeply of the fresh cold air of Parnassus; let us strum our guitars and clash our cymbals, and whirl like dervishes in the eternal hubbub of Forms and Ideas.[3]

. . .

1. Flaubert often shouted aloud *(gueulait)* the sentences he was writing. He called his study his *gueuloir*.

2. *Madame Bovary*, Part II, Chapter 9.

3. This note of exaltation and gratitude is reminiscent of the prayer of thanksgiving on the Nile (p. 122, n.1), and joins it among the exceptions to the oddly phrased remark by Henry James in *Notes on Novelists:* "[Flaubert's] case was a doom because he felt of his vocation almost nothing but the difficulty."

To Louis Bouilhet

[Croisset, December 26, 1853]

. . .

How is our poor Muse? What do you think about her? What does she say? She writes me less often. I think that at bottom she is tired of me. Who is to blame? Destiny. For I feel my conscience perfectly at ease in this whole affair, and consider that I have nothing to reproach myself for; and as for her being tired of me, so would anyone else be, in her place. There is nothing lovable about me, and when I say lovable I use the word in its deepest sense. She is indeed the only woman who has loved me. Is that a curse sent her from heaven? If she dared, she would say I do not love her. She is mistaken, however.

It is probable that Flaubert's letter of Monday, December 26, crossed one that Bouilhet had written to Paris the previous Saturday. Bouilhet's letter did more than merely answer some of Flaubert's recent questions. If Flaubert, as he had been saying in his last two letters, sincerely, or even partially, believed that Louise was tired of him, Bouilhet gave him cause to change his mind.

[Paris, Saturday, December 24, 1853]

. . . I have just been having impossible, interminable conversations with her. *You* are "an egoist, a monster," and many other things besides. Apart from the deadly boredom of such confidences, they cast me in the role of a fool. The Muse's intentions seem to me neither frank nor disinterested. This display of emotion masks a great egotism that I find repellent. For the sake of physical pleasure she has jeopardized the future of her daughter, her darling daughter, her charming daughter, etc.

Do you want me to tell you what I feel? Do you want me to say straight out what she is after, with her visits to your mother, with the comedy in verse,[1] her cries, her tears, her invitations and her dinners?

She wants, and expects, to become your wife![2]

I was thinking so without daring to formulate the idea to myself, but the word was boldly uttered to me, not by her, but as positively coming from her. That is why she refused the Philosopher.[3]

All that seems to me monstrous. There is nothing physically wrong with her: she is frustrated and furious. Now I see her game. She is playing every possible card—your friends, DuCamp in the past, me

204

today, pleasant acquaintances,. Babinet, Préault, etc., and finally your family. That is the culmination, the last scene of the comedy (in verse).

She knew from me that your mother was in Paris. She came to invite me to dinner that day, and I saw no reason to keep your family's presence a secret from her. Whereupon she proposed—wrote me, half an hour later—that I talk about her to your mother, tell her how she loves you, etc. I declared in no uncertain terms that I would do nothing of the sort, and that I wanted no such commissions.

In short, *cher vieux adoré*, at this moment I am extremely exasperated. To such a point that I don't know whether I shall continue to see the Muse as hitherto. She has been very obliging to me, but it was all done for so obvious a purpose that I am ashamed. I shall send her some suitable present as thanks for her help in finding me a place to live, and gradually, without any fracas, I will let her go. Perhaps I am taking too dark a view of things. Write me by return. Give me your advice, as sage and as friend.

Tomorrow, Sunday, I am to dine with her. She will want to see your letter. I will refuse; perhaps we shall quarrel. I don't give a damn. From the moment your future is at stake I ignore the niceties: I want no one to meddle with that.

.   .   .

Our poor Muse is making enemies of all her acquaintances, past and present. No one here takes her seriously. She makes herself wantonly ridiculous. I am distressed by it all, because at bottom I am fond of her, and it is always sad to be disappointed.

Louis Bouilhet (Flaubert's "cher bougre") and Louise Colet were probably jealous of each other. Flaubert (Bouilhet's "cher vieux adoré") had facetiously assured Louise that he himself was not the object of Bouilhet's "passion" that recent Sunday, October 28; and Bouilhet, in the present letter, speaks of Louise's wish to marry Flaubert as though it were a crime, rather than the normal ardor of such a woman to possess the man she loved in her way—as he had possessed her in his. A futile "game," undoubtedly, considering how well she knew him; but scarcely "monstrous."

1. A play by Louise, never performed and its text now lost, entitled *Les Lettres d'amour*. One of its characters (ignoble) was modeled on Victor Cousin, and another (flatteringly admirable) on Flaubert. (J.B.) Flaubert found it a lamentable work and said so in several letters to Louise.

2. The French reads: "Elle veut, elle croit devenir ton épouse!"—to which Bouilhet has added the parenthetical remark: "Le vers y est, ma foi!"—meaning that he had unwittingly written an alexandrine.

3. Victor Cousin was now Honorary Professor at the Sorbonne, having been deprived of his post in the Ministry of Public Instruction by the Imperial regime. Continuing to believe himself the father of Louise's daughter, he contributed regular sums for the child's support. Recently, according to Louise, he had proposed marriage.

To Louise Colet

[Croisset,] Wednesday, 11 P.M. [December 28, 1853]

. . .

Do not worry, pauvre amie, my health is better than ever. Nothing that comes from myself ever harms me. It is the world outside that hurts me, agitates me, wears me down. I could work for ten years, uninterruptedly, in the austerest solitude, without suffering as much as a headache; whereas a creaking door, the face of a bourgeois, a ridiculous suggestion, give me palpitations, upset me.[1] I am like those Alpine lakes which roughen under valley breezes, gentle winds that blow over low-lying ground; but great gusts from the mountains pass over them without ruffling their surface, and serve only to chase away the mists. And then, is one ever harmed by what one enjoys doing? A vocation patiently and candidly pursued becomes almost a physical function, a way of existence that occupies one's whole being. Excess holds no dangers for those who by nature tend to exaggerate.

. . .

Have you ever remarked how all *authority* is stupid concerning Art? Our wonderful governments (kings or republics) imagine that they have only to order work to be done, and it will be forthcoming. They set up prizes, encouragements, academies, and they forget only one thing, one little thing without which nothing can live: the *atmosphere*. There are two kinds of literature: one that I would call "national"[2] (the better of the two); and the other, "individual" —works produced by gifted writers. For the first to be realized, there must be a fund of opinions shared by the mass of the people, a common bond such as does not now exist; and for the full development of the second, there must be *liberty*. Nowadays, however, what can we say, what can we talk about? This situation will worsen: I dearly hope I am right. I prefer absolute Nothing to evil; dust, rather than putrefaction. And eventually there will be a revival, a new dawn. We shan't be here to see it. But who cares?

. . .

1. Flaubert had written Louise two weeks before, when his mother and Caroline were away, that the increased solitude at Croisset was "charming" and "superb." "I hear no human step, no human voice, I don't know what the servants are up to, they wait on me like shadows. I dine with my dog . . ."
Sadistic "tactlessness" of that kind has been more characteristic of Flaubert when writing to Louise than the innuendo the present letter seems to carry, in its mention of a "ridiculous suggestion" and the "stupidity" of authority in matters of art. (In addition to her government pension, Louise had been awarded three prizes by the French Academy, and the following year was to win her fourth.) It was probably Bouilhet's letter of December 24, about Louise's "game," that generated the change of tone.
2. Flaubert is here referring to his concept of Greek art as "the very constitution of an entire people," as expressed in his letter of April 24, 1852 (see p. 158).

[Croisset,] Monday night, 1 A.M. [January 2, 1854]

. . .

Bouilhet was here Friday night, Saturday, and yesterday morning. He will come again on Wednesday for the rest of the week. So far, we have had time only to talk about ourselves; most of it was taken up with the *Fossiles* and *Bovary*.[1] He was pleased with my fornication scene. However, before said passage I had one of transition, eight lines, which took me three days and doesn't contain a superfluous word—but which I have to do over again because it's too slow. It is direct dialogue, which I must change to indirect, and there isn't room to say what needs to be said. It must all be very fast and incidental, to be as though thrown away, almost unnoticeable in the book. Following which I still have three or four corrections to make—infinitely small, but they will take me all next week. How slow! How slow! No matter: I keep going. In fact I've taken a long step ahead, and feel a great inner relief, which makes me quite gay and cheerful, even though tonight I was literally sweating from the effort. It's so hard to undo what has been done, and done well, in order to insert something new in its place without revealing the joint.

. . .

Preoccupation with morality makes a work of imagination so false and boring! I am strongly attracted to criticism. The novel I am writing sharpens my ability in this respect, for it is above all a work of criticism, or rather of anatomy. The reader will be unaware, I hope, of all the psychological workings concealed beneath the form, but he will feel their effect. Another side of me longs to write great, sumptuous things—battles, sieges, descriptions of the fabulous ancient Orient. Thursday night I spent two lovely hours with my head in my hands, thinking of the bright multicolored walls of Ecbatana.[2] Nothing has been written about all that. How many things still float in the limbo of human thought! It isn't subjects that are lacking, but men.

. . .

1. In other words, they had as yet had no time to look at Louise's *La Servante*, which she had finally consented to let them "edit." Whatever suggestions they may have made, the poem as printed remains immensely overlong, scurrilous, and generally deplorable. Louise's defiant publication of so sorry a work unquestionably played a role in the now imminent rupture.

2. Today the city of Hamadan, in Iran. "The Medes were again obedient [to Deioces] and built the city now called Agbatana, the walls of which are of great size and strength, rising in circles one within the other . . . The number of the circles is seven, the royal palace and the treasuries standing within the last. The circuit of the outer wall is very nearly the same with that of Athens. Of this wall the battlements are white, of the next black, of the third scarlet, of the fourth blue, of the fifth orange; all these are coloured with paint. The two last have their battlements coated respectively with silver and gold." (Herodotus, *History*, I, c. 98. Translated by George Rawlinson.)

As we now know, it was Salammbô's Carthage that would eventually emerge from Flaubert's "lovely hours" of meditation.

To Louise Colet

. . .

In your note that came this morning, you ask me to reply to your letter of last Friday. I have just reread it; it is here, lying open on my table. What kind of answer can I give you? You must know me as well as I know myself, and you keep bringing up things we've discussed a hundred times without getting anywhere. You even reproach me for the affectionate expressions—you call them "bizarre"—that I use in my letters to you (though it seems to me I do not overindulge in sentimentalities). I will be even more sparing of them in the future, since they "make you gag." Let us go back, start over again. I will be categorical, explicit:

1. About my mother. Yes: your guess is correct. It is because I am persuaded that if she were to see you she would behave coldly toward you, less than politely, as you put it, that I prefer you not to see one another. Besides, I dislike this confusion, this bringing together of two very dissimilar kinds of affection. (You can picture what kind of woman my mother is, in this respect, when I tell you that she will never visit her elder son without invitation.) Besides: what would be her pretext for calling on you? When I told you she would visit you, I had at last overcome a tremendous obstacle, after several days of parleying, because I wanted to please you. You took no account of that, and rushed most inopportunely to reopen an irritating subject, one extremely antipathetic to me, on which I had expended great effort. I would have gone on, but you told me not to. Too bad. Now once again I beg you: leave this alone. When the time is ripe and an occasion presents itself, I will know what to do. Your persistence in this matter strikes me as very odd. Your continually asking to meet my mother, wanting me to bring her to your house, wanting her to see you, seems to me just as peculiar as though she, on her side, were to want me not to see you, not to have anything to do with you, because, because, etc. And I assure you that if she were to open her mouth concerning such matters she would soon shut it again.

Next question: financial. I am not "sulking" about this at all. I am not playing a game. I never hide my money (when I have some). There are few people as meagerly off as I who have such an air of wealth about them. (I do give the impression of being rich: that is quite true.) This is unfortunate, as it can cause me to be taken for a miser. You seem to consider me niggardly because I don't offer assistance when I am not asked. But when did I ever refuse? (No one knows the trouble I have sometimes gone to to oblige a friend.) You say I never feel a spontaneous urge to be generous? I say that is not true, that I am quite capable of such impulses. But this is no doubt a strange delusion. Didn't Du-Camp, too, once tell me: "Your purse strings are stiff from disuse"?

To sum up: I told you that I will *always* oblige you, and yet I keep saying I haven't a sou. That seems suspect to you, but I deny none of it, and I repeat it again. Let me explain. It is quite true that I haven't a farthing. (At the moment, 20 francs must carry me through till February.) Don't you think I would buy

100 copies of Leconte's book, etc. if I could? But one must first pay one's debts. Of the 2000 francs I have coming to me this year,[1] I already owe almost 1200. On top of that there are my trips to Paris. Next year, in order to live in Paris I shall have to dig deep into my capital. *That is unavoidable.* I have decided on a certain sum for living expenses in the city. Once that is used up, I'll have to resume my present existence, unless I earn something—a supposition I find absurd.

But, but!—pay close attention to this *but:* if you needed it, I would find money for you anyway, even if I had to pawn the family silver. Do you understand me now?

As for finishing *Bovary,* I have already set myself so many dates, and been mistaken so often, that I refuse not only to speak of it, but to think of it. I no longer have any idea, and can only trust in God. It will be finished in its own good time, even if I die of vexation and impatience—which might very well happen were it not for the fury that sustains me. Meanwhile I will come to see you every two months, as I promised.

Now, poor dear Louise, do you want me to tell you what I really think, or rather what you really feel? I think that your love is wavering. Your dissatisfactions, the sufferings I inflict on you, can have only that cause; for as I am now, so I have always been. But now you see me more clearly, and your judgment is a reasonable one, perhaps. I don't know. However, when you love a person *completely* you love him just as he is, with his faults and his monstrousnesses; you adore even his scabs, and the hump on his back; you love to inhale the breath that poisons you. The same is true of the spiritual aspect. Now, I am "warped, squalid, selfish," etc. You know, you'll end up by making me insufferably proud, always finding fault with me as you do. I think there cannot be a mortal on this earth less commended than I; but I will not change. I will not reform. I have already erased, corrected, blotted out or suppressed so many things in myself that I am weary of it. Everything has its end, and I think I'm now a big enough boy to consider my education complete. Now I have other things to think about. I was born with all the vices. I have radically suppressed some, and kept the rest on a starvation diet. God alone knows the martyrdoms I have undergone in this psychological training-school; but now I give up. That path leads to the grave, and I want to live through three or four more books; so behold me crystallized, immobile. You say I am made of granite. I admit it. But if my heart is inflexible, it is at least firm, and never gives way. Desertions and injustices do not change what is engraved on it. Everything that is there remains; and the thought of you, whatever you or I may do, will not be effaced.

Adieu—a long kiss on your beloved forehead.

1. Flaubert's personal income came from property left him by his father; he had no expenses while living at home. In her letter of "last Friday," Louise had characterized her many complaints as "further proof of [my] love." Flaubert had lent her 800 francs, which she had so far been unable to repay.

To Louise Colet
[Croisset,] Wednesday midnight [January 18, 1854]

.   .   .

This week I reread the first act of *King Lear*. Shakespeare frightens me the more I think of him. In their entirety, I find his works stupendous, exalting, like the idea of the planetary system. I see only an immensity there, dazzling and bewildering to the eye.

But I well know, pauvre chère amie, that we cannot always live with our noses pointed at the stars! No one suffers more than I from the necessities, the penuries, of life. My flesh lies heavy—some 75 thousand kilograms of it—on my soul. But when I urge you to renounce action, I don't mean that you should live like a brahmin. I mean merely that we should immerse ourselves in real life only up to the navel. Let movement be confined to the region of the legs: let us not be passionate about picayune, ephemeral, ugly, or mortal things. If we have to seem to be moved by all that, then we can pretend to be: but let us only pretend. Something filmier than a cloud and more resistant than a cuirass is needed to protect those natures that are rent by a mere nothing and vibrate from top to bottom at the slightest touch. We have to carry the burden (let us not forget it) of *all* other people's sufferings. And how can the vase be expected to stay full when you shake it by both handles? Brothels provide condoms as protection against catching the pox from infected vaginas. Let us always have a vast condom within us to protect the health of our soul amid the filth into which it is plunged. The pleasure is diminished, it is true, and sometimes the sheath splits.

.   .   .

It is tempting to let the epistolary record of the liaison end there, with the vision of Shakespeare, the flattering evocation of twin special souls, and the distasteful metaphor, all combining to epitomize the Flaubert whom Louise had perhaps been "cursed," as he put it, to love. But "the union of this ever diverse pair" still had a short time to run.

The possibility of Louise's association with a magazine was still in the air, and with Flaubert she sometimes talked of what might be printed in it. "There is something quite new and charming that could be done for your magazine," he wrote her in January 1854, "something that could almost be a literary creation and which hasn't occurred to you: an article on fashion. I will explain what I mean, in my next."

In the manuscript of *Madame Bovary*, Flaubert had already written several passages that touched on women's fashions; and fashion was to play a crucial, even diabolical, role in the last part of the novel. He had introduced the lovely young Emma, still a girl on her father's farm, opening her parasol of "rosy iridescent silk" on a day of thaw. There was a picturesque description of clothes worn at a country wedding. At a fashionable dinner party in a château,

"Madame Bovary was surprised to notice that several of the ladies had failed to put their gloves in their glasses," which meant that unlike provincially bred Emma, these sophisticates saw no reason to signal that they did not drink wine in public. There was Emma as she danced: "Her hair, drawn down smoothly on both sides and slightly fluffed out over the ears, shone with a blue luster; in her chignon a rose quivered on its pliant stem, with artificial dewdrops at the leaftips. Her gown was pale saffron, trimmed with three bunches of pompom roses and green sprays." In the end, many of Emma's fatal debts were to be for clothes.

Now Flaubert sent Louise his suggestions for a fashion article—incorrigibly inflicting on her, as a preamble, yet more passages to do with himself or with Shakespeare.

To Louise Colet

[Croisset,] Sunday night [January 29, 1854]

.   .   .

Do you know how many pages I have written this week? One, and I cannot even say a good one. A quick, light passage was needed, and I was in a frame of mind better suited to gravity and unhurried exposition. What trouble I am having! What an atrociously delicious thing we are bound to say writing is— since we keep slaving this way, enduring such tortures and not wanting things otherwise. There is a mystery in this I cannot fathom. The writer's vocation is perhaps comparable to love for one's native land (of which I have little, by the way), a certain fated bond between men and things. The Siberian in his snow and the Hottentot in his hut both live content, not dreaming of the sun or of palaces. Something stronger than they keeps them attached to their miserable environment, while we flounder about in our search for Forms. Whether poets, sculptors, painters or musicians, we perceive existence as refracted in words, shapes, colors or harmonies, and we find that the most wonderful thing in the world.

And then I was overwhelmed for two days by a scene in Shakespeare (the first scene in Act Three of *King Lear*[1]). That man will drive me mad. More and more all the others seem like children beside him. In that scene all the characters, wretched beyond endurance and completely crazed by their sufferings, go off their heads and talk wildly. There are three different kinds of madness howling at once, while the Fool cracks jokes and rain pours down amid thunder and lightning. A young gentleman, whom we have seen rich and handsome at the beginning of the play, says this: "Ah! I knew women, etc. I was ruined by them. Distrust the light sound of their gown and the creaking of their satin shoes, etc." Ah! *Poésie françoyse!* How clear your waters run in comparison! When I think of how faithful we are to those busts—Racine! Corneille! And other talents just as mortally boring! It makes me groan! I long (another quotation from the Bard) to "tread them into mortar and daub the walls of a jakes with them."² Yes, it bowled me over. I could think of nothing but that scene on the heath, where wolves are heard howling and old Lear weeps in the rain and tears his beard in the wind. It is when one contemplates such peaks that one feels small: "Doomed to mediocrity, we are humbled by transcendent minds."³

But now to talk about something other than Shakespeare: about your magazine. Well, I think that everywhere, apropos of everything, Art has its place. Now who, up to the present, has dabbled in writing about fashion? Dressmakers! But just as upholsterers have no understanding of furniture, cooks little understanding of cuisine, and tailors none whatever of costume, so dressmakers have no idea of Art. For the same reason, portraitists paint bad portraits (the good ones are painted by thinkers, by creators, who alone know how to *reproduce*). The narrow specialization in which they spend their lives blinds them to the very significance of their specialty, and they constantly confuse the accessory with the essential, the trimming with the cut. A great tailor might be an artist, as in the XVIth century goldsmiths were artists. But mediocrity is creeping in everywhere: the very stones under our feet are becoming dull, and our highways are boring beyond words. Perish though we may (and perish we shall in any case), we must employ every means to stem the flood of trash invading us. We must take flight into the ideal, since we can no longer dwell in marble halls and wear the purple, recline on hummingbird-feather divans, enjoy swansdown carpets, ebony chairs, tortoise-shell floors, solid gold candelabra, lamps carved in emerald. And so we must raise our voices against gloves made of shoddy, against office chairs, the mackintosh, cheap stoves, against imitation cloth, imitation luxury, imitation pride. Thanks to industrialism, ugliness has assumed gigantic proportions. How many good people who a century ago could have lived perfectly well without Beaux Arts now cannot do without mini-statues, mini-music and mini-literature! Take a single case: the ominous proliferation of bad drawings by lithography. And the extraordinary notions of the human anatomy those lithographs convey! On the other hand, cheapness has made real luxury fabulously expensive. Who is willing these days to buy a good watch? (It costs 1200 francs.) We are all fakes and charlatans. Pretense, affectation, humbug everywhere—the crinoline has falsified the buttocks. Our century is a century of whores, and so far what is least prostituted is the prostitute.

But since our purpose here is not to sermonize the bourgeois (who aren't even bourgeois any more, for since the invention of the public bus the bourgeoisie is dead; they sit there in the bus alongside the "lower classes" and not only think like them and look like them but even dress like them: take the fashion for coarse cloth, the new styles in overcoats, the jerseys worn for boating, and the blue work shirts for field sports, etc.)—still, since there is no question of sermonizing them, this is what I would do: I would accept it all, and write straight from the democratic point of view: point out that nowadays everything is for everybody, and that the greatest possible confusion exists for the good of the greatest number. I would try to establish *a posteriori* that consequently there is no such thing as fashion, since there is no authority, no rule. In the past it was known *who* set the fashions, and every fashion had some sense to it. (I would return to this point later: it would be part of a history of costume—which would be a very good thing to write, by the way, a totally new subject.) But now there is anarchy, and everyone is free to follow his own caprice. Perhaps from this a new order will emerge.

And here are two further points that I would develop. This anarchy is the result, among a thousand other things, of the historizing tendency of our epoch. (The Nineteenth Century seems to be taking a survey course in history.) Thus in the space of less than thirty years we have seen vogues for the Roman, the Gothic, the Pompadour and the Renaissance, and something remains of all that. So: how take advantage of this for beauty's sake—or, forgive the pun, for our Beauties' sake? I see it this way: by studying what form, what color, is suitable for a given person in a given circumstance. This involves the ability to sense a certain harmony between color and line. The great courtesans and the true dandies are particularly good at this: they do not dress in obedience to fashion magazines. That is the art such a magazine must address itself to if it wants to be new and realistic. Study, for example, how Veronese dresses his golden women, what ornaments he places on the necks of his negresses, etc. Isn't there such a thing as a "seemly" way of dressing? Isn't there a libidinous way, or an elegiac, or a provocative? On what do such effects depend? On an exact harmony, so subtle as to be unnoticeable, between features and facial expression on the one side, and apparel on the other. A further consideration is the relation between costume and function; and some forms of the beautiful are rooted in this utilitarian idea. For example, the majesty of church vestments: the gesture of benediction is stupid without wide sleeves. The Orient is de-Moslemizing itself by adopting the frock-coat. They can't even make their ablutions any more, poor things, what with their buttoned cuffs! Similarly, the introduction of the *sous-pied*[4] will sooner or later cause them to give up the divan (and perhaps even the harem, for such trousers also have *buttoned flies*. For the importance of the fly, see the great Rabelais.) As for the *sous-pied*, it is now being given up in France because of the proliferation and speed of commercial business. Note that the stockbrokers were the first to adopt spats and low-cut shoes: the *sous-pied* hindered them from rushing up the steps of the Exchange, etc. And is there anything stupider than the "fashion bulletin," which reports what costumes were worn *last* week, so that the reader can wear them *next* week, and which sets rules for everybody? Not to mention that to be well dressed, everyone must dress in the way best suited to himself. It is always the same question, the question of poetics. Each individual piece of work contains its own innate poetics, and each of these must be discovered.

So: I would attack and put to rout that idea of a general fashion. I would rampage against stove-pipe hats; and against dressing-gowns with designs of palm-leaves, and those "bonnets grecs" embroidered with flowers.[5] I would terrify the bourgeois and the bourgeois spirit. The fashion for corsets must go —hideous things, revoltingly lubricious and excessively inconvenient at certain moments. I have sometimes suffered grievously because of corsets!!! Yes,

I have suffered greatly from those nothings, which a man "mustn't talk about" (because that "isn't done" by the virile type we are all supposed to pattern ourselves on, at the risk of being considered eunuchs). There are certain styles of interior decoration, certain costumes, certain colors in clothes, shapes of chairs, borders on curtains, that make me really sick. In the theatre I never see the coiffures of women "en toilette" without being nauseated, because of all the fish glue veneering their hair, etc.; and the sight of actors wearing gloves from Jouvin even when playing *William Tell* is enough to make me hate the opera. What imbeciles! What about expressive movements of the hand—what happens to them, constrained in a glove? Imagine a statue wearing gloves! Styles must always say something; they must express, to the greatest extent possible, the soul of the wearer.

Enough talk about rags, no?

Ah! I have spent many hours of my life at my fireside, furnishing palaces, dreaming of liveries, for the day when I would have a million a year! I have seen myself wearing buskins studded with diamonds. I have heard horses neighing at many an imaginary porte-cochère, harnessed to equipages that would make all England die of envy. Such banquets! Such sumptuously decked tables! Such service, such good fare! Fruit, from every country in the world, poured out of baskets made of its own leaves! Oysters were served on beds of seaweed, and all around the dining room ran an espalier of flowering jasmine alive with exotic birds.

Oh! Our ivory towers! Let us climb them in our dreams, since the hobnails on our boots keep us anchored here below!

In my entire life I have *never* seen anything luxurious except in the Orient. There you find people clad in rags and swarming with vermin, yet with gold bracelets on their arms. The Beautiful is more useful to them than the Good. They cover themselves with color, not with cloth. Their need for smoking is greater than that for food. Admirable predominance of the Idea, whatever else may be said.

So—adieu, it is very late; je t'embrasse, à toi.

1. What follows is in *Lear*, Act III, not Scene I, but Scenes II and IV. Only if one is to consider the Fool mad, which Flaubert seems not to do, can one conceivably find here "three different kinds of madness howling at once"; and the paraphrase is inaccurate, for the "young gentleman" (Edgar) does not say he was ruined by women, nor was he. Flaubert's inexactitudes concerning these scenes which he had apparently been reading only recently, and yet his undoubted enthusiasm for them, are the subject of interesting comment by Sartre (*L'Idiot de la famille*, II, 2034 et seq.) Flaubert was still reading Shakespeare with the help of a French translation. Three years later, while reading *Macbeth*, he would write to Louis Bouilhet: "If I persist a little longer, I will be able to understand . . . Shakespeare very well." Flaubert's Shakespeare was rather like his Greek. As for his impatience with the French classics, see his contrasting remarks to Louise about Corneille (p. 92).

2. *Lear*, Act II, Scene II. The French here in the letter is: "Je voudrais les broyer dans un pilon, pour peindre ensuite avec les résidus les murailles des latrines."

3. "Nés pour la médiocrité, nous sommes accablés par les esprits sublimes." From Montesquieu, *Dialogue de Sylla et d'Eucrate*, which Flaubert and Louise had read together almost a year before (see p. 156).

4. A strap attached to the bottom of the trouser leg and passing under the foot, to keep the trouser trim.

5. What we would now call men's "paisley" dressing gowns; and, to be worn with them, at home, small round "Greek" caps, sometimes tasseled.

In another sense, too, it was late—too late for the faltering liaison to last much longer. Even after Bouilhet's warning about Louise's "game," Flaubert continued for a time to use her as his outlet—for chronicle, ideas, protests, and his brand of affection; talking to her, as it were, from the solitude of Croisset, seeing her occasionally in Paris and presumably making love. But the last surviving letters (about a dozen of them[1] after the letter concerning fashion) do not go beyond April 1854. There follows a gap of almost a year. Then, in March 1855, in circumstances whose immediate details are unknown, Flaubert wrote his real "ultima."

1. Omitted from the present volume, these abound in outrages·
"You ask for love, you complain that I don't send you flowers. Flowers, indeed! Go find some nice fresh-faced young boy with perfect manners and all the right ideas. I am like the tiger, who has bristles of hair at the tip of his glans, which lacerate the female."
"You tell me you are hardly ever troubled by erotic thoughts. I can make you the same confidence: I confess I no longer have any sexual urge, thank God."
"I have always tried (but I think I failed) to turn you into a sublime hermaphrodite. I want you to be a man down to the navel; below that, you get in my way, you disturb me—your female element ruins everything."
Yet, along with this heightened abuse, there are some fine Flaubertian strokes:
"I am like Egypt: in order to live, I need regular floods—of style."
"Sentences must stir in a book like leaves in a forest, each distinct from each despite their resemblance."

To Louise Colet

[Paris, March 6, 1855]

Madame: I was told that you took the trouble to come here to see me three times last evening.

I was not in. And, fearing lest persistence expose you to humiliation, I am bound by the rules of politeness to warn you that *I shall never be in.*

Yours,

Tuesday morning.   G.F.

On that sheet of Flaubert's blue notepaper Louise has dashed down the words "lâche, couard et canaille"—"poltroon, coward, cur."

It must have been about this time that Flaubert was describing, in his novel, the way in which a lover he had created, the brutal gentleman-farmer Rodolphe Boulanger, chose to break with his mistress, Emma Bovary. "Then," the passage about Rodolphe's letter of rupture to Emma reads, "looking around

215

for something to seal the letter with, his eye fell on the signet ring [given him by Emma] with the motto *'Amor nel Cor.'* 'Scarcely appropriate under the circumstances, but what the . . .' Whereupon he smoked three pipes and went to bed."

The coarse-grained, uncultured Rodolphe is scarcely to be identified with his creator Gustave Flaubert. Yet there is something redolent of "smoking three pipes and going to bed" in Flaubert's manner of breaking with the mistress— importunate and intolerable though she had become—whom he had loved, known long, and confided in most intimately. This brutality toward Louise is emphasized in a detail of the rupture he invented for Rodolphe and Emma: for Flaubert himself had received, as a gift from Louise, not a signet-ring but a cigar-holder, inscribed with the words "Amor nel Cor."

In *Madame Bovary*, Emma reads Rodolphe's letter "through, now and then giving an angry sneer." Louise Colet was in no sense the "model" for Emma Bovary; and yet (to anticipate), when the novel was published and Louise read it, she was inevitably made to think of herself in the scenes of lovers' meetings and in Emma's vehemences. She expanded the angry sneer she had written on Flaubert's letter of rupture into a poem, printed in a Parisian magazine, with *Amor nel Cor* as its title. Intended to be bitter but achieving, alas, only mawkishness, the poem is an embarrassing justification of Flaubert's warning against putting one's "heart's dross" on paper. Certain of its lines refer to a novel, written by the brutish recipient of the woman's gift, as "un roman de commis voyageur"—a novel for traveling salesmen.

With her "lâche, couard et canaille," Louise makes her exit from Flaubert's correspondence, except as a memory occasionally evoked in letters to people who had known them both. Flaubert seems never to have seen her again; she once glimpsed him in a crowd. He heard of her as a voice reported speaking ill of him to friends, and as a writer of fiction who used him as a model for characters in novels, much as she had excoriated Alfred de Musset in her poem, *La Servante*.[1]

Because of the cessation of letters to Louise, the composition of the last third of *Madame Bovary* is scarcely recorded. But now the great drama of the novel's publication was imminent.

1. Louise Colet continued her career as poet, novelist, and journalist until her death in 1876. She became an ever more outspoken feminist, was never well off, and displayed courage in adverse circumstances. Often these were of her own making: she quarreled with almost everyone, including her daughter Henriette, and left, on the whole, a reputation entitling her to be more fitly remembered not as "Penserosa" (the title of one of her early books), but rather, perhaps, as "Clamorosa." Henriette, who inherited Flaubert's letters to her mother, sold them to a publisher in the early 1900s. They have been printed in various editions of Flaubert's correspondence ever since, culminating in that of the Bibliothèque de la Pléiade, definitively edited by Jean Bruneau.

VII

Publication, Trial, Triumph
1856-1857

$\mathbf{A}$T THE TIME of the final rupture between the lovers, Louis Bouilhet, in Paris, had had his second long poem well received and had almost completed an historical drama in verse. Flaubert had himself taken an apartment in Paris for the winter of 1854-1855, and he did the same the next winter. He and Bouilhet saw each other constantly, had affairs with Parisian actresses, and afforded each other professional help and consolation, Flaubert sustaining and scolding the rather timid Bouilhet in the face of repeated rebuffs by theatrical producers, and Bouilhet continuing his role of "midwife" as *Madame Bovary* neared its conclusion.

In one of his last letters to Louise Colet, in 1854, Flaubert had written:

> I think I have taken a big step—made the *imperceptible* transition from psychology to drama. Now that I'll be in the midst of action, the passions I depict will be conveyed more effectively. I'll no longer have to use so many half-tones. This will be more amusing, for the reader, at least . . . When will the blessed day come when I will write the words "The End"? Next September it will be three years that I've been at work on this book. That's a long time, three years spent on the same idea, writing in the same style (especially when the style is one which expresses my personality as little as that of the Emperor of China), living continuously with the same characters, in the same surroundings, clobbering oneself to maintain the same illusion.

Now, a year later, he was still at it. There were times when he found his labor on the last chapters almost intolerable. "I am working badly, quite without any taste for it, or rather with *dis*taste. I am profoundly sick of this task. It is a real pensum for me now," he wrote Bouilhet from Croisset in September 1855. "My wretched novel won't be finished before February. This is becoming ridiculous. I don't dare mention it any more." What he was writing, and what he saw about him, intensified his misanthropy: "I feel waves of hatred for the stupidity of my age. They choke me. Shit keeps coming into my mouth, as from a strangulated hernia . . . I want to make a paste of it and daub it over the nineteenth century, the way they coat Indian pagodas with cow dung." And he told Bouilhet: "You know, about six weeks ago my mother made a remark I find sublime, enough to make the Muse hang herself out of jealousy at not having thought of it herself. 'Your mania for sentences,' my mother said, 'has dried up your heart.' "

Especially for the later chapters of the book, those dealing with Emma's extravagances and promissory notes, and the resultant forced sale of the contents of the Bovarys' house, he made detailed use of a strange document concerning his old friend Louise Pradier.[1] (He continued to see this other Louise from time to time, and the tone of his occasional letters to her was always quite formal: "Chère Madame," and so on—in order, Jean Bruneau thinks, that she might share them with her mother and sister, who were well known to Flaubert and his family. This formality was in strong contrast to the nature of his other relations with the lady, who seems to have remained good natured and easygoing in her "disgrace.")

The completed manuscript of *Madame Bovary* in Flaubert's hand bears the dates "September 1851-April 1856."

FLAUBERT and Maxime DuCamp never fully recovered the degree of friendship that had preceded their disagreement over Flaubert's chosen way of life, but the bitterness of that episode had abated, and DuCamp was one of the first to be shown the completed novel. Although, as will be seen, he had strong reservations, he seems not to have found it the "total fiasco" he had prophesied to Louise Colet; in any case, he kept the "pledge" he had made to Flaubert five years before, and offered to print it in the *Revue de Paris* in six bimonthly parts and to pay Flaubert two thousand francs. Flaubert accepted, asserting in a letter to his cousin Olympe Bonenfant in Nogent that the sum proved him to be "an excellent businessman."[2] DuCamp, for his part, was to boast for the rest of his life of being the first publisher of *Madame Bovary*.

Delivery to the *Revue* was delayed because Bouilhet, on rereading the manuscript as a whole, advised some cutting, and Flaubert reluctantly removed thirty pages. After the novel had been read by Léon Laurent-Pichat, one of DuCamp's codirectors on the *Revue*, DuCamp sent Flaubert a letter whose tone and content will surprise no serious creative writer who has had to do with publishers and editors of magazines:

July 14, 1856

Cher Vieux: Laurent-Pichat has read your novel, and I enclose his remarks about it. You will realize when you read them how I must agree, for they reproduce almost all the observations I made to you before you left. I gave the book to Laurent with no comment beyond a warm recommendation; it is not by collusion that we harass you along the same lines. The advice he gives you is good—the only advice, let me say, that you should follow. Let us take full charge of the publication of your novel in the *Revue*; we will make the cuts we think indispensable; and later you will publish it in a volume in whatever form you choose: that is your affair. My personal opinion is that if you do not do this, you will be gravely compromising yourself, making your first appearance with a muddled work to which the style alone does not give sufficient interest. Be brave, close your eyes during the operation, and have confidence—if not in our talent, at least in the experience we have acquired in such matters and also in our affection for you. You have buried your novel under a heap of details which are well done but superfluous: it is not seen clearly enough, and must be disencumbered—an easy task. We shall have it done under our supervision by someone who is experienced and clever; not a word will be added to your manuscript, it will merely be pruned; the job will cost you about a hundred francs, which will be deducted from your payment, and you will have published something really good instead of something imperfect and padded. You are doubtless cursing me with all your might at this very moment, but you may be sure that in all this I have only your own interest at heart.

On that letter Flaubert scrawled "Gigantesque!"; and retorted to DuCamp that the novel was to be published as it was or not at all. After some dispute it was agreed that only one passage would be omitted—that describing the careening course, through the streets of Rouen, of the erotic cab containing Emma and her lover Léon. That, DuCamp flatly said, was "impossible."

The first installment, originally scheduled for July or August, finally appeared in the issue of October 1, 1856.

1. Among the Flaubert papers in the Municipal Library of Rouen, Mlle Gabrielle Leleu found, and summarized in 1947, a manuscript entitled *Mémoires de Madame Ludovica*, an account of Louise Pradier's debts and adulteries written by an unnamed woman. The American scholar Douglas Siler, who published the document in full in 1973, has identified the author as a friend of Mme Pradier's, a certain Mme Louise Boyé. It is not known how the document came into Flaubert's possession. One of Flaubert's major "scénarios"—outlines—for *Madame Bovary*, recently discovered by Dr. Siler (who is preparing an edition of Pradier's correspondence), is none other than a partial summary of the *Mémoires de Madame Ludovica*.

2. It is difficult to assess the "real" value of Flaubert's 2000 francs (magazine payment for four and a half years' work) except by comparing it with certain incomes of the time. The reader will recall Flaubert's writing to Alfred LePoittevin in 1845 that Louise Pradier, cast out by her husband, was living "wretchedly" on 6000 francs a year. Jacques Desmarets, in *La France de 1870* (Hachette, 1971), lists the following annual averages: "bourgeois," 13,000 to 17,000; artisans and shopkeepers, 1600 to 1800; minor officials, 1000 to 1200; laborers and shop employees, under 1000. According to Theodore Zeldin, in *France 1848-1945*, a doctor might expect to average 3000 francs a year in 1842, a good Parisian carpenter could earn 1300 francs during the early Second Empire, and an *agrégé de l'université* (a particularly qualified teacher in a lycée) began at 2200 francs and could rise to 6600.

To Leon Laurent-Pichat

Croisset, Thursday night. [October 2,] 1856

Cher Ami

I have just received *Bovary*,[1] and first of all want to thank you for it (I may be vulgar, but I am not ungrateful); you did me a service by taking it as it is and I will not forget it.

Confess that you thought me and still think me (more than ever, perhaps) wildly ridiculous. If some day I come to agree that you were right, I promise you faithfully that I will make you the most humble apologies. But you must understand that this was a *test* which I wanted to make; let us hope that what I learn from it will not be too much of a jolt.

Do you think that this ignoble reality, so distasteful to you in reproduction, does not turn my stomach as it does yours? If you knew me better you would know that I abhor ordinary existence. Personally, I have always held myself as aloof from it as I could. But aesthetically, I wanted this once—and only this once—to plumb its depths. Therefore I plunged into it heroically, into all its minutiae, accepting everything, telling everything, depicting everything, pretentious as that may sound.

I am expressing myself badly, but well enough for you to understand the general trend of my resistance to your criticisms, judicious as they may be. You were rewriting my book. You were damaging the inner poetics that determined the pattern (as a philosopher would say) of its concept.

In short, in acting out of deference and not out of conviction, I would have considered that I was failing in my duty to myself and to you. Art requires neither complaisance nor politeness: nothing but faith—faith always, and freedom.

1. I.e. the first installment in the *Revue de Paris*.

The installments of *Madame Bovary* made a considerable impression from the beginning. The night of November 6, 1856, Bouilhet's play, *Madame de Montarcy*, was acclaimed at the Théâtre de l'Odéon. The two friends were jubilant about their simultaneous success.

However, as serialization proceeded, the editors of the *Revue de Paris* received an increasing number of protests from subscribers, especially readers in the provinces, outraged by the novel's "immorality"; and during November they learned that because of certain passages the government "examiner of books and periodicals"—Napoleon III's censor—had asked the Department of Justice to prosecute the magazine and Flaubert for "outrage of public morals and religion." When Flaubert opened his copy of the issue of December 1, he found the newest installment headed by an editorial note: "The editors find themselves obliged to omit from this installment a passage which they consider unsuitable for publication in the *Revue de Paris*. They hereby advise the author of their action and assume full responsibility for it."

And the *Revue* asked Flaubert to make more cuts.

To Leon Laurent-Pichat

[Paris,] Sunday. [December 7, 1856]

Mon cher Ami

First, thank you for disclaiming personal responsibility; I therefore now address not the poet Laurent-Pichat, but the *Revue*, an abstract personality, whose interests you represent. This is my reply to the *Revue de Paris:*

1. It kept the manuscript of *Madame Bovary* for three months, and thus it had every opportunity, before printing the first line, to know what to make of it. The alternatives were to take it or leave it. The *Revue* took it, and must abide by the consequences.

2. Once the agreement was concluded, I consented to the elimination of a passage which I consider very important, because the *Revue* claimed it presented a risk. I complied gracefully, but I will not conceal from you (and now I am speaking to my friend Pichat) that that day I bitterly regretted having had the idea of publishing.

Let us speak our minds fully or not at all:

3. I consider that I have already done a great deal, and the *Revue* thinks that I should do still more. *I will do nothing:* I will not make a correction, not a cut; I will not suppress a comma; nothing, nothing! But if the *Revue de Paris* thinks that I am compromising it, if it is afraid, the simple thing to do is to stop publication of *Madame Bovary* at once. I wouldn't give a damn.

Now that I have finished addressing the *Revue*, let me point out one thing to my friend:

By eliminating the passage about the cab you have not made the story a whit less shocking; and you will accomplish no more by the cuts you ask for in the sixth installment.

You are objecting to details, whereas actually you should object to the whole. The brutal element is basic, not superficial. Negroes cannot be made white, and you cannot change the *blood* of a book. All you can do is to weaken it.

Needless to say, if I break with the *Revue de Paris* I shall nevertheless remain a friend of its editors.

I know how to distinguish between literature and literary business.

The *Revue* replied that if Flaubert would not make the new cuts, they would. He threatened suit, but was dissuaded by a lawyer friend in Rouen: the law, it appeared, was on the *Revue's* side. He then asked that the last installment be canceled. The *Revue* refused, but consented to his prefacing it with a note:

> Considerations which it is not in my province to judge compelled the *Revue de Paris* to omit a passage from the issue of December 1; its scruples having been again aroused on the occasion of the present issue, it has thought proper to omit several more. Consequently, I

hereby decline responsibility for the lines which follow. The reader is asked to consider them as a series of fragments, not as a whole.

Gustave Flaubert

On December 26, Flaubert signed a contract with the publisher Michel Lévy for the publication of *Madame Bovary* in book form, giving Lévy the rights to the novel for five years in return for the sum of 800 francs.

Meanwhile, the government proceeded with its charge.

To EDMOND PAGNERRE[1]

[Paris, December 31, 1856]

My dear Pagnerre:

You know better than anyone else that I have published a novel in the *Revue de Paris*, since in your newspaper you wrote very amiably about me in that connection. Now I stand accused of having "outraged public morals and religion" in that book. I have already been interrogated by the examining magistrate, and it is very probable that I shall be summoned to court on a criminal charge. I shall be sentenced in any case, and this is why:

I am a pretext. The government is out to destroy the *Revue de Paris*, and I have been chosen as its instrument.[2] The situation is this: If the case is dropped, I will have saved the *Revue de Paris*; if it is not dropped, I face ruin.

Our friend Cormenin,[3] in whose presence I am writing this, tells me that you are an intimate friend of M. Abbatucci.[4] Do me the service of writing to him and explaining the situation as it really is.

I think I have written a book that is moral by its effect as a whole. As for details, I am being blamed for a scene of Extreme Unction which is copied almost word for word from the Missal. The ridiculous character in my novel is a Voltairean, a materialist philosopher (like the Garçon!).[5] I do not preach adultery or irreligion, since I show, as every good author should,[6] the punishment incurred by immoral behavior.

If I am sentenced, it will be impossible for me ever to write a line again. I will be watched; and a second offense would bring me five years in prison. Besides, it is not pleasant to be sentenced for immorality. It puts one in the company of the Alexis Duponts or the Hervés.[7]

So be a good fellow and do what you think proper to extract me from this hornet's nest.

Write the Minister telling him who I am as a man and what kind of book I have written. If they want to nab the *Revue*, there are plenty of opportunities. But they should leave me in peace to write my little stories.

Adieu, thank you in advance, for I am counting on you.

1. A Bonapartist, editor-in-chief of *Le Journal du Loiret*, published at Orléans. Flaubert had known Pagnerre as a boy in Rouen. DuCamp had urged Flaubert to seek help from all the Bonapartist friends he could think of. (J.B.)
2. DuCamp and his fellow editors believed this (the magazine had received one or two

warnings), and they had apparently persuaded Flaubert it was so. But Jean Bruneau thinks that although the *Revue de Paris* was unquestionably in disfavor with the government because of the liberalism of some of its articles (it was, in fact, later suppressed), the target at this time was really Flaubert and his "immoral" book. See Flaubert's own mention of "Jesuits" on p. 225.

3. Louis de Cormenin, a former codirector of the *Revue de Paris*.

4. Charles Abbatucci, senator and Minister of Justice.

5. For the "Garçon," see p. 2. Pagnerre, Flaubert later told his niece Caroline, had been "one of the creators of the Garçon. That is a free-masonry one doesn't forget."

6. It is difficult to know whether Flaubert is being totally ironic here or suggesting to his old friend that these words be repeated to the important senator and Minister of Justice.

7. Dupont, a singer, and Hervé, an actor, had been arrested for abusing young children of both sexes. Dupont, sixty years old, hanged himself. (J.B.)

Despite the rigorous press censorship of the period, the affair of *Madame Bovary* and the *Revue de Paris* did not go unreported. Throughout January, Parisian literary journals commented on the scandal facing the *Revue*. In its issue of January 3, 1857, the Brussels newspaper, *L'Indépendence Belge*, which was sometimes forbidden the French mails, carried a "Paris letter" entitled "Madame Bovary et ses persécuteurs," with a sequel on January 27. Flaubert, who from his solitude at Croisset had expressed his contempt for the press, now found himself *in* the press. The rhythm of his life radically changed, he "plunged into the fray"—as he had once reminded Maxime DuCamp he was capable of doing if the affair were "of short duration and something that I enjoy." He busied himself preparing his defense, writing letters like the one to Pagnerre, soliciting help from friends and acquaintances who might influence government officials. His brother Achille, through the Prefect in Rouen, saw to it that the Ministry of Justice was informed of the Flauberts' being "an important family, whom it might be dangerous to attack because of the approaching elections"; a powerful defender was found in the prominent trial lawyer Antoine-Marie-Jules Senard, who had been a friend of the elder Dr. Flaubert. Nevertheless, the government persisted in its case. Flaubert continued defiant and outspoken. "At any moment," he wrote to his brother in mid-January, "I expect the summons that will name the day when I am to sit— for the crime of writing in French—on the bench usually occupied by pickpockets and prostitutes."

To his brother Achille

[Paris, c. January 20, 1857]

I am very surprised not to have received my summons; there is a delay: are they hesitating, perhaps? I think so; the people who have spoken on my behalf are furious; and I hear that one of my protectors, who is a *very* highly placed personage, is becoming "enraged," and threatens to "smash some windows at the Tuileries." The outcome will be favorable, I am sure, whether the affair is quashed or whether I go on trial.

The various steps I have taken have been very beneficial, in that opinion is now on my side; there isn't a literary man in Paris who hasn't read me and doesn't defend me; they are all sheltering behind me—they feel that my cause is theirs.

The police have blundered. They thought they were attacking a run-of-the-mill novel and some ordinary little scribbler; whereas now (in part thanks to the prosecution) my novel is looked on as a masterpiece; as for the author, he has for defenders a number of what used to be called "grandes dames"; the Empress, among others, has twice spoken in my favor; the Emperor said, the first time, "They should leave him alone"; and despite all that the case was taken up again. Why? There begins the mystery.

While waiting, I am preparing my statement, which is simply my novel itself; but I am cramming the margins next to the incriminated passages with embarrassing quotations drawn *from the classics*, to show by means of that simple parallel that for the past three hundred years there hasn't been a line of French literature that couldn't be indicted as undermining morality and religion. Have no fear: I shall be quite calm. As for not appearing at the trial, that would be a retreat; I shan't say anything, but will sit next to Senard, who will need me there. Besides, I can't afford not to display my criminal countenance to the populace.

I thank you and Pottier[1] for your future visit. Come and dine with me in my Venetian oubliette. I'll provide a bundle of straw and some chains, and have my portrait painted as "the author in fetters, sitting on dank straw in his dungeon"!!!

It is all so stupid that I have come to enjoy it greatly.

As you see, nothing is certain as yet: we must wait.

By the middle of next week you should receive some pieces by me published in *L'Artiste*. There will be four numbers in all, containing fragments of *La Tentation de Saint Antoine*.[2] If I should forget to send them, remind me: the last fragment will appear next Sunday.

Adieu, cher frère, je t'embrasse.

1. Conservateur of the Rouen Municipal Library.

2. Immediately after finishing *Madame Bovary*, Flaubert had taken up his manuscript of *Saint Antoine*, and during the summer and fall of 1856 he "corrected" it—a process which resulted in its being cut by half. When *Madame Bovary*, appearing in the *Revue de Paris*, showed signs of becoming a *succès de scandale*, Théophile Gautier urged Flaubert to lose no time in publishing the new version of *Saint Antoine* in the magazine *L'Artiste*, of which Gautier was one of the editors: "It's a good idea to keep dropping tons of bricks on those stupid bourgeois, without interruption." The new *Saint Antoine* appeared in the issues of December 21 and 28, 1856, and January 11 and February 1, 1857.

To Alfred Blanche[1]

[Paris, January 23, 1857]

This is to inform you that tomorrow, Saturday, January 24, I shall honor by my presence the swindlers' bench in Room 6 of the Criminal Court, at 10 A.M. Ladies are admitted; decent and tasteful dress required.

I am not counting on anything like justice. I shall be sentenced, and perhaps given the maximum—sweet recognition for my labors, noble encouragement to literature.

I dare not even hope that proceedings will be postponed for a fortnight: Maître Senard cannot appear for me either tomorrow or a week from now.[2]

But one thing consoles me for this nonsense: namely, having met with so many expressions of sympathy for myself and my book in so many quarters. I count yours among the first, dear friend. The commendation of certain enlightened minds outweighs the dishonor of criminal prosecution. And I defy the whole French judiciary, with its gendarmes, and the whole Criminal Investigation Service, including its informers, to write a novel that will please you as much as mine.

Such are the proud thoughts that will keep me company in my dungeon.

If my work has real value—if you find that you have not been mistaken about it—I pity my prosecutors. This book that they are seeking to destroy will survive all the better for its very wounds. They are trying to shut my mouth: their reward will be a spit in the face that they won't forget.

Some day, perhaps, you may have occasion to speak to the Emperor about these things. You could cite my trial as illustrative of the inept turpitudes taking place under his rule.

Which doesn't mean that I am becoming a wild man of the Opposition, and that you will soon be having to seek my release from Cayenne.[3] No, no: don't worry. In my deep immorality I stand alone, with no love for any party or clique, not even allied to any coterie, and—naturally—supported by no one. I am detested by the Jesuits in short gowns as much as by the Jesuits in long gowns; my metaphors irritate the former, my frankness scandalizes the latter.

That is all I had to tell you. That, and that I thank you again for your kind help. It has proven useless, for anonymous stupidity has shown itself more powerful than your devotion.

1. A very high Imperial official—Secrétaire Général du Ministère d'Etat. His family was prominent in medical circles in Rouen and Paris. (J.B.)
2. The trial was postponed until January 30.
3. At that time a penal settlement for political offenders.

To his brother Achille

[Paris,] Sunday, 6 P.M. [January 25, 1857]

My trial is definitely fixed for next Thursday; there are chances for, and chances against; nothing else is being talked about in the literary world.

Today I spent a whole hour alone with Lamartine, who paid me the most extravagant compliments. Modesty prevents me from repeating the ultra-flattering things he said; what is certain is that he knows my book by heart, understands all I mean by it, and has a clear perception of me as a writer. He will give me a laudatory letter to be offered in court; I am also going to get certificates as to the morality of my book from a number of the most established literary men; Senard says this is important.

My stock is rising; I have been asked to write for the *Moniteur* at 10 sous a line, which for a novel like *Bovary* would amount to about 10,000 francs. Such is the result of prosecution.

Whether I am sentenced or not, my position is now assured.

It was Lamartine who initiated the courtesies: that surprises me considerably —I would never have expected the bard of Elvire[1] to conceive a passion for Homais.

. . .

Adieu. I haven't an idle moment. I have appointments all day, and at night I write and correct proofs.[2]

1. A name which appears frequently in Alphonse de Lamartine's *Méditations poétiques.* Flaubert considered Lamartine soft, both as poet and as politician. "What a mediocre man that Lamartine is!" he had written to Louise Colet a few years before. At the trial, Senard was able only to mention some of the flattering things Lamartine had *said* about *Madame Bovary* to its author—for to Flaubert's displeasure Lamartine never sent the promised letter.
2. Of *La Tentation de Saint Antoine.*

To his brother Achille

[Paris, January 30, 1857]

Mon cher Achille

This morning you should have received a telegram from me sent by one of my friends, saying that the Court will announce its decision a week from to-morrow. Justice still hesitates! . . .

Maître Senard's speech was splendid. He crushed the attorney from the Ministry of Justice, who writhed in his seat and made no rebuttal. We flattered him with quotations from Bossuet and Massillon, smutty passages from Montesquieu, etc. The courtroom was packed. It was marvelous, and I was in fine form. At one point I allowed myself personally to contradict the attorney, who was immediately shown to be acting in bad faith, and retracted. In any case, you will see the rest of the proceedings word for word: I had a stenographer (at 60 francs an hour) taking it all down. Senard spoke for four hours without interruption. It was a triumph for him and for me.

He began by talking about Father, then about you, and finally about me; then followed a complete analysis of the novel, refutation of the list of charges and of the incriminated passages. Here he was particularly strong: the attorney must have been given a good dressing-down after the session.[1] But the best was the passage about Extreme Unction. The attorney was completely discomfited when Maître Senard took a Missal from under his seat and read from it. The passage in my novel is nothing but a *softened* reproduction of what is in the Missal: we certainly stuffed them with a famous bit of literature.

Throughout his speech, Senard spoke of me as a great man and treated my book as a masterpiece. He had about a third of it read aloud. He made the most of Lamartine's commendation. "You owe him not only an acquittal, but apologies!" was one of the things he said. And: "Ah! You are attacking the second son of M. Flaubert! . . . No one, M. l'avocat général, and not even you, can give him lessons in morality!" And when the attorney talked nonsense about one passage, Maître Senard replied: "I do not question your intelligence, but I am struck by your obsession [with adultery]."

All in all, it was a proud day, and you would have enjoyed it had you been there.

Say nothing; keep quiet; after the verdict, if I lose I will appeal in the *Cour d'appel*; if I lose there, in the *Cour de cassation*.

Adieu, cher frère, je t'embrasse.

1. By his superiors at the Ministry of Justice.

The decision was announced on February 7, 1857. The Court was unable to resist a certain amount of "literary" comment, and expressed its preference, at once stern and wistful, for literary works which deal less with life as it is than with life as it should be; but in the end it stated: "In the circumstances, be it known that it is not sufficiently proven that Pichat, Gustave Flaubert, and Pillet [the printer of the *Revue de Paris*] are guilty of the offense with which they are charged; the Court acquits them of the indictment brought against them, and decrees a dismissal without costs."

To MAURICE SCHLESINGER[1]

[February, 1857]

Mon cher Maurice

Thank you for your letter. I shall answer briefly, for all this has left me so exhausted physically and mentally that I haven't the strength to walk a step or hold a pen. The fight was hard, but I finally won.

I have received very flattering compliments from all my confrères, and my book is going to sell unusually well for a writer's first. But the fact is, I am infuriated whenever I think of the trial: it has deflected attention from the novel's artistic success, and I dislike Art to be associated with things alien to it. To such a point that all this row disgusts me profoundly, and I hesitate to publish *Madame Bovary* as a volume. I long to return, and forever, to the solitude and silence I emerged from; to publish nothing; never to be talked of again. For it seems to me impossible in the present day to say anything, social hypocrisy is so ferocious!!!

. . . The volume I was going to publish after my novel, a book that cost me several years of painstaking research and study, would send me to the penitentiary![2] And all my other plans have similar drawbacks. Do you realize now what a bad joke my situation is?

.   .   .

1. The Schlesingers were now living in Baden.
2. The first installments of *Saint Antoine* in *L'Artiste* had appeared in time to be quoted by the Public Prosecutor as further evidence of Flaubert's immorality. Serial publication continued to the end, however, without interference. Although Flaubert apparently did have some fear that he might eventually be prosecuted for this work as well, his decision not to publish it as a volume at this time was probably largely motivated by continued dissatisfaction with the work itself. *Saint Antoine* would finally appear as a book only in 1874, still further shortened, and intensified, to the form in which it is now known.

To EDMOND PAGNERRE

[c. February 11, 1857]

If I haven't replied sooner to your congratulations, it is because I was so utterly exhausted for several days following my political bouts that I could neither take a step nor hold a pen. I am still numb and dazed, and not a little anxious about my future books. What can I write that would be more inoffensive than my poor novel?

I am even hesitant about publishing it as a volume, because I want to restore the passages deleted by the *Revue de Paris*—all of them inoffensive, in my opinion. The cuts were idiotic, and create a lubricious effect utterly foreign to the book.

The Prosecutor still has two months in which to appeal. Could you find out definitely from Abbatucci whether he intends to appeal? Must I wait the two months? How am I regarded? Who has it in for me? I'll end up like Rousseau, believing in a Holbachian conspiracy. Because, although everyone I saw personally was favorably disposed, underneath there was an incomprehensible determination to get me.

Meanwhile, Lévy is after me to publish. I don't know what to do.

People advise me to omit some of the passages picked out by the prosecution. But that is *impossible* for me. I will not commit absurdities to please the authorities—not to mention that I find such a method of handling the matter a real bit of asininity.

Such is the sad plight of your unfortunate friend. You know I expect you to dinner one of these days, on the "boulevard du crime."[1]

1. Flaubert was spending the winter in lodgings on the Boulevard du Temple, nicknamed "le boulevard du crime" because of its numerous theatres specializing in melodramas. Possibly he was facetiously implying that he himself was one of the boulevard's "criminals."

The Ministry of Justice did not appeal the verdict, but it was doubtless out of prudence that book publication was delayed until mid-April. In this first edition of 6750 copies, *Madame Bovary* was printed in two volumes, with a dedication to Louis Bouilhet and a note of thanks to Maître Senard.[1]

During and after serialization, Flaubert had received letters and comment from readers unknown to him—responses which, whether in their praise or in their moralistic shock at the author's unwavering, intransigent view of society,[2] anticipated the flood of conflicting reviews that would greet the published book. More than once he was asked who had been his "model" for Emma Bovary. Among those who wrote asking that question was a literary spinster in Angers, who sent him some of her fiction and, apparently, a portrait of herself. She and Flaubert never met, but maintained a correspondence for many years.

1. The note reads, in part, "After the detailed analysis you gave of my novel in your magnificent pleading, I find it has acquired a kind of authority such as I myself never supposed it to possess."

2. Predictably, comment from sources close to the Church or the regime was particularly hostile. Flaubert wrote to Bouilhet on October 8, 1857:

"Have I told you, apropos of success, that the curate of Canteleu [the parish that included Croisset] is thundering against me? He snatches my book from his parishioners' hands! I confess I enjoy this immensely. No praise has tickled me more. Now nothing is lacking: attack by the government, abuse by the press, hatred from the priests. *Taieb! Buono!*"

Some of the dismayed critical reactions to *Madame Bovary* read like confirmations of Flaubert's own vow made when he was not yet eighteen: "I will simply tell the truth, but that truth will be horrible, cruel, naked." (See p. 9.)

To Mademoiselle Leroyer de Chantepie

Paris, March 18 [1857]

Madame:

I hasten to thank you: I have received everything you sent. Thank you for the letter, the books—and especially for the portrait: that was a delicate thought, and I am touched by it.

I am going to read your three volumes slowly and carefully—in the way, that is, I am sure they deserve.

But I am prevented from doing so for the moment, because before returning to the country I am busy with some archaeological work dealing with one of the least-known periods of antiquity—a task which is preparation for another. I am going to write a novel whose action will take place three centuries before Christ. I feel the need of leaving the modern world: my pen has been dipped in it too long, and I am as weary of portraying it as I am disgusted by the sight of it.

With a reader as sympathetic as you, Madame, frankness is a duty. Therefore, in answer to your questions: *Madame Bovary* has nothing "true" in it. It is a totally invented story; into it I put none of my own feelings and nothing from my own life. The illusion (if there is one) comes, on the contrary, from the *impersonality* of the work. It is a principle of mine that a writer must not be his own theme. The artist in his work must be like God in his creation—invisible and all-powerful: he must be everywhere felt, but never seen.

And then, Art must rise above personal affections and neurotic susceptibilities! It is time to banish anything of that sort from it, and give it the precision of the physical sciences. Nevertheless, the capital difficulty for me remains style, form; the indefinable Beauty *resulting from the conception itself*—and which is, as Plato said, the splendid raiment of the Truth . . .

To his cousin Olympe Bonenfant

[Croisset, June 14, 1857]

I see I haven't replied to your last letter, which came more than a month ago, in the midst of the flurry of publication. Everything is going smoothly, and if I hadn't been a fool I would now be well off, since my publisher has already sold 15 thousand copies, which at two francs a volume makes 30 thousand francs, and sales keep increasing. In *sum*, I'll have let slip the *sum* of 40 or 50 thousand francs.[1]

Voilà. It's true that I am being showered with honors. I have been attacked and commended, vilified and extolled. But I wouldn't mind having made a little cash.

·   ·   ·

1. On August 31, 1857, Lévy voluntarily gave Flaubert an extra 500 francs.

Flaubert's letters to only two of *Madame Bovary*'s many reviewers have been preserved: those to Sainte-Beuve and Baudelaire. He may have written to others, but the notice paid his novel by those two writers meant more to him, for different reasons, than the rest of the critical comment.

The article by Sainte-Beuve (whom Flaubert had met through Théophile Gautier) was especially valuable because of the critic's eminence and respectability: his literary feuilleton had for a number of years appeared every Monday in the semi-official *Moniteur Universel*, which had a national circulation among the upper bourgeoisie. To a young writer, favorable notice by Sainte-Beuve was the opening of the door. His article on *Madame Bovary*, which he had cautiously delayed writing until specifically asked to do so by the newspaper, appeared on May 4, 1857. Although not remarkably penetrating, it nevertheless exalted Flaubert above other novelists of his generation: "One precious quality distinguishes M. Gustave Flaubert from the other more or less exact observers who in our time pride themselves on conscientiously reproducing reality, and nothing but reality, and who occasionally succeed: he has *style*. He even has a trifle too much."

Its closing words were picked up by the caricaturist Lemot in a celebrated cartoon: "Son and brother of eminent doctors, M. Gustave Flaubert wields the pen as others wield the scalpel. Anatomists and physiologists, I find you on every page!"

To Charles-Augustin Sainte-Beuve

Tuesday night [May 5, 1857] Croisset, near Rouen.

Monsieur et cher maître

I am covered with confusion: I have just read your article in the *Moniteur*. How can I express to you all the feelings it evoked in me, and all the pleasure it gave me? To tell you I found it splendid would border on the ridiculous, seeing that you treat me as a friend—that is to say, with the closest attention and the highest praise.

In four newspaper columns you have repaid me for all my labors. Now I have my recompense. Merci, Monsieur, merci.

What an exquisite pleasure it is for me, remembering how I read *Volupté* and *Les Consolations* at college, that one of the men one looks up to should condescend to interest himself in my thoughts and take me by the hand.[1]

But please let me enlighten you on a purely personal point. Do not judge me by this book. I do not belong to the generation you speak of: at least, not in ways of feeling. I insist that I belong to *yours*—I mean the good generation, that of 1830. It represents everything I love. I am a rabid old Romantic—or a fossilized one, whichever you prefer.

I regard this book as a work of pure art, the result of an inflexible resolve. Nothing more. It will be a long time before I write anything else of the kind. It was *physically* painful for me to write it. Now I want to live—or rather resume living—amid less nauseating scenes.

Next winter, will you allow me to come some evening and sit with you by your fire, for a good talk about our beloved literature, which so few care about in this day and age? I will ask you, apropos of *Bovary*, some practical advice— the kind that is worth more than all the theories and aesthetics in the world. It will be a pleasure and a lesson.

Looking forward to that honor, let me assure you that I am

Most gratefully yours—

1. Flaubert may well have read Sainte-Beuve's novel and poems while at the college, although, as Jean Bruneau points out, there is no mention in the early letters of his doing so. The first reference to Sainte-Beuve in the correspondence is in a letter to Louis de Cormenin of June 7, 1844: "I am flattered to see that you agree with me in hating Sainte-Beuve and all his group." And to Louise Colet, in 1852, Flaubert calls him a "lymphatique coco"—Sainte-Beuve having expressed the wish, in one of his *Lundis*, that Louis Bouilhet, as poet, would "stop picking up the butts of Alfred de Musset's cigars."

Although a number of Charles Baudelaire's poems had been published in magazines, he was known at this time to comparatively few readers, and to them chiefly as art critic and translator of Poe. Before meeting him, and before reading any quantity of his verse, Flaubert had expressed, in a letter of 1854 to Louise Colet, an imperative for modern writers calling for much the same poetic temper that Baudelaire was soon to display so powerfully. "We must make a break with the tail-end of Lamartinism, and adopt an impersonal poetics; or if we choose to practise a subjective lyricism it should be unfamiliar, reckless, in short so intense as to be an absolutely new *creation*. But as for saying weakly what everybody feels weakly, No."

When novelist and poet became acquainted through Théophile Gautier, it was not strange that they found each other's "poetics" admirable, and Baudelaire undertook to review *Madame Bovary*. Meanwhile, on June 25, 1857, *Les Fleurs du mal* was published, and Flaubert wrote to Baudelaire as he had not previously written to anyone his own age.

To CHARLES BAUDELAIRE

Croisset, July 13 [1857]

Mon cher Ami

I began by devouring your volume from beginning to end, like a kitchen-maid pouncing on a serial, and now for the past week I have been rereading it line by line, word by word, and I must tell you that it delights and enchants me. You have found the way to rejuvenate Romanticism. You resemble no one —the greatest of all virtues. The originality of your style springs from the conception; each phrase is crammed to bursting with its idea. I love your sharpness, with the refinements of language which enhance it, like damascene work on a fine blade.

These are the pieces which struck me most: Sonnet XVII, *La Beauté*, for me a work of the highest quality; and then *L'Idéal, La Géante* (which I already knew), No. XXV:[1]

> Avec ses vêtements ondoyants et nacrés,

Une charogne, Le Chat, Le Beau navire, A une dame créole, Le Spleen, which went straight to my heart, its tone is so right. Ah! How well you understand the boredom of existence! Of that you may boast without false pride. I won't go on, lest I seem to be copying your table of contents. But I must tell you that I am utterly enchanted by LXXV, *Tristesses de la lune:*

> . . . Qui d'une main distraite et légère caresse
> Avant de s'endormir le contour de ses seins . . .

and I deeply admire the *Voyage à Cythère*, etc. etc.

As for criticisms, I make none, because I am not sure that I should agree with them myself after a quarter of an hour. In short, I am afraid of mouthing ineptitudes that I would immediately regret. When I see you this winter in

Paris, I shall merely ask you a few humble, tentative questions.

To sum up, what I love above all in your book is that in it Art occupies first place. Furthermore, you write of the flesh without loving it, in a melancholy, detached way that I find sympathetic. You are as unyielding as marble and as penetrating as an English fog.

Once again, a thousand thanks for your gift; I shake your hand warmly.

1. Flaubert read the first edition of *Les Fleurs du mal.* Some of the numberings are different in later editions.

Further sympathy was created between Flaubert and Baudelaire by a juridical coincidence, news of which reached Flaubert in the country.

To Charles Baudelaire

[Croisset,] Friday, August 14 [1857]

I have just learned that you are being prosecuted because of your book. Apparently I am rather late in hearing about this. I am in ignorance of everything, for I live here as though I were a hundred thousand leagues from Paris.

Why? Against what have you committed an "offense"? Religion? "Public morals"? Have you been "brought to justice"? When will that be? Etc.

This is something new, to prosecute a book of verse. Up to now the bench has left poetry severely alone.

I am deeply indignant. Give me details about the affair, if it is not too much trouble, and accept a thousand very cordial greetings.

To that letter, and to another from Flaubert suggesting certain lines of defense, Baudelaire replied:

Cher ami

I am sending you this short and hasty note before five o'clock merely to express my contrition at not having replied to your affectionate words of sympathy. But if you knew into what an abyss of puerile business I have been plunged! And the article on *Madame Bovary* again postponed for a few days! What an interruption in one's life a ridiculous misadventure can be!

The comedy was played out on Thursday. It was a lengthy affair.

Result: 300 francs fine for me, 200 for the publishers, suppression of Nos. 20, 39, 80, 81, and 87.[1] I will write you at greater length tonight.

Baudelaire's review of *Madame Bovary* was delayed not a few days, but almost two months, appearing in *L'Artiste* for October 18, 1857.

1. The verdict was later revised, and those poems are now included in all editions.

To Charles Baudelaire

I thank you very much, mon cher ami. Your article gave me the greatest possible pleasure. You entered into the arcana of the book as though my brain were yours. It is understood and felt to its very depths.

If you find my book stimulating, what you wrote about it is no less so, and we will speak about it all when we see each other, in six weeks.

Until then, once again a thousand greetings.

Baudelaire had written in his review that following the death of Balzac, interest in the novel had disappeared; Flaubert had now revived it. And Baudelaire proceeded to expound what he thought must have been in Flaubert's mind when he conceived *Madame Bovary:*

> On a banal canvas, we shall paint in a style that is vigorous, picturesque, subtle and exact. We shall put the most burning and passionate feelings into the most commonplace adventure. The most solemn utterances will come from the most imbecile mouths.
>
> What is the very home of imbecility, the most stupid society, most productive of absurdities, most abounding in intolerant fools?
>
> The provinces.
>
> Which of its inhabitants are the most insufferable?
>
> The common people, incessantly engaged in petty employments, the very exercise of which distorts their ideas.
>
> What is the tritest, the most prostituted, human situation, the most broken-down barrel organ of all?
>
> Adultery.

"To accomplish the tour de force in its entirety," Baudelaire continued, "it remained for the author only to divest himself (to the extent possible) of his sex, and to become a woman. The result is a marvel; for despite all his zeal as an actor he was unable to keep from infusing male blood into the veins of his creation, and Madame Bovary, in the most energetic and ambitious aspects of her character, and also in her strong predilection for reverie, remained a man."

In another paragraph he praised Flaubert for being the first to utilize hysteria, "that psychological mystery," as the "base and bedrock of a literary work"; and he ended by saying: "It would be easy for me to show that M. Gustave Flaubert has deliberately concealed, in *Madame Bovary,* the lofty lyrical and ironic faculties manifested without reserve in *La Tentation de Saint Antoine,* and that the latter work, the secret chamber of his mind, remains clearly the more interesting for poets and philosophers."

Some of Baudelaire's remarks sound much like Flaubert himself as we have read him in the correspondence, and the review may well have benefited from conversations between the novelist and the poet. Perhaps Flaubert had said to Baudelaire, as he was to say to others, "Madame Bovary, c'est moi, d'après moi!": "Madame Bovary is myself—drawn from life."

Flaubert must have particularly enjoyed the references to his beloved *Saint Antoine*. For now he was engaged on the project he had announced to Mlle Leroyer de Chantepie—a project which would display, he hoped, all the extravagance he had lavished on the saint, enhanced by the control he had learned from portraying the sinner. Another of the "three subjects" he had listed in his letter to Bouilhet from Constantinople was assuming modified form. Much as his "Flemish" novel had become *Madame Bovary*, so *Anubis*, "the story of the woman who wants to be laid by the God," was emerging as *Salammbô*, the story of the Carthaginian princess whose golden chainlet of virginity is snapped by a giant mercenary—a man she persuades herself may be a god in disguise.

APPENDIX I

A Self-Portrait
of Louise Colet[1]

Paris, Saturday, June 14, 1845

Why begin this diary today, instead of ten years ago, when I arrived in Paris —when I was full of enthusiasm, eager to see everything, still with my illusions about great men, about feelings, about fame?

Now I am thirty-four, no more, no less. I have grown stouter, my figure is no longer very slender, but still elegant, well shaped. My bust, neck, shoulders, and arms are extremely beautiful. I am still admired for the smooth curve of my throat and chin: too smooth, perhaps, for the outline of my face is blurred as a result, and lacks length, looks too round. I remedy this defect by the way I wear my hair—very long curls over the temples, which fall to my shoulders, partly covering my cheeks. I am often complimented on my luxuriant hair (very light chestnut: it was quite blonde when I was a child): a coiffeur arranges it skillfully every day. And yet my hair is one of the scourges of my vanity: it is beginning to go white (and when I say "beginning," I should mention that I found white hairs ten years ago.) The short hairs on the temples are almost entirely white. I brush longer hair over them and lacquer it in place. Every Saturday I have any other white hairs plucked out. "Memento mori," I always say with a laugh on those occasions, or rather "Memento vivere." I have been doing this for three years, and my hair is so abundant that the thinning leaves no trace. While my hair is being dressed I read or write, so no time is wasted. Thanks to the care I take, I manage to conceal my white hair so well that no one believes me when I speak of it . . . I have a high forehead, very well formed, very expressive; my eyebrows are thick, elegantly arched; my eyes, dark blue, large, very beautiful when they brighten in response to a striking idea or perception, but they are often tired by work or dimmed by tears. My nose is charming—dainty, distinguished, unusual. My mouth is small, fresh-looking, though not remarkable in shape. My smile is particularly pleasant—kindly, naive, I am told: I have never seen myself smile. My teeth are beautiful, in excellent condition, and I have all of them except one rear molar that I had extracted, being unable to stand the pain. My legs are perfect, slender at the ankle; my feet are very small, finely-boned, and the contrast between them

237

and my tall, strong figure is greatly admired. My hands, too, are slender, white, fine. Quite a long portrait! I think I am hardly worth the trouble: some day I'll be more concise. As for my moral portrait, it will emerge from the following pages.

1. This self-portrait is the opening section of the fragmentary Memoranda, or "Mementos," of Louise Colet, reproduced by Jean Bruneau in the Pléiade edition of Flaubert's correspondence from the autographs and typewritten copies in the Musée Calvet at Avignon. All the other "Mementos" of Louise Colet translated in the present volume are from the same source.

Flaubert and Syphilis

Theodore Zeldin, in *France, 1848-1945*, quoting contemporary sources, writes as follows about syphilis in Flaubert's day:

> It was indeed a major blight on the country. Flaubert, in his *Dictionary of Accepted Opinions*, defined it as being almost as common as the cold: "More or less everybody is affected by it" . . . Half of syphilitics caught the disease between the ages of fourteen and twenty-one. In the bourgeoisie a tenth caught it at school . . . Visits to prostitutes started at school. On holidays and the Thursday half-day the brothels swarmed with schoolboys.[1]

Flaubert was no exception. One of his letters to Ernest Chevalier, written two months after his seventeenth birthday (see p. 9), tells of visiting a Rouen brothel, and he may have been infected with syphilis even before entering Law School in Paris. Alfred LePoittevin furnished him with the addresses of a number of Parisian "houses" and the names of some of the girls. The painful chancres mentioned in the letter to Bouilhet from Constantinople (p. 129) resulted from subsequent, recent, probably nonsyphilitic venereal infection. There was little medical knowledge of venereal diseases at the time. Mercury; which could produce painful effects of its own, was the standard treatment for syphilis, and Flaubert was one of the many who "spent one night with Venus and the rest of their lives with Mercury." In August 1854, when he was almost thirty-three, approaching the end of *Madame Bovary*, he wrote to Louis Bouilhet:

> Laxatives, purges, derivations,[2] leeches, fever, colic, three sleepless nights—gigantic nuisance—such has been my week, cher monsieur. I have eaten nothing since Saturday night, and only now am I beginning to be able to speak. To put it briefly, Saturday night my tongue suddenly began to swell until I thought it was transmuting itself into that of an ox. It protruded from my mouth: I had to hold my jaws open. I suffered, I can tell you. But since yesterday I am better, thanks to leeches and ice.

You should have had a letter from me Saturday morning—it must have gone astray. For a week I was hideously sick. Terrific mercurial salivation, mon cher monsieur; it was impossible for me to talk or eat—atrocious fever, etc. Finally I am rid of it, thanks to purges, leeches, enemas (!!!), and my "strong constitution." I wouldn't be surprised if my tumor were to disappear, following this inflammation: it has already diminished by half. Anyway . . . I won't go to consult the great Ricord[3] for another six weeks. Meanwhile I'll keep stuffing myself with iodide.

Flaubert was fortunate that with him the disease did not take the course it did with Jules de Goncourt, Baudelaire, and Guy de Maupassant, all of whom died of paresis in their forties. The extent to which syphilitics infected women with whom they had intercourse during the contagious stage of the disease; the infection transmitted, in turn, by infected women; the effect on children; the personal and social wretchedness—all are part of the history of the disease before the discovery of penicillin.

1. Vol. I, pp. 304, 306.
2. An old medical term. Blistering, cupping, or other means of "withdrawing inflammation or morbid humor from a diseased part of the body." (O.E.D.)
3. "Possibly the single most successful doctor of the nineteenth century was Philippe Ricord (1800-89), personal physician to Napoleon III and the national expert on syphilis. Born in Baltimore, the son of a bankrupt French shipowner, he rose to become Paris's busiest and possibly richest doctor. His house in the rue de Tournon contained five large salons for his patients to wait in . . . His *Treatise on Venereal Diseases* (1838) did rightly distinguish between gonorrhea and syphilis, but he insisted that the latter was not contagious through secondary lesions: he continued to administer his incorrect doctrine to all the rich of Europe, despite the discoveries of the more obscure Joseph Rollet of Lyon (1856)." (Zeldin, I, 24-25, with a footnote mentioning Paul Labarthe, *Nos Médecins contemporains* [1868], 44.)

APPENDIX III

A Letter from
Maxime DuCamp

[Paris,] Wednesday, October 29, 1851.

To answer everything in your letter, mon cher vieux, would take me six months, and I would have to send you a volume of analyses. So I will only take up a few of your points and the last paragraph. For the rest, I would have to compose a complete treatise on your anatomy (concerning which I think you are often mistaken), and I do not want to do that: the task of dissecting and quartering is deeply repugnant to me,[1] and besides, what purpose would be served?

The matter of publication is very complex, despite its apparent simplicity. Do you merely want to publish? That is easy. Or do you expect to "arrive" by publishing? That is not easy. You know as well as I that we are no longer living in the days when one became famous overnight by writing *Les Truands* or *L'Ecolier de Cluny*.[2] The literary movement, or rather the passion for literature, is a thing of the past; art has fallen on evil days; philosophy and politics have completely usurped its place, and we must resign ourselves to spending many a long day in the dark before seeing the light again. Only in the theatre is it still occasionally possible to become a star overnight, without previous experience. If you want to arrive (I mean secure recognition), you must dig your tunnel quietly, like a miner, and blow up the citadel at a moment when such a thing is least expected. That requires careful preparation of the ground. Will you do it? I doubt it. In this, you are the way you tend to be about everything: you have a violent desire for things when they are impossible or impracticable, and as soon as you have them you are disgusted with them simply because you have them. You used to think a great deal about how you would begin: you wanted to make your mark, you wanted to obtain an instantaneous success and win the support of artists and journalists—that was actually your idea, as I recall. What you expected to do at great expense, I am doing now with nothing —and this is perhaps the real reason why you are offended by my remarks. You think my conduct undignified; you think I should have simply set down my prose and waited quietly with folded arms for admirers to come forward. No! Since I have made a start, since I want to get somewhere, I am not going to

241

falter in my purpose. I am on my way: bon voyage! My pistols are in my pockets, I have spent a long time charting my route, and woe to him that stops me! I know I am playing a dangerous game: my life is at stake, and it is up to me to win. You were surprised, on your return from England, to find me so unaccustomedly busy, and you confided your surprise to Gautier. He gave you a very silly answer: had you really known what I am like, you would have understood me without consulting anyone else. Do you remember Rastignac's words in *Le Père Goriot?* What he says so grandly, I say in a smaller way: "A nous deux, maintenant!" I have finally got hold of something—a center of activity where I can do what interests me, let off some of my superabundant steam: I have a very serious campaign to wage; a life-or-death struggle is in the balance. A literary revival is in the offing, and I am determined to be part of it—as a captain, not a private. A month ago I was worried, tormented, actually afraid. Today I am calm and confident: I have won my first battle.[3] I worked, and what is more I put others to work under my orders; and with my very first assault I have breached the walls of the citadel to which I have been slowly and quietly laying siege since 1847. Are you prepared to do all that? You always push things to their wildest extremes: you say, not quite in jest, "I was not made to be a waltzer." But mon Dieu! Who is suggesting anything of that kind? However, what you need above all is to learn the art of living, of which you are utterly ignorant. That ignorance has already done you greater harm than you can realize, and in your dealings with others it will make you inferior to many a talentless cretin.

You tell me: do what you like with me; make up my mind. That is impossible; I refuse; I cannot take charge of people's souls. Even though you may misunderstand me and take it out on me, I must leave you in your uncertainty; I could show you the two sides of the question, but especially in your case I will never tell you what course to follow. Nevertheless, whatever decision you make, whatever path you choose, I am always here; and believe me, I will spare you the hardest part. Whenever you want to publish, you will find your place ready and reserved—something that few can count on. Never for a moment have I separated you from myself in my thoughts: I have worked for the three of us—Bouilhet, you, and myself. That has long been the case, without your ever suspecting it.

If you publish, what will you publish? Your fragments of *Saint Antoine*, with one or two exceptions, are the kind of thing the public finds boring, and that is to be avoided above everything else; and besides, they are only fragments. What your mother said is right: if you have written something good, publish it. Like her, I can say no more than that. I have made my own success, I am going to make Bouilhet's; send me something good and I will make yours. This is all very serious and important, I know, and I cannot give you a single counsel.

You tell me that because it is to your taste, and after much deliberation, you have *chosen* the life you lead; but in this you are completely deluded. You passively *accepted* that way of life, and it has become your second nature. You accepted it first out of necessity, because of your illness; then out of duty, because of the deaths in your family; and finally, above all, because of the blind hatred of change you carry about with you and because you were afraid of your mother's unspoken reproaches. With her, you have never dared break what early became a habit. The proof of this is the happiness you have experienced whenever you have been able to get away. You enjoy having a good time—don't deceive yourself; and you expressed a profound truth when you wrote me that you consent to be active only when activity brings you pleasure: that is very true.

Your way of life involves two great drawbacks:

1. It has tied you to your mother, hand and foot. It has given you the terrible habit of depending on others where your everyday life is concerned, and of thinking only of your *subjective* self and never of your *objective* self.

2. It has encased you completely within your own personality. You know how *you* live, but not how others live. Look about you as you may, you see only yourself; and in everything you have written, you have portrayed only yourself.

Those are the two great flaws in your way of life; and the fact is that it is weighing on you, boring you, and making you think that you "hate life," whereas it is simply *your* life that you hate.

All this is not irremediable: far from it. We live at a time when it is dangerous to isolate ourselves from contemporary intellectual currents. This winter I am going to take courses at the Conservatory, and if I were younger I would study sciences, in order to understand what is going on. Such things are useful, if only to enlarge one's vocabulary. Solitude is beneficial only to the very strong, and to them only when they deliberately seek it for the completion of a task. Are we very strong? I doubt it; and we can never learn too much from others.

If you want to succeed, to arrive, I will say more: if you want to be truly yourself, come out of your hole, where nobody is going to look for you, and move into the daylight. Rub shoulders with the world; contemn it just enough to stand above it; but through this contempt, learn to observe by frequenting it. If you are the stronger, turn it to your advantage. Listen carefully to what it has to say; get to know it; and then talk down to it, and make it listen to you.

Who of all of us had a more favorable start than you? No one. Your life was free of cares, you had money and were known to be in comfortable circumstances, you had the shelter of your mother's house, the certainty that great sacrifices would be made to encourage you, a name made illustrious by your father and already familiar to the public. What have you done with all that? Nothing—and you are thirty years old. If you haven't made a beginning within two years, I don't know what the end will be.

Nowadays we no longer believe in unknown great men. From anyone who claims to have special qualities we pitilessly demand that he show us what he can do, and if he comes up with nothing we have our doubts about him. Be careful not to emulate those pregnant women who tighten their corsets in order to look thin and in so doing give themselves a miscarriage: that is fatal.

As yet, nothing forces you to publish; but if you want to publish eventually, make haste to prepare. As I already said, your place will be kept for you: I have given you my pledge. And the day you come to occupy it you will do as I have done: you will fling yourself so ardently and fiercely at the dish from which others are timidly nibbling, that they will all give way without even so much as trying to stop you.

Now, if you find your way of life adequate, and it leaves you with no regrets, if your work makes you happy, if you are satisfied with what you are writing and feel no need for anything else, if you are so filled with your own personality that you are content to be a great man for yourself alone, I have nothing to say: except that—since happiness comes first—you will do well to continue as you are.

So: as for advice, I give you none and can give you none. This is too serious a matter for me to have the right to do so. I cannot lure you on to a path that is perhaps not the one for you: I do not want to be your tempter. On one occasion[4] I was that, and once is enough. All I can tell you is that if you resolve to publish, I will help you with all my strength, with all my heart, with all my intelligence, with everything I know of life, with all my connections, with all my friends, with all my power, with all my influence: six months from now I will perhaps add "with all my authority." In short, count on me for everything —except to make your decision.

Do not doubt yourself—that would be wrong; but at the same time continue to scrutinize yourself with great diffidence. Self-confidence is a splendid thing only when legitimized by success; otherwise it is merely harmful, and makes others laugh while reminding them to be modest about themselves.

In short, when you are alone with your conscience you must know better than anyone else what you have to do. You must know, especially, what you *want* to do, and that is what must guide you.

So there you are, cher vieux: make up your mind. At this moment you have two possible options:

On the one hand, complete immersion in your own personality.

On the other: the need to publish something *good* within two years.

That, I think, is a brutal résumé of your position. Make your choice; and as soon as you have a goal, move toward it without looking back and without straying from your path.

One more word and I will have finished with this long letter which has been very painful for me to write and which I would never have undertaken had you not put my back to the wall.

My harsh words hurt you, you say, and you attribute them to your "normandisms." You are mistaken. Later, when we are real sheiks,[5] we will talk about all that. All I can tell you now is that I had been loving you for qualities that you do not possess. When I realized that, I had to redirect my friendship

244

to that new nature I discovered in you; and—I tell you this from the bottom of my heart—that was a painful experience which disturbed me for a long time. It was then that I gave vent to those harsh utterances you reproach me for and which I regretted as soon as they were said; it was then that I felt bitter words spring to my lips and—because of my impetuous nature—escape from me despite my constant attempts to suppress them.

Adieu, cher enfant. Think carefully about all this; think about it coldly—it is almost like a medical consultation. And whatever happens, never forget that I am

Always yours,

Maxime DuCamp

Thursday night [October 30, 1851]

1. Flaubert had written to Louise Colet in 1846, during one of DuCamp's visits to Croisset: "In the mornings he goes to the Hôtel-Dieu to watch the doctors operate and amputate. He enjoys that." (DuCamp's father, like Flaubert's, had been a well known surgeon.) Flaubert, in his letter of October 21, 1851, to DuCamp (see pp. 147-149), to which the present letter is the reply, had "asked for it," though perhaps—as is usually the case—not really wanting it; and in the present letter one does not sense that psychological dissection was in fact any more repugnant to DuCamp than physical surgery. Although the tone and level are in places deplorable, much of what DuCamp says is quite sensible. Even—or perhaps especially—knowing Flaubert as he did, he can be excused for not knowing he was offering *common* sense to a genius.

2. *Les Truands et Enguerrand de Marigny, 1302-1314, Histoire du règne de Philippe-le-Bel*, by Lottin de Laval (Victorien Pierre Lottin), (1832; second edition 1833). *L'Ecolier de Cluny, ou le Sophisme, 1315*, by E. Roger de Beauvoir (Edouard Roger de Bully), (1832).

3. The successful launching of *La Revue de Paris*.

4. Perhaps the occasion mentioned on pp. 151-152, n.1.

5. In a letter to his mother from Egypt, Flaubert had defined the term "sheik" as he and Maxime used it between themselves:

". . . the sheik is a certain type of elderly [French] gentleman, inept, living on his income, very respectable, very set in his ways, more or less senile, always asking us questions about our trip such as the following:

" 'And in the towns you've been visiting—is there a little social life? Are there clubs, where you can read the newspapers?'

" 'Are railroads making headway? Is there a main line nearby?'

" 'I sincerely trust socialist ideas haven't made inroads?'

" 'Is the wine good, at least? Are there some special vintages?'

" 'The ladies are . . . friendly?' . . .

"All that in a tremulous voice, with an air of imbecility. Sometimes we do a double-sheik —i.e. two sheiks in dialogue."

WORKS OF RELATED INTEREST

This brief bibliography is restricted to selected works in English or English translation. A number of other works are cited in the connecting texts and footnotes.

Brombert, Victor. *The Novels of Flaubert: A Study of Themes and Techniques.* Princeton: Princeton University Press, 1966.

Flaubert, Gustave. *The Dictionary of Accepted Ideas,* translated by Jacques Barzun. New York: New Directions, 1954.

    November, translated by Frank Jellinek. New York: The Serendipity Press, 1967; Pocket Books, 1967. London: Michael Joseph, 1966.

    Intimate Notebook, 1840-1841, translated by Francis Steegmuller. New York: Doubleday & Co., 1967. London: W. H. Allen, 1967.

    The First Sentimental Education, translated by Douglas Garman. Berkeley, Los Angeles, London: The University of California Press, 1972.

    Madame Bovary, translated by Francis Steegmuller. New York: The Modern Library.

Levin, Harry. *The Gates of Horn: A Study of Five French Realists.* New York: The Oxford University Press, 1963.

    "A Literary Enormity: Sartre on Flaubert." *Journal of the History of Ideas* 33, no. 4, October-December 1972.

Starkie, Enid. *Flaubert: The Making of the Master.* New York: Atheneum, 1967.

Steegmuller, Francis. *Flaubert and Madame Bovary.* Chicago: University of Chicago Press, 1977. London: Macmillan, 1968.

    Flaubert in Egypt (translated and edited). London: The Bodley Head, Ltd., 1972. Chicago: Academy Chicago Limited, 1979.

Zeldin, Theodore. *France 1848-1945. Volume I: Ambition, Love and Politics. Volume II: Intellect, Taste and Anxiety.* Oxford: Clarendon Press, 1973, 1977.

INDEX